# Myth and Memory

*Edited by John Sutton Lutz*

Myth and Memory:
Stories of Indigenous-European
Contact

**UBC**Press · Vancouver · Toronto

15 14 13 12 11 10 09 08 07      5 4 3 2 1

Printed in Canada on ancient-forest-free paper (100% post-consumer recycled) that is processed chlorine- and acid-free, with vegetable-based inks.

---

**Library and Archives Canada Cataloguing in Publication**

Myth and memory : stories of Indigenous-European contact / edited by John Sutton Lutz.

Includes bibliographical references and index.
ISBN 978-0-7748-1262-7 (bound); ISBN 978-0-7748-1263-4 (pbk.)

1. Indigenous peoples. 2. Europe – Colonies – History. 3. Acculturation. 4. Indian mythology. I. Lutz, John S. (John Sutton), 1959- I

JV305.M98 2007                   305.8                   C2006-907043-1

---

Canadä

UBC Press gratefully acknowledges the financial support for our publishing program of the Government of Canada through the Book Publishing Industry Development Program (BPIDP), and of the Canada Council for the Arts, and the British Columbia Arts Council.

This book has been published with the help of a grant from the Centre for Studies in Religion in Society, University of Victoria.

UBC Press
The University of British Columbia
2029 West Mall
Vancouver, BC V6T 1Z2
604-822-5959 / Fax: 604-822-6083
www.ubcpress.ca

# Contents

# Acknowledgments

This volume was fostered in the rich intellectual environment of the Centre for Studies in Religion and Society at the University of Victoria, then under the direction of Harold Coward. Harold suggested the model of inviting scholars from a range of disciplinary perspectives to come together as a team to work on a book that would be enriched by their interaction. Harold was "midwife" to this book, but in no way responsible for the slow delivery! He was helped by the fantastic staff at the centre: Moira Hill and Connie Carter, Leslie Kenny, and his successor Conrad Brunk.

Thanks to the centre, the Social Sciences and Humanities Research Council of Canada, the Vice Presidents Academic and Research, and the Dean of Humanities at the University of Victoria, the colloquium "Worlds in Collision: Critically Analyzing Aboriginal and European Contact Narratives" was held at Dunsmuir Lodge near Victoria, in February 2002. In addition to the team of authors represented here, a broader collection of experts, indigenous and non-indigenous, presented their work. I wish to thank all the participants at that colloquium for their wisdom and for enriching this volume. Nicholas Thomas and two anonymous reviewers also improved the chapters.

The Mowachaht-Muchalaht people, represented by Margarita James, welcomed the book team to their territory and took us to Yuquot, Captain Cook's "Friendly Cove," on the west coast of Vancouver Island, where the conversation between native and newcomer on this coast began, and where we began ours. The book-writing team, whose works individually are wonderfully distinct, have collectively charted a new direction in this field. My thanks to Judith Binney, Keith Thor Carlson, J. Edward (Ted) Chamberlin, Nora Marks Dauenhauer, Richard Dauenhauer, Michael Harkin, Ian MacLaren, Patrick Moore, and Wendy Wickwire for their remarkable efforts and their patience.

Thank you all!
John Sutton Lutz

# Myth and Memory

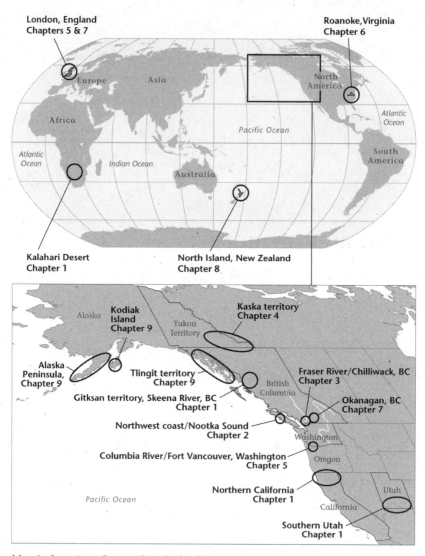

London, England
Chapters 5 & 7

Roanoke, Virginia
Chapter 6

Europe   Asia
Africa
Atlantic Ocean
Indian Ocean
Australia
Pacific Ocean
North America
Atlantic Ocean
South America

Kalahari Desert
Chapter 1

North Island, New Zealand
Chapter 8

Alaska
Kodiak Island
Chapter 9
Yukon Territory
Kaska territory
Chapter 4

Alaska Peninsula,
Chapter 9
Tlingit territory
Chapter 9
British Columbia
Fraser River/Chilliwack, BC
Chapter 3

Gitksan territory, Skeena River, BC
Chapter 1
Okanagan, BC
Chapter 7

Northwest coast/Nootka Sound
Chapter 2
Washington

Columbia River/Fort Vancouver, Washington
Chapter 5
Oregon

Northern California
Chapter 1
Utah
California

Pacific Ocean

Southern Utah
Chapter 1

*Map 1*   Locations discussed in the book

# Introduction: Myth Understandings; or First Contact, Over and Over Again
*John Sutton Lutz*

First contact.

The words leap off the page into the imagination. Between who? What happened? How do we know what happened?

Whether we are thinking science fiction or historic encounters, such as Columbus and the "Indians," James Cook and the Hawaiians, or Martin Frobisher and the Baffin Island Inuit, the questions are the same, the curiosity intense. The moment of contact between two peoples, two alien societies, marks the opening of an epoch and the joining of histories. What if it had happened differently? Would our world be different today? From our distance, the historic moment of contact seems so pregnant with possibilities, so full of hope and fear, and often, so laden with disappointment for what might have been.

But contact stories are not just about the past and the "might have been." Contact stories grab our attention because they also explain how things are now, and they contain a key to how they might be. For settler peoples, they are origin stories, the explanation of how the immigrants got "here," and they are the opening paragraph of a long rationale for displacing indigenous peoples. For indigenous peoples, they are a prologue to the process in which their world was turned upside down. For both, the stories are the opening act in a play that is still unfolding. Is it a story of progress or one of dislocation? Is it about bringing the gifts of civilization or robbing the wealth of the land? Depending on one's viewpoint, the plot of the play and the blocking of the performance vary dramatically. Each needs its own opening scene.

All over the world, settler populations and indigenous peoples are engaged in negotiations regarding legitimacy, power, and rights. In New Zealand, Australia, and Canada, this takes the form of litigation and negotiations concerning treaty and Aboriginal rights. In the United States, it is manifest in a struggle over cultural property, archaeological sites, and human remains. At root, these are all struggles over what is an accurate recounting of what happened – about history – about what we believe. The stakes are huge. The legitimacy of the settler nations and indigenous claims to be the rightful owners or caretakers of the land and resources are based on these contact stories.

Comparing indigenous and explorer accounts of the same meetings brings the collision of fundamentally different systems of thought into sharp relief. Europeans and indigenous people had (and in some cases, still have) incommensurable beliefs about what motivated behaviour, about fate, about trade, about reality. The juxtaposition of multiple systems of knowing challenges our culturally specific meanings of event, of time, of place, of narrative, and of history itself. Immediately, we are asked to evaluate written versus oral traditions and then, even more challenging, to decide between explanations based on different notions of what is real and what is imaginary.

First contact *and* the imaginary are, it turns out, closely linked. When we look for that moment of "First Contact" in historical encounters, that moment when two peoples stumbled upon each other unexpectedly – when two cultures were caught off-guard by the novelty and strangeness of "the other" – it retreats into the imagination. What we find instead is that Europeans did not discover the unexpected. They went into new territories full of expectations, ideas, and stereotypes: what they found was – in large measure – what they expected to find. It was not the "new" that they encountered so much as what the popular myths of the day suggested they would find. Christopher Columbus found "the Indies" and Indians; Jacques Cartier found the rapids that marked the entrance to "La Chine" – China. Martin Frobisher, who found "gold" on Baffin Island, was one of many whose gold, when smelted, was no more than dross.[1]

We often think of Christopher Columbus' 1492 landfall as the "real first, first encounter." Yet we know that the Norse had been to North America in the years around 1000 and that European fishermen had been fishing the Grand Banks off northeast America for a long time before Columbus. But even if Columbus had no knowledge of his predecessors, his encounter was the product of expectations conditioned by imaginary worlds conjured up long before his arrival. Columbian scholar Peter Hulme argues that, rather than strictly reporting what he saw, Columbus produced a "compendium of European fantasies about the orient." Hulme shows that the descriptions in Columbus' text are grounded in the European discourses of "Orientalism" and the savagery of "the other," which Columbus drew from his reading of Marco Polo and the classical writers Pliny, Homer, and Herodotus.[2] The classical accounts, which passed for factual knowledge in their time, of monsters and cannibals, formed the foundation for Columbus' descriptions of the "West Indies." Recent work on Marco Polo shows that his eyewitness accounts were ghostwritten and were probably fables derived from other jailed travellers.[3] Columbus' account, imbued with all these mythological associations, is now studied as a factual record of the contact moment. So, the first, "first contact story" is also, in Hulme's words, "the first fable of European beginnings in America."[4]

The inability to see the new world with fresh eyes is also evident from the illustrations that were attached to Columbus' writings and those that followed him. In the engravings, the people, the flora and fauna and geography, all look European. The visual references are to the classical era of the ancient Greeks rather than the new "Americans."[5] Europeans did not see their "new worlds" with fresh eyes; they saw them through the lenses of their ancient stories.

Nor was the experience any more novel to the peoples of the Americas or the South Seas. For the indigenous people, whose old worlds became new to Europeans, even the very first of the documented voyages were not their first encounters with strangers. Five hundred years before Columbus, northern Europeans – Vikings – had built one and probably more settlements on the eastern shores of America. Possibly, other undocumented strangers had come from the east. Almost certainly, indigenous Americans had intermittent visitors from the west.[6]

Yet even these visitors were not new, for the indigenous peoples of the Americas and the Antipodes had extensive experience with visitors from a spirit world, the place from which they imagined many of the early Europeans had come. Moreover, many had prophets who had foretold the arrival of these unusual visitors. Rather than being something new, these strangers were usually seen as something old – the dead returned, ancient people or spirits revisiting.[7] Like the Europeans, indigenous people drew their new encounters from, and into, their old mythologies.

So, for both parties, there was always an element to first contact that was not new contact. It was a performance pantomimed on the beaches, riverbanks, or decks around the globe, following ancient scripts as each side drew the other into its own imaginative world.

To call first contact an "event," then, is partially misleading, for several reasons. Although, using European records, we can date many encounters to a chronological moment, the meaning of that moment depended on the long sweep of the centuries-old stories that the participants brought with them. And very clearly, from the earliest encounters, stories spread among European seafarers and throughout Europe so that subsequent voyagers already "knew" what to expect. The latter-day voyagers sailed with the stories of Columbus and his successors as cargo, setting the stage for the next series of first encounters, over and over again. Similarly, the stories travelled vast distances along the coast and inland among indigenous peoples. As Europeans moved along the coasts, or up rivers, and as indigenous people ventured down, there were succeeding sets of first encounters; each, in some measure, being a product of the last.

Oral narratives will often unsettle the European notion that an event is a discrete and bounded incident. Indigenous people may frame the event differently with different causality and temporality, and oral narratives sometimes consider a series of related happenings (in terms of their world view) in a single story.[8]

Instead of thinking of a "first contact" as an event, Mary Louise Pratt offers the more useful idea of a "contact zone." We can think of the contact zone as, first, a space across which one could map a moving wave of first contacts, and second, as a temporal zone – an extended period over which the encounters happened. We could also expand the notion to include the zone of discourse where stories of first contact play out.[9]

Temporally, we can often clock the opening of various contact zones. But when did they close? If a contact zone is a period in which two cultures were meeting each other for the first time, in the Americas this may span the period from the Viking encounter around 1000, or if you prefer, the Columbian encounter of 1492, into the mid-twentieth century when all the Arctic and Amazonian peoples had finally met Europeans. If we think of the contact zone as the period in which two cultures are still struggling to figure each other out, a zone in which miscommunication and conflicting mythologies govern interrelationships as much as shared understandings, these zones lasted even longer. The chapters in this book argue that we are still in that contact zone.

Not only are settler populations and indigenous people still meeting in zones of mutual incomprehension, a case ably made by J. Edward Chamberlin's lead chapter, they are also still creating and telling new contact stories and challenging the old ones, as the chapters by Keith Thor Carlson, Patrick Moore, I.S. MacLaren, Michael Harkin, Wendy Wickwire, and Judith Binney, all demonstrate.

This book takes a critical look at how contact stories have been and are being told and used. Although a few anthologies of contact stories do exist, as do some excellent examinations of historical encounters informed by contact stories, few scholars have examined first-contact stories as a genre or an ongoing "contact zone." In the 1940s, R.G. Collingwood wrote that each generation of historians rewrites history in the light of the concerns of the day.[10] Today, what is most important to a new generation and a much more inclusive range of storytellers is the contact narratives themselves, and the currency these stories have.

Natalie Zemon Davis identified four strategies that the current generation of scholars is using to move the European from the centre of contact stories. First, they describe the "gaze," revealing European attitudes and images of non-European peoples as "projections of anxieties" or elaborations of European categories. Second, they privilege both indigenous people and

Europeans as actors and reactors, primarily in terms of resistance and domi-nation. Third, they examine what Richard White has called "the middle ground," a space of shared and contested meaning focused around exchange and mixture. Fourth, they look at cultures in contact with each other in "terms of absolute simultaneity, radical contemporaneity ... seeking signs of the common human experience" but "insisting at the same time on the existence of strong and concrete cultural difference and the importance of divergent context." The chapters in this volume draw particularly on the last three strategies but offer another possibility: identifying the mythology and the history embedded in stories that emerge from both indigenous and European contact accounts, treating both as equally credible and incred-ible. Several chapters in this volume develop yet another strategy: focusing primarily on how indigenous people have recorded, verified, and used con-tact stories within their own oral and written literatures.[11]

This book stems from a meeting of ten diverse scholars, a mix of histori-ans, anthropologists, linguists, and literary scholars. It is an attempt to bring them into a dialogue with each other as well as the stories, and to create a critical mass of commentary.[12] The scope is international: the narratives come from New Zealand, the eastern and western seaboards of the United States, subarctic Canada, and the Kalahari. As a reflection of the active scholarship in the area, several examine the northeast Pacific. Each focuses on a par-ticular time and place, and all contemplate the larger issues raised by first encounters. Four themes run through the book, each an avenue to under-standing the contact zone: currency, performance, ambiguity, and power.

**Currency**

In Chapter 1, J. Edward (Ted) Chamberlin invites us to think about the notion of "currency." Currency speaks of time and of belief. As he says, "currency," the kind minted and printed by governments, has value only if people believe in it. Like the coin of the realm, stories have currency only if people believe in them. Chamberlin highlights *the* key question, because all the chapters in the book ask us to re-examine what we believe, and why we believe some stories and not others. Several of the chapters here focus on this kind of currency, the question of belief.

In Chapter 2, John Sutton Lutz develops this line of inquiry by examin-ing both the contact events and the ensuing stories. He contrasts the so-called realist tales told by the settler societies with the myth-linked stories that have been passed down or have arrived in a dream to the current gen-eration of indigenous people in the northeast Pacific. Contact narratives are all about belief, and Lutz argues that the "rational European stories" that pass for realist accounts are in fact as rooted in a European mythology as others are in an indigenous "myth world."

One of the great reservations about engaging indigenous contact accounts is their connection to the world of storytelling. In an oral culture, can one tell truth from fiction, and if so, how? In Chapter 3, Keith Thor Carlson looks at the importation of contact stories and other oral histories into the contemporary world of the courts, and considers the dilemma of two competing oral histories. We have established criteria with which to evaluate competing texts written in a Western tradition, but we are ill-equipped to evaluate indigenous stories. Through a decade of research with the Stó:lō (pronounced Stah-lo) First Nation near Vancouver, Canada, Carlson describes the Stó:lō criteria for accepting or rejecting oral histories. When they want to use the courts or the court of public opinion, how should the different oral accounts be judged as more or less true?

Carlson's chapter identifies Stó:lō tests for historical accuracy. These are not based on probability or corroborating evidence in the sense that most non-indigenous historians or courts would use. For the Stó:lō, the corroborating evidence is the reputation of the storyteller and the genealogy of the story as traced through previous narrators. The cultural and physical risks of mistelling an account are high among the Stó:lō, and this has served to preserve the culturally relevant information in stories over long time spans. Both Carlson and Wendy Wickwire, in Chapter 7, point out that in the indigenous traditions they study, there is no notion of fiction. Like scholarly writing, these oral cultures have clear rules that govern where embellishment is allowed and where it is not.

Wendy Wickwire's chapter also focuses on the question of belief. Her chapter maps out the historiography of Harry Robinson, a brilliant indigenous historian from the Okanagan Nation in British Columbia, with whom she worked for over a decade. After his death, she returned to those of his stories that she had set aside as not fitting into the ethnographic mode. They offer an indigenous exploration of why white colonists are dominant (they have no regard for the truth), a validation of an indigenous world view, and a prophecy for a more balanced future relationship. In presenting them, Wickwire asks us to reinterpret Boasian anthropology and to reconsider the relationship between indigenous and non-indigenous views of our own history.

Stories have another kind of "currency" in the sense that they are all of our time. When we retell, or even reread contact accounts, we bring them into our time and place. The very act of bringing them to us transports us into the contact zone. As E.H. Carr noted a long time ago, "History is not the past: it is the consciousness of the past used for present purposes." The stakes tied up in contact stories are very much about today.[13] As historians and the courts have moved toward understanding and giving more credibility to oral narratives, the question of how we deal with conflicting stories within the oral tradition becomes more urgent. Wickwire, Chamberlin, and Carlson all raise the issue of whether we can develop the listening skills to evaluate them.

In Chapter 4, Patrick Moore invites us to take a closer look at how indigenous people, in this case the Kaska of the Subarctic, classify stories. He finds that linguistic clues separate "true" historical narratives from those that are told more to entertain or poke fun. Moore notes how place and time (what Mikhail Bakhtin called "chronotope") are characterized differently in the different genres of stories. From his chapter, we discover the range of acceptable renderings of the past in a Kaska world view.[14]

European contact performances fall into a range of genres, from the scientific to the epic, from the novel to the comic book. Both Carlson and Moore point out that indigenous traditions also have their range of genres. Moore develops in a Kaska context the notion suggested by Lutz that, in interpreting novel experiences, each culture has access to certain cultural forms only. Moore, and Judith Binney in Chapter 8, focuses on intertextuality – the relationship of stories or texts to each other. Moore finds that several contact stories relating the novel appearances of Europeans are transposed onto long-standing vision quest narratives or pre-existing formulas for humorous stories. He also draws our attention to the different understanding and importance of time in indigenous and immigrant stories. So, stories also have another kind of currency: they flow over time and across space. How they flow is through the magic of performance.

### Performance

Something was always exchanged on first contact. Often the exchange included goods, but it always involved attempts at communication, usually very deliberately contrived. Even indigenous people, who often had less time to prepare for the encounters, were quick to assemble their chiefs or ceremonial speakers, don their regalia, and marshal their symbols of wealth and power. Both sides to the encounter had much at stake: trying to suggest that they were powerful though not threatening, and interested in exchange though not to be bested.

Typically, the parties would speak to each other without any comprehension; then they would turn to gesture. Often the contact events themselves were elaborately staged, intensely theatrical, performances. The performances were pantomimed, they were sung and danced, they were spoken, and they were enacted. Symbols such as flags and masks, uniforms and effigies were invoked and exchanged. As Stephen Greenblatt observed, these first meetings were "very often contact between representatives bearing representations."[15]

Not only were the first-contact events themselves performances, a focus of the Lutz chapter, but the retellings of these stories are also performances. Indigenous historical performance has given priority to the spoken form, to song, dance, and art. Although some groups, such as the Aztecs, have been writing their history for centuries, most adopted writing as a mode of performance in the last century. Wendy Wickwire, Keith Thor Carlson, Patrick Moore, and Judith Binney all stress the performative aspect of indigenous storytelling in their chapters.

Storytellers in the modern European tradition wrote down their narratives. We have been accustomed to treating these exploration accounts as first-hand eyewitness reports, and we often accord them more weight than the mediated stories told by oral transmission. The "I/eye was there" nature of these accounts is what accords them so much credibility. Yet, in Chapter 5, I.S. MacLaren probes one of these "I saw" European stories, a well-known record by the famous "Indian painter" Paul Kane, and points out that neither Kane nor most of the explorers upon whom we rely actually wrote the texts published under their names. Moreover, some of the Kane material was borrowed from other writers, and some was exaggerated or fabricated to place Kane near or at the centre of events. This and MacLaren's other published work cast exploration narratives – so-called realistic accounts – as performances for an audience, often written by a team of creators.[16]

For our great public events, we turn these narratives over to playwrights, musicians, poets, and screenwriters, who rewrite them yet again, so we can perform our history in pageants, grand commemorative occasions such as the American bicentennial, Olympic opening ceremonies, or the opening of parliaments, or in religious events such as Easter services. We sing them in our national anthems and our pop music; we dance them in our ballets as well as in street rap. We also perform them, in plays, in poems, in historical novels, and in academic monographs; we perform them in art and we print them on our currency. We perform for ourselves and we perform for the others as a way of creating and solidifying our individual and collective identities.[17]

The "arrival story of Europeans" in the Arctic or the Pacific, the founding of this state or that city, which we find in history books, travel guides, poems, plays, and songs, are good examples. In Chapter 6, Michael Harkin focuses specifically on how one contact event, the establishment and disappearance of the Roanoke Colony on the eastern seaboard of the United States, has been shaped and reshaped to give legitimacy to the settler population. These storytelling performances self-consciously retell the encounter, compressing and sometimes re-ordering timelines, shifting or conflating places, and transposing people – in effect, telescoping time and space into a poetic unity. They are, in Chamberlin's words "ceremonies of belief" as well as "chronicles of events." These are the so-called charter myths that nations, as well as ethnic and social groups use to justify their presence, their occupation of land, their denial of inheritance, and their rights to dispossess and oppress others who, they would claim, have a less legitimate story. Harkin's chapter shows how even a colony that disappeared without a trace can be used to legitimate a subsequent settler population.

Obviously, performance requires artifice. By definition, it cannot be true, since it is meant to be a representation, yet its power rests in its ability to make us believe. Performance is the creation of meaning, recreating and referring to events that are now distant. To invoke the past, we must resort to art. In theatre, the invocation is achieved through costumes and set. In text, it comes through descriptive re-creations, by speaking in the voice of a witness from the past, or in appropriating another language. The intent of this is not simply to deceive, as Chamberlin reminds us, but to deceive to tell the truth. We are all familiar with the notion that fiction can sometimes be truer than a recitation of facts. This preference goes back at least to Aristotle, who favoured poetry over history because the former was the "vehicle of universal and essential truths" whereas the latter "merely trafficked in the contingent, specific, unique, superficial facts."[18] Performances always leave room for ambiguity.

## Ambiguity

The most piquant of ethnographic moments are those of first contact, as Greg Dening writes in his book *Performances,* because of their "extravagant ambiguity." Each side was left to guess what message the other was trying to convey. Each side continually revised its attempt to communicate, looking for signs of recognition from the other. These were "real" ethnographic moments in the sense that each side was looking for cross-cultural clues about meaning and motivation, though often through very narrow lenses. Of course, misunderstanding was communicated as often as was meaning. Sometimes these could cause offence, but so often, the extravagant ambiguity of the moment allowed each side to make what it pleased of the messages coming from the other.[19]

Inevitably, communication means translation. Even gesture and gesticulation require translation, as travellers well know. Anyone who has waved "bye-bye" in China, only to have the departing party return, or who, in a South American country, has tried to signal affirmation by making the North American "OK" sign (bringing the thumb and forefinger together) will have experienced the cultural specificity of gesture.

Also inevitably, there is some exchange of language; and over time, specialized interpreters of language begin to mediate and funnel the exchange. Often, as Richard Dauenhauer and Nora Marks Dauenhauer suggest in Chapter 9, translators were people already "in between." Some were captives on one side or the other, others were the offspring of sexual contacts that so rapidly became part of the wider intercourse. It might seem that the presence of translators, especially as they gained fluency in each language, would reduce the ambiguity. In writing of the archetypical translator, Cortes' Doña Marina, Stephen Greenblatt remarks that language is the companion of empire. Of course, to some extent he is right, but the translators also have their own part to play in creating spaces of misunderstanding and undermining the European project.[20]

Translators became the bottleneck though which communication between whole societies began to flow; as a result, a single person often had enormous influence on the outcome of contact encounters. The translator was always, by definition, something of a hybrid. Translators, as Lewis Hyde notes, may earn their pay from one side or another, but some of that pay always comes from existing in the "in-between." The translators always had an agenda of their own, and this filter, or perhaps more accurately, this muddiness injected into the process, was part and parcel of the contact encounters. Hyde points to an old Italian pun – "'traduttore, traditore/translator, traitor' to remind us that the translator who connects two people always stands between them."[21]

The Dauenhauers' chapter is unique in the North American context and rare elsewhere. Its focus is the translators themselves, three men who connected Russia to the Tlingit inhabitants of America for over thirty years of the contact zone. One, a hostage rescued from the Tlingit, had a Russian father and a Tlingit mother; the other two, Tlingit themselves, were captured as boys by the Russians. Their hybrid identities meant that both sides, Tlingit and Russian, would ask the same questions regarding them: Where does their loyalty lie? Should we believe them? How should we interpret what they say?

The issues of translation and ambivalence are still with us now in the contact zone. When we deal with indigenous accounts, and even with many of the European accounts, we do so through translations from one language to our own. But even texts originally written in our own language can need translation from their time to ours. Over many lifetimes, words come and go from circulation, their meanings shift, and the references that were once common knowledge become obscure. We perform the role of translators when we enter the contact zone. As the chapters in this book show us, translators are transformers, transforming not only words but ideas and even whole cosmologies into something that "makes sense" to us. In Western and many indigenous mythologies, this kind of linguistic transformation has been seen as the work of the Trickster, since misunderstanding is so often injected. As Hyde says, "Translation from one language to another is Eshu-work, Legba-work, Hermes-neutics," and we may add, Coyote- and Raven-work. When we translate, we perform the Trickster/Transformer's work.

The Trickster figures prominently in most non-Christian traditions. In the Pacific Northwest, the Nuxalk people tell us that the Creator thought one language would be enough for all peoples, but Raven, the Trickster, made many languages, to have more sport in the spaces of misunderstanding.[22] The chapters by Wickwire, Chamberlin, and Lutz engage the role of tricksters in contact encounters.

If extravagant ambiguity was present at the first encounter, it has only grown with each retelling of the stories: "Native and Stranger each possessed the other in their interpretations of the other. They possessed one another in an ethnographic moment that was transcribed into text and symbol ... They entertained themselves with their histories of their encounter."[23]

In Chapter 6, Harkin looks at how the story of the "Lost Colony of Roanoke" has become entertainment and symbol, at how the ambiguity has been stretched to engage settler audiences while it tells them a story that they need to hear. In Chapter 1, Chamberlin very much focuses on "how the uncertainties of representation (whether something is there or not) and of communication (whether we believe the teller or the tale) generate the very certainties to which we give assent" in the oral and written texts of religion, law, science, and the arts.

In Chapter 8, Judith Binney focuses on how Ngai Tuhoe and Ngati Whare, two Maori tribes living on New Zealand's North Island, interpreted their encounters with Europeans through their own historical/prophetic ideas of "shelter." One narrative tells of the "mythical" white *kawau* (cormorant); others draw on biblical constructs. She shows how these narratives are continually redeployed to suit new situations. She calls this kind of history, which interweaves Maori narrative forms (including prophecies and story frameworks from mythologies) with those heard, and often read, about Maori and European cultures (the Bible, anthropological accounts, white histories), "plereomatic history."

Plereomatic history is easily recognizable in oral history, but the concept applies to European contact stories as well, where it is sometimes called "intertextuality." When Columbus left Europe with the writings of Pliny and Marco Polo as cargo, or when James Cook sailed the South Pacific with Francis Drake in his library and other accounts partially remembered in his head, each produced contact stories that were plereomatic. Within Columbus' "first-hand" inscriptions were European mythological patterns and stories read at second hand. In the same vein, the works that Harkin discusses are plereomatic. These histories of Roanoke interweave myth-forms, eyewitness recollections, and second-hand interpretations.

The notion that all contact narratives are a mix of eyewitness observations and remembered prior accounts and myth-forms helps us understand why, even in the verbatim records of the European explorers, we can find ambivalence. The ambivalence is the space between what they saw and what their cultures permitted them to see. In the hybridity of the text, as Homi Bhabha has argued, we can also seek a reflection of the indigenous voice. In the cracks in the European logic within these texts is the space of the "out-of-power language." Here there is also a recognition that, even as Europe imposed its own stereotypes and myths on the "native," a dialogue was going on.[24] As the European world begins to alter the indigenous, something, including fragments of the indigenous myth-world, is being transmitted to Europe, becomes reinterpreted, and starts to act on the Europeans.[25]

### Power

The ambiguity in the performance of contact stories opens a gap in which one can sometimes discern what lies at their heart: the workings of power within and between cultural groups. This is true from several aspects. At a literal level, it is evident when we think of the balance of power in those contact moments the accounts describe. On one hand, as Harkin shows, the story of Roanoke is told to suggest the longevity and legitimacy of European settlement in Virginia. It can also be read against the grain, so to speak, as a story about indigenous power, and the inability of Europeans to survive in their "new world" without help from indigenous people who remained comfortable and powerful in their "old world." Although it is seldom explicit in the contact narratives, between the lines it is apparent that in North America, at least well into the sixteenth century, indigenous people had the power to determine the success or failure of new European settlements.[26]

Power is also at the heart of contemporary retellings. If contact stories are kept alive, it is because they have continuing importance – a role to play in each of the respective performing communities. Binney, Moore, and Wickwire describe how narratives function to redress power relations between native and newcomer. They offer insight into how history is generated and understood by a people, and look at how some indigenous people respond to political and economic domination in story. Indigenous storytellers may challenge the legitimacy of the arrival of Europeans or explain it as the working out of a supernatural process that belongs in their own mythology, as in the case of the Robinson stories in Wickwire's chapter. The accounts may poke fun at the Europeans, levelling the playing field so to speak, as the Kaska stories do in Moore's chapter. Humour and irony are common strategies to challenge and reorder hierarchies of power.[27]

Contact stories are reperformed in the context of settler nations to naturalize the presence of Europeans in former indigenous spaces, but they also have a more fundamental role to play in supporting European ways of knowing. Mary Louise Pratt has written about how exploration is tied to the expansion of science in the eighteenth-century Enlightenment. She shows how science provided Europeans with a way of knowing the world.[28] Since then, Europeans have attempted to universalize a specifically European world view which they call "scientific" or "rational."

In Chapter 5, I.S. MacLaren gives a concrete example of how contact narratives, themselves performances and imaginary productions, were used in the nineteenth century by Herbert Spencer as part of the foundation for the modern scientific discipline of sociology. Like Linnaeus, who, a century before, had used travellers' accounts of Patagonian giants, Amazons, and other mythological creatures to build his taxonomy of animals, Spencer avidly combed the exploration accounts of his day to create a science of society that would distinguish Europeans from "primitive" cultures. Spencer's description of so-called primitive societies was the foundation on which he based his idea of Europe's progress. One of the groups he chose to make his "scientific comparison" was the Chinook people of what is now the Oregon-Washington border in the United States. As MacLaren shows, Spencer's main source was the eyewitness narrative of Paul Kane – only Paul Kane did not write the section in his book on the Chinook people. Kane's published narrative actively exaggerated his encounters with the indigenous people of the Pacific Northwest, and his ghostwriter(s) freely plagiarized from other travellers, whose own accounts bordered on the apocryphal. From its birth, sociology, like science and the other social sciences more generally, drew on the mythologized interpretations of Europe's contact with the other. Then, "scientific knowledge" was used as a marker of European superiority over indigenous mythology and superstition, and part of the larger rationale for colonization.

## Conclusion

Contact – the moment when the match hits the striker, sparks fire the tinder, a flash of light illuminates an encounter. It is the moment when stories begin; we seem to be drawn to the moment – the story – like moths to a flame.

All the writing in this book, ironically, is about listening. Collectively, the chapters offer an introduction to the range of acceptable renderings of the past in some indigenous and European cultures. John Sutton Lutz, I.S. MacLaren, and Michael Harkin all remind us that the European contact accounts are stories too. Keith Thor Carlson, Patrick Moore, Wendy Wickwire, and Judith Binney show that indigenous stories are history. The Dauenhauers invite us to look at the people who were themselves the point of contact between cultures, and J. Edward Chamberlin writes about the difference between hearing and listening. Listening is the stage of comprehension, of paying attention, which follows acknowledging sounds. If we know how, we can listen to written accounts too, hearing old stories in new ways and unsettling our familiar notions of first contact and all the history that follows.

Contact narratives (especially European) are sometimes taken as history and sometimes (especially indigenous ones) as myth. They are sometimes taken as works of literature or of science. In fact, these are not separate categories. Myth and history, science and fiction, are not exclusive but complementary and inseparable ways of knowing. Contact stories were and are all of these things.

The encounter moments, so full of misunderstandings, were worked into both science and myth. In each culture, the stories are now part of education, history, folklore, and "common-sense" knowledge that guides our understanding of current events. Such stories, as the great indigenous storyteller Thomas King reminds us, "assert tremendous control over our lives, informing who we are and how we treat one another as friends, family, and citizens."[29]

Critically reading/hearing contact stories means engaging "myth understandings." Rethinking contact narratives means rethinking the relationship between history and myth, an activity that, as Jonathan Hill has argued, should not be reserved solely for scholars. It is a road to understanding our "own modes of mythic and historical consciousness" and how they differ from those in other societies. And this is what it takes, writes Michel Foucault, to "free thought from what it silently thinks, and so enable it to think differently."[30]

When we read or listen to contact stories, we are immediately spirited into the contact zone where different cultures are meeting. We become the translators. And as the Dauenhauers show, translators inevitably change meanings. We cannot help but put our own spin on the accounts, which have themselves been spun by someone else. This is discouraging news if we are looking for absolute truth about the past, but if our goal is understanding past and present, there is something very encouraging in this knowledge.

The hopeful part is that, for us, like those we read about, something is communicated at contact, in spite of all the transformation and misunderstanding. In spite of all that is lost in translation, something of the encounter between strangers, something about the other, is transmitted. Something of the contact moment is absorbed and each of the parties is changed, sometimes profoundly, sometimes only by the addition of a story. Either way, contact narratives show us that we have the capacity to get glimpses of a world beyond the horizon of our own cultures, beyond the fences of our minds. Every story we read or hear changes us. The contact zone is a place of hope.

# 1

# Close Encounters of the First Kind
*J. Edward Chamberlin*

The Canadian two-dollar coin struck to commemorate the establishment of Nunavut – the name of the mainly Inuit (Eskimo) community in the north of Canada that received quasi-provincial status in 1999 – has a picture of the queen on one side and an Inuit drum dance on the other. It is the quintessential image of encounter and its perennial paradox: state power and indigenous sovereignty, with their backs to one another.

This coin opens up a couple of other issues, often lost sight of in our preoccupation with narrative. First of all, the initial encounters between Natives and newcomers were not always chronicled in stories, but sometimes in songs or dramatic performances, in music or in dance. One of the reasons we routinely discredit each other's accounts may be that we misinterpret their form, mistaking a dog for a clumsy cat, as it were, or a coin for a silly stone. The ceremonies that celebrated first encounters – the stories and songs and dancing and drumming and paintings and carvings – depended upon traditions of imaginative exchange, which, like any currency, were worthless unless someone believed in them. But crediting someone else's currency doesn't come naturally ... until we are actually in their country, and have no choice.

I talked about crediting a currency. Credit means simply "he or she believes"; but exactly what is it that we believe when we believe in a currency? When it comes to that two-dollar coin, the choice would seem to be simple: the monarchy or Inuit culture. But most of us don't believe in either. And yet we credit the currency.

One of the reasons we do so is that we believe that someone or something "backs," or underwrites, it. For commercial currency, it used to be gold; now we believe it's the government, or the gross national product. But who or what backs the currency of the stories and songs of first contact? Reality? or the literary imagination? A history of events? or a tradition of performance?

There is no single answer, of course; but for us to get beyond a melodrama of Them and Us, there has to be a shared sense of the importance of the question, and of the really quite extraordinary act of faith that any currency calls for, whether it is a piece of paper, the sound of a word, or the movements and masks of a dance. Otherwise, our traditions of imaginative expression become nothing more than minor local currencies that either nobody credits or everybody uses with a tourist's genial contempt.

What is fundamental here is the arbitrariness of *all* currencies, which is to say of all traditions of expression. "By the meaningless sign linked to the meaningless sound we have built the shape and meaning of western man," said Marshall McLuhan.[1] He was talking about words and images, and how we recognize them as representations of ideas and things; but he could have been talking about all the ceremonies of belief that make up our imaginative and spiritual lives. And he should have said humankind all around the world, for it is in the embrace of arbitrariness – and the artifice of assigning significance – that we ultimately constitute our communities. Often these seem silly to those who don't grow up in them; but it is these arbitrary forms of imaginative currency – language being only the most obvious – that hold us together even as they keep others apart.

All of this is bound up with questions about mirroring and making, as well as about meaning and motive, which are the stock-in-trade of all our work. I'll begin with a story told by the folklorist Barre Toelken.[2] It has to do with an armband of tiny glass beads stitched on buckskin, made for him by a friend from one of the southern Oregon coastal tribes. He was wearing it when a woman from one of the northern California tribes came up to him and said "that's very pretty, nice beadwork, but you know of course it's not an armband. It's a basket." And he said, understandably enough, "well, you certainly couldn't carry much in it. It's something you put on your arm." This is Toelken's account of the rest of their conversation:

> I tried to explain to this old lady that this really wasn't a basket. This was an armband. She very patiently tried to explain to me that it is too a basket and not an armband. She said, "Of course it is an armband. Anybody can see that, but it is really a basket." And she went on to explain that the Indian people in this area of California and southern Oregon have been making baskets for generations, for thousands of years, but they very seldom make these baskets any more because the distinctive kind of grass they need is almost never available any more. It's the shoot that comes up after a fire. In the old days the people in the area used to ... burn off the underbrush every year which would provide a new growth of grass which would attract animals like deer and other small animals ... Baskets became known in many of the tribes not simply as things to hold food in or things that might be made up of certain design, but ... symbolic of the process of interaction between people and nature. Not just items but something beyond items. And when that grass was no longer available because the forest service keeps

the forest from burning off every year so these shoots are not there any more, at least not in enough abundance to make baskets, but people can buy beads, they started converting to another medium the same designs that were once used in the baskets, but of course now there are different requirements. The medium is different. It looks different. The shape is different. The stuff is different. You might say the thing itself has become something different. But the idea has been maintained.

Then Toelken told another story, about a woman he invited from a northern California tribe to come to the University of Oregon, where he was working at the time, to teach basket weaving. Many students, especially local craftspeople, enrolled in the four-week class. By the end of the third week, a number of them, who had paid quite a bit to take the class and wanted to learn how to weave from somebody who really knew the traditional way, were becoming quite frustrated because they hadn't yet done any basket weaving. All they had learned was some songs. "We love these songs," they said to her, "but when do we get to the baskets?" The Aboriginal weaver looked confused and said, "that's what we're doing. A basket is a song made visible."

Just when his audience was about to feel a more or less respectful distance from all this basket business, Toelken talked about bowls, specifically the chalice used in Roman Catholic and other Christian Communion ceremonies.

It's a cup to hold liquid. Now what's your response if you happen to be standing around a church and a visitor from another country, say from China, comes along. He's got a rented car. Suddenly something goes wrong with the car. He decides to drain the water out of the radiator, or the oil out of the oilpan. He rushes around looking for something to put the liquid in. He goes into this unlocked building and sees this nice big container for liquids up on a table in the front, and so he carries it out and starts to put it under his car. Do you say "Well, go ahead. Nobody is using it in a religious service right now. Go ahead and drain your oil, and we'll clean up later." Most of us would say "Wait a minute. You can't do that. That's a chalice. That's a sacred item." And the visitor is going to say, "I don't know. It doesn't look sacred to me. It's for holding liquids. I need it very badly. See, I've got problems with my car. What's wrong with this society? This is backward." And you're going to be saying to him, "Look, no, no. That's a cup, sure enough, but that's a cup that means something else."

To many of us these are well-known sorts of stories, of a type that defamiliarizes familiar objects and thereby forces us to look at them in a new light – making strange so that we can make believe. This is what art always does, in fact, and when I raised earlier the possibility that lyric and dramatic modes may sometimes be as significant as narrative ones when it comes to representations of first encounters with others, I was thinking about how different modes of expression are premised on different forms of defamiliarization, each of which establishes different borderlines between reality and the imagination. Also, they are backed for belief by different assumptions about representation.

We are mainly concerned in this book with representation in language, so I will focus my comments there. In doing so, I want to turn our attention to the dynamics of listening and reading, instead of speaking and writing, and to replace the power politics of oral and written traditions that are the darling of postcolonial studies with the deep contradictions that lie at the heart of all verbal and visual representation.

One of these, which preoccupies historians, has to do with whether such representations are true or not. We will come back to this, for it troubles us especially when our accounts are in conflict. But there is another, equally perplexing, contradiction that has to do with an uncertainty about whether we live in or outside of our representations. This is both an ancient unease and a very contemporary one. It is bound up with contradictory ideas about whether language creates our thoughts and feelings or merely conveys them, and it has an interesting connection with first encounters. It used to be said that all words were originally metaphors, each embodying the sudden wonder of an encounter with something strange, and transforming it into what the twentieth-century philosopher Ernst Cassirer (following the nineteenth-century philologist Max Mueller) referred to as a "momentary god."[3] The god then becomes the word, according to this theory, in the same way that the wafer and the wine become the body and the blood of Christ in the Christian Communion. Theologians call it transubstantiation. Literary critics call it metaphor. We might as well call it a contradiction, and a pretty unnerving one at that.

Yet we often seem remarkably comfortable with it. Not necessarily with the Communion service, of course, though lots of people the world over believe in something like this within their various religions. But even those who do not, those who are unlikely to believe in things such as transubstantiation, routinely repeat the creed of their faith in defiance of the very dubious things that it contains and the doubt that is in their hearts. I mean no disrespect by this; for at the moment of saying so, they *do* believe.

There's something else here. These moments of encounter, transubstantiated into words, become communal as soon as they become language. That is, they are shared with others. So, of course, are the ceremonies that commemorate these encounters, which typically involve some sort of congregation. When you think about it, it is rather odd that we would want to say questionable things when others can hear us. Surely we would want to keep these moments – when we are challenged to "believe it or not" – strictly private. And yet we regularly go public with them; when we sing our national anthems, to take a secular example, we use words and phrases about people and places that we would almost certainly question in any other context. We say we believe when maybe we really don't ... except right at that moment, the ceremonial moment when the border is crossed, the covenant is renewed, and the challenge is to "believe it *and* not." At other times, it all degenerates into soggy wafers and some old wine, or a chalice that could be mistaken for an oil can, or some maudlin and melodramatic (and often brutally mistaken) words about home and native land.

*All* chronicles of events, it turns out, are ceremonies of belief. That is how language works; and once again, an old theory of language may help us here. Those first words I just mentioned – the resonant metaphors, the momentary gods – soon slip into conventional use. They become currency, like a two-dollar coin, and we lose our consciousness of their arbitrariness. They become what Ralph Waldo Emerson used to call fossil metaphors, for the life has gone out of them ... until singers and storytellers bring it back, making old words new again, turning the currency back into gold, refreshing language by restoring the wonder of metaphor and the strangeness of that moment of encounter.

Strangeness is the key. It signals that we are about to cross a border. I think the problem with some stories and songs from other cultures is not their strangeness, which part of us always welcomes, but the fact that we miss the signals they give that we are at the border; or we mistake them for signals of something else. This happens *within* communities often enough; but it is especially the case across cultures, where distinctions between myth and history, for instance – and the different arbitrariness or strangeness in the storytelling style of each – may be marked quite differently. In theatre, the stage itself provides a signal of the strange world we are entering, which may be why theatre travels fairly well across cultures. Most of us know all about entering a space in which Hamlet is both the Prince of Denmark and Laurence Olivier, or the figure dancing before us is both Raven and Uncle Fred.

Which is where metaphor, the basic trick of language, comes in: saying something is something else that it obviously is not, simultaneously allowing us to live in two worlds and undermining our ability – and, at least momentarily, our need – to distinguish between them.

Barre Toelken tells a story about living in southern Utah with his wife's family when he became very ill, contracting pneumonia. There was no doctor, no physician nearby. But there was a medicine man, a Native American diagnostician. The family called him in, and he concluded that Barre was suffering from a particular malady whose cure would be the red-ant ceremony. So a man who was very well versed in that ceremony, a seer, a kind of specialist in the red-ant ceremony, came in and administered it to him. Soon after that, he recovered completely.

Not long afterwards, Toelken, who was very curious about what had taken place, said to his father-in-law, "I wonder about the red-ant ceremony. Why is it that the diagnostician prescribed that particular ceremony for me?" His father-in-law replied, "Well, it was obvious to him that there were red ants in your system, and so we had to call in a seer to take the red ants out of your system." Incredulous, Toelken said, "Yes, but surely you don't mean that there were red ants inside of me." His father-in-law looked at him for a moment, then said, "Not ants, but ants."[4]

The Kiowa writer Scott Momaday, author of the novel *House Made of Dawn,* once used this story to describe how a traditional Indian view of nature involved bringing man and nature into alignment, first of all to achieve some kind of moral order and then to enable a person "not only to see what is really there, but also to see what is *really* there. Unless we understand this distinction," we will have difficulty understanding the Indian view of the natural world.

This kind of contradiction can be found in all cultural traditions – it is the basis of story and song in the sciences as well as in the arts – and unless we understand what Toelken and Momaday are saying, we may have difficulty understanding not just the Indian but *any* view of the natural world, including our own. There is also an interesting connection between Toelken's diagnostician and contemporary critical theory. The word "semiotics," popularized by Umberto Eco (author of the novel *The Name of the Rose*), comes originally from medical diagnostics, and simply means the interpretation of "signs." Hippocrates, the founder of medical science, first used it to refer to a patient's symptoms. Semiotics has become not so much the study of truthtelling as of everything that can be used in order to deceive us. If something cannot be used to tell a lie, Eco once suggested, it cannot be used to tell the truth; it cannot, in fact, be used to "tell" at all.[5]

We are discussing deep contradictions here, but they are ones we all know about. I want to use the example of tracking to underline how ancient this knowledge is, and also to shift attention (as I promised to do) from the cultural politics of speaking and writing to the cognitive dynamics of listening and reading. It is now generally argued that reading rather than writing signalled a change in human consciousness, as new reading practices followed the development of print technologies and nourished the great Renaissance innovations in reading the Book of Nature and the Book of God, which became modern science and Protestantism. But even scholars as attentive to ethnocentric epistemologies as Michel Foucault assume that it is only relatively recently that sign systems such as language have come to be understood as representations. I am convinced that the cognitive and cultural advances we associate with the development of reading practices in medieval and modern Europe were in fact flourishing thirty thousand years ago in the highly sophisticated reading practices of hunter-trackers around the world, who had an understanding of the contradictions of representation that was as complex as anything we might associate with the Renaissance.

The one thing trackers know when they see a track is that the animal isn't there. That's all they know. And they know that's all they know. This knowledge is at the heart of hunting and tracking; and it is at the heart of reading. I am not talking here about the ability of trackers to see animal signs, which paradoxically has led most commentators to miss the point. The systematic recognition of signs by traditional trackers is remarkable. But it is not reading. Rather, it is a necessary preliminary, the way recognizing a script or hearing a speech sound is. It is the first half of the process. The other half is how these signs are made to signify. Reading is qualitatively different from seeing, just as listening is from hearing; and in the case of reading, it involves learning to recognize the difference between a thing and the (always arbitrary, and sooner or later conventional) representation of a thing – the difference between a bear and the word "bear" or the spoor of a bear. This is what tracking is all about. It is also what we do when we learn how to read. We learn that the word's the thing. Which is to say, we learn that it is *not* the thing.

Like texts, then, tracks must be invested with arbitrariness in order to be read, for it is this arbitrariness that creates the distance that allows for the recognition of words or signs as representations. This is what we talk about when we identify the literary sign as the site of a relationship between the self and the other, creating difference. This is also what we should be talking about when we consider stories and songs of first encounters.

With familiarity, of course, we tend to naturalize all signs, whether we are engaged in hunting or hermeneutics; but we retain an awareness of their artifice, their arbitrariness, when we read them. That is why poetry is useful: it restores arbitrariness to language. We can find an interesting illustration of this in eighteenth- and nineteenth-century dictionaries and encyclopaedias in which definitions of poetry always included an exemplary speech by an Indian chief. Of course, we could call this romantic nostalgia. But we could also see in it an instinct (which we have all but lost) for the necessary artifice of any engagement with otherness.

We need constantly to remind ourselves how the uncertainties of representation (whether something is there or not) and of communication (whether we believe the teller or the tale) generate the very certainties to which we give assent in any story or song. Only then will we realize how our culturally conditioned awareness of artifice and otherness is linked with our cognitive awareness of arbitrariness and difference, and how this connection provides us with an understanding of texts, and of the reality they represent.

Let's take a moment to listen to Oscar Wilde, the godfather of all commentary over the past hundred years on the imaginative artifice of representation and the social construction of reality. "Where, if not from the Impressionists," he wrote,

> do we get those wonderful brown fogs that come creeping down our streets, blurring the gas-lamps and changing the houses into monstrous shadows? ... The extraordinary change that has taken place in the climate of London during the last ten years is entirely due to a particular school of Art ... Things are because we see them, and what we see, and how we see it, depends on the arts that have influenced us. To look at a thing is very different from seeing a thing. One does not see anything until one sees its beauty. Then, and only then, does it come into existence. At present, people see fogs, not because there are fogs, but because poets and painters have taught them the mysterious loveliness of such effects. There may have been fogs for centuries in London. I dare say there were. But no one saw them, and so we do not know anything about them. They did not exist until art had invented them. Now, it must be admitted fogs are carried to excess. They have become the mere mannerism of a clique, and the exaggerated realism of their method gives dull people bronchitis. Where the cultured catch an effect, the uncultured catch cold.[6]

With all the wit there is wisdom in this argument, and in its most famous aphorism, Wilde's signature song: "life imitates art." In another part of the essay (mischievously titled "The Decay of Lying") in which this passage appears, Wilde proposed that "the telling of beautiful untrue things" is the proper aim of all storytelling, and that the liar "is the very basis of civilized society." Perhaps this is why the Trickster – from the Greek god Hermes and the west African (and now West Indian) spider Anansi to the crafty Coyote and unreliable Raven of Native America – is at the centre of so many traditions of story and song.

Children know all about this, for they learn when very young about the contradictions of truthtelling. "It was, and it was not" is how storytellers of Majorca begin their stories. "Once upon a time" is how many of us begin ours, conjuring up both time immemorial and bedtime. Among the herders and hunters of southern Namibia and the Kalahari, where I have been working for the past few years, the word "*/garube*" is used; it means "the happening that is not happening." (Their language is Khoikhoi, the majority language of southern Namibia and widely spoken in the Northern Cape of

South Africa.) Interestingly, the root of ǀgarube is /*garu*, which means inconsistent speech by a sober person, the kind of speech or story that hovers between the accidental and the deliberate. It is not necessarily serious; and it is assumed that a story in such speech will be understood only by those who recognize the uncertainty of motive behind it. There is a prefix, /*gu*, which is sometimes used to intensify this sense of uncertainty; it refers to a story told by a dying person to someone else as his or her inheritance. Stories don't get much more serious, or more motivated, than that. Which creates an interesting convergence. The combination /*gu*/*garu* is used by Khoikhoi speakers to refer to stories that nestle between fact and fiction, between intentional seriousness and unconscious fantasy; and some Khoikhoi speakers in Namibia, who have been Christians for hundreds of years, use it to refer to the Bible, a contact narrative par excellence.

"Infinity is a place where things happen that don't," say the mathematicians, reminding us that this is the realm of the sciences too (since physicists give wonderful descriptions of atoms as miniature galaxies with colourful planets, curious moons, and remarkable orbits – and then admit that nobody has ever actually seen one).[7] The novelist E.L. Doctorow was once criticized for bringing characters together in his historical novel *Ragtime* who could not possibly have met in real life. "They have now," he replied. The German theatre critic Joachim Fiebach talks about how in certain stories words such as "ancestor" need to be translated very carefully, because they imply a dichotomy that many of us really don't accept. Then he quotes a Zulu expression, "father is departed, but he is." *Did the Greeks Believe Their Myths?* asks the French classicist Paul Veyne in the title of his book. Yes and no, he answers.[8]

At the end of *Portrait of the Artist as a Young Man,* James Joyce has his character vow "to forge the uncreated conscience of his race." The word "forge" is carefully chosen to catch the contradiction: it's both a forging and a forgery. The original Greek word for a trick was *dolos,* and the first trick was baiting a hook for a fish. Hermes, the messenger of the gods in Greek mythology, began his career when he was one day old by stealing cattle from Apollo, which he then barbecued but didn't eat, thereby making the point that some things are valuable not because they are useful but because they are special. Or, if you are a thief, because they belong to someone else. Lewis Hyde, in a book called *Trickster Makes This World,* catches the character of this kind of imaginative sleight of hand when he says that "Hermes is neither the god of the door leading out nor the god of the door leading in – he is the god of the hinge."[9]

Borders and hinges. Along with crossroads, these are among our most compelling images of the place where stories and songs work their magic. They are also, notoriously, places of conflict. Let's turn to an illustration of what can happen there, this time in a recent encounter. When the Gitksan

and Wet'suwet'en peoples of the northwest of what is now British Columbia, Canada, went to court to confirm jurisdiction over their territory in
what has become known as the *Delgamuukw* case, they told the history of
their people in the stories and songs that represent their past – *ada'ox* and
*kungax* they call them. One of the Gitksan elders, Antgulilibix (Mary
Johnson), was telling her particular ada'ox – the cycle of stories and songs
that were in her custody – to the court. At a certain point, she said that she
must now sing a song. The judge, Allan McEachern, was flummoxed, for
the request seemed to him to flaunt the decorums of his court. He tried to
explain how uncomfortable he felt having someone sing in his court. He
also said that it was unlikely to get him any nearer the truth that he was
seeking. He asked the lawyer for the Gitksan whether it might not be sufficient to have just the words written down, and avoid the performance. Met
with a dignified intransigence, he finally agreed to let Mary Johnson sing
her song; but just as she was about to start, he fired his final salvo. "It's not
going to do any good to sing it to me," he said. "I have a tin ear."[10]

Judge McEachern was roundly criticized for his comments, both by the
wider community and by the Supreme Court of Canada, which later heard
the case on appeal. It was indeed a stupid thing to say, for he wasn't the least
bit interested in the song or its music anyway. But it was also a smart thing
to say; for he *did* have a tin ear, and he couldn't have listended to the music
even if he *were* interested in it. Most of us go through life assuming that we
could make not only music but meaning out of Mary Johnson's song. For
the Mary Johnsons of the world, it is a sinister assumption. It is an assumption that understanding sophisticated oral traditions comes naturally to the
sympathetic ear. It doesn't. Just as we learn how to read, so we learn how to
listen; and this learning does not come naturally. It requires what the literary critic Northrop Frye used to call an educated imagination.[11]

For there is nothing remotely natural about listening. Hearing, yes; but
not listening. We recognize this distinction when it comes to seeing and
reading, but are less aware of it when it comes to hearing and listening. And
yet reminders are all around us, such as the strict protocols of almost all oral
traditions in which only certain people can tell certain stories to certain
people in certain places on certain occasions wearing certain regalia – like
judges, or priests. Or in which (as in ancient Greece) a lyric had to be sung,
an epic recited, a dramatic performance spoken.

Frye has written a lot about reading; but in one of his notebooks from the
1940s, he turned his attention to listening. "Learning to listen to music
easily and without panic is a valuable discipline," he proposed, "essentially
the removal of the barriers of panic and laziness." This is what Judge
McEachern could not or would not do. When confronted by the music of
Mary Johnson's testimony, he panicked; in courtly language, he said it made

him feel "judicially embarrassed."[12] And he was lazy, for he didn't want to be bothered to learn the listening protocols, much less the language, within which the song made sense. He knew they were there – he had moved the court from Vancouver to Smithers and had waived the venerable hearsay rule to accommodate them – but he couldn't be bothered to go any further.

Belligerent conservatives ask better questions than sympathetic liberals, which is why I am interested in Judge McEachern, his tin ear, and his tendentious "why not just write it down." He said something else as he dismissed the case. He said he believed Mary Johnson, but not her ada'ox. Another stupid statement. Certainly none of *us* would have said it. But it picks up that central question: do we believe the singer or the song? Far from being the product of twentieth-century arrogance, this reflects an ancient uncertainty that is right at the heart of many great traditions of pronouncement and performance, such as those of religion and poetry and law. And it bedevils our response to stories and songs of first contact.

From our discussion of credit, we know that belief and truth are not synonyms. With music, much of its power has nothing to do with what we call truthtelling, which may be why the judge was so uncomfortable. But we all know what it is to "believe" in a piece of music, even though we might not use that word (or, like Judge McEachern, might not be ready to give credit because we don't recognize the currency). Music and speech have long been linked in discussions about the origins of language, but surprisingly little attention has been paid to how we listen. Frye's offhand remark provides a useful point of entry, one which retains the imaginative as well as the instrumental dimension of listening. Panic and laziness conjure up a set of aesthetic counterparts that have long been accepted in the critical analysis of literary texts but which hold across disciplines: engagement and detachment; familiarity and strangeness; sympathy and judgment; the mystery of performance and the relative clarity of commentary. It may be useful to bring these to bear on contact situations. The uncertainty that defines listening – that leaves us hovering between story and storyteller, and wondering whether bearing witness is what the speaker does or the listener – is perhaps an ontological as well as an epistemological condition. Whatever the case, learning to listen is a complex and cognitively sophisticated process, which is why school (or its early equivalent) is one long lesson in the discipline of listening, of sitting silently while being taught to manage the twin menaces of panic and laziness, known in the teaching trade as anxiety and boredom; and of learning how to believe in the arbitrariness of it all.

And then there is the matter of truth. The Nobel laureate Halldor Laxness, on the eleven-hundredth anniversary of the settlement of his native Iceland, suggested that Icelanders have descended as much from books as they have from men. He was referring to the great sagas that have a central place in their literary tradition, and which have become their history, true within one of those narratives of nationhood that we all live by. Laxness poked fun at the invention of Icelandic genealogies which traced pedigrees back to Homer's Troy, and he described the storytelling of one Arngrimur Jonsson, who in the late sixteenth century set out to counteract the belief that Icelanders were the descendants of robbers, murderers, and slave owners with another version, straight from the sagas of medieval Iceland, in which they came from a long line of aristocratic heroes, noble commoners, and poets. In due course, his history changed northerners' sense of themselves. "Before Arngrimur's time," said Laxness,

> nobody seems to have asked whether the sagas were "true" or not. It is not very likely that the problem had ever come up. Arngrimur was the one who discovered that question, as well as the answer to it: all true. To a people enjoying true literature, it was an irrelevant question to ask, and the answer incomprehensible; a question inconsistent with your mental makeup – and with the world you live in. Like all great art, the saga is too great a truth in itself to be compared with reality. Such people were never born in the world who talk, or for that matter act, like the characters of, say, *Njal's Saga*.[13]

How then to judge the truth of a story or a song? How to decide whether we are in the realm of the imagination or in reality? One trick is to see things from different perspectives, recognizing that stories and songs work in two ways: they express their meanings in more or less direct communication; and they reveal them in what might be called fields of force. Most good ones do something of each; and listening and reading almost always involve both. Our unease with other people's stories and songs is often caught up in our uncertainty about the dynamics of expression and revelation, which is essentially the same uncertainty that bothered Judge McEachern about whether truth inhered in the telling or the tale, and whether the song represented reality or not.

Behind both of these is the uncertainty that I mentioned at the beginning of this chapter. When we bear witness about someone or something, our own credibility is always being judged; but a judgment is also being made about whoever or whatever certifies or backs our testimony. Though we don't always recognize it, it is often the ceremony itself that certifies the commentary; which once again brings us back to the role of the community – or those who are paid by it, such as priests and professors – to confirm that the ceremony is properly performed. Identifying the ways in which texts are underwritten by the artifice (a.k.a. the arbitrariness) of that ceremony and the assent of the community may do more than anything else to help us understand other people's stories and songs, and to judge their truth.

But though the notion of contradictory truths may be troubling to many of us, it shouldn't be. We routinely accept all sorts of contradictions. Think of two painters sitting early one evening across the harbour from a ship at anchor there. One of them, working in one particular mode of truthtelling, paints the ship according to the knowledge that she has of it – for instance, that it has twenty-seven portholes, and is grey. The other, working in an equally creditable tradition, paints seven portholes, because that's all he can see in the twilight; and he paints it in unlikely tones of pink and green, because that's what it looks like from where he's sitting at that hour of the day. He knows it's wrong; but he also knows it's right. The so-called Impressionists in the nineteenth century, who were sticklers for truth as they saw it even when what they saw was a pink cathedral, used to call this "seeing with an innocent eye," one undirected – unsocialized might be the current term – by painterly conventions and viewer expectations.[14]

Which is the true portrait? Both are determined as much by conventions of style – or ceremonies – as they are by any certainties; and either, taken out of its frame of reference, can be made to seem false or foolish. On the other hand, both are believable; and people believe both, praising each for its authenticity and authority.

Every imaginative tradition has allegiances both to the facts of experience, which in a sense are part of us, and to the formalities of expression, which are separate from us. To life and to art, we might say. Two truths? Perhaps; but instead of two truths we might say two stories, which together help us chart the convergence of reality and the imagination, showing us how conventions of visual or verbal representation are best understood not in isolation but by seeing where they meet others, and the world.

Let me give an illustration from two traditions of stories and songs, one ancient and the other contemporary. The Gitksan people of northwest British Columbia have lived in the mountains fishing and hunting and farming and trading for thousands of years. They have a story that tells of changes to one of the river valleys, near the mountain called Stekyooden, across from the village of Temlaxam.[15] It was once the centre of their world, one of those places that bring peace and prosperity to the people who live there.

This valley nourished the Gitksan so well that they became unmindful of their good fortune and forgot the ways that the mountains and the rivers and the plants and the animals had taught them. The spirit of the valley, a grizzly bear called Mediik who lived by Stekyooden, warned them and gave them many signs of his anger; but they ignored these warnings, until finally he got so angry that he came roaring down from the top of the mountain. Grizzlies running uphill are breathtakingly fast; I've been chased by one, and he looked like a freight train impersonating a gazelle. But because their front legs are short, grizzlies sometimes tumble coming downhill, and Mediik brought half the mountain with him, covering the valley floor and the village of Temlaxam and all the people there. Only a few survived, those who were out hunting in the high country or berry picking on the opposite slopes or doing the hard work that makes for an easy life.

This was just about thirty-five hundred years ago. Over time, the people returned to the valley, and although never the rich and fertile home it once had been, it always held its place in their history; and they remember the great grizzly and the lesson he taught them. Today the stories of the Gitksan move out from that valley like spokes from the hub of a wheel or children from their parents. It is the centre of their lives, the place they came from, and the place to which they return their thoughts and their thanks. Their present-day claims to the territory arise from the claims that the valley has on them, and the story of the grizzly and the slide confirms both claims.

Several years ago, when the Gitksan decided to assert their claims in court, they told this story. They told it with all the ritual that it required, for, as Mary Johnson reminded the court, the stories and songs that represent their past are about belief, and therefore need ceremony.

So do all stories, they realized. They also realized that the story of the grizzly and the sacred mountain called Stekyooden and the village of Temlaxam, which in their minds confirmed the presence of their people in that place for millennia, might not be believed by the judge, schooled as he was in stories of a different sort. So one of their leaders, Neil Sterritt, suggested they draw on another storyline to complement their own. They had geologists drill under the lake (now called Seeley Lake) that fills the valley, take a core sample, and analyze it. A scientific ceremony. The geologists discovered soil and plant material which matched that high up on the mountain slope, exposed where the grizzly had taken down the hillside – or where the earthquake had produced the slide that brought down half the mountain. And the sample dated from the exact time when the Gitksan story said the grizzly grew angry with the people in the valley, thirty-five hundred years ago.

The court was inclined to see the scientific story as confirming the legendary one. However, the elders of the Gitksan were at pains to persuade the judge that each story was validated by the other; that neither had a monopoly on understanding what happened; that the storyline of geology was framed by a narrative just as much the product of invention as the story told by their people; and that each storyteller's imagination – whether telling of tectonic plates or of grizzly outrage – was engaged with discovering a reality that included much more than the merely human.

The story of the grizzly is a very old one, hardened on an anvil of ancient tellings and tested by memories that disputed it for much longer than our seismic and sedimentary theories. The Gitksan believe both of them. Both, for them, are true. "Bear" and bear, as it were. Both are necessary for their people to live their lives. And both are revealed in stories.

The Mediik story may seem familiar to many of us, of course, because it is the story of a flood; *the* flood, for the Gitksan. Nonetheless, its power comes not from that connection, nor from the fact that flood stories are very common across cultures, but from the way it complements other historical and scientific accounts and yet still insists on its own authority, without discrediting others.

# 2

# First Contact as a Spiritual Performance: Encounters on the North American West Coast

*John Sutton Lutz*

> The first thing they did when they approached within about musket shot of the ship was to begin singing in unison to their motet and to cast feathers on the water ... [T]hey make a particular signal. They open their arms, forming themselves in a cross, and place their arms on the chest in the same fashion, an appropriate sign of their peacefulness.[1]

This first meeting of native and stranger, Haida and Spaniard, on the northeastern Pacific shores in 1774 was, like first meetings everywhere, brimming over with danger and possibility. Both peoples sought to minimize the danger and maximize opportunities. Without a common language, both did so by performing for the other.

Despite all their differences, the natives and strangers engaged in plays that contained many of the same messages and wrestled with similar questions. What gestures to make that would not provoke? What costumes to wear to inspire the appropriate awe or respect? What face to put forward to show the right mixture of strength and openness? What precautions to take to indicate readiness but not fear? What steps to take to prevent treachery? What gifts to offer to suggest one's wealth and interest in trade?

The first encounters between indigenous people and the Spanish and British along the northwest coast of North America in the eighteenth century were largely peaceful.[2] That they began this way hinged on the messages exchanged by speech and gestures, music and armaments, dress and deportment that comprised the contact performances. Undoubtedly, what was sent via the performance was imperfectly received by the audience, and the response to the misunderstood message was no doubt also misunderstood in a cycle of confusion. At the first meeting of the Spanish and Haida, the pilot Martinez recorded, "I asked them a thousand questions [by signs], all having to do with whether we could cast anchor, but they did not understand me, and their replies were to say that they had plenty to eat and drink if we would come ashore."[3] Still, the overwhelming desire for peace and the increasingly refined messages on both sides ensured that the misunderstandings did not cause offence.

Greg Dening has written about the theatricality which is always present in intercultural contact and "is intense when the moment being experienced is full of ambivalences. The 'encounters in place' of natives and strangers to the Pacific, 1767 to 1797, were full of such charades that were directed at producing effects in others." It was, he says, "a time of intensive theatre of the civilised to the native" but also, as I emphasize here, of the native to the stranger.[4]

A sailing ship is visible to the shore, and shore to the ship, long before it arrives, so both native and stranger had some time to choreograph their first messages. Even on those rarer occasions where natives and strangers stumbled upon each other without warning, performances were quickly improvised, each drawing upon earlier ceremonies where, in different contexts perhaps, they had performed for others. The strangers and natives performed their wealth and their interest in exchange for each other. That both were trading peoples, each with a cultural imperative to acquire wealth through exchange, goes some way to explaining the peacefulness of these encounters. But they also, I will argue, performed their spirituality – their mythology – for each other. These were not just diplomatic and trading encounters, they were spiritual encounters as well. Even more than their mutual desire for gain, it was the spiritual that, in large measure, determined the peaceable outcomes.

I have deliberately chosen the word "spiritual" for its capacity to encompass the vastly different religious beliefs of Europeans and indigenous peoples. Europeans were governed both by their religious beliefs and more secular cultural mores when they met indigenous people, the former obviously spiritual, but the latter also infused with moral guidelines based in religious teachings. Indigenous people made less of a distinction between the sacred and the profane. For the peoples of the northeastern Pacific shores, spiritual power animated the whole world, and every action had a spiritual component.[5]

The first contact was not so much "an event" for both European and indigenous peoples as an initiation of a dialogue which, once commenced, could not be easily broken off. To the limited extent that these contact texts have been compared before, they are usually seen as speaking past each other. Here I want to look at them as speaking to each other, and so in context with their counterparts across the cultural divide. Since the interactions were comprised of a series of performances, each in response to the other, it ought to be fruitful to see the early contact accounts as part of a single dialogue, a "contact situation" that encompasses both native and stranger.[6]

One of the most obvious difficulties is comprehending the performances of the indigenous participants. One must of necessity enter into a world that is distant in time and alien in culture, attempting to perceive indigenous performance through their eyes as well as those of the Europeans.[7] Clearly, this is a challenge that can be met, at best, only partially. But this difficulty we are at least aware of. The key and usually unremarked problem is that we have insufficient distance from our own and our ancestors' world view. The hidden, and so more rarely engaged challenge, is to step outside and see one's own culture as alien and to discern the mythic in the performances of one's own histories.

Treating the contact situation as a single analytic field means putting both parties under the same ethnohistorical lens, asking the same questions of the different stories, regarding the relationship of spirituality to history, and of myth to history. When we do this, we find that both Europeans and indigenous peoples situated their contact encounters in mythohistorical frameworks imbued with and coloured by their spiritual beliefs. The "mythic and historical modes of consciousness" were interwoven in the records of both native and newcomer.[8]

Spirituality has long been out of fashion in contact stories told in history and anthropology, a result of two generations of scholarship that have denigrated its importance. An earlier generation of scholarship portrayed the contact encounter as a meeting between a technologically sophisticated, intellectually complex, rationally oriented Europe with a simple, primitive, and spiritually credulous indigenous population.[9] That many indigenous peoples initially confused Europeans with supernatural beings was held out by Europeans as a sign of their own superiority and the simple ignorance of indigenous people. It made Europeans feel good if, in the stories about these encounters, the explorer, be he Captain Cook or David Livingstone, was received as a god in the eyes of the Natives. Whether or not indigenous people thought of the Europeans as gods, European observers were hoping to see themselves in that role.

No wonder, then, that a generation of scholarship has been written against this tradition. From the 1960s and '70s on, scholars have taken pains to describe the sophisticated nature of indigenous cultures, the dark side of the so-called Enlightenment voyages, and the downside of the explorers. This scholarship emphasized indigenous agency and rationality, arguing that indigenous people drove hard bargains with Europeans and made only those deals which they considered favourable.[10] This view largely inverted the assumptions of the previous generation. In its well-meaning attempt to be relativist, it implied a universal rationality across the European-indigenous cultural divide. This scholarship emphasized how smart and rational indigenous people were; it also downplayed indigenous belief systems and their role in shaping the indigenous response to the immigrant. Yet "rational" is a code for particular cultural beliefs – individual maximization and utilitarianism – historical constructions culturally specific to western European nations and their offshoots. This attribution of rationality to other peoples was not the cultural relativism to which this generation of scholars aspired: in fact, it achieved the opposite – a projection of European ideals to the rest of the world, "reproducing rather than critiquing the cultural and political hegemony of western industrialized societies."[11]

When, in 1981, Marshall Sahlins stepped beyond the dichotomy of the canny/credulous, rational/irrational Native in attributing the murder of Captain Cook to the spiritual beliefs of the Hawaiians, it is no wonder that he was jumped on by Gananath Obeyesekere and that their debate has been so polarized. Obeyesekere, as a spokesperson for the (postmodern wave of the) second generation, misread, as did some other indigenous people, what Sahlins was doing, and believed he was hearkening back to the first generation.[12] The postmodern critique surely tells us that what is considered reasonable behaviour in one culture – propitiating the nature spirits before embarking on a voyage, for example – would be irrational behaviour in another. In my view, Sahlins led a third generation of contact studies, looking at how people behaved "rationally" within the context of their own cultural definitions.[13] Moreover, a closer look at the Europeans would show that their rational behaviour was also determined, in part, by their nonrational spiritual beliefs.

Let me relate to you a contact story now.

This story, first recorded at Port Simpson on British Columbia's north coast in 1860, refers to the first arrival there of Europeans in 1787. The version I quote was told in 1916 by Ts'msyen (Tsimshian) George McCauley to anthropologist William Beynon:

The people were all living on the south end of Pitt Island. Here they gathered their winter food of halibut and fur animals, seals and otter ... One day, two Gitrhala [Gitxaała] men set out from their village to fish for halibut and were so absorbed in fishing that they failed to notice a large boat approaching. When one of them looked up, he saw a huge being with many wings approaching towards them. They at once thought it was a monster which lived in the nearby rocks. They were at the time fishing over a spenarnorh ("abode of monster") from which a huge Raven used to emerge (a crest of "Arhlawaels, Kanhade"). They thought that the monster had now taken a new form and was approaching to do them harm. So they drew up their fishing lines, which were made of kelp (mawrh) and paddled in for the shore. There, they thought they would be safe. The man that was sitting in the stern had the rope of the canoe fastened around his waist. Then they landed, the man in the bow of the canoe ran up into the woods, and the man in the stern got up and tried to follow, but failed to untie the rope from his waist. It tightened and he fell down and was overtaken by these strange beings, who resembled human beings. They came up to where he was lying and untied the rope, and he now set up and looked at them and became frightened. To protect himself he urinated in his hand, and rubbed the urine all over his body. The Gitrhala used to protect themselves from monsters and supernatural beings and ghosts, by rubbing themselves with their urine, thus breaking off any bad influence of the supernatural beings. If anything appeared to do them harm they would throw their urine at it. The urine was always kept close at hand in their houses and never wasted. These strange men now picked him up and made motions for him to come down to the canoe. They pointed first to the canoe and then to the halibut, and then to their mouths. This they kept on doing while saying "Soap," which they gave him and took a halibut from the canoe. The Gitrhala man thought that they were giving him a name. Then they made signs for him to cut the halibut up for them. So he took his knife of albatross bill and began to cut up the fish. These strangers took the fish from him and cut it up quickly. He was then frightened on seeing their weapons for cutting. These strangers then motioned him to build a fire, and he went down to his canoe and brought out his firing outfit (gyins), and began to build a fire. He worked a long time. Meanwhile, these men had gathered some moss and got their flint-lock revolvers, and set it off. When the Gitrhala man heard the report, he fell right over and "died" (sadaek, suddenly died, meaning fainted away). As he came to, he saw a huge fire burning, and now knew that these men were supernatural. So to give himself double protection, he again urinated in his hand and bathed his body. The men came to him and made motions for him to cook fish. He then went down to his canoe and got his cooking box and set stones in the fire, and filled his box up with water. As soon as the stones were hot, he put the halibut in and then the hot stones in the cooking box and kept on changing the stones. The strangers looked on for a while, and then one of them went down to the boat and got a large pot and put water in it and put the whole halibut in the pot and then boiled it on the fire. The Gitrhala man was now much frightened. When the fish was cooked, the men got out something else out of another pot which the Gitrhala man thought to be maggot (this was rice), and began to eat. They poured upon the rice black stuff which the Gitrhala knew to be the rot of people (this was molasses). They made motions for him to eat, but he was so afraid that he could not move. He now saw that they were eating and that they would not harm him. So he called out to the other man, "Come on down. They are eating. They won't touch anybody."

They were eating the rot of people, along with maggots, and they were also eating adaeran (a fungus growth on trees) much like a mushroom, very dry, and large. These were biscuits.

After these men had finished eating, they made signs to the Gitrhala to show them where they lived.[14]

Some years later, George McCauley again told the story to Beynon, but this time added a continuation about how the supernatural monsters then visited the village. The strangers came ashore and were treated to a series of dances which showed the Gixaała (formerly called Kitkatla) chief's spiritual power. Then the villagers were invited onto the water being:

> They saw many fearsome things, they saw hanging down among the ropes many human skulls all around this monster and these skulls had ropes running through the eyes of the skulls and when the ropes moved they gave a groaning and moaning sound. When the Gitxałas saw these things they were very much afraid ... After they had been here some time, one of the [white] men came with his supernatural horn, which he blew and then all of the super[natural] beings danced, all dancing around the great chief of the supernatural beings.[15]

Finally, the story relates that the chief exchanged his name with the captain of the ship, and that henceforth the chief used the name Hale.

Clearly, we have performances within performances. George McCauley was engaged in storytelling in front of an audience, Beynon. He tells of a series of performances, at first improvised, as the first encounter was unexpected, and then ritualized and formalized as dances were performed and names exchanged.

But were they spiritual performances?

Indigenous peoples on the northwest coast and their ethnographers tell us that when Europeans arrived, the Native people lived in a world where there was no firm divide between the natural and the spirit world. The astronomical and meteorological phenomena, the plants and animals, even rocks and the sea, were all alive and cohabited in a world with human beings and their ancestors. Many of these other-than-human beings had another manifestation in their own parallel worlds which was human-like. Thus, the salmon lived in the water but could take off their fish skins when at home and live as humans do, and likewise the other creatures. Their homes were parallel worlds under the sea, in the sky, and over the horizon; in one of these parallel universes, the dead also lived. Spirits could be enlisted by properly prepared individuals to help, but they could also harm. People could communicate with the other-than-human beings in certain states of heightened vulnerability and awareness – dream states, fasts, or quests – and in these circumstances the spirits of humans could move into the other universes and return.[16]

The oral histories of the Ts'msyen are full of supernatural encounters and lessons on how to deal with them,[17] so when a strange vessel sailed into the Gitxaała territory in 1787, there was no doubt about what this item was. It appeared over a spot associated with a supernatural being and the super-natural trickster, Raven. There was only one rational thing to do. Douse oneself in urine.

The Gitxaała account is a rich one, and variants of it have been recorded several times, the first in 1860, probably within the living memory of a few who were young in 1787. Owing to the relatively late timing of contact events in the north Pacific and the structured form of storytelling among the people living here, there are many such accounts from the west coast. In the course of this research project, I have identified close to two hundred different surviving accounts, recorded between 1789 and the present, of how indigenous people perceived the arrival of Europeans on the west coast of North America.[18]

When we look at a large number of these accounts, we see a wide variety of stories, not surprising given the amazing diversity of indigenous cultures on the west coast. But the Gitxaała account related above has something in common with almost all of them. Europeans are shown as associated with the spirit world.

This is not to suggest that Europeans were seen as "gods." Indigenous people here had no gods that they worshipped. Instead, they were aware of a wide variety of spirits that could take human form. In the stories of various peoples, Europeans and their ships were interpreted as having various links to the spirit world. They were commonly associated with the parallel world in the sky (from which many indigenous groups traced their ances-try), the land of the dead, the tricksters Raven and Coyote, or other "trans-formers" who had the power to change their form.

For example, several Nuu-chah-nulth stories have been recorded about the arrival of Captain James Cook's vessels, the first British ships to make landfall on the shores of the Pacific Northwest. In several of these accounts, Cook's ships were described as having come from the sky, more particularly from the moon, according to some. "Everything pointed to confirm the shamans' statements that these were the moon men. They wore yellow, had a brass band in their caps, brass buttons and epaulets that shone like the moon." The moon was the most powerful of all the spirits in Nuu-chah-nulth cosmology.[19]

An account of Cook's arrival recorded by E.O.S. Scholefield from Chief George of Nootka Sound offered several supernatural explanations:

At first they thought it must be an island appearing, but as the object grew larger they saw it was some kind of watercraft. The ship was going quickly and making great waves. Then it was thought that it must be the work of Haietlik, or the lightning snake, making it move so quickly, and that the snake was working under the water; but others thought it must be the work of Quaots (the supreme deity of the Nootkans) and therefore a supernatural manifestation. Some of them thought it was magic, and some thought it was a salmon that had been changed by magic.

The association with the supernatural Qua-ots (*kāʔōts*), who was supposed to have arrived at the beginning of time in a copper canoe, might have been suggested by the copper sheathing Europeans used to prevent teredo worms from devouring their wooden ships.[20]

A version of this story recorded by Mary Amos from Machalat Peter goes on to say that only men who had been sexually abstinent for ten months were considered pure enough to approach the being. These were led by a female shaman who hailed the ship, "Hello you, you spring salmon, hello you dog salmon, hello coho salmon." In this story, the strangers were salmon people. After this encounter, the Tahsis *(tcesis)* people performed the "white man dance" whenever they had a feast, to reaffirm their connection to this spiritual event; the dance involved, among other things, wrapping their legs up as if they were wearing pants and holding burning sticks in their mouths.[21]

The Cook stories have the great advantage of reminding us that we ought not to be surprised by conflicting versions of the same event. This is particularly true on the northwest coast, where stories, especially accounts of supernatural encounters, were secret knowledge owned by specific families.

The theatrical nature of the first contact was also recorded by Captain Cook's officers:

After we had anchored the boats came alongside without hesitation but none of the Natives chose to venture on board ... as they had no Arms and apperd very friendly we did not care how long they staid to entertain themselves, & perhaps us; a man repeated a few words in tune, and regulated the meaning by beating against the Canoe sides, after which they all joined in a song that was by no means unpleasant to the Ear ... As they were now very attentive & quiet in list'ning to their diversions, we judg'd they might like our musick, & we ordered the Fife and drum to play a tune; ... they Observd the Profoundest silence, & we were very sorry that the Dark hind'red our seeing the effect of this music on their countenances. Not to be outdone in politeness they gave us another song, & we entertained them with a French horn, to which they were equally attentive.[22]

Indigenous accounts of the first encounters with Europeans, coming from different parts of the Pacific's northeastern shores, have a spiritual component in common. I will mention just a sample of the more accessible ones. Squamish Andrew Paull's account of the meeting with George Vancouver near the site of the present city of Vancouver stresses the fact that Vancouver arrived at a spiritually potent time. According to Paull, the Squamish believed a disaster would befall them every seven years; Vancouver's arrival coincided with the seventh year, so special steps were taken to propitiate him.[23] Revealing a common motif in the indigenous narratives, Squamish Louis Miranda and Philip Joe related that the strangers on the ship were thought to be from the land of the dead – because of their pale faces and they way they were wrapped up tight in their clothes, like corpses in a blanket.[24] Several Nlaka'pamux accounts of their meetings with Simon Fraser identify him as the "sun"; others suggest he was a manifestation of the transformer-trickster Coyote. Many accounts say that the European ships were thought to be a supernatural bird, the Clatsop and Tlingit identifying it with Raven, the Trickster and Transformer.[25]

The names that indigenous people gave the Europeans are revealing of the link to the spiritual and suggest more than just a brief association of the two. The Nuxalk were divided on the opinion of whether the whites were people returned from the land of the dead or people from the sky. They called whites Qomcua, after a supernatural being who lived in the sky. Catharine McClellan notes that the Yukon Dene described the first whites they encountered as Cloud people, from their pale faces and the assumption that they came from the sky; a Tsimshian name for whites has the same origin.[26]

Secwepemc (Shuswap) called Europeans "Spetê´kɬ," the "Old Ones" or "Ancient Ones" in Shuswap language, because they were thought to be associated with the powerful transformer beings who once travelled through their land. Carrier Dene called the Europeans "Needo" and the Tsilhqot'in "Midugh," meaning, literally, "above us," possibly suggesting a celestial origin.[27]

The appearance of the Europeans was a novel manifestation, but it was not a threat to the indigenous spiritual ordering of the world. These strangers had a place in their world, inhabited as it was by the supernatural. Clearly, indigenous people were processing the new through the familiar, a principle Anthony Pagden calls *attachment*.[28] Rather than immediately destabilizing traditional beliefs, the arrival of Europeans was merely part of the ongoing proof of these beliefs.

Europeans too came to these encounters with a spiritual helper. For them, the encounter with the Pacific coast of America stemmed in part from an Enlightenment interest in science, a power play in an imperial game, a seeking after material advantage, and an imperative of their own spirituality. These were not separate interests: spirituality and religion intertwined with science, empire, and trade, and so, for Europeans too, the encounter was a spiritual one. For some of the voyages of exploration, one of the explicit purposes was evangelical. In other cases, even those where profit or science were the primary objectives, Christian spirituality and the eighteenth-century understanding of God and man's relationship to him underlay the whole enterprise.

This is most obvious on the Spanish missions. The Spanish voyages all carried priests aboard on a reconnaissance of souls, looking for information about the indigenous people and the possibilities for establishing missions. The instructions issued to the first European voyage under Captain Juan Perez were to enlarge the king's territories "so that their numerous Indian inhabitants ... may receive by means of the spiritual conquest the light of the Gospel which will free them from the darkness of idolatry."[29] We get a sense of how their Catholic spirituality pervaded their world view from the first observation of the Haida, noted in the epigraph on page 30. The Spanish recorders, priests, and officers all described the Haida as forming themselves in a cross as they approached the ship. Captain Perez described them as singing a motet, meaning "a vocal composition in harmony, set usually to words from Scripture, intended for church use." The priest, Father Juan Crespi, noted that a short time later, when a second canoe arrived, "night had fallen, and we were all reciting the rosary of Our Lady of the Immaculate Conception ... Seeing that no attention was paid to them, because we were at prayers, the people in the canoe began to cry out, and they continued shouting until such time as the daily recital of the rosary and special prayers to some saints were concluded and the hymn of praise, which caused great admiration on their part, was sung."[30]

The invocation of Spanish spirituality was nowhere more explicit than in their performance of acts of possession/dispossession. When, on 30 June 1790, the Spaniard Manuel Quimper was rowed ashore at Royal Roads, near what is now Victoria, British Columbia, he read the act of possession, which starts, "In the name of God, the Trinity, the Maker and Creator." John Kendrick describes the procedure: "Having disembarked with most of the seamen and soldiers and carried ashore a Cross which they adored on their knees," the troops bore it in procession, singing a litany. When the procession ended, they planted the cross in a mound of stones, under which they placed a bottle sealed up with pitch which contained the "Acta de Possesion." The reason for taking possession was given: it was "to bring the word of the Holy Gospel to the Barbarous Nations so that they might escape the snares of the Demon and their souls might be saved."[31]

Less transparent but no less significant was the pervasive spirituality of the age of exploration in the Pacific on board the British Protestant ships.

The eighteenth century is normally thought of as the Enlightenment and the Age of Reason; the spiritual is often downplayed. But the spirituality of the Enlightenment, in spite of a few well-known examples, was not materialism, or neo-paganism; it was a new, more inquisitive and expansive Christianity.

The eighteenth century witnessed the rise of Western Protestant missionary activity and the establishment of a plethora of denominational missionary agencies. Examples include the Society for the Promotion of Christian Knowledge, founded in 1698, the Baptist Missionary Society of 1792, the London Missionary Society of 1799, and the Church Missionary Society of 1797.[32]

R.S. Sugirtharajah notes that the creation of these missionary societies was contemporaneous with the founding of the trading companies such as the Hudson's Bay, the East India, and the Dutch East India Companies.[33] This was also the period of the exploration of the Pacific.

Enlightenment Christianity had two countervailing impacts on the contact experience. On the one hand, the new emphasis on science as a way to understand God's plan was the spiritual foundation for the voyages of British explorers Cook and Vancouver, of the Spaniard Malaspina, and the Frenchman La Pérouse. It was as if the kings of Europe had taken up King Solomon's proverb that "The Glory of God is to conceal a thing, but the glory of the king is to find it out."[34] Cook and Vancouver were not religious men, but neither were they atheists. Their journals testify to their belief in Providence and God's blessing of their mission. Their instructions enjoined them to reflect glory on their king, and it was not necessary to state that theirs was not only a Christian king but the head of their church. Their instructions required them to show the Natives "every kind of Civility and Regard," in line with their faith, but also to facilitate the pursuit of science.[35]

The other side of European spirituality was the inferior position it ascribed to indigenous people. In this view, the uncivilized and unchristian indigenous people were not the equals of Europeans. While James Cook was probing the far reaches of the Pacific, European intellectuals were engaged in a battle over whether man had been created in a single or a multiple genesis. If the genesis had been single, as the Bible describes, indigenous people at best represented a stage of civilization that Europe had transcended a thousand years before; at worst, they had degenerated from the divine image that God himself had set on the earth. The polygenesis approach argued that indigenous people, like other non-Europeans, were not descended from Adam; they were not made in God's image, but from other inferior creations and so were not fully human.[36]

Both the single and polygenesis approaches, however, left no doubt that Christian Europeans were superior to all non-Christians. Lack of Christianity was the criterion that marked *terra nullius*, or "empty land": according to

European "law," lands not claimed or occupied by a Christian nation were "empty" and so open for claim by any Christian country. The spirituality in Europe's formal religious acts, such as the adoration of the cross and the rituals of possession, was also performed in its laws and the mixture of scientific investigation, paternalism, and disdain with which Europeans first greeted indigenous people. Christianity is to Europe what the transformer stories are to the indigenous west coast of North America. Indigenous rationality rested on the transformer myths as European rationality and assumed superiority rested on Christian mythology.

The recontextualization of the first contacts as spiritual encounters for all parties helps explain why they were largely peaceful. The coincidence of the particular European and indigenous spiritual views was a prerequisite to peaceful trading. The specific conjunction helps explain why Cook was feasted here and eaten in Hawaii. Perhaps the best proof of this is the rarer situations where one side or the other did not make a spiritual connection, or where an aggressive spirituality disposed one party to violence instead of peace.[37]

When, in 1775, the Quinault first met Europeans between the mouth of the Columbia and Cape Flattery at the entrance to the Juan de Fuca Strait, they showed no special awe of them. It was these two landings of Spaniards, from the *Sonora* under Bodega y Quadra and the *Santiago* under Bruno de Hezeta, that constituted the first European landing on the northeast coast of the Pacific (south of Alaska). Hezeta, who went ashore at 4:30 in the morning of 14 July to read the act of possession, met six unarmed indigenous men who traded salmon and other fish to the Spaniards for beads. A few miles to the north, the *Sonora* sent a boat ashore with seven well-armed men to replenish the water supply and cut some poles. Quadra reported that "When they arrived on land, some three hundred Indians, falling upon them treacherously, had surrounded the boat and knifed those who were in it." Evidently, all seven Spaniards were killed.[38]

The Quinault and their immediate neighbours to the north, the Makah, had no dread of the spiritual power of Europeans. They exhibited this again in 1808 when a Russian ship was wrecked on their shores and the survivors, including a woman, were enslaved, the usual practice with strangers.[39] The Quinault experience suggests a possible outcome when no spiritual link was made with the Europeans.

There is a plausible explanation for why the Quinault were unusual in their response to the Europeans: they had met offshore strangers before. In 1833, a dismasted Japanese fishing ship washed across the Pacific and wrecked itself on their coast. The three Japanese crew members who remained alive were promptly enslaved. Probability suggests that in the two thousand years that the Quinault had occupied these shores, this was not the first such arrival. The Quinault name for these exotic strangers was "wandering people." The Clallam, also neighbours to the Quinault, called them "men who washed ashore," a name that predated the arrival of Europeans. Most likely, the Quinault (and Clallam) were integrating Europeans into a pre-existing category of seaborne strangers, and not the spiritual world.[40] In west coast societies, strangers – people with no kin connections – had no standing, and attacking, killing, or enslaving them would not constitute a transgression of social norms.[41]

As contact increased between native and stranger on the west coast, the integration of the "other" through the "spiritual world" ebbed. On the European side, the expeditions to the Pacific northeast became more specialized. Initially, the explorers were replaced by the merchants. Merchants were also a product of European spirituality but tended to emphasize the inferior place ascribed to indigenous people in European culture, rather than the paternalism and scientific curiosity that characterized the voyages of discovery. The result was an increase in the level of violence inflicted by Europeans on indigenous peoples. Later, the merchants were replaced or augmented by missionaries. Clearly, spirituality was the overriding concern for the missionaries, and thus the mission-led interactions with indigenous people were at the peaceful extreme of the continuum. As the forerunners of the Canadian and American states were formed, the government took on and reflected the conflicted spiritual views regarding indigenous people. Since then, the spiritual and mythological elements in the European approaches to indigenous people have changed but have not disappeared.

On the indigenous side, increasing familiarity with Europeans altered their understanding of the European links to the supernatural but did not destroy them. Indigenous associations of the European and the spiritual persisted in variable forms, and from people to people, long after the early contact experience had ended. The continuance of these beliefs, which has been not been sufficiently acknowledged in studies of this process, obviously requires a full examination in its own right. But since this longevity speaks to the importance of the spiritual at first contact, let me outline an argument for that persistence.

Distinctly indigenous views of the spirit world survive today in many indigenous communities. This is evident from the statements of indigenous people themselves, from the persistence of the winter spirit dances in many communities, the ongoing potlatch exchanges, the Shaker Church, and the use of good and bad "medicine" to help or harm people. The evidence is also statistical. A 1972 survey of Indian bands in the Fraser River drainage of British Columbia asked "does anyone in your band think the salmon spirit is important now?" Representatives of 32 percent of the bands said yes, and the positive responses ranged from a high of 43 percent in the upper Fraser drainage to a low of 13 percent in the urban Fraser Valley.[42]

If the belief in the spirit world is different and less widespread than it was 250 years ago, does this mean that a more or less linear decline occurred in such beliefs? Not likely. Although it may have taken only a short acquaintance with Europeans for indigenous people to decide that they did not come from the salmon world, the land above, or the land of the dead, and that they were not manifestations of Raven or Coyote, it took a long acquaintance before Europeans and their goods lost their association with the supernatural.[43] The place of the European stranger has shifted in indigenous cosmology, but probably not as rapidly as some have suggested.[44] Likewise, the place of indigenous people in European cosmology has shifted, but slowly, unevenly, and incompletely. When Europeans found a densely occupied "empty land," they were not immediately prompted to re-evaluate their belief systems. When they found indigenous people working hard, this sight did not immediately undermine the myth of the "lazy Indian."[45]

It is in the nature of belief systems that they change slowly, and that their strength is precisely in incorporating the novel into the familiar. In explaining to themselves what was happening and what had happened, indigenous people (and Europeans) had nowhere to turn but their own mythic consciousness. If Europeans were not from the land of the dead, or the sky, alternative explanations which were consistent with indigenous cosmologies were quickly developed.[46]

As Dening points out in the context of the South Pacific, "The waves of diseases that swept over Indigenous People reinforced cultural beliefs rather than challenged them. They believed that it was sorcery that caused them even as they associated them with Europeans." On the northwest coast, the oral histories also tell of smallpox as a supernatural disease, sometimes linked with Europeans, and sometimes not. Fur traders used their association with supernatural powers to threaten and control the local peoples. And when Frances Densmore was collecting songs among the peoples of the northwest coast in the 1920s, she recorded the spirit songs that had saved many people from dying of smallpox.[47]

Moreover, indigenous people, like Europeans, were perfectly capable of understanding their spiritually linked ideas on a number of levels. When we say that something is supernatural, we may mean that it is of the spirit world, or that it is far beyond the ordinary, or that it has characteristics we would normally associate with the spirit world – perhaps one of the meanings invoked in the popular tourism slogan "Super, Natural British Columbia." Likewise, we must assume that indigenous people were and are perfectly capable of holding metaphoric and literal meanings of their spiritual beings at once.[48] Calling the newcomers the "Old Ones" does not necessarily mean they were literally thought to be the Old Ones. It may mean that they had characteristics that invoked the stories of the Old Ones, and so they seemed to be associated with them. This is particularly true, given that their main spiritual actors – Coyote, Raven, and Mink – were tricksters with lusty sexual appetites and the full range of human frailties that constantly caused them trouble.[49]

In a coastal indigenous society, wealth came from having powerful spiritual helpers. The wealth of Europeans, and especially their access to metal goods and weapons, implied that if they were not spiritual beings themselves, they had powerful spiritual allies. A full generation after the first encounters, the Tsimshian were still telling stories of meeting supernatural Europeans.[50] Europeans also appear in the indigenous pictograph and petroglyph rock art associated with spiritual encounters.

That indigenous people remained interested in European spiritual powers even a century after first contact will come as no surprise to those who have read the recent work on indigenous relationships with missionaries on the northwest coast. In most cases, missionaries were invited into indigenous communities by community members who sought them out. Some indigenous people, anxious to obtain help from a white ally, saw economic benefits from association with the missionary. Few were interested in replacing their own spiritual beliefs and powers with Christian ones. They sought to add the spirit powers of the whites to their own.[51]

For a time after first contact, European goods also had a connection to the supernatural, so even the exchange of goods had a spiritual context. We see this especially in the indigenous ritual use of copper associated by the Nuu-chah-nulth with the spiritual figure Qua-ots. Indigenous people often incorporated European trade goods into their spiritual ceremonies and used them as items of adornment to show a link to the Europeans themselves.[52] The use of pants in the white man dance mentioned above, or the fact that the Chinook called buttons by the name they used for stars, are examples. European items worn to signify a connection to Europeans include one of the two spoons taken from Perez's ship on its brief halt near Hesquiaht. This was worn as an adornment around the neck of a chief until purchased by Captain Cook; the first axe head traded in Haida Gwaii was also used as an ornament on a necklace.[53] Such associations endured for a century at least.

One example of the lasting association of Europeans and their goods with spirit powers comes from the accounts of a Stó:lō man, Old Pierre, given to anthropologist Diamond Jenness in the 1930s. Old Pierre talked about the persistence of the belief in spiritual helpers and noted that the steam engine and the locomotive were particularly potent spiritual helpers among the dancers with whom he was associated. Irving Goldman, working with the Ulkatcho Dene in the 1940s, found that objects from the "white world," such as a spring mattress, were held in special veneration, used as status symbols, and not slept on. Catharine McClellan, working with Tutchone elders in the 1970s, heard them recall that their shamans had spirit helpers that came from tobacco, 30-30 shells, angels, books, and mirrors, as well as the more "traditional" natural helpers.[54]

The recognition that the first and ongoing contacts between native and stranger were spiritual encounters as well as material ones asks us to rethink the contact history of the northeastern Pacific coast. Indigenous and European peoples did not have a spiritual view of each other at one moment and a rational view the next, nor did they have to choose between one or the other. In most cases, as Jonathan D. Hill points out, "mythic and historical modes of consciousness complement rather than oppose each other." Myth can, has, and does provide the foundation for understanding history.[55]

This reinterpretation asks that we take spirituality seriously. To do this, we have to re-examine our joint history. An ethnohistory of any contact event asks that we probe the extent to which the European as well as the indigenous history was recorded and performed in a language steeped in its own spiritual mythology. Understanding the spiritual component of contact events, and the stories that have arisen from them, should bring a better understanding of the misunderstandings embedded in those foundational first encounters.

# 3

# Reflections on Indigenous History and Memory: Reconstructing and Reconsidering Contact

*Keith Thor Carlson*

Half a century ago, the historical philosopher R.G. Collingwood posited that the historian's ultimate goal was to re-create the conscious thoughts of a person from another era.[1] We know that in attempting to meet this objective, historians have occasionally committed some of the worst acts of intellectual colonialism, appropriating and misrepresenting the motivations, intentions, understandings, and voices of marginalized people from past eras. And yet the fault lies, perhaps, less in the exercise than in the failure to meet Collingwood's criteria. For him, the elusive objective could be achieved only through a careful questioning of one's sources and the application of what he referred to as "inferential" knowledge. Toward the same end, while advocating a similar method of intellectual questioning which he refers to as "dialogic reading," Dominick LaCapra has emphasized the moral obligation historians have to the people they seek to understand and depict. For LaCapra, the dialogic process "refers in a dual fashion both to the mutually challenging or contestatory interplay of forces in language and to the comparable interaction between social agents in various specific historical contexts."[2] Dialogic reading recognizes "that projection is to some extent unavoidable insofar as objects of inquiry are of intense concern to us because they pose questions that address significant values or assumptions."[3] Thus, LaCapra suggests that we consider multiple meanings, often shaped by cultural context, for terms and expressions that might otherwise appear self-evident. Reasoning along similar lines in his remarkable and oft-cited essay "Thick Descriptions," Clifford Geertz points out that the anthropologist is "seeking in the widened sense of the term in which it encompasses very much more than talk, to converse with ... [Natives], a matter a great deal more difficult ... than is commonly recognized."[4] In these regards, anthropologists and historians are engaged in very similar exercises. What historians seek to accomplish across a temporal divide, ethnographers strive to realize between cultures. The ethnohistorian seeks to do both.

The ethnohistoric exercise can never be merely academic. Whereas the forces of globalism have long compelled indigenous people to try and see the world as the colonizers do, representatives of colonial society have only recently begun to recognize the value of inverting this paradigm, of appreciating the value of indigenous knowledge and ways of knowing. To engage in this counter-colonizing process is to move toward creating an intellectual middle ground, an academic contact zone where good measure can be given to the tales of traders as well as the Transformers, and where the epistemological walls between modernist and postmodernist, between First and Second Nations, can be breached by the construction of ever thicker descriptions of metaphorical understanding – descriptions that might permit us, as the other's other, to at least begin to learn how Natives think, about history and memory, for example.[5]

In seeking this goal, academics are not operating in intellectual isolation. In Canada, for example, the Supreme Court of Canada recently acknowledged the validity of Native oral history in its judgment in *Delgamuukw v. British Columbia* (1997). In Canadian jurisprudence, oral history is no longer merely equated with the Western legal concept of "hearsay." In a somewhat related decision of the previous year *(R. v. Van der Peet)*, the same judicial body determined that where an Aboriginal community demonstrates that an activity had been an integral part of its ancestors' society prior to the assertion of British sovereignty (which in British Columbia was 1846),[6] that activity could be protected as an Aboriginal right.

Many scholars and lawyers have rightly hailed these decisions as important and just. Taken together, they potentially validate not only Aboriginal historical experience, but also the way in which that experience is known or understood. In particular, they emphasize the significance of the contact era and the contact experience. Yet I know from experience that, since *Delgamuukw,* expert witnesses and First Nations organizations who have tried to introduce Native oral history into the courts have found that the legal forum remains unable or unwilling to adequately deal with Aboriginal oral history on terms that are meaningful to the Native people and societies who have created and preserved them.[7]

Much of the cause for this disjuncture lies in the assumption found within the 1997 *Delgamuukw* decision that Native oral histories work in fundamentally the same way as Western history, and that these bodies of indigenous knowledge will therefore necessarily supplement and enrich an existing historiography and jurisprudence derived from what are largely archival-based understandings of past happenings. Raising the methodological and epistemological problems of this assumption is not to suggest that Western and Native forms of historical understanding are necessarily incompatible or set in incongruous opposition to one another. Nor should this concern be too quickly associated with the sort of relativistic approach that sometimes leads to all historical narratives (Western and other) being disregarded as equally invalid portals for better understanding genuine past happenings. Rather, the fundamental dilemma seems to hinge on the issue that, as Native oral histories assume a greater presence in Canadian courts and politics, the narratives and the cultures they represent might find themselves increasingly abused in a manner not dissimilar to the way that victims of sexual crimes have often found themselves doubly violated by the courtroom cross-examination experience.[8] If, for example, oral history is seen as contradicting or running contrary to evidence gleaned from documentary sources, how will the courts determine the relative validity of the two bodies of evidences? Already we are seeing that the judicial system considers those oral histories that lack documentary confirmation to be a subordinate order of information and interpretation. Perhaps more to the point, if, in litigation involving an inter-tribal dispute, two competing or contradictory Aboriginal oral histories are presented, will the courts be equipped to assess the contending narratives' relative validities by criteria that have indigenous import? The same question applies more broadly to historians as we encounter, interpret, and use Native oral history in various academic, political, and legal contexts.

This chapter makes no claim to having fully penetrated an indigenous epistemology. Rather, it is the product of sustained dialogues with both documents and people that aspires to set a foundation from which future analysis can be launched and future dialogues started. It is based upon more than a decade of intense social and professional interaction with Coast Salish people living along the lower Fraser River watershed in southwestern Canada. In order to better understand the way in which Central Coast Salish society functions within history, I begin by exploring the way that history functions within Central Coast Salish society. I use contact narratives as the primary vehicles for communicating this analysis. First, I provide a brief outline of the two types of Coast Salish historical knowledge (and an explanation as to why I feel the standard ethnographic descriptions dividing them into two separate bodies of information relating to two separate periods of history are inappropriate). Next, I engage in an analysis of the indigenous discourse over the importance of "keeping the stories right." What does this cultural mandate mean in terms of historical accuracy and legitimacy, and do such concepts transcend cultures and time? I conclude with a comparative look at the role of memory and "authorities" within the functioning of Coast Salish and Western history.

Among the Coast Salish, history is a serious matter. It continues to be used to validate social and political status, as well as personal and collective identity. The upper class (which Wayne Suttles argues made up the majority of the population at first contact) is known in the Halq'eméylem language as *smela:lh* – literally "worthy people." When asked to define the meaning of worthy people, fluent elders typically explain that it refers to "people who know their history." Lower-class people, by way of contrast, are called *s'texem*, a term translated as "worthless people," because they have "lost or forgotten their history."[9]

Knowing one's history serves a number of important social, economic, and political functions. Ownership and regulatory rights to productive family fishing grounds or berry patches continue to be inherited today. Without detailed genealogical history linking a person to such sites, one would be "worthless" in a very real sense of the word. Likewise, leadership was largely hereditary and, either formally or informally, it largely remains so in many Coast Salish communities. In the distant past, certain men, who might best be thought of as "genealogy founders,"[10] rose to prominence after performing great feats. Genealogical ties to these men, and memory of their heroic actions, are important components in succeeding generations of leaders' claims to their own prominence. In a similar manner, certain ritualists were trained to memorize (and occasionally supplement) the epic sacred stories of creation describing the establishment of order in what was a chaotic world. These people were especially valued because their vocational knowledge was considered to augment and reinforce the genealogical narratives relating to property and leadership, and because the stories they protected and transmitted were the basis of inter-tribal social and diplomatic relations. For example, indigenous historians discussing the important actions of the Transformers as they created the tribal ancestors of one community often refer to the important and necessary movements of those same characters to other regions for the acquisition of power or some other key resource.[11] Individual tribal histories, therefore, are inextricably linked together as chapters of a larger supra-tribal history that informs the collective consciousness of a much broader region and serves as the basis for the establishment of more formal socio-economic and political alliances.[12] Thus, in a way that is often difficult for outsiders to appreciate, the Coast Salish world remains anchored to a foundation of shared memory and historical understanding, constructed from overlapping and shared oral history and historiography.

In a society where history is regarded as the arbitrator of so many facets of identity and power, conflicts inevitably arise over matters of historical interpretation. The most intense and disruptive conflicts might be best thought of as history wars, that is, as clashes wherein one group challenges the historical legitimacy of another's historical claim to hereditary rights and prerogatives.[13] For the Coast Salish, where, until recently, European-style literacy played no role in the transgenerational transmission of historical information and knowledge, historical validity remains intrinsically linked to personal and collective family reputations. People are sources of history,[14] and given this, few things are more important than an individual's reputation as a historical expert.

The Central Coast Salish method of constructing and conveying oral history, as well as the techniques used to determine historical legitimacy, is complex. As I understand it, the Coast Salish have two distinct categories of historical narratives: the first, called *sqwelqwel*, often translates as "true news"; stories from the second group are referred to as *sxwoxwiyam*, which are often interpreted as legends or "myth-age" stories. Typically, Western observers have regarded sqwelqwel as the more legitimate form of history based on memories of real events, and sxwoxwiyam as fictitious stories. Because outsiders generally consider sqwelqwel to be based on actual happenings, there is an assumption that they are more stable than sxwoxwiyam, that is, less prone to manipulation and change. Such distinctions, however, do not exist in the minds of the Coast Salish. Wayne Suttles has shown that both types of historical narratives are regarded as equally real, but what is less appreciated is the fact that the indigenous rules governing their usage impact their mutability, and that such matters are important to the indigenous people who depend on these narratives to interpret the past so as to make sense of the present.

A metaphor that perhaps approximates the indigenous understanding of the concepts of sqwelqwel and sxwoxwiyam history, and their relationship to one another, might be that of a single play unfolding simultaneously on two separate stages. On the first stage occurs the drama of the physical world with which most of us are familiar. On the second are depicted the actions of the *xa:xa* (sacred or taboo) realm of the spirit world. The spiritual actors on the second stage are able to observe the actions on the first, but the physical actors on the first generally cannot see the characters and happenings of the second. Actors from one stage can, and occasionally do, move through obscured passageways and enter the action on the other stage. Access points for beginning the journey from the physical stage to the spiritual stage are found at various xa:xa places located throughout the physical landscape, but only specially trained people can successfully negotiate the arduous and danger-fraught journey into the spirit world. Spirit actors, meanwhile, can and do enter the drama of humans, often emerging into the physical world through these same xa:xa portals. Their visits can be short or lengthy. The play's "author" and "director" is Scha-us, the "Great First," or Creator.[15] However, he has revealed the drama's full script only to the spirit beings on the second stage, and so his directions are opaque to all humans except the shamans who have made the journey to the spirit world. These ritualists may occasionally hear the Director's directions, but more often they learn of the Great First's intentions second hand from their associates in the spirit world.

Thus, Coast Salish history is one filled with significant points of interpenetration between the two dimensions of sqwelqwel and sxwoxwiyam. In the ancient past, the penetrations were so frequent as to make the two dramas essentially indistinguishable – the passageway separating the stages was often open and visible, so to speak. More recently, the drama occurring in the sxwoxwiyam spirit realm has played a slightly less prominent role in the ongoing drama of contemporary Coast Salish human history, or sqwelqwel.

Sqwelqwel represents a body of historical knowledge/memories that generally consists of information about past happenings to which the speaker has some direct connection. That is to say, sqwelqwel describes events that happened to a particular individual or to someone the conveyor of the information knew or knows. Among the most important sqwelqwel are those relating to family history. As mentioned, genealogy stories link the present generation to important figures from the past; as such, they are among the most valued of the sqwelqwel narratives. Recently, in discussing the integrity of historical genealogy narratives with two elderly fluent Halq'eméylem-speaking women, I was told that in the past there were people who were recognized as the keepers and communicators of all family histories. These people, typically but not exclusively men, were referred to as *sxá:sls*, which they translated as "he who keeps track of everything."[16] The sxá:sls' task, as they understood it, was to "take care of everything our grandparents taught [showed] us."[17] In the mid-1930s, a Coast Salish elder known as Old Pierre from the Katzie Tribe on the lower Fraser River explained that prior to the assertion of non-Native legal hegemony, whenever a dispute arose as to the proper form and content of such a historical narrative, it became necessary to "summon two old men who belonged to different villages, but were both well versed in local histories" to discuss and reconcile the differing historical interpretations.[18] Severe variances in historical interpretation, Old Pierre maintained, required the defender of a particular version of history to enlist two additional "lawyers" to plead his case, after which, as the anthropologist Diamond Jenness recorded, the adjudicating "old men retired to consult in private. Whatever decision they reached was final."[19]

Sqwelqwel stories are not exclusively about genealogy. They can range from the common to the spectacular. A discussion of where one was last night and what one ate for dinner is just as much a part of the sqwelqwel discourse as a riveting account of how someone once killed a grizzly bear using only a small sharpened bone as a weapon.

In instances where the historical action within a sqwelqwel does not directly involve the story's teller, it is expected that a connection with the events and the speaker will be created through a process perhaps best thought of as "oral footnoting." That is to say, the audience will expect speakers or tellers to explain how they know what they know. Someone relating a sqwelqwel about an incident that occurred a century ago, for example, might preface the narrative by saying something like, "This story is about my great-grandfather. I was told this story by my grandmother, who did not see the actual events but learned of them from her father's brother (my great-grand-uncle), who was with my great-grandfather when it happened." The validity of such stories is not necessarily assessed against criteria of extant evidence. Nor is the question of "probability" (as generally defined by mainstream Canadian society, i.e., not supernatural) generally considered important. Rather, validity is primarily determined according to the status of the teller in relation to the listener and the various individuals (historical conveyors and actors) identified through the oral footnoting process. Thus, a particularly detailed and horrifying story one elderly woman shared describing how her great-aunt had been kidnapped, raped, and impregnated by a *sasquatch*[20] from which she had ultimately escaped was believed to be an accurate account of real happenings by all the listeners I spoke with afterwards. It was perceived thus not only because sasquatches are thought to be real,[21] but because the speaker and her family were highly regarded. They were well trained, they knew not to lie: as the other people realized, this family understood that its cherished status would drop should it ever be caught lying. Cognizant of this, the elder was trusted to speak truthfully in order to maintain her family's social standing.

This, however, is not to say that sqwelqwel are immutable. According to Coast Salish people, the decision to enrich a sqwelqwel so as to make it entertaining is not incorrect. Nor is it the sole prerogative of the speaker to decide when a sqwelqwel will be enhanced. This is not to say that the accuracy of a story is simply a function of the social situation in which the speaker finds him- or herself (sqwelqwel are not simply responses to the perceived needs of an audience or listeners). Rather, many Coast Salish consider that on certain (possibly most or all) occasions, sqwelqwel are composed and shared not only with the intention of telling people how things happened or what happened, but also to create special spiritual contexts. Emotions are generally regarded as being directed or guided by omnipresent ancestral spirits. People are happy because the ancestors want them to be happy. People are sad because the ancestors want them to be sad (that is, to mourn, or to grieve, or to solemnly contemplate). People who act in accordance with ancestral guidance can generally expect to live healthy and fulfilling lives. Elders often refer to those who do not as examples of

people whose troubled lives and inner turmoil are the products of a dislocation from their ancestors' spirits.

Thus, exaggeration and intentional manipulation of sqwelqwel can and
does occur, even by high-status speakers. Although status and careful oral
footnotes help establish a speaker's integrity, and therefore the perceived
validity of a narrative, what appears to be of vital importance is the intent
behind the speaker's utterances. Is the relating of particular past happenings designed primarily to convey historical fact (or a particular lesson), or
is it intended more to communicate some other kind of message? Is the
history meant to be humorous, and if so, is the humour more important
than the facts? Funny stories are not infrequently exaggerated (perhaps it
would be more accurate to say that certain aspects of particular stories are
emphasized and then enriched) for the purpose of making them funnier.
Listeners generally understand and even expect that such narratives are being
somewhat manipulated to create and communicate humour, and therefore
to create a happy social and spiritual atmosphere. This most typically occurs when the original action was considered devoid of humour as it was
occurring, but in hindsight became funny. For example, one Coast Salish
man shared a sqwelqwel that had all of his extended family and guests at a
dinner gathering literally shedding tears of laughter. He recounted how one
night, while returning from an evening of somewhat excessive socializing
at a local pub, he was surprised by the sudden appearance of a deer's reflective eyes in his car's headlights. "Luckily for me I'd been drinking, and so I
was only driving about 20 miles an hour," the speaker chuckled as he introduced his sqwelqwel:

> I slammed on the brakes and screeched to a halt about fifteen feet from the
> deer [everyone at the table begins to laugh because they know car tires
> don't screech at twenty miles per hour]. That deer just stood there frozen in
> the headlights. I thought to myself, "Now here's a situation. A deer just
> sitting there and me without my rifle." Well, what could I do? I got out of
> the car and walked toward the deer. It just stood there – stupid like [speaker
> imitates the look on the deer's face]. I looked toward the side of the road
> and there was a good-sized rock [gestures to indicate a rock about the size of
> a softball]. I picked it up and walked up to that deer, and WHAM! I hit it up
> side of the head. Well, you should've seen it jump. You should've seen *me*
> jump! But I grabbed hold of that big deer and took another swing with the
> rock. But that deer was tough. He started dragging me away, so I swung
> again. [At this point the speaker has jumped up from his chair and is mov-
> ing about the room in very animated fashion, alternating between his ac-
> tions and those of the deer. People at the table are laughing extremely hard
> and wiping away tears.] Finally, the deer stopped moving. I had done *it*! I'd

hunted a deer without a rifle – just like a real Indian, eh? But I still had a problem. I didn't have a rope to tie the deer down [on the hood of my car]. But I had to get that deer home right then. If I didn't, some white guy might come along. Then there'd be trouble, eh? [Speaker pauses and people at table stop laughing to ponder this important point.] If a white guy came along he'd probably take credit for killing that deer with a rock himself and take the deer home to *his* wife! [Everybody bursts out laughing at the irony.] So I hoisted that deer up on the hood of my car and started driving. Slowly, slowly, slowly along that old bumpy pot-holed road. Then, I guess one of those potholes woke the deer up! He wasn't dead, he was just knocked out! He slid off the hood of my car and started staggering around the road so I jumped out to get him [speaker again emulates the wobbly deer's actions, and then his own unsteady movements]. I found another rock and I gave that deer a *real* good hit. He was dead this time for sure. So I hoisted him back on the hood and started off again. When I got home I told everybody [all extended family living in the immediate area] to come out and see my deer: "I've been huntin' with a rock," I said. They wouldn't believe me. But when they checked that deer over they couldn't find no bullet holes *and* no crushed bones like there would be if I'd hit him with my car. No sir, I killed him with a rock. I killed him with a rock twice![22]

After he finished speaking, and while all of us sitting around the big kitchen table were still laughing, the speaker's brother-in-law looked at him incredulously, smiled, and asked if the story was true. "Course, it is," he replied with a smile, then added, "Would an Indian lie when a white man's listening?" At this point he looked directly toward me, the only "white man" at the table. "You sure would," his sister interrupted with an accusing tone – after which there was a long awkward pause as the room grew silent before she added with a smile, "You never owned a car. You had a truck!" Everybody laughed again.

Interactive historical accounts like this illustrate not only the function of fiction within true stories, but also the manner in which our presence as outsiders affects what is being told and how it is being told. They challenge us to consider seriously our roles in both the ethnographic and the historiographic processes. Viewed in this light, contact was not only a moment that occurred when representatives of an Aboriginal society first met a representative of a non-Native community, but a series of moments that occurs repeatedly, and yet somewhat distinctively, each time people speak across cultures.

Of course, spirits are not exclusively, or even primarily, interested in guiding historical discourse simply in order to establish mood and social context. Ancestral spirits are also considered to be regularly listening to (that is, monitoring) the actions, thoughts, and spoken expressions of the living –

especially if acted, thought, or spoken in front of open fires after dark.[23] People are particularly careful not to dishonour their ancestors by lying, for ancestors may take reprisals for actions or words that disgrace them. In order to avoid creating even the perception in the minds of the ancestors that someone might be speaking of the past in an inappropriate manner, many contemporary elders still avoid speaking of the recently deceased, or even uttering their names, after dusk, except in appropriate spiritual and ceremonial contexts. Improper historical utterances might be inadvertently interpreted by ancestral spirits as beckoning; "called" spirits who are not properly greeted have a tendency to become confused – a condition that creates an imbalance in the spirit world. Confused ancestral spirits frequently assume that they were summoned because one of the living is suffering or lonely, and so, with the best of intentions, the ancestor might take away the person's soul to comfort it in the spirit realm – a condition which, if left untreated by a shaman, is fatal. Concern for such matters is, at least rhetorically, especially strong among the hereditary "upper class," who, as Suttles has documented and my own fieldwork confirms, claim to have more extensive training and knowledge of metaphysical matters.[24]

Not all alterations of historical speech are for effect or the result of carelessness. Despite taboos, people will occasionally exaggerate or even fabricate elements of a sqwelqwel. Although lying is generally regarded as an expression of people's improper attempts to enhance their status, and therefore beyond what ancestral spirits would endorse, it nonetheless occurs – and not only for those reasons. One relatively recent and illustrative example of this involves a man whom I shall call John Doe.

I first spoke with John Doe in 1992 while working on an eight-month contract with the Stó:lō Tribal Council. I had been asked to conduct archival and oral history research into the question of "traditional Coast Salish leadership." My academic training had been principally in archive-based history. Interestingly, as I later learned, though I considered my inexperience in anthropology and oral history a serious deficit in my skill set, it was, in large part, what initially made me attractive to the Tribal Council leadership. Justice Allan McEachern had recently delivered his ill-conceived and now infamous *Delgamuukw* decision in which he rejected oral history and the evidence of anthropologists in favour of what he deemed the superiority of historical insight gleaned from documentary evidence. Of course, McEachern's interpretation of archival documents as objective voices from the past which spoke for themselves, and of historians as readers who simply pluck quotes, was, as Robin Fisher pointed out, an example of the sort of historical enquiry that Collingwood had earlier dismissed as "scissors and paste" history.[25] Nonetheless, it apparently was at least partly responsible for briefly transforming people with history graduate degrees into hot commodities: "We were told [by the courts] that historians are what we need to win land claims court cases," the Tribal Council's executive director of Aboriginal rights and title later explained to me, "and so we decided we'd hire an historian."

During the course of my research, I ultimately conducted repeat interviews with thirty-one people who had been identified for me as knowledgeable elders and cultural experts. Through their generosity and patience, I came to appreciate and expect that elders' oral traditions would not necessarily contain the elements historians used to assess the legitimacy of Western archives-based histories. Rather than referring to specific first-hand historical observations or records (something impossible in oral histories discussing events beyond the personal memories of the present generation), the Salish elders emphasized their relationships to both the historical actors and the various sources (earlier generations of "tellers"). Thus, in those stories that were not simply the recounting of events within the teller's own life, elders often validated their narratives by referencing the person from whom they had heard the story, and, where possible, with additional references to the antecedents of that source ("I heard this story from my great-uncle, who heard it from his uncle – who was my great-great-grandfather").

On other occasions, when the links between the various generations of sources were perhaps not as well known to the teller, elders were generally careful to provide contextual information about the central figure discussed within the historical narrative, such as his or her relatives, family status, and other notable facts. In either case, the elders were providing what might best be thought of as "oral footnotes" – references that in highlighting the link between themselves and the historical actors, and/or the various intergenerational transmitters of the story, served to sustain and enhance the status of both. In this way, the validity of the historical action/actor was linked to, and in part a product of, the status of the conveyors of the historical information, and vice versa.

Although he was not originally on the list provided by Tribal Council officials, one of the organization's employees suggested that I interview John Doe. Apparently, he professed to have much knowledge about traditional leadership. Upon further enquiry, I learned that John Doe perhaps possessed a great deal of historical knowledge on a range of topics. But when I asked some of the elders I had already interviewed for their opinion, I learned that more than a few people regarded him and his historical information with suspicion. My enquiries were greeted with responses ranging from conspiratorial smiles and short answers such as "Ah, don't listen to him; he tells strange stories; nobody really believes him" to faintly veiled anger:

"He's a damn liar, I don't know why he makes those things up. It only hurts us all."

In the late 1980s, I was told, John Doe had begun to assert that he had important historical information which was unknown to others. On many occasions, and to a host of different people, he allegedly claimed, among other things, that he was able to trace his genealogy back twelve generations (most Coast Salish, I learned, generally consider knowledge of seven or eight generations to be the maximum extent of pertinent genealogical information, and so this seemed both remarkable and unprecedented).[26] He also claimed that he knew of a Spanish fort that had been established near Yale in the lower Fraser Canyon in the late eighteenth century (a generation before the 1808 arrival of Simon Fraser, thought to be the first European to visit that region). John Doe also allegedly contended that he had visited, and therefore knew the location of, several archaeological sites that contained astounding and unparalleled finds. One of these was a hermetically sealed clay-lined "pithouse" that had been abandoned centuries earlier, but which was still in perfect condition and filled with wonderfully preserved artifacts. Another was a deep vertical cave on a mountaintop that he alleged was the birthplace and home of X̱á:ls, the Transformer, and into which John Doe supposedly claimed to have been lowered two hundred feet on a rope.

Although certain people looked upon John Doe's claims to privileged historical and cultural information with suspicion and even disdain, not everyone did. Among a different segment of the local Aboriginal population, John Doe was increasingly regarded as having been selected by the ancestors as a special carrier and conduit of historical information. As such, he was acquiring a reputation as both a cultural leader and historian. Moreover, even people not associated with him were pointing out that if his information was true it might be of assistance in advancing Aboriginal rights and title. The existence of such remarkable archaeological sites in such remote locations, for example, could be used to support the Aboriginal claim to the land and its resources by showing that the current population's ancestors had made use of the resources in a wide territory. The Spanish fort was of particular interest. The Tribal Council's director of fisheries, its cultural researcher, and its land claims lawyer individually approached me to enquire whether the story of the fort might be true. If the Spanish had established themselves on the mainland of British Columbia, they reasoned, there might be supportive archival documents. Such documents, if they existed, might describe "traditional" Coast Salish activities that could be used to reinforce arguments for recognition of certain Aboriginal rights – in particular the right to the commercial sale of salmon.

I expressed my reservations, explaining that there was no reference to a Spanish fort on the BC mainland in any of the historical literature with which I was familiar. Even so, I agreed to look into the matter, first by talking directly with John Doe and then enquiring among other elders and cultural experts to see if his account of the Spanish fort could be corroborated, or, alternatively, explained in other terms. Negative evidence (in this case the absence of archival documents) would not justify concluding that something had not existed or happened, especially if an oral tradition maintained that it had.

When I first met with John Doe, he explained that he preferred not to discuss the matter of traditional leadership with a non-Native outsider, but he agreed to speak with me on a host of historical topics, including the pithouse, the Transformer's cave, and the Spanish fort. Respecting his wishes, I confined my questions to these topics. During our conversation, however, he made it clear that he would not reveal the details about how to find the pithouse or cave; nor would he divulge to anyone how he came to learn about the Spanish fort.

In my follow-up conversations with other elders, I was unable to identify anyone with information about a pre–Simon Fraser Spanish fort. It became apparent that many viewed John Doe not as blessed with special powers of perception and knowledge, but rather as a weaver of creative works of fiction. One person criticized him as someone who had too little training in historical and cultural matters to have legitimately learned such detailed information. Another hinted that the inadequacies (low-status ancestry) of John Doe's character made it unlikely that the spirits would have favoured him with the gift of such knowledge. Still another dismissed the Spanish fort account as untrue, not because he knew the fort did not exist, but rather because he was familiar with other of John Doe's historical narratives (those relating to cultural matters), which he claimed to "know" were false, and so dismissed the fort story as well. Indeed, what appeared of most concern to everyone who criticized John Doe was his rising popularity. How and why, they wondered, could other Aboriginal people not recognize that his descriptions of cultural history were liberally peppered with creative embellishments? And they worried that perhaps this lack of recognition was yet another indication of culture loss; perhaps people were losing the traditional skills needed to determine what was real and what was false – what was good history and what was not.

Significantly, for the purpose of comparison with Western historical methods, the various indigenous critiques of John Doe's history did not necessarily involve the checking of evidence. Initially, at least, none of his Coast Salish critics seems to have asked him to share his twelve-generation genealogy, to provide details about the Spanish fort (such as where it was located and when it was established), or to take people to the archaeological sites and cave. Instead, they generally asked, "Well, who did he get that stuff [information] from? I never heard that before. Who told him that?"

John Doe's evidence was deemed unreliable not because he had failed to produce the physical evidence, but because he had consistently failed to use adequate oral footnotes to validate the manner in which he had acquired his knowledge. In other words, he was being discredited because he failed to trace his knowledge through recognized experts or authorities, and in this was proving himself "unworthy" in some eyes. As one widely respected elder observed, "A 'good person' would tell us how he knows that stuff; who told it to him."[27]

A few years later, in the mid-1990s, John Doe began adding information to his historical narratives. Earlier, he had refused to provide details, arguing that he had been entrusted to protect the history. Ordinarily, among the Coast Salish, such an argument carried a great deal of weight. Aspects of knowledge, especially spiritual and historical knowledge, are widely considered "private." To publicly share such information so that others may use (or misuse) it is to weaken its import, and by extension to lower the teller's status.[28]

And yet, in this case, perhaps John Doe felt that he could silence his critics only by verifying the authority behind his evidence, even if this meant revealing all of it. Accordingly, and to many people's surprise (for they had assumed the information was orally transmitted to him), he explained that his knowledge was in large part derived from archival documents he had read in the 1970s at the Aboriginal Resource Centre's archives. It was in the archives, John Doe revealed, that he had read a 1894 publication by Franz Boas, in which the prominent North American anthropologist had recorded a detailed Coast Salish genealogy.[29] John Doe apparently had added the four succeeding generations of information to Boas' existing list, thereby establishing the link to himself. This was certainly an example of accurate research and a legitimate and valid act, but he was criticized for treating the published material as though it were his own private preserve, even keeping it from members of his extended family. A non-Native employee at the resource centre had also allegedly been with John Doe when he visited the archaeological sites. In fact, Doe asserted that this employee had lowered him on the rope into the deep cavern. Additionally, the story of the eighteenth-century Spanish fort had also originated with the archives, for it was there, John Doe revealed, that he had obtained old documents proving the fort's existence.

Although these facts briefly aided John Doe, ultimately, they could not withstand the persistent public scrutiny. When one elder slyly pointed out that, as far as she could remember, the resource-centre employee was not physically capable of making the strenuous hike to the remote mountaintop cave, let alone lowering a man of John Doe's robust stature two hundred feet into a crevice and then pulling him out again, the newly acquired shine faded from John Doe's sqwelqwel. By noting the flaws in the cave story, people were implying that John Doe probably told untruths about the other information as well. Over time, even a few of his former supporters joined those who did not take his stories seriously, perhaps for the simple reason that his failure to meet the indigenous criteria for legitimacy subsequently called into question the worthiness of his facts on all subjects.

Although John Doe's sqwelqwel was ultimately deemed illegitimate and therefore unimportant to most Coast Salish people, readers might be interested in further information regarding the Spanish fort. The fact that, in the early-to-mid 1990s, he had spoken of the fort's existence with a number of graduate students, some of whom recorded the story as a Coast Salish oral history, makes this perhaps all the more relevant. Indeed, this was a major concern of some of the political leaders and elders who knew of John Doe's discussions with the students: "Did the non-Native students believe him?" Although they hoped not, they also worried that if the students *dis*believed him, they might, by association, dismiss all Aboriginal oral history as false or made up. Moreover, an examination of the place of John Doe's historiography in connection with the Spanish fort provides a convenient segue into a treatment of other sqwelqwel pertaining to the contact era, which in turn provide an entrée into discussions of the functioning of the second genre of Coast Salish historical knowledge – sxwoxwiyam.

　　Although John Doe never showed me the copied documents he allegedly received from the archives, I suspect, having reviewed the Aboriginal Resource Centre's archival cartographic holdings, that he based his Spanish fort assertion on a reading of nineteenth-century maps. In 1814, David Thompson produced a map of the northwest coast and Columbia Plateau for the North West Company.[30] Much of this map was based on Thompson's own first-hand observations, but the portion depicting the stretch of the Fraser River between its junction with the Thompson River and the Pacific Ocean is derived solely from Thompson's reading of Simon Fraser's 1808 journals. On this portion of the map in bold print is a notation reading, "To this Place the White Men have come from the Sea." Additionally, on a number of maps produced in the 1850s, the word "cañon" appears adjacent to the river near present-day Yale.[31] One can imagine how, collectively, such evidence could be taken to infer that the Spanish had come from the sea to establish a garrison. "Cañon," however, is not (as one could be forgiven for assuming) a reference to military cannons, but the Spanish word for "canyon." It depicts the point on the river where an adventurer from the sea could expect to encounter cataracts and rapids, indicating the entrance to the Fraser Canyon. Thompson's reference to white men from the sea is likewise apparently derived from his reading of Fraser's journal. The Scots explorer noted that, upon arriving at a village near present-day Yale, he and his men were escorted to the shore near Lady Franklin Rock and there "informed ... that white people like us came there from below." Fraser recorded that he was then "showed indented marks which the white people made upon the rocks" (marks Fraser dismissed as "natural").[32]

It is interesting that Fraser and his men were brought to this spot and told the story of the "scratch marks." Today, local Coast Salish historians still bring visitors there to explain how the marks were made by X̱á:ls (one of three bear brothers and their sister who collectively are referred to as X̱ex̱á:ls, or, in English, as the Transformers). Together and independently, the Transformers had incredible powers of alteration that enabled them to change people into objects. The world takes its present form largely because of the actions of the Transformers. One of the best-known transformer stories recounts how X̱á:ls made the scratch marks near Lady Franklin Rock while engaged in a battle with an "evil Indian doctor" who was sitting on the opposite shore of the river. Each time X̱á:ls "used his power against the Indian doctor he grit his teeth and scratched a mark into the rocks with his fingernails."[33] The competition continued for some time until X̱á:ls eventually transformed the evil doctor into stone. X̱á:ls is believed to have left the marks on the rock as a lasting legacy of his work.[34] These "transformer sites," as they are popularly called, are located throughout the Coast Salish landscape and serve as sacred mnemonic devices as well as spiritually potent places where properly trained shamans can acquire sacred historical information.

A few entries earlier in Fraser's journal is a telling reference to his understanding that the "the respect and attention, which we generally experience, proceed, perhaps, from an idea that we are superior beings, who are not to be overcome."[35] Wendy Wickwire has recently demonstrated that Simon Fraser was not incorrect in this assumption: the oral history of the Interior Salish living immediately upriver from the scratch marks demonstrates that people initially thought Fraser to be the returning Transformer.[36]

For the Coast Salish, this interpretation is corroborated most clearly in the oral history recorded ca. 1894 by C.F. Newcombe, a collector who was travelling through the region purchasing Indian "curios" for various North American museums. Newcombe met with Chief Pierre Ayessick of Hope and asked him to share any stories he knew regarding the arrival of Simon Fraser in his community. The following is my transcription of Newcombe's scribbled recording of Ayessick's "first contact" sqwelqwel:

A long time ago when tribes had left winter villages to go to Yale for summer for salmon, news came from above from Big Canyon that men of different race were coming. The people were troubled.

It was thought that they must be people spoken of in the old stories. They were getting scared. They thought that because they were the people spoken of in the old stories by their grandparents when they appeared they would help the good people and be their friends, but if bad the[y] would turn them into stone, or animals or birds.

A meeting of all the people came together and it was decided to try to please the newcomers and they all, men women and children ... [bathed?] in the river and painted their ... [faces and] their bodies with red berries as paint *(soqnat),* which grows at the base of fir trees.

Then the chief sent messengers to ... [meet?] the strangers at Big Canyon and to invite them to come down. They walked along the river trail over the rocks. They found them camping with a number of boxes of ... [?] which were thought to hold small-pox or miracle medicines. The visitors came on at once, the Indians helping them by packing boxes etc. along the trail. When the party got to Yale all the people were crowded the ... [better?] to receive them and gave them ... [?] and all kinds of food. When the Yale people saw them they remembered that some time before a visitor to them from the Columbia river country had described the way of the white people ... [?] and they then found that they were the same, ... [?] and ... [?] they were easy in their mind.

Hope's grandfather, the head chief, lent a canoe and the chief lent a second one. These were then of great value because they used to ... [?] of slave and ... [?].[37]

Ayessick clearly appears to frame the story of Fraser's arrival within the context of the sacred narratives of X̱exá:ls, the Transformers (the "people spoken of in the old stories"). His narrative represents a sqwelqwel about what was believed to be a sxwoxwiyam. Likewise, the Reverend Thomas Crosby, the first Methodist missionary to establish himself along the lower Fraser River and apparently the first European to become genuinely fluent in the local Halq'eméylem language, noted that according to the Coast Salish people he spoke with in the 1860s, Simon Fraser was initially regarded as the "pure white child of the sun." Aboriginal leaders allegedly carried Fraser "on their backs and set him down on mats in places of honour." And after his departure, the local Coast Salish were remembered as having "danced to the sun-god for days in token of their appreciation of the visit of his son."[38]

Thus, in deciphering Thompson's map, John Doe appears to have fallen into the same trap as Thompson did in his reading of Fraser; he accepted the text at face value and overlooked the possibility that his ancestors probably interpreted the first non-Natives they met within their own epistemological framework. Fraser and his men not only looked different physically, but they dressed oddly and were in possession of technology that could not be readily explained with reference to existing indigenous experiences. Confronted with this new situation, the Coast Salish did what anybody would do under similar circumstances: they tried to fit the newcomers into their existing historical understandings. Coast Salish people knew that X̱á:ls, the Transformer, had been different; he had special powers; he had travelled up the Fraser River after appearing from the ocean below; and he later ascended to the sky and journeyed with the sun after he reached the eastern sunrise.[39] Although subsequent colonial incursions led the Stó:lō to revise and abandon what might be thought of as their initial "European equals Transformer" thesis, it seems clear that at least initially they regarded Fraser and his crew as the returning X̱exá:ls.[40]

Ultimately, it seems, there was no Spanish fort, but beneath the text on the nineteenth-century maps and within the interpretation provided by John Doe as subsequently critiqued by members of his community, there resided not only a fascinating account of a first encounter, but also cultural clues that provide glimpses into the way in which Coast Salish historical sqwelqwel knowledge functions. Both indigenous and Western historical techniques ultimately came to the same conclusion about the validity and utility of John Doe's historical information and interpretation by using their own separate criteria. Certainly, the Coast Salish did not need an outside academic to tell them whether the history was correct. The risk is that outsiders (and here I'm referring particularly to the courts) who are not familiar with the indigenous mechanisms for assessing legitimacy might apply Western methods only to dismiss John Doe's narrative and, by extension, end up dismissing or discrediting the broader community and society that he appeared to represent.

⋘⋙

The second type of historical narrative, as mentioned above, is called sxwoxwiyam. As noted, sxwoxwiyam are typically set in an age when the world had not yet been put in its permanent form, when people and animals could speak to one another, and when dangerous "Indian doctors" with powers of transformation dominated the social and physical landscape. Into this world dropped the *tel swayel* (sky-people) who become the "first people" of various tribal communities. Other people already existed, but the world was too chaotic for them to be considered the founders of contemporary communities. The sky-people began the process of fixing the world into its current stable form, but they did not finish the job. The world was next visited by X̱exá:ls, the Transformer siblings who travelled through the world completing the work begun by the sky-people: dispensing with bad Indian doctors (although their work was sometimes morally ambiguous), creating other "first people" for additional tribal groups, bestowing special technical or ritual knowledge, and generally "making the world right."

Early Western observers and ethnographers have classified sxwoxwiyam histories variously as "legends," "folktales," and "myths." Such terms, though perhaps useful initial efforts at creating metaphors of cross-cultural understanding, unfortunately served to convey the impression that the narratives were fictitious accounts akin, perhaps, to contemporary Western society's conception of Greek mythology or European fairy tales (that is to say, stories of fantasy without anchor in historical reality or personal memory).

More recently, Wayne Suttles has chosen to refer to sxwoxwiyam as "myth-age" stories, a definition that more clearly situates them as a genre of knowledge through which Coast Salish existence in, and relationships with, the world are explained historically.[41] However, this definition too, it seems, has served to overly reinforce the impression that sxwoxwiyam exclusively describe the distant past – the age when the Transformers lived and acted – as opposed to a time when people believed that the transformer stories were true historical accounts. This distinction is significant, for though Suttles (like Jan Vansina[42] and Julie Cruikshank,[43] among other sensitive scholars) went to great length to emphasize that many contemporary Coast Salish continue to believe in the validity or reality of sxwoxwiyam, he nonetheless presented these narratives as though indigenous people thought of them as about a distant by-gone era. In this regard, the metaphor implied is that sxwoxwiyam are to Coast Salish people perhaps what Old Testament stories are to contemporary practising Christians – largely true, if fantastic, accounts of real events from a distant and different time when God played a much more active role in human affairs – that is, stories of past miraculous events that are unlikely to happen today. Perhaps a more indigenous understanding might be reflected in saying that sxwoxwiyam are to contemporary Coast Salish people what New Testament stories appear to have been to early Christians living in the generations immediately following Christ's crucifixion: miraculous and true stories that occurred not only in the distant past, but recently, and which might occur again today or tomorrow. In this regard, they might be better thought of as sacred histories *rather* than myth-age accounts.

Among the Coast Salish, and especially among the social and spiritual elite, great emphasis is placed on "keeping the sxwoxwiyam stories right," in unaltered form. Indeed, contrary to popular non-Native impressions, the obligation to retain integrity in sxwoxwiyam is greater than that associated with sqwelqwel. Today, Stó:lō people who incorrectly tell a sacred history are seldom publicly sanctioned, but, as mentioned, they are still often spoken of behind their backs as "low class." In addition, they are typically referred to as "people who don't know right from wrong," or, and perhaps more tellingly, as too influenced by white society. As one respected authority on cultural protocols recently explained, "Some of our own people today think our Transformer and origin stories are like fairy tales; things you can make up or change. Well, they aren't. It's not right to tell school teachers to encourage students to 'make up' legends about coyote, or mink, or black bear. Today, people are forgetting this. This seems to be especially the case with some of our people who have gone off to university and gotten degrees."[44]

But there is more than ridicule at stake with regard to maintaining the integrity of sxwoxwiyam. Indicative are the protocols and sanctions Sally Snyder observed and recorded in 1963, even among her supposedly "acculturated" Coast Salish informants, people she described as being "compulsive about telling stories 'right.'" As Snyder discovered, "If a story was imperfectly recalled it was wrong for ... [people] to 'guess,' meaning to pad, improvise, paraphrase or omit. It was better not to tell it at all for it was dangerous to omit scenes and to shorten myths. Nubile women in the audience might then give birth to deformed children, incomplete or malformed like the abbreviated or truncated story. And shortening of myths would shorten the lives of all listeners."[45]

The rigid protocols for ensuring accuracy and preventing the altering of a sacred historical narrative should not be too quickly equated with a prohibition on certain people either acquiring new (or remembering forgotten) information to supplement existing narratives, or creating entirely new sacred historical narratives. Although Salish people could neither guess nor improvise content and meaning, nor edit or shorten a sacred historical narrative, without risking community sanction for endangering their audience, evidence suggests that sxwoxwiyam could (and can), under certain circumstances, be supplemented. That is to say, the "right people" can acquire certain types of sacred historical knowledge by visiting special sites where they access the metaphysical tunnels that lead to special locations in the spirit world where knowledge and information can be "remembered." Typically, such acquisitions are associated with what are popularly, and somewhat problematically, referred to as "vision quests." Katzie elder Old Pierre acquired such information in 1936 for the anthropologist Diamond Jenness when, during the course of an interview, he could not remember certain important material. He retrieved it the following morning by sending his spirit to the site of a large boulder known to possess historical knowledge. The spirit forces associated with the rock then provided the elder with the information he required.[46]

Moreover, and again only under special circumstances, it appears possible that entirely new sacred histories can be added to the indigenous canon or historiography. Like Christian biblical texts, sxwoxwiyam cannot be altered, but whereas the elite of the Christian Church have concluded that additional "books" cannot be added to the New Testament (no doubt much to the chagrin of individuals such as Metis leader Louis Riel and Mormon founder Joseph Smith), properly trained and sufficiently respected Stó:lō spiritual leaders can, under special circumstances, add to the body of sacred oral histories. In this context, it is probably important to restate that such narratives are not exclusively about the distant past. Rather, they are a distinct set of historical discourses, and some of the information they convey pertains to the very recent past, potentially as recent as a few moments ago.

The following incidents illustrate the nature of a particular form of Salish historical memory. On separate occasions two elderly Coast Salish men shared information with me about aspects of their "contact-era" history. Each insisted that he had acquired it through means that might appear rather unconventional to a Western historian: in nightly dream sessions, certain ancestors had provided them with information that the spirit world wanted to ensure was not "forgotten," and which would be made available to their community through both their voices and my writings. In one instance, the elder shared information concerning traditional leadership in a series of well-organized lecture-like discussions that he delivered over the course of a number of weeks. Not only had he more detailed knowledge on the subject than any of the other thirty-one people I interviewed, but his information also corresponded to a remarkable degree with that in early unpublished non-Native historical and ethnographic observations and obscure anthropological publications. Ultimately, although I looked for alternatives, I could find no way to account for his historical knowledge except on his terms – a fact that obviously amused him; by then a close friend, he actually encouraged me to look for alternative sources for his knowledge "if it would make me feel better."[47]

How then does Coast Salish history function? Is it incompatible with Western ways of knowing about the past? Among R.G. Collingwood's many insightful contributions is his insistence that unverifiable statements by "authorities" cannot be history, and that therefore, "an historian [who] accepts the testimony of an authority and treats it as historical truth [in the absence of verifiable evidence] ... obviously forfeits the name of historian."[48] Additionally, in Collingwood's opinion, memory is not, and cannot be, history, "because history is a kind of organized or inferential knowledge, and memory is not organized, not inferential."[49]

Collingwood's categorization of authorities and memory could be taken to disqualify Aboriginal oral history as a less valid window on the past. Neither authorities nor memory, however, are necessarily only as Collingwood describes them. Even in the Western world, reliance on memory has been equated with an absence of creative genius only within the last few hundred years. In a recent and thoughtful study, Mary Carruthers has demonstrated that medieval European society equated memory with intelligence and creativity. Although contemporary geniuses are said to possess "creative imagination [Collingwood's 'referential knowledge'] which they express in intricate reasoning and original discovery, in earlier times geniuses were said to have richly retentive memories, which they expressed in intricate reasoning and original discovery." Thomas Aquinas, for example, was reported to have dictated to three secretaries on three different subjects simultaneously, not because he was necessarily smarter than other people (though no one would deny Aquinas' intelligence), but "because he had organized his thoughts and committed them to memory before hand."[50]

In cultural situations where primary documents cannot be reviewed, as in an oral or memory-focused society, the ideas informing what constitutes legitimate history may be rather different, but not necessarily less valid, than those in contemporary Western society. Members of such communities typically rely upon authorities rather than reference to evidence as sources of both historical information *and* historical knowledge – not necessarily the same thing. Such authorities were/are not mere receptacles of unprocessed historical data, as Collingwood posits; instead, they might best be thought of as the non-literate equivalent of an archives and historian combined into a single being. Communities dependent on memory for the processing and transmission of knowledge, such as those of medieval Europe or contact-era North America, therefore, developed elaborate mnemonic techniques to allow complex information to be preserved across time in unaltered form so it could be recited and interpreted for members of contemporary society in a manner that was meaningful. They also developed sophisticated, if mysterious, means of acquiring lost or forgotten information about the past – information that not only supported earlier narratives, but also aided in interpreting them. These techniques allowed specially trained individuals to retrieve and retain vast amounts of material. Other techniques allowed these same people as well as untrained members of their communities to discern good information about the past from bad. Exploring how such matters functioned can provide us with important insights into indigenous ways of remembering and knowing.

Viewed in this light, the onus placed on an indigenous keeper of history to "keep the stories right" is all the more impressive. For one thing, it dwarfs the academic checks and balances placed on a contemporary Western scholar, not only in terms of the obligation to keep track of information, but, more importantly, in terms of relating material in a fashion that will meet changing societal needs, while at the same time ensuring that its factual components are not compromised. Consider, by contrast, the repercussions visited on a Western academic who fails to maintain the integrity of his or her historical narratives. Mild sanction might include the diminishment of reputation. Within the legal context, the historian's expert-witness testimony might be deemed, at best, unreliable, at worst, perjury. Should the fraud remain undetected, the historian must at least live with the knowledge that he or she is partly responsible for a court decision that punished the innocent and let the guilty go free. On a wider scale, the historian's compromised information and analysis will mislead those people who use them to design contemporary actions. Coast Salish people listening to a historical narrative, on the other hand, face real dangers should the speaker compromise its integrity. It is not just the speaker's honour (and that of his or her family) that is at stake, but the physical well-being of the listening community. A more dialogic form of historical communication is difficult to envision.

Can Canadian courts and Western historians ever truly appreciate indigenous history on genuinely indigenous terms? Probably not. As the contact narratives from two centuries ago illustrate, the epistemological gulfs between natives and newcomers are formidable. But perhaps this is acceptable so long as it is recognized that other ways of knowing, though different, are not necessarily inferior. The point, really, is not to think *like* another, or speak *for* another, but to think in ways that allow us to speak *with* another in a manner that recognizes differences as opportunities for improving understanding.

We cannot begin to incorporate indigenous historical perspectives into our Western historiography until we consider the meanings of oral accounts in their own settings. Aboriginal groups have their own methods of classifying history – methods that distinguish between good and bad, between stories that cannot be altered and those that can. Each Aboriginal group has its own way of distinguishing the based-on-fact, the fictional, and the true, or what Dell Hymes has classified as the "could have been, should have been, and must have been."[51] It is important for us to distinguish between what is real and what is true, and to be aware that such a distinction may not exist for some people, or that certain people's definitions may contrast with our own. If oral histories are to be accorded appropriate respect in academia and the courts, this will have to be achieved with the consultation and interaction of each cultural group, for it is from within the group that the nuanced methods used to determine the specific indigenous tests appropriate to the case under consideration emerge. Historically, we have tried to bridge the epistemological gulf separating native from newcomer so that we can acquire an understanding of the "other." Perhaps a more appropriate and rewarding course might be to meet the other in the unstable intellectual middle ground and from that more tenuous position work collectively in an attempt to understand one another.

# 4

# Poking Fun: Humour and Power in Kaska Contact Narratives

*Patrick Moore*

Recent studies by historians and anthropologists have drawn attention to the characteristics of different types of oral historical narratives.[1] Their concern with more accurately describing genres of narrative accounts reflects a desire to understand the significance of the stories from a Native perspective, and, in some cases, a need to mediate between oral accounts and the standards of evidence for legal proceedings. Scholars such as Julie Cruikshank, Robin Ridington, and Wendy Wickwire, who have conducted long-term research with Native storytellers, have shown that there is often no clear demarcation between contemporary events and the events of distant or mythological time in either Native conception or Native narrative accounts.[2] Researchers have moved beyond the classification of narratives as myths and folktales that was used by Boas and others, but now need to further refine their analyses of the ways in which stories are used and classified by Native people.

Like the scholars mentioned above, I have also conducted long-term research with Native storytellers. My earlier research, with Dene Dháa (Slavey) storytellers in northern Alberta, concerned traditional narratives of mythic times and historical accounts of Native prophets.[3] More recently, I have worked with Kaska storytellers in the Yukon. My research has focused on the linguistic features of the narratives; in particular, it has examined how these features relate to distinctions between types of stories and the ways that different types of stories are used. Although this chapter describes the features of Kaska narratives, it has general implications for the study of oral historical accounts since similar issues have been raised concerning narratives from different regions. Many Native historical accounts, for instance, make reference to traditions of mythological events.[4] Like Kaska accounts, those from other regions respond to historic and contemporary power imbalances between Natives and non-Natives, and these stories may also take a humorous approach to historical events.

## Distinguishing Myths and Historical Accounts

In Chapter 3 of this volume, Keith Thor Carlson discusses two categories of Coast Salish narratives: the *sqwelqwel*, often translated as "true news," and the *sxwoxwiyam*, often interpreted as legends or "myth-age stories." He argues that these two types of narratives do not refer to well-bounded sets of mythical as opposed to historical incidents, since the spirit world described in the sxwoxwiyam often impinges on historical events. Similarly, Kaskas distinguish *sa'ǎ gudeji*, "long ago stories" (stories of mythological events), from *sa'ǎ t'ene gudeji*, "stories of recent times." They are reluctant, however, to isolate the events of mythic times in the distant past since they have continuing relevance for contemporary events. As in the Coast Salish stories cited by Carlson, shamans, who are called *nédet'ē* "dreamers" in Kaska, have continuing access to the spirit world and to past and future events. These spiritually powerful individuals take a leading role in many Kaska historical narratives, including the account of "Tés Ní'ā," below.[5] Furthermore, all Kaskas do not classify stories in the same ways. Some narrators say that even incidents involving giant animals that preyed on people occurred *sa'ǎ t'ene* (just recently).

One characteristic of Kaska narratives, however, may give an indirect indication of whether a story depicts a historical incident in the Western sense. Kaskas have a long history of interaction with surrounding Native groups, as well as with non-Natives. In historical accounts, some characters may speak another language, or belong to another group. Even if the ethnicity or language of the characters in historical accounts are not mentioned, storytellers can usually identify their affiliation. In contrast, the Kaska stories that are most clearly mythical do not mention the ethnic affiliations of the characters, or the language they speak. Although Kaskas view mythological and historical events as overlapping and interpenetrating, much like Coast Salish and other groups,[6] features of ethnicity and language may provide an indirect indication about whether a story depicts historical events in a Western sense.

## Humorous and Non-humorous Accounts

Two genres of Kaska historical narratives can be distinguished on the basis of their content, structure, and the purposes for which they are told. I will refer to one genre as *humorous narratives*, since they elicit laughter from Kaska audiences; the other type will be referred to as *non-humorous narratives*. The former could also be called first-contact stories since they portray either the first time Kaskas met Euro-Canadians, or similar sorts of encounters with strangers (such as black soldiers in the Second World War) or new technology (such as airplanes). The choice of the term *humorous narratives* is not ideal since these stories also function as a form of serious social commentary.

Humorous accounts of first contact that have been recorded with other groups in the Yukon and Northwest Territories show similar characteristics.[7]

The structure of the humorous accounts differs from the non-humorous accounts in describing a single scene, often the scene of first contact with Euro-Canadian traders. In contrast, the non-humorous accounts typically consist of multiple scenes depicting events that occurred over a longer period of time. The humorous accounts feature stereotypical images of dictatorial Euro-Canadians and backward, somewhat timid, Native people. This humour has a serious side as well, since it makes reference to the power imbalance between Euro-Canadians and Native people. Many non-humorous accounts are also critical of Euro-Canadians, but they focus on the details of the specific offences they have committed.

Two Kaska stories, representing different narrative genres, are presented below, and their structure and content are contrasted following the stories themselves. Mida Donnessey's story, "The Hudson's Bay Airplane," is an example of the humorous genre of Kaska historical narratives; its structure and content are similar to the humorous first-contact stories about the arrival of white traders at Frances Lake, such as those that have been recorded with Alfred Caesar (1999) and Liza Magun (1999).[8]

### The Hudson's Bay Airplane

My uncle said that some Kaska men came to Lower Post. They were working on a boat, and from Lower Post they took food up the river. They hadn't gotten into the boat yet, the first time the Hudson's Bay traders came. They hadn't seen white people yet; my uncle hadn't worked with them yet. My uncle and all of them were young, all of them, even Uncle Tom. They hadn't seen white people the first time when they packed food, he said. It was tasty for the white people, but when the white people made soup with some of it, the Kaskas didn't eat any.

"We hid from that plane when it landed," Daddy said. "What's coming after us?" they said, as they all ran away and hid under the stumps.

Some of them were even up in the trees. "They are coming to kill us," they said.

"'Come here! Who are you?' the white people called out to us." [Daddy said.] They spoke a different language, they say. They just kept bothering people like that, they say.

"You all come down and gather here together," they said. That's how the Hudson's Bay traders gave Uncle Tom his name. "Liard Tom, you come down from up in that tree!" they said to him.

He didn't know what they were saying because they were speaking English.

Uncle Sambo ran off too. "Sambo, you come down too," the Hudson's Bay man told him. Uncle Tom said that was when they gave him his name. Those Hudson's Bay men gave English names to everyone. "Let your name be like that," he said. He made up Uncle Tom's name like that, and Uncle Sambo's, all of them: Stewart and all of them. Old Stewart and all the rest were hiding from those men under stumps. They gave all of them white man names: Grandpa Alec and Captain, all of them.

"Captain, come down from there!" they said to him, he said. That's how the Hudson's Bay [men] gave them their names, when they climbed up in trees to flee from the airplane.

"Will they kill us?" they said.

"No!" said the Hudson's Bay men. That's how they made that store at Lower Post.

The Hudson's Bay man set traps to show all of them how to do it. They set traps like that. They had metal traps and the Hudson's Bay men showed them how to set them. The Kaskas only knew about deadfalls, not steel traps.

"You all shoot with this," he said to them and showed them a shotgun. They shot with that shotgun. Some didn't know how to fire it and they were knocked backwards by the recoil. "It will sound like, 'Buff!' when it goes off," they said.

Now, people are engaged in useless arguments over land. They are saying we Kaskas should give away this land. God made this earth for us. We'll make our living from it; we'll eat from it; we'll drink from it.

There was no purpose in the Hudson's Bay men coming to us. That man spoke to the Kaskas as though he was God, they say. A long time ago people were afraid. People were afraid like animals. The Hudson's Bay men tried to make Kaskas like white people, they say.

"We won't kill you," they said. Just like you [Pat Moore] learn our language, long ago some Kaska learned to speak English. Some understood the way the Hudson's Bay men talked there, they say.

Mary Charlie's story "Tés Ní'ā 'Standing Walking Stick [Mountain]'" is an example of the non-humorous genre of Kaska historical narratives.[9] It begins with an encounter between a shaman and a Hudson's Bay trader at Pelly Banks, which is located at the confluence of the Pelly and Big Campbell Rivers approximately 200 kilometres northwest of the town of Watson Lake, Yukon, and ends by describing events relating to the 1850 starvation and cannibalism of the company traders there, a tragedy that can be confirmed by the Hudson's Bay Company archival records.[10]

### Tés Ní'ā "Standing Walking Stick [Mountain]"

A Kaska elder became angry with a white man and took off from Pelly Banks. The white man had boiled a Canada goose, and the broth was still on the stove of his cabin. The old man was visiting the white man and with a cup he dipped out some of the broth, they say.

The white man was offended by this and thought to himself, "Why did that man dip inside that pot?" The white man got up and walked over to the Kaska man. He then picked up the pot, walked outside, and poured the broth out on the ground. The old man drank some broth from the pot, and the white man poured it out on the ground to keep it from him, which made the old man angry.

"He treats me just like his dog!" the old man yelled when he went outside. "He poured the broth outside to keep it from me when I only wanted to drink some of that nice broth. He treated me just like his dog! He poured the broth out to keep it away from me."

That is what the old man said. That old man really yelled, they say. From there, the old man went back up along the Pelly River.

The old man continued on from there. From Pelly Banks he continued on up the valley; he must have been traveling with some other people. He must have traveled with someone as far as Pelly Lakes, what they call Gēs Mené' "Salmon Lake" or Tú Désdés Mené' "Clear Water Lake" in the Kaska language. People were living there, way up in the mountains. While they were traveling along, the old man went off by himself.

Finally, he started out toward his destination. From there, he went up on the mountain, they say. He walked up on the mountain on the caribou moss, they say. He was walking like that, and his footprints were plainly visible in the moss where he walked. Far up on the mountain the old man came to rocks, they say. He stuck his walking stick in the rock there, they say. He stuck his walking stick right into the rocks. His walking stick was standing there angled toward him, and he took one last step right beside the walking stick then. He stuck his walking stick in the rock on top of that mountain and then stepped beside the walking stick. Right there was his last footprint, in the rock beside his walking stick. There was no more.[11] That's why they named it Tés Ní'ā "Standing Walking Stick Mountain," they say.

From then on, there were no more tracks. From then on, winter came and never let up. The caribou and moose just about vanished and the people starved, they say. There was no food and people even killed each other.

Finally they were all exhausted, but, even so, one man continued on, even though he was completely exhausted. His wife and children were following behind on his trail and he walked on, they say. His wife had set one rabbit snare when they camped, and she caught one rabbit, and was carrying the broth from the boiled rabbit in a pot, as she walked along her husband's trail.

Her husband was up ahead hunting for two caribou – a cow and a calf. He was following their tracks where they had traveled on the snow. He came to the top of a high bluff, they say. From there he looked out across the valley below and thought, "What is that down below? It looks like caribou tracks still going ahead, far across the valley. How will I ever make it that far? I'm already falling over with hunger." He was thinking this as he looked out, and then he started to cry. Behind on his trail, his children were following after him. He was walking, trying to kill something for his wife and children. When he came to the top of the bluff, he sat there crying. He saw the tracks far across, but it was too hard for him to go on.

Then God took pity on him. As God thought to himself, "This poor person," the caribou turned back toward him. That's the way it was. When he saw the tracks disappearing way down below, he was sitting there crying. From far below, the two caribou came back up towards him, they say. That was the cow caribou and its calf, which had run off before.

He killed them on top of the bluff. He cut off the ears of the caribou, cooked them by the fire, and ate them. He cut up the caribou, and after that, he cut off the caribou ears. He cut them off, he ate just a little bit, and then he collapsed, they say. He collapsed right beside the fire.

"After a long time, I finally raised my head. I must have been there a long time," he said, they say.

If even one drop of blood dripped on the snow, he put it inside the caribou stomach, they say, because he knew what it was like to be without food. He started back toward his family then. He put on his pack again, and started out.

When his children saw him, they leaped up to greet him, even though they were staggering from hunger. "Dad killed something for us!" they said, and they jumped up to meet him.

"You must all be happy about what I was able to do," their father said. "I am alive for you. I am still walking! What do you have to say?"

Finally he collapsed, but he soon regained consciousness, they say. Then, from there, they all went to the caribou kill. They didn't throw anything away, not even the smallest pieces of meat. Even the bones they boiled in water, they say, so they could drink the broth.

The man who killed the caribou was still worried. He was worried about those white men who lived down at the trading post at Pelly

Banks. Unfortunately, it was impossible for him to understand English. He just couldn't understand what they said. He couldn't understand one word of English. For this reason, he never really spoke to those white men, but still he felt sorry for them. He thought to himself, "They might die. They might die," he thought.

He put on his pack again, they say, even though he didn't have any strength left. He was so weak that he was staggering as he walked. He started off, they say; starting off toward them with his walking stick, they say. He put things for them in his pack, and put it on again. "They might still be alive, so maybe I will pack some meat back to them," he said. "You stay here with the children," he told his wife, and she stayed there with them.

He traveled way down by Pelly Banks and noticed that there were deadfall traps set up near there. Someone had cut up meat to bait the deadfall traps. They had set them up like that, with bait on the trigger-stick, and the man thought to himself, "Why does the meat look like that? What kind of meat did they use on the trigger of those marten deadfalls?" That's what he was thinking as he walked along down there. Because he was smart, he realized what was going on, and even though he suspected something was wrong, he continued to walk along.

Finally he came to their house. He entered and found only one man sitting there. The other one was missing. "Where could he be?" he thought. "What has happened to him?" He was worried about what might have happened to that missing man, and as he thought about it he became afraid. "This man must have killed him because he had no food, and he might do the same thing to me." He was thinking. "Why did I come here?"

He was really frightened, and then across the room from them he noticed something covered up. He could see a little bit of something exposed, and it looked like human flesh. He was afraid for his life because of what he could see, and he thought, "What happened to the other man? His partner must have killed him."

Then the white man realized that his visitor was afraid, and he said, "Why are you afraid of me? We were starving and I killed him. I ate him, and because of that I am still alive." To reassure the man, the trader offered him some bullets, saying, "I'll give you some bullets," and he held out a handful of bullets. The man took them and put them in his pocket. The white man gave him a small sack of bullets and thanked him for bringing meat saying, "Things turned out well because you packed meat here to me."

The man hastily threw the shells in his pocket and started off. As soon as he reached the door, he started running. Even though he was weakened from hunger, he ran as fast as he could. He ran until he reached his wife, and told her, "I packed meat back to those white men so they could survive. One of them was eaten; the other one killed him." Because of what had happened, both the man and his wife were afraid. "He told me, 'Pack food back to me!'" the man told his wife.

There was no one in Pelly Banks at that time who they could tell about what the man had done, they say. That's what they say, traditionally. That person who took food to them couldn't speak English himself. They say it was like that for Pelly Banks people, they would pack food to anyone who needed it. It was *ā'i* (taboo) what those white people had done, they say. They say that people should not be overly proud. They say the white men did that. They bothered with things which are taboo according to Indian law, and insulted people.

We say, "There is our country; let's go back."

## Contrasting Features of the Two Genres

The prototypical first-contact stories portray the arrival of white traders in Kaska territory, particularly that of traders at Frances Lake. The event described in Mida Donnessey's story, the arrival of the first airplane at Lower Post, British Columbia, occurs at a much later date, but the scene is described in much the same way as earlier scenes of first contact. The normal course of everyday life is suddenly disrupted by the appearance of the airplane, and the Native men who are present run for cover behind windfall stumps and hide in the trees.

The white traders start ordering people about as soon as they get off the plane, and they give English names to the men who are hiding, without even thinking of learning their Kaska names. The white traders christen the Kaskas as they call them out of hiding: "Liard Tom, you come down from up in that tree! Sambo, you come down too!" The amusing portrayal of bossy white people and fearful, somewhat backward, Native people is typical of this genre. The humour has a more serious side, however, since it makes reference to the real power imbalances between whites and Natives that have existed historically, and which are part of contemporary society.

The white traders in "The Hudson's Bay Airplane" also bring trade goods, much like the early explorers. Descriptions of the introduction of new foods and new technology, such as guns, are common to these humorous narratives. Many of the stories describe how Kaskas were introduced to guns by white people, even though guns were introduced by Tlingit and Tahltan before white traders established direct trading relations with Kaskas. The Tlingit and Tahltan encountered by Robert Campbell at Dease Lake and along the Stikine River in northern British Columbia in 1838, for example, were well armed, and Kaskas at Frances Lake were familiar with guns when traders arrived there in 1840.[12] The Kaska terms *úne* (gun), *etūtĕ'* (bullets), *dāne* (money), *súgunĕ'* (flour), *ts'īk* (tobacco), and other terms are Tlingit loanwords, providing further confirmation of the extent of Tlingit influence.

At the end of her story, Mida Donnessey explains why she finds this incident relevant for contemporary concerns. She declares that the white assumption of authority was unjustified at that time, and that in the context of land claims negotiations, their domination of Native people is still unjustified.

The differences between the humorous genre of Kaska narratives and the non-humorous stories are evident when "The Hudson's Bay Airplane" is compared to "Tés Ní'ā." The story of "Tés Ní'ā" describes events that occurred within a decade of direct contact with white traders in this area, and at a much earlier date than the events in "The Hudson's Bay Airplane." The white traders are negatively portrayed in the non-humorous account, but the focus is on their violations of the fundamental rules of social respect, what Kaskas call *ā'i* "respect, taboo." Their suffering comes as a consequence of insulting a powerful Kaska shaman. The sudden onset of winter in "Tés Ní'ā" relates to a belief that is shared by many Native groups in this area, that shamans were able to travel between the summer world of ordinary reality and a snow-covered spiritual domain. Cruikshank cites similar beliefs among Southern Tutchone and Tagish:

> A recurring metaphor in narrative presents the world as incorporating two parallel realities: one in a dimension that underlies the secular, material, temporal world of everyday life; the other is a domain that could more aptly be called superhuman and timeless. At the beginning of time, the narratives state and restate, a physical boundary – the horizon – separated these dimensions. On one side of the horizon was a snow-covered winter world where everything was white. On the other side was the summer world full of colour and warmth. Eventually the animals trapped on the winter side conspired to puncture the boundary so that the world as we know it could be brought into balance through its alternating seasons. In narrative, however, these dimensions remain distinct and must be negotiated repeatedly by all thinking beings and particularly by shamans, who are more likely to travel between dimensions. Everyone has access to such journeys; the differences between the powers of a layman and a shaman are of degree rather than kind.[13]

Kaskas recount the Pelly Banks cannibalism incident to criticize the values of the traders, but the more important point they make is that Euro-Canadians are ultimately part of the same social and natural systems as they themselves. The story is grounded in Kaska beliefs about respect, the spiritual powers of certain individuals, and the influence of relations that were established in mythic times on contemporary events. The Kaskas in this story are not portrayed as fearful or backward; indeed, they are clearly more capable than the white traders since they are able to secure food.

In the humorous historical narratives, both Native people and white people are captured in scenes that make them appear silly. The exaggerated fear of the Kaska men hiding from the airplane is one example. Similar examples can be cited from other Kaska historical narratives, which cannot be included for lack of space.[14] In the excerpt below, Kaska elder Alfred Caesar makes a Hudson's Bay Company trader look ridiculous. In typical fashion, the trader assumes the authority to do as he pleases, and rummages through a cache belonging to the Native people. Alfred Caesar describes how the trader discovers women's panties made of groundhog skin in the cache, a sexual image that serves to poke fun at the white trader. His reference to "Cold wind just like nothing!" presumably refers to the Kaska women wearing these items and not to the trader himself.

> "I see a cache!" He [the trader] said. He went to that cache and lots of bare-footed children ran off in the bush. The Hudson's Bay man started to take things down out of the cache. There were all kinds of things in there: moose skin, caribou skin, groundhog skin pants, and panties – women's panties made out of groundhog skin. They said that they hardly noticed the cold wind when they had those on! Cold wind just like nothing![15]

In contrast, the offence that the Pelly Banks traders commit in acting disrespectfully toward the Kaska medicine man in "Tés Ní'ā" is not taken or portrayed in such a lighthearted manner. The inclusion of humorous incidents would diminish the gravity of their offences, and thus Mary Charlie sets a serious tone in keeping with the nature of the subject matter.

The humorous appeal of the first-contact stories derives from the exaggerated stereotypes of white and Native people, and the parody of relations between the two groups. The humour is never straightforward, however, since the reality of oppression by whites is not really laughable. Keith Basso has described Western Apache joking portrayals that arose in a similar context of domination by whites.[16] He finds that the joking performances are intentionally ambiguous and may either be taken seriously or as jokes. He says that they convey messages about two sets of relationships: one that exists in the immediate discourse context (between the person who tells the joke and the person with whom she or he is joking), and one that concerns an absent relationship (the generic nature of relations between Native people and Anglo-Americans).[17] Similarly, there is ambiguity as to how the humorous Kaska historical narratives are to be interpreted. The amusing images of bossy white traders and backward Native people may be taken either literally or as a general indictment of white domination. Basso says that the social criticism that is implicit in these sorts of performances addresses the wider social imbalances between Anglo-Americans and Natives, rather than some specific case:

> However, what is communicated about the latter [the messages concerning white-Native relations] can be interpreted without explicit reference to situational features. As Paul Ricoeur (1973) has suggested, messages about absent phenomena may be analytically decoupled from the perishing occasions of their transmission, and be treated as *cultural texts* – as what Clifford Geertz (1975:48) has neatly described as "stories people tell themselves about themselves," or turning again to Western Apache joking imitations, as statements by Apaches for Apaches that are about Apaches and the kinds of dealings they have with Anglo-Americans.[18]

He says that Western Apache joking imitations of white people were first performed by children in the 1930s, after a school was constructed near their community, and later by adults, starting in the post-war period when more whites came into Apache territory. The exact historical origins of Kaska humorous narratives are unclear, but, as with the Apache, the influx of whites, particularly during and after the Second World War, would have made the theme of white domination especially significant.

Humour is a common response to oppression in other communities as well. Robert Cochran, for example, in "'What Courage!': Romanian 'Our Leader' Jokes," finds that jokes about the infamous dictator Ceauşescu arose as a response to government domination: "Romanians, asked about life in their country, very often answer by telling jokes. Political jokes, in particular, are important in Romania, offering a traditional, if largely covert, means of self-expression to a mightily constrained people. They are oblique testimonies, revelations made with forked tongue. Jokes about the nation's longtime ruler, Nicolae Ceauşescu are especially numerous, and address a wide range of contemporary issues."[19] Similarly, Geneva Smitherman describes some of the humorous forms that have arisen in African American communities in the United States focusing on insults levelled at a person's mother, a form of verbal play traditionally called "the dozens," a "play in the dozens," now also referred to as "snaps" and familiar to a wider audience in a more light-hearted form as "yo-momma" jokes. The more serious forms of this game of insults are designed to test an individual's ability to endure verbal abuse and respond creatively in kind:

> For a people trying to survive under an oppressive racist yoke, the dozens provided a way, to borrow from Ralph Ellison, to "change the joke." The game functioned as an outlet for what countless blues people and Jess B. Simple folk called "laughing to keep from crying." It was a form of release for the suppressed rage and frustrations that were the result of being a Black

man or woman trapped in White America. Despite economic discrimination and racist insults against your personhood, you could ill afford to be hot; the dozens taught you how to chill. As well, the game taught discipline and self-control; it was a lesson in how to survive by verbal wit and cunning rhetoric, rather than physical violence.[20]

Like the jokes, joking games, and joking impersonations of other oppressed groups, such as those of the Apache, Romanians, and African Americans discussed above, the humorous Kaska narratives make reference to a more complex and oppressive reality.

## Structure

The structure of the humorous narratives differs from that of the non-humorous accounts in ways that are related to the purposes for which they are told. The former, like the Apache joking impersonations of the white man described by Basso, address general inequalities rather than a specific incident. The latter, however, focus on specific details as a way of building a larger case. The examples of the two genres that have been presented here, "The Hudson's Bay Airplane" and "Tés Ní'ā," take similarly critical views of white traders, but they do so in different ways. The humorous narrative, "The Hudson's Bay Airplane," operates in a surreal context of exaggeration and stereotypes that invites the listener to interpret the story as having a more general meaning beyond the events described. The non-humorous story, "Tés Ní'ā," in contrast, is solidly anchored in descriptive details, and since the relations of cause and effect are complex and dramatic, the listener is not prompted to seek an alternative meaning.

These differences in purpose and conceptual organization relate in turn to the ways that the two genres are staged. Most of the humorous stories focus on a single scene, but the non-humorous narratives usually consist of a series of scenes that take place at several locations over a longer period of time. The events of "The Hudson's Bay Airplane," for example, occur in a single day; those of "Tés Ní'ā" play out over nearly a year.

Mikhail Bakhtin suggested that space and time may be represented differently in different genres, and used the term *chronotope* to refer to the ways that space and time are characterized in a particular work.[21] Although Bakhtin was primarily concerned with literary genres, there are also interesting differences in the ways that space and time are characterized in oral narratives. The humorous and non-humorous genres contrast, for instance, with respect to linguistic devices that are central to the depiction of space and time. These relate to the devices required to stage the multiple scenes of the non-humorous accounts, as opposed to the single scene of the humorous ones. The distinctions also relate to the surreal sense of time, place, and action in the humorous stories, which the narrator uses to motivate the listener to interpret the accounts as being symbolic of more general conditions of inequity.

In the non-humorous accounts, the extensive use of temporal connectives such as "then," "up to there," and "finally" relates directly to the need to link multiple scenes. Postverbal particles such as "past," "before," and "then" are also far more common in these stories than they are in the humorous ones. Temporal relations between actions are indicated in the non-humorous stories through the use of subordinate constructions, such as "'He treats me just like his dog!' the old man yelled when he went outside," in which one action (yelling) is described as occurring while another (going out) is in progress. This type of subordinate construction is far less common in the humorous accounts.

In Kaska narratives, time is rarely referenced in terms of specific dates or quantified units, such as days or months, but every verb makes reference to whether actions are complete (perfective), incomplete (imperfective), ongoing (progressive), planned (optative), or unrealized (future). In non-humorous accounts, perfective verbs indicating completed action predominate, as appropriate for historical events. For example, in Mary Charlie's story "Tés Ní'ā," 76 percent of the verbs are perfective forms, 8 percent are imperfectives, and the remainder are of other types. In the humorous accounts, however, imperfective verbs, which indicate actions that are taking place or unrealized, are often as common as perfective forms. In Mida Donnessey's story "The Hudson's Bay Airplane," 45 percent of the verbs are perfective, 47 percent are imperfective, and the remainder are of other types.

Imperfective verb forms are used extensively in "The Hudson's Bay Airplane" and other humorous accounts for reasons that relate to the overall sense of the stories. The extensive use of imperfective verbs contributes to the sense that these events are not solidly anchored in the past, but are rather ambiguously past and present. This prompts the listener to interpret the description as being symbolic of ongoing inequities since the details are not fixed in time. On a specific level, imperfective verbs are used to describe unrealized action, thereby indicating that the arrival of the whites interrupts the normal flow of activity. For instance, Mida Donnessey, in describing the arrival of the first airplane at Lower Post, says the Native men "hadn't gotten into the boat yet," using an imperfective verb. The normal course of events, in which the men would have boarded the boat and travelled upstream, is cut short by the arrival of the airplane. In the humorous accounts, imperfective verbs are also used extensively in quoted commands, a device which has the effect of making the commands seem more immediate to the audience. Although both genres use quoted speech, the humorous accounts make more extensive use of commands in order to emphasize the bossiness of the whites.

Customary verbs, which are employed to express habitual or repeated action in Kaska, are used only in an imperfective form. These verbs prompt the listener to interpret events as symbolizing ongoing conditions. In the humorous account "The Hudson's Bay Airplane," for example, the customary form of the verb "spill out" is used to indicate that the Native men regularly threw out the food they were fed by their white employers. Interestingly, the serious account "Tés Ní'ā" also mentions soup being spilled out. In this case, however, it is the white trader who spills out the broth after a Kaska man, visiting the post, helps himself to a cupful. As is consistent with the structure of the non-humorous accounts, the trader's actions are not described as habitual, but rather as a singular offence with serious repercussions.

In the serious historical narratives, the passage of time is often implied by the movement of individuals or groups. There are also significant differences between the two genres in the use of directionals, deictic expressions that indicate direction of movement, location, and relative distance. These terms have important narrative functions in Kaska, indicating the social roles of characters, and whether actions are central events or asides to the main action. In the serious accounts, the directionals index the point of view of the focal character in any scene, and the class of directionals that indicate forward movement predominates in these stories. The use of directionals in the humorous accounts is limited because most of the action occurs at a single location. In "The Hudson's Bay Airplane," the directionals reflect the spatial perspective of the white people rather than the Natives; for example, the white people use the term for "coming from up above" in commanding the Kaska men to come down out of the trees. There are no directionals reflecting the Native spatial perspective in this particular story. The use of directionals in this case serves to reinforce the commanding position of the whites, while also implying that their arrival is associated with an unnatural reversal between Native and white perspectives on the world.

Michael Harkin has proposed that similar sorts of contact narratives among the Heiltsuk make reference to a dramatic transformation in the way the Heiltsuk conceived of history and historical events, which occurred with the arrival of white people. He says, "But it is arguably not a type of technology per se that the Heiltsuks acquire – either axes or European clothes or the steamship – but in fact a new historicity."[22] He proposes that certain stories reflect or refer to a pre-contact mode of conceiving time, which is then changed to a linear Western mode of conceiving time with the arrival of Europeans.

Although the two genres of Kaska historical narratives depict time and space in different ways, they may be equally well-established narrative traditions. Such differences relate to the purposes of the accounts and not to historical changes in the way Kaskas conceive of history. Both genres are well established at present, and there are non-humorous stories of events that preceded white contact.[23] There appears to be continuity in the way that the non-humorous narratives represent space and time, but it is less clear whether the humorous stories and their mode of representing time and space are recent developments. Since they concern first contact, their way of portraying time and space might be thought to have developed in response to contact with white people. This seems unlikely, however, because similar ways of depicting time and space are found in humorous mythic stories about idiotic giants and cannibals, such as Edzedutsie, stories that are not associated with the arrival of Euro-Canadians. The two narrative genres and their associated modes of depicting space and time both may be well-established discourse forms.

Structural variances also define the two genres. These relate to the differing manner in which they make their point. The humorous accounts are not meant to be taken at face value, whereas the non-humorous ones are supposed to be taken more literally. These distinctions are not absolute, however, as some humorous narratives draw on the conventions of the non-humorous ones, as discussed in the section on intertextuality below.

The purposes for which the humorous accounts are told relate to the nature of their humour, as described in the sections on content and structure above. In contrast, the non-humorous stories provide a more carefully constructed case against Euro-Canadian values and practices. They often describe the ways that non-Kaskas violate the principles of á'i (respect, taboo) which constitute sacred codes for proper behaviour. The non-humorous accounts also typically include detailed descriptions of the consequences that result from these offences.

**Genre and Intertextual Gaps**

Although the humorous narratives differ from the non-humorous ones in content, structure, and purpose, some stories contain features of both genres. Similar sorts of difficulties in establishing absolute criteria through which to identify generic differences served to undermine the older categorical approaches to the study of genre.[24] More recent approaches to the topic emphasize the relations between genres.[25] Julia Kristeva, for example, credits Mikhail Bakhtin with anticipating recent views of the importance of intertextuality, the production borrowing between historic and contemporary genres:

> Bakhtin was one of the first to replace the static hewing out of texts with a model where literary structure does not simply *exist* but is generated in relation to *another* structure. What allows a dynamic dimension to structuralism is his conception of the "literary word" as an *intersection of textual*

*surfaces* rather than a point (a fixed meaning), as a dialogue among several writings: that of the writer, the addressee (or the character), and the contemporary or earlier cultural context.[26]

Similarly, Charles Briggs and Richard Bauman, in their article on genre and intertextuality, emphasize that structure, function, and meaning are not merely features of any single discourse, but are also "products of ongoing processes of producing and receiving discourse."[27]

The humorous Kaska genre employs intertextuality to make amusing references to other sorts of discourse. Moving between genres also prompts the listener to consider an account at something other than face value. When the genre of the story itself is ambiguous, this serves to alert the listener that nothing should be taken for granted. In addition, intertextuality is a form of innovation that is used by narrators to maintain humorous appeal. This creative drive for innovation is characteristic of humorous performances in other cultures as well, as with the joking discourses in the African American community that are described by Smitherman above.

One of the most popular humorous Kaska stories, Amos Dick's "The Boy Who Found White People," for example, playfully reverses the usual roles of Natives and whites.[28] In this story, a Kaska boy travels south from Frances Lake, Yukon, to Fort St. John, British Columbia, to learn about modern technology from traders, reversing the usual scenario in which white explorers discover the Natives. His epic journey has parallels to accounts of vision quests, and its structure resembles the non-humorous accounts because it includes multiple scenes over a long period of time.

### The Boy Who Found White People

Grandpa Pelly Smith told me a story about Frances Lake. A long time ago people used to stay there, nearly a hundred people were living there.

"People fought with each other," Grandpa said. "It happened in the springtime, early springtime at Frances Lake," he said.

At that time a young boy paddled down south with a spruce bark canoe. That's when he found white people down there.

*Arthur John:* I thought they were fighting with people from Telegraph Creek [Tahltans].

*Amos Dick:* People fought with each other, they say. They must have fought each other down there; people killed each other. Then, one boy left by himself. He paddled down with a spruce bark canoe. He paddled and paddled.

"It doesn't matter if I die then. It's fine even if I die," he thought.

He went far away, down by Fort St. John somewhere. There was a log cabin there; there was a cabin. He went up the bank from the river, and found an axe and a stove at the cabin. He had never seen those kinds of things. There was a log cabin there, the boy said. The trail was well worn, and there was a good axe there. Kaska had no matches at that time, and the boy didn't know about matches. He only used a flint fire striker to make a fire. He saw a pot there, and he used it to go get water, and then he made a fire.

He set a net for fish. They made fish nets out of sinew; that was the kind he used. (They used the sinew from along the tenderloin, that's what they used to make fish nets.) Having netted some fish, he put the pot on the fire, and boiled some fish for himself.

There was a horse trail there. Horses, *gǘndấn,* horses. He went along beside the trail to where there was smoke from a fire coming up. People were chopping firewood. He went up a hill towards them, they say. There was a white man there, one white man, *skukāni* (white man). He had never seen that kind of person before. He went to take a closer look. That boy had a moose skin jacket, moose skin moccasins, and everything. He had long hair, arrows, *k'ấ* (arrows) and everything. He went to take a closer look at the three white people. He saw them, and then the white men saw him. One of them ran into the cabin.

Two of the three white men came to him. "Come on!" they told him.

The boy responded, "Come on!" He repeated the same thing they said to him because he didn't understand English. The white men came to him and took him with them.

"It doesn't matter if they kill me," the boy thought. "It's fine, even if they kill me."

Then they started to teach him. They taught him. They taught him all the time for eight years. He had to write and everything.

"You are the only survivor," they told him.

There were lots of people long ago, but people fought too much. The boy went down there with a canoe, and then for eight years he was with those men while they went trapping with steel traps and everything. Eight years passed.

"Go get your friends," they finally told him one day.

"Yes, I'll do it," he said.

They gave him a shotgun and everything. They gave him a fish net and everything. He pulled everything back with a big loaded toboggan in the month of March. He must have pulled his load back to where the Tahltan were living. People started to gather when they saw him coming and he walked toward them. When he was almost to them, he shot the shotgun "Bo!" and people ran off, they say.

"It's me," he said. "I've been gone for eight years, and finally I've come back to you," the boy said.

They gathered around him again.

"Gee, you've been gone eight years," they said to him.

"I ran off because people were getting killed," he said. "They killed lots of people, over a hundred people were killed."

He took out a pot to show them. He took out a pot, a cup, a frying pan, and everything they had given him.

"*Usá'* (Pot)," they said. "Shotgun."

"I met some white people way down there," he said. "They gave me a fish net, and everything, snares and everything, even a shotgun."

"Gee, what happened to your shells, they're no good," they said to him.

"Do you want to see it? I'll shoot a tree," he said. "Ba!" it sounded.

*Arthur John:* Shot right through that tree, eh?

*Amos Dick:* Yes, that's the way they brought back those things from the white men. It might have been two hundred years ago. I don't know what year it was when people fought each other. It was a long time ago. People fought each other all the time. They killed each other with arrows; they would fight over nothing.

*Arthur John:* Funny why they fought anyway. I can't figure it out.

*Amos Dick:* I don't know either.

*Arthur John:* A long time ago, they didn't have anything to fight about, but still they fought and fought all the time. People had to watch themselves.

At the beginning of this story, Amos Dick refers to a non-humorous account of warfare in the Frances Lake region.[29] That warfare in this area had resulted in the deaths of Natives is confirmed in two 1843 letters written by Robert Campbell, the Hudson's Bay Company trader who established the first post in the southern Yukon at Frances Lake in 1842.[30] The Kaska boy, perhaps orphaned because of these conflicts or perhaps simply fleeing the region, travels south in a spruce bark canoe.

Just before telling the story, Amos Dick indicated that the boy went to the Fort St. John area to find out about the white people who had reportedly arrived there. When the boy thinks "It doesn't matter if I die then. It's fine even if I die," the listener is alerted that he is on a vision quest, for this is exactly what people say in Kaska accounts of vision quests. When the boy reaches his destination, his wishes are fulfilled when he receives a vision of the white man's bounty. The boy's Native goods, the fire striker, sinew nets, arrows, and skin jacket and moccasins, are carefully contrasted with the goods he discovers – the matches, twine fish nets, pots, and axes. When he finally approaches the white men, he again thinks of his quest: "It doesn't matter if they kill me. It's fine, even if they kill me." The boy is then educated by the white men for eight years, a part of the story that refers to the later system of Native residential mission schools.[31] After this time, they generously supply him with trade goods to take to his homeland, just as, in many vision quest accounts, the person receiving the vision is supplied by the animal spirit people before returning home. Arriving home after his eight-year absence, he shows people everything he has learned. The description of people being frightened by a gun, for instance, is common to the humorous accounts. "The Boy Who Found White People" makes extensive use of the features found in other sorts of narratives, including the multiple scenes of most non-humorous accounts and the structure and content of vision quest stories. It has a high degree of what Briggs and Bauman call *intertextuality*, and Amos Dick chooses to highlight these connections to other types of narratives.

In contrast, narrators of non-humorous accounts do not emphasize the ways in which their material draws on other sources. They prefer that listeners take the description of events at face value and have a serious attitude toward the story as a whole. Although short amusing incidents may be included, care is taken to preserve a serious tone for the narrative as a whole. Humorous accounts can successfully take on the form and content of a non-humorous one, but the latter do not borrow from the former to the same extent.

Both genres refer to Euro-Canadian discourse about Kaskas and other Native people, another form of intertextuality. These counter-discourses are similar to the Maori stories cited by Judith Binney in Chapter 8, which incorporate features of European discourse. A Kaska example of this occurs in "The First Time We Saw White People," a story told by Liza Magun which disputes a claim by Anton Money that he was the first white person seen by Kaskas at Frances Lake. She says, "'That was the first time that the Kaskas saw white people,' Money said. That's what Money said, 'I was the first white person they saw,' he said. He said that for nothing; it wasn't true."[32] Similarly, Mary Charlie's version of the cannibalism incident at Pelly Banks responds to the prominence of Native cannibalism in the historical and anthropological literature.[33] Amos Dick's account of a Kaska man on a vision quest to find Euro-Canadian traders can also be seen as a response to Euro-Canadian discourses of discovery.

The characteristics of the humorous Kaska genre lend support to Briggs and Bauman's proposal that some innovative genres make more extensive use of intertextuality, and that the relations to other types of narratives are highlighted in these cases.[34] The non-humorous genre, in contrast, is more conservative, and narrators tend to downplay intertextuality in it.

## Conclusion

Scholars who are using oral accounts of historical events need to carefully research the full range of narrative traditions in the region where they work. This requires detailed consideration of the linguistic features that constitute a style for the various types of accounts, and of how the stories are used in the communities. Unfortunately, researchers are often restricted to a small number of sources; their ability to assess linguistic features may also be limited. Without this understanding, however, it is difficult to establish the significance of the accounts. Catharine McClellan, for instance, expressed some of the confusion she experienced regarding the significance of the amusing first-contact stories she recorded with Southern Tutchone:

> At first I thought these stories in which the natives laugh at themselves might be a rather recent phenomenon developed on the part of a minority group trying to ingratiate itself with the whites. However, the fact that the white man or white men's goods are always involved may really be incidental. Now I wonder whether the stories may represent a genre of humor which is old in the oral literature of both the interior and the coast, but which may have received new impetus with the arrival of the whites.[35]

McClellan was able to reach this level of perception only after noting the similarities between many different humorous accounts.

The identification of narrative genres through the study of their structure, linguistic features, and functions is a necessary first step to understanding historical narratives. This type of study also provides the keys to further research concerning larger social issues, such as the history of power relations between Natives and non-Natives, and Native responses to political and economic domination. Briggs and Bauman propose that intertextuality is not only a key to unravelling the creative links between genres, but also to revealing relations between performance genres and the power structure of a society.[36] The non-humorous Kaska accounts downplay intertextual features and are associated with traditional Native values. The humorous stories are a more innovative form of criticism that freely uses features of other narratives. Similarly, genres of oral narratives from other areas can be expected to vary in their management of intertextuality, providing an indication of the social perspectives of the narrators. Careful examination of the aspects of historical narratives for even a single group, such as the Kaskas, reveals the complexity and sophistication of these accounts. The humorous material, though characterized by a simple structure, is nonetheless a creative response to conditions of social inequity. Further understanding of the types of oral narratives and of the relations between them will contribute to a more sophisticated use of these sources as historical evidence, and to a comprehension of how they are used in the communities in which they are performed.

# Herbert Spencer, Paul Kane, and the Making of "The Chinook"

*I.S. MacLaren*

The odd trinity of names invoked by the title of this chapter[1] has much to do with the mid-nineteenth-century circulation of knowledge throughout the British Empire, and with one prominent means – the book – by which knowledge was authoritatively transmitted. Although this chapter focuses on Pacific Northwest coast peoples in what is now part of the United States, the case study is equally representative of a process in which European explorers and travellers came to speak for imperial interests as their narratives of encounters with peoples and lands around the world were both prepared and disseminated by publishers at the imperial centre. The objects of those accounts, whether they were Native Africans, South Americans, or Asians, all underwent representation by this process in much the same way as did Native North Americans.

Paul Kane (1810-71) was an itinerant Irish-Canadian painter of coaches, houses, and signs who began his travels in eastern North America, painting portraits. Englishman Herbert Spencer (1820-1903) was a journalist, philosopher, and sociologist of the highest rank. What they shared was the world of London publishing, where knowledge circulated freely and was consumed avidly. As a theorist of how societies function and fail to function, Spencer, the father of English-language sociology, was, as it were, a prominent armchair traveller. How he put to use the knowledge transmitted to him by travel books such as *Wanderings of an Artist among the Indians of North America,* published in 1859 under the name of Paul Kane, is as much a concern of this discussion as is the question of how the representation of Native peoples named Chinook came about in a book ostensibly written by Kane, who painted them and their lower Columbia River homeland for a few months in 1846 and 1847.[2]

Like Herbert Spencer, researchers who study the compositions of explorers and travellers commonly suppose that, in the centuries prior to the advent of the professional travel writer, people who explored or travelled were as inclined to write as they were to journey or voyage. Much of our under-standing of the Euro–North American perspective of the "contact zone" created when cultures met and collided issues from the "documents" that were published under the names of people – usually men – who travelled afar.[3] That understanding may be mistaken, for hastily drawing a straight line between travel and narrative, that is, between eyewitness observer, on the one hand, and recorder, on the other, is precarious. Not only is the contact zone fraught with "enormous" problems of communication, but also the records of what occurred at contact are deeply conflicted.[4] And yet it seems to be human nature, if not always scholarly procedure, to overlook the complexity of the textual evidence in favour of clearer claims based on the inferred authority of the eyewitness.

Kane's book marks a good example of what has been termed the "written-by-committee-syndrome." Explorers and travellers were usually chiefly people of action. Books about their movements were demanded of them, but de-mand alone could not transform them into authors. Most needed to be helped into print, and all such help, if it came from those who remained at the publishing centre, necessarily altered the texts if it did not contaminate the eyewitness account. The "help" of which explorers and travellers osten-sibly stood in need was furnished by people who had seldom ventured out of England. Notorious long before the 1850s were the hack and ghostwriters of London, centred in Grub Street, with its lowly housing and pittance-paying piecework. To them regularly fell the assignment of ascribing hu-man worth or peculiar novelty to people and their lifeways across the world. The reliability of the eyewitness traveller thus became and should remain for contemporary scholars a complex matter of some considerable doubt.

Herbert Spencer made novel use of the literature of exploration and travel. Borrowing the term *sociology* from Auguste Comte, the Englishman had sanc-tioned its use and rendered it authoritative by employing it often in his writings about functionalism and systematic philosophy. Spencer argued for a science of society, an all-inclusive system by which to study and com-pare all social organizations and processes in all ages, to arrange a vast number of historical and contemporaneous facts into dependable, if rigid, catego-ries. He conceived of society "as an organism. Research and exposition were directed largely by the biological analogy."[5] By championing functional-ism, he asserted the need to "analyze structures such as kinship or activities such as rituals in terms of their functions for maintaining the society."[6]

Of course, Spencer did not go far without confronting opposition to his approach. In particular, his emphasis on materialism and determinism, together with his de-emphasis of metaphysics and ethics, brought his work under sharp scrutiny even as it established a place for itself in most universities by the onset of the twentieth century. Only in the early 1970s was his brand of sociology displaced because of its "excessively classificatory or typological theories that pigeonholed phenomena in terms of their functions."[7]

Under Spencer's direction, *Descriptive Sociology* was published as fifteen large folio volumes in London by Williams and Norgate between 1873 and 1919. The project involved him in a collaboration with James Collier (1846-1925), David Duncan (1839-1923), and Richard Scheppig (1845-1903). This compendious work's title suggests that no interpretation need occur in this science, indeed, that it must be resolutely avoided. In the work's "Provisional Preface," Spencer speaks of the need for "data" about a variety of societies, that is, non-interpreted and non-interpretive information that would lead to the production of tables that would enable comparisons among societies. Raw empiricism may not have been the foundation of positivism in the original use of that term by Comte, but *Descriptive Sociology* consummately exemplifies the methodology and the ideology of positivism. "Systematic descriptions" were vital; without them, Spencer wrote, "the Science of Life could make no progress."[8] Thus, even as he was developing a social evolutionary model on which he based his famous *Principles of Sociology* (1874-96), Spencer was overseeing the necessary methodology for it: the collection of data about what he regarded as primitive societies. Ultimately, from that data, he gave the world the theory of social progress ("societies evolve from lower to higher forms and progress from simple and undifferentiated to more complex types"),[9] including the idea of the survival of the fittest, or social Darwinism: "different social groups, including races, were at different states of evolution; the more advanced groups were destined to dominate groups less 'fit.'"[10] His work, it is well to remember, was very influential; sales of his titles rivalled those of the novels of Charles Dickens in the same era.

Only the sixth volume of *Descriptive Sociology* is dedicated to North America. In the thirty categories by which societies are studied, such as "Superstitions," "Laws of Intercourse," and "Aesthetics," ten groups are regularly mentioned – Esquimaux, Chinooks, Snakes, Comanches, Iroquois, Chippewayans, Chippewas, Dakotas, Mandans, and Creeks. Almost without exception, the data compiled comprise excerpts from narratives of exploration and travel. Because this selection of groups seems highly arbitrary, it perhaps depended chiefly on the books available to Spencer's team of compilers, including David Duncan, who was responsible for the sixth volume.

The Chinook are described under twenty-six of Spencer's thirty categories. In amassing their "data" on Chinook and Clallam, Spencer and his compiler relied heavily on *Wanderings of an Artist among the Indians of North America* (hereafter, *Wanderings*), more, in fact, than on any other single source. Spencer had published the first volume of his *Essays, Scientific, Political, and Speculative* with Longman, Brown, Green, Longmans, and Roberts in 1858, the year before the same London house published *Wanderings*. As is well known, Spencer's adherents, although not Spencer himself, believed that "best interests" of society could be advanced by ridding it of the inefficient and making room for the "better"; dedicated as Kane may have been to Native peoples, *Wanderings* nevertheless resolutely presented the most sensational of Native lifeways and, often, exposed them to ridicule and/or censure. The single most commonly excerpted source for the data of *Descriptive Sociology*, it served well Spencer's ideological concern to make room for the "better."

Of the ninety-two excerpts for Chinook (eighty-nine) and Clallam (three) in *Descriptive Sociology*, thirty-three come from *Wanderings;* that is, of all the data about these two groups in this definitive compendium, more than one-third (35.87 percent) derive from the book of a person who spent ten months west of the Rocky Mountains and between three and four months in the lower Columbia River Valley. Twenty-three excerpts come from Chapter 12, three from Chapter 13, five from Chapter 14, and two from Chapter 15 of *Wanderings*. Under the category of "Superstitions" in *Descriptive Sociology*, the Chinook are represented by twelve excerpts, six of them from *Wanderings*. This pattern is more or less the case for the other categories in which the Chinook are included.

In and of itself, the over-reliance on a single source gives one pause about Spencer's methodology, but the further matter of published travel and exploration literature's unreliability also suggests that the search in works of that genre for unimpeachable data is, if not misplaced, then certainly insufficiently qualified. The case of Kane's book is particularly illustrative of the risk that Spencer and his team were running.

Paul Kane has become a significant figure of English-white-Canadian history and culture. Famous in his lifetime as the author of *Wanderings* and as the painter whose works illustrated Canada's display at the Paris Exposition universelle of 1855, he was rendered prominent and authoritative through his membership in the Canadian Institute and marriage into a prosperous family. In our day, reproductions of his oil-on-canvas paintings may be found at many historical sites in eastern and western Canada and the western United States. Scholarship has regularly accorded him attention, although, until recently, he and his work have been regarded fairly straightforwardly; for example, *Wanderings* has been deemed a "classic of Canadian travel literature."[11] Tributes to his fame as a hero of the early Canadian West take many forms: in Alberta, a St. Albert high school bears his name; a book devoted to him topped the 1971 best-selling list for non-fiction;[12] a 1971 Canadian stamp commemorated the centennial of his death;[13] an Edmonton, Alberta, park is named for him; and a documentary film about him – the third – has recently been completed and broadcast.[14]

Yet, basic questions continue to emerge in research regarding him, and others persist. An abiding concern is the relation between Kane himself and the author of *Wanderings,* which was published under his name in London in 1859, eleven years after his 1846-48 travels from Toronto to Vancouver Island and back. Studies of Kane's field notes and portrait and landscape log, now in the Stark Museum of Art in Orange, Texas, have called Kane's authorship of the book into question, or, at least, have queried the likelihood of his identity as the lone or most significant author. However, the identity of his collaborators or editors or ghostwriters remains unknown.

Comparative studies have focused on the content and prose style of the three key works associated with Kane: these include his own field notes and portrait and landscape log;[15] the draft manuscript of *Wanderings,* which is written in two different hands, neither of them Kane's;[16] and *Wanderings* itself, which presents a persona of Kane as a gentleman, which he was not, and a disgusted authority on repulsive Native North Americans, which also he was not. The great mystery is how a man who travelled and lived among First Nations peoples for more than two years, and who seemed determined to return west as soon as he had spent one winter back in Toronto, could have represented them as pejoratively as the draft manuscript and book do, entirely at odds with his own notes and logs.

Could Kane have muzzled himself as he saw this evolution, amplification, and transformation occur? One cannot be sure, but one can be more certain that Kane's case is hardly exceptional. Jacques Cartier, the "discoverer" of Canada, comes to mind straightaway, as do Samuel Hearne and Captain James Cook, the arctic and Pacific explorers. So do Alexander Mackenzie, the first white man to cross North America, John Hanning Speke, who searched for the source of the Nile, and a host of other explorers and travellers.[17]

Although the London publishing house did much to ready Kane's book for publication, its draft manuscript, which was completed in eastern North America, not in England, had already begun to exhibit great modification of the field writings, so that credit or blame in this case cannot be ascribed entirely to Grub Street writers. Because only the notes and logs are in Kane's hand, it is tempting to insist that they alone should be regarded as the base text and the others – draft manuscript and book – a corruption of it. However, this evaluation requires qualification: the multiple versions need to be studied together, held in tension, in order to permit the emergence of patterns of differences, if they exist, and to enable the assessment of the diverse purposes that they served for their varying audiences.

Prominent in the Chinook chapters of *Wanderings* is a man whom the book calls Casanov (d. 1848), but whom most texts call Cassino. Based at Fort Vancouver (now Vancouver, Washington), he was the leader of the lower Columbia River people during the 1830s and 1840s, when a series of epidemics diminished their numbers by startling degrees – perhaps as much as 70 percent. According to *Wanderings,* when Casanov's son died of consumption, he followed Chinook tradition by ordering that one of his own wives, the dead boy's mother, be killed as an expression of his grief. Near the end of the anecdote, the author remarks that "Casanov assigned to me an additional motive for his wish to kill his wife, namely, that as he knew she had been so useful to her son and so necessary to his happiness and comfort in this world, he wished to send her with him as his companion on his long journey."[18] With this passage, which asserts eyewitness status for Kane, *Wanderings* implies that Casanov told him directly not just about that second motive but also about everything that the artist learned concerning the event. However, only the book and "The Chinook Indians," an article credited to Kane and published several times in the mid-1850s,[19] include the sentence. By contrast, the draft manuscript contains a version of the anecdote but no claim that Kane heard it directly from Casanov.[20] Meanwhile, there is no basis for any of this account in Kane's portrait log entry for Casanov.[21] His own record of the man was confined to a sketch portrait. It was exhibited in Toronto's Old City Hall in November 1848, shortly before Casanov died, a month later, on 10 December.[22]

In fact, the writer of "The Chinook Indians" and of *Wanderings* excerpted this word-picture from an earlier source, an account written by Samuel Parker (1779-1866), the chaplain who, a decade before Kane's arrival at Fort Vancouver, had officiated at the burial of Casanov's son on 2 February 1836. Essentially, this section of *Wanderings,* which simply refers to the chaplain as reading the service at the grave, is a slavish paraphrase of Parker's book. This earlier account includes the details that Casanov had decided to kill the boy's mother, that she was "most assiduous in her attention to him," that she was the "most beloved" of Casanov's several wives, and that he reasoned "that the greater the sacrifice, the greater the manifestation of his attachment to his son, and the more propitiatory to his departed spirit" – all of which are repeated in *Wanderings.*[23] The woman's escape to Fort Vancouver, her eventual return to "Chenook Bay," and the subsequent murder of another woman end Parker's account as they do the one in *Wanderings.*

Parker's *Journal* was first published in 1838, and had been reprinted several times before Kane began his travels. Perhaps Kane read it while at Fort Vancouver but his own writings make no note of it. The author/editor of "The Chinook Indians" and of *Wanderings,* apparently discontented with the draft manuscript's version in which Kane merely learns of Casanov's plan, decided that Kane should hear about it directly from the instigator himself.[24] So *Wanderings* resembles "The Chinook Indians" but differs from the draft manuscript in its inclusion of the sentence that claims eyewitness status for the persona of Kane: "Casanov assigned to me an additional motive for his wish to kill his wife."[25]

Does *Descriptive Sociology* excerpt this passage, problematical though it is? Yes, under the section titled "Superstitions." It is the prominent excerpt of the dozen in that section.[26] The attestation of the eyewitness lends to Spencer's data an unimpeachable empirical force about Chinook superstition.

At least this account can be traced to someone who was at Fort Vancouver, and who might have heard of Casanov's plan to kill his wife, a plan that was never carried out. Other excerpts from *Wanderings* included in *Descriptive Sociology* leave more room for doubt regarding Spencer's reliance on the book for his data. A discussion of their unreliability, however, requires a clarification of the evolution of the description of Chinook people that appears in *Wanderings*.[27]

Learning that Kane's book amounts to more and less than he encountered requires a familiarity with the means by which the book came gradually into print. Of course, Kane's enduring art has always implicitly extended authority to words published under his name, even if, as has been remarked often, only his field sketches, not his stylized studio oil paintings, possess a historical authority.[28] Even on its own terms, however, *Wanderings* commanded respect. In 1859, it was the first publication about the entire western regions of northern North America ostensibly written by someone not in the employ of the fur trade, and it assumed significance when it was issued in three other languages. It can be and for some time was regarded, therefore, as a disinterested account of life during the last decade of the Hudson's Bay Company's domination of the fur trade.

Although it concerns Native peoples, it contains only one sustained example of the sub-genre called "Manners and Customs," the precursor of ethnography. One expects to find this sub-genre in books of travel outside Europe as early as the sixteenth century. It is the logical narrative result of the assumption held by Europeans and, in the case of western North America, also by eastern North Americans that their travels, written up and disseminated from the publishing centre of one or another imperial or national power, would serve to bring into existence remote peoples whose realms were about to be assimilated. "There could," one veteran scholar of European explorations of North America has put it, "be no real discovery of North America unless, and until, there was a written record of that discovery."[29] That record functioned as the prominent means by which English-speaking nations claimed territory; the "Manners and Customs" section in the published record often served to illustrate to all those parts of the world dominated by the myth of progress that the backward occupants of said territory should be "civilized," which was to say, displaced.

The "Manners and Customs" passage of *Wanderings* claims to treat the Chinook Indians.[30] However, much of the passage, which forms the book's twelfth chapter, offers under the name of Chinook details about other peoples Kane encountered over a broad swath of the Pacific Slope and on both sides of the Cascades. So the manners and customs of many ethnic groups are presented together almost exclusively under one name. Moreover, one gross error shows that the writer(s) of the chapter possessed less than a firm grasp of the material. At one point, the Chinook are called "Flatheads."[31] Although their practice was indeed to flatten the forehead at birth, in the nineteenth century, the homeland of the Flathead, who did not practise the flattening of the forehead, was the interior Columbia Plateau, hundreds of kilometres distant from the Chinook, as far as Spokane lies from Portland. Although it is not infrequent in nineteenth-century publications, the confusion of Chinook with Flathead, whose only common characteristic is their residence west of the prairies/plains, probably did not originate with Kane himself; his field notes exhibit no such confusion.[32]

In fact, an examination of Kane's own field notes and logs (the only writings in his own hand) reveals that Kane remained almost silent about the Chinook. Although he did a great deal of sketching and collecting of artifacts while on the lower Columbia River, he simply stopped writing in his field notebook once he arrived at Fort Vancouver, and did not resume daily entries until he left. However, his portrait and landscape logs did continue through this period of December 1846 and the first three months of 1847. Occasionally, Kane forgets in which book he is writing, so a passage that sounds like a field note can appear in one of these two logs, whose primary purpose is to record not his travels, but information about the subjects he sketched. And, of course, many of those sketches have survived. But it could be that the "Manners and Customs" section was added to the draft manuscript to fill a void in the field writings detected either by Kane himself or by others who worked on that part of the text. The draft manuscript contains a great deal of information not found in Kane's field notes or logs, and, occasionally, not in *Wanderings,* either; in addition, the book itself includes details that appear in no earlier version.

For this particular section of the book, moreover, there are yet further variants: that is, to the field notes and logs written by Kane as he travelled, the draft manuscript, not in Kane's hand, and *Wanderings* itself, we must add "The Chinook Indians," the article mentioned above. Published twice in 1855 and once in 1857, before the release of *Wanderings* but probably after the completion of the draft manuscript (or so it appears – the manuscript's completion date has not been fixed), the article contains the book's section on the Chinook. For this reason, this part of the narrative is more bibliographically complex than any other.

Before the article was first printed, it was given as an address to the Canadian Institute in Toronto. The date of the address is unclear. When it was published, in the July 1855 issue of the *Canadian Journal,* the institute's own publication, it appeared with the statement "Read before the Canadian Institute, March 14th." However, in the institute's annual report for 1855, the list of "Communications" gives the date of the address as 31 March.[33] It is also mentioned in the minutes for the institute's meeting of 31 March, which were published in the May 1855 issue of the *Canadian Journal.* These minutes alone clarify that, although the paper was "communicated by Mr. Paul Kane," it was "read by Mr. G.W. Allan" (1822-1901). By that year, Allan was Kane's Toronto patron. He had commissioned one hundred oil-on-canvas paintings from Kane and had nominated the painter for membership in the illustrious Canadian Institute.[34] Together with the first published version of the paper, these minutes confirm that its presentation was complemented by a display of Kane's collection of artifacts and "several admirable oil paintings."[35]

In 1856, two other sections of the draft manuscript also appeared in *The Canadian Journal* as articles under Kane's name. Titled "Notes of a Sojourn among the Half-Breeds" and "Notes of Travel among the Walla-Walla Indians," they were printed only once each. Before their publication, they too were read as papers at meetings of the Canadian Institute in Toronto. However, like "The Chinook Indians," one at least – the Walla-Walla paper – was probably not read by Kane; according to the manuscript (handwritten) minutes of the meeting, this task was undertaken by Allan, his patron.[36] The title of "Notes of a Sojourn among the Half-Breeds" matches that of an address read before the Canadian Institute on 13 November 1855. Kane's name appears as the author under the title of this article, as it does under those concerning the Chinook and the Walla-Walla.[37] Still, the statement "Read before the Institute" might be misleading, but, equally plausibly, might not. Consider this: the December 1855 issue of the *Canadian Journal* containing the institute's annual report for that year mentions the "Conversazione at Moss Park; the residence of G.W. Allan, Esq.," held on 13 November, and notes that a paper was read by Paul Kane, Esq., 'Notes of a Trip to Lord Selkirk's Settlement on Red River, Hudson [sic] Bay Company's Territory.'"[38] On the face of it, this statement seems straightforward enough. However, when we examine the institute's records for Kane's Walla-Walla paper, lingering doubts arise concerning its validity. According to the handwritten minutes for the institute's meeting of 5 April 1856, Kane's paper regarding the Walla-Walla Indians was read by Allan. However, the published version of the minutes, which appeared in the July issue of the *Canadian Journal,* gives no indication that anyone other than Kane was involved: "The following

Papers were then read: 1. By Paul Kane, Esq. – 'On the Habits and Customs of the Walla-Wallas, one of the North American Indian Tribes,' from the Journal of the Author."[39] In the end, the question of who read the papers remains as unresolved as that regarding their authorship; moreover, how closely the presented papers resembled the subsequently published articles remains equally unclear.

Further examination of the content of *Wanderings* and "The Chinook Indians" thus proceeds from an awareness of a considerable body of sources about the "Chinook," all allegedly Kane's work. The twelfth chapter of *Wanderings* opens with the following sentence: "Fort Vancouver, the Indian name of which is Katchutequa, or 'the Plain,' is the largest post in the Hudson's Bay Company's dominions, and has usually two chief factors, with eight or ten clerks and 200 voyageurs, residing there."[40] The name "Katchutequa" first appears only in the draft manuscript, though with a different spelling, where an interlineation (writing inserted between the normal lines of text) that is not in Kane's hand occurs in the passage that describes Kane's arrival at Fort Vancouver on 8 December 1846. It reads, "the Indian name of which Kachoutqua means the Plain."[41] Nowhere in Kane's field writings can one find this name, and it is not mentioned elsewhere in the draft manuscript or any version of the thrice-published article. Hudson's Bay Company trader William Fraser Tolmie (1812-86) remembered that the site of Fort Vancouver was "named by the Tshinook Skit-so-to-ho, and by the Klikitat Ala-si-kas, or the place of mud turtles," but he, a contemporary of Kane, made note of this name only in an unpublished source.[42]

"Katchutequa" does not appear often as an alternative name for Fort Vancouver in other books or manuscript sources, but it seems to have been a legitimate one, although not one that always referred to the immediate vicinity of Fort Vancouver. Anthropological linguist Michael Silverstein suggests that "Katchutequa" might be a truncated form of "Chilluckit-te-quaw."[43] This word appears to originate with the explorers Merriwether Lewis (1774-1809) and William Clark (1770-1838), who led Thomas Jefferson's appointed expedition to the lower Columbia River in the fall of 1805 and the winter and spring of 1806. Lewis and Clark used "Chilluckittequaw" to denote the Wishram people, who lived upriver from but on the same (north) bank as Fort Vancouver, which, of course, was not established until another two decades after their travels.[44] In the only edition – Biddle's – of Lewis and Clark's narrative that was available to people on the Columbia in the early nineteenth century, "the Friendly village" is the name given by the explorers to a Wishram settlement, encountered on 29 October 1805, just upriver from the site of present-day Lyle, Washington, at the mouth of the Klickitat River.[45] However, the term Chilluckit-te-quaw was a misnomer: David and Kathrine French surmise that "Lewis and Clark had tried to elicit a name [for the place from the local people] but instead evidently recorded a word that was a description of their own elicitation process (the act of pointing)."[46] Silverstein suggests that, regardless of whether or not it was a misnomer, "there was, indeed, either a continuing tradition in the usage of at least a truncated form of this Lewis and Clark term among Whites ... or ... Kane or some source of his had access to it, though how and when/where the truncation of the first syllable took place, is the question."[47] How the term migrated nearly one hundred kilometres (sixty miles) downriver to the site of Fort Vancouver is another question, unless the fluid movement of peoples on the lower Columbia River at different seasons answers it.[48]

Another possible source for "Katchutequa" is Chinook Jargon: its name for Fort Vancouver, something like *qitsutxwa* or *chùtxwa*, was recorded as *kitsothot* and *kitsotkwa* in the twentieth century.[49] But both possibilities raise the further question of how Katchutequa made its way into the draft manuscript, and there found for itself a new meaning: the "Plain." If that is not enough perplexity, one is left wondering why the spelling in *Wanderings* ("Katchutequa") diverged from "Kachoutqua" in the draft manuscript.

This instance exhibits how it is that one seldom reads through even the first sentence of a chapter of *Wanderings* without encountering a bibliographical intrigue, the investigation of which requires diversions into the expertise of other disciplines. The straightforward correspondence between what eyewitness travellers saw and heard, and what is claimed in accounts published under their names is an illusion all too often. Relying on published narratives of exploration and travel as authoritative texts is hazardous if one aims at a clear understanding of how worlds collided. The genre, it is well to remember, rose to prominence along with the novel in the eighteenth century, and it has as much to do with the goals of the novel – to enlighten and to entertain – as it does with non-fiction prose genres.[50] Still, this genre seldom proves to be entirely illusory and misleading.

In its "Laws of Intercourse" category, Spencer's *Descriptive Sociology* includes two excerpts for the Chinook, one of which is the description from *Wanderings* of Chinook Jargon, which is called a patois. The passage explains the origin of "Clak-hoh-ah-yah," which it gives as a common salutation of the Chinook, "originating, as I believe, in their having heard in the early days of the fur trade, a gentleman named Clark frequently addressed by his friends, 'Clark, how are you?' This salutation is now applied to every white man, their own language affording no appropriate expression."[51] In his own writings, Kane makes no claim to have mastered Chinook Jargon and does not mention this salutation; it first appears in the draft manuscript, where the spelling is given as "Clach hah ahye."[52] The three versions of "The Chinook Indians" include this derivation but use slightly different spellings, *"Clah*

*hoh ah yah"* in the two versions published in the *Canadian Journal,* and *"Cha hoh ah yah"* in the *Daily Colonist.*[53] Botanist David Douglas, for whom the Douglas fir is named, recorded being hailed in 1825 by the salutation *clachouie,* meaning "friend," but, unlike the draft manuscript, the article, and *Wanderings,* he did not associate it with the English salutation "Clark, how are you?"[54] No earlier instance of this definition of the expression in Chinook Jargon has yet come to light.[55]

Three of the five excerpts about the Chinook in the category of *Descriptive Sociology* called "Aesthetic" derive from *Wanderings.* The most notorious concerns a culinary delicacy called Chinook olives, which was apparently made from acorns deposited in a hole dug in the ground and fermented over four or five months by regular applications of human urine.[56] *Wanderings* seems to be the only nineteenth-century published source of information about this Chinookan practice, and it has been oft-quoted.[57] The source of it has been traced but not found. The possibility of the practice must be allowed: the use of urine as a fermenting agent has a history in many cultures; although urine itself contains no yeasts, its release of nitrogen can stimulate wild yeasts in the soil environment, thus randomly initiating fermentation. Ethnobotanical research confirms that urine was used to leech tannins in acorns. That such a practice was widespread among Chinookan peoples and those of other cultures on other continents is not at issue today.[58] In Spencer's day, if not in Kane's, the use of urine by a Parisian baker and German brewers was noted by John Bourke,[59] in both of whose works this passage from *Wanderings* is also cited by way of Spencer's volume.[60]

Chinook olives are first mentioned in the draft manuscript, which claims that both males and females of a household must deposit all their urine in the hole.[61] The three versions of "The Chinook Indians" do not retain this specification of genders, and *Wanderings* implies that only men are contributors. *Wanderings* exhibits similar fastidiousness in omitting the detail, found in the draft manuscript and the article, that "even should a member of the family be sick and unable to reach [the hole] for this purpose the fluid is carefully collected and carried thither."[62] As well, the draft manuscript and the article contain an appended account, *not* repeated in *Wanderings,* about the Chinook wife of a white trader who could not readily be brought to abandon her taste for the delicacy.[63]

Meanwhile, no basis can be found in Kane's writings for the excerpts from *Wanderings* used by Spencer that describe the Chinookan stick game of chance[64] and the immolation of slaves.[65] Indeed, of the thirty-three passages excerpted as data from *Wanderings,* twenty-two, or 66 percent, have no basis in Kane's own notes and logs; the remaining eleven, or one-third, have at best a slight basis.

The degree of concern arising from the representation of the Chinook in a single book of travel, which was rehearsed as "data" in an academic publication, serves as a caution about the straightforward reading of travel narratives and their sub-genre Manners and Customs. Nowhere are the repercussions of ignoring this instance of variability and unreliability more sharply displayed than in *Descriptive Sociology*. Scholars who approach narratives of exploration and travel with the understanding that eyewitness-equals-author-equals-authority embark on a hazardous enterprise. Textual concerns ought to be a focal point of cases in which both publications and their manuscripts have survived. The collision of worlds was often exacerbated in the narrative record of the cultures whose high esteem for the printed word's authority did not preclude textual manipulation to meet the exigent needs of the day. If editors and ghostwriters knew – and many did – that a purple patch regarding Native sloth, barbarity, indecency, or superstition would help sell a book, why would the addition of one to every chapter, as occurs in *Wanderings,* not promise to mask a book's narrative deficiencies, heighten its popularity, and guarantee increased sales? The publishing mechanism played as vital a role in the project of European empires as television does today in the project of the American empire. Scholars can ably detect the bias of television and film; scholars of the collision of worlds in earlier epochs need to be persuaded that the bias of print requires scrutiny and assessment, book by book. Otherwise, understandings that depend on published sources will remain as much their hostages as Herbert Spencer and his team unwittingly became of their "data."

# 6

# Performing Paradox: Narrativity and the Lost Colony of Roanoke

*Michael Harkin*

The distinguished historian David B. Quinn, in his edited collection of source materials published around the quadricentenary of the Lost Colony – the early British colony on Roanoke Island in what is now Dare County, North Carolina – pleads that we ignore the myth that has grown up around Roanoke, and concentrate instead on the real historical actors and events of the 1580s.[1] We intend to ignore his advice. The purpose of this chapter is to begin to explore the mythmaking process that, especially in the last century and a half, has interpreted and reinterpreted the Lost Colony to various groups.[2] Indeed, we reject the simple distinction between real history and myth, embracing instead what Marshall Sahlins has called the "mytho-praxis" of history.[3] Simply put, this means that mythmaking, or, less pejoratively, narrative production, plays a role not only in the post-hoc interpretation of events, but in their shaping as well. A pragmatics of mythmaking is essential to the sort of reinterpretation of key events in the contact between societies that I propose here. In particular, events of "first contact," whether or not they are truly that in a larger historical context (which they were not in the case of the Lost Colony – the Portuguese pilot Simon Fernandes and several members of the party had previously met coastal Algonquians, some of whom had extensive prior contact with Europeans and other Native groups) are especially susceptible to topoi, or culturally constructed stereotypes. Such topoi are particularly productive of ongoing narrative transformations of the basic model. I draw further on the historian Greg Dening's notion of "performance" as a re-presentation of events in the historical consciousness of a group.[4] Thus, through iterations and reiterations, especially in the mode of theatricality, historical events are not only remembered but, to use Dening's apt term, "consummated." They are in a sense completed, but only to the extent that they may provide a starting point for a further cycle of performance and consummation. Moreover, the commemoration of one set of events may provide a ground for further historical events, and for a historical consciousness that purposely conflates eras and actors. Just as the Heiltsuk conflated the coming of the white man with both the advent of the steamship in central British Columbia and the "mythtime" period of frequent contact between humans and supernatural beings, so Tarheels (native North Carolinians) have associated the Lost Colony with the rise and fall of slavery, post–Civil War industrialization, and the ethnic and cultural diversification of the state in the late twentieth century.[5]

As I will argue, this narrative production consisted of a series of representational moments, both contemporary with the colony and in the centuries following, that portrayed paradoxical qualities of the original colony itself and of the society that ultimately sprang from it. In part because of the paradoxical nature of the colony, caught between a military and a commercial-expansionist idea of colonization, between the seasonally productive tidal zone and the shelter of the mainland, and, of course, between two radically different cultural worlds, the Lost Colony has been called into service to address other paradoxical issues in the history of the Carolinas and Virginia, and more broadly the South and American society as a whole: in particular, race, ethnicity, and identity.

A common means, in European culture and beyond, of portraying paradox is through gender and sexuality. As the historian Mary Fuller has recently shown, the gendering of Roanoke, and "Virginia" more broadly, was quite clear.[6] Not only was this stretch of mid-Atlantic coastline considered feminine, but it was also a sexualized (if resistant) femininity, as equated in John Donne's famous poem "To His Mistress Going to Bed" with the body of his lover:

> O, my America, my Newfoundland,
> My kingdom, safest when with one man mann'd,
> My mine of precious stones, my empery;
> How am I blest in thus discovering thee![7]

This image of courtly love and love at court, as epitomized by Sir Walter Raleigh's wooing of the Virgin Queen herself, provides a mental model for the discovery and conquering of the land itself. In contrast to the north Atlantic and the colony of Newfoundland, which predated Roanoke, "Virginia" was seen as desirable and maidenly, while the former was a utilitarian servant, producer of codfish, good for sustenance but little else.[8] The wild imaginings of Roanoke and later Jamestown as the source of untold wealth of the sort that is decidedly non-utilitarian, such as gold, "precious stones," and, of course, tobacco, clearly flows from the Elizabethan mindset, which separated women into such distinct categories. Such a dualistic notion of femininity represents a deep structure of Elizabethan culture, which is deployed in a variety of novel contexts. This process is evident in Arthur

Barlowe's 1584 account, from the initial survey of the area, of Roanoke as an unspoiled virgin: the scrubby, marginal land of the Outer Banks, the chain of barrier islands which includes Roanoke, is transformed into a land of great sweetness, firmness, and abundance.[9] Thomas Hariot, another member of the expedition, produced his "Brief and true report of the new found land of Virginia" explicitly to drum up interest in the area, employing similar tropes. In the broader context of Elizabethan exploration, promoters of colonization, such as Richard Hakluyt and Raleigh, made extensive use of such imagery drawn from courtly poetry.[10] The colonizer was thus in the same position regarding the new found land as was the courtly lover with respect to his beloved. The explicit connection between "Virginia" and the Virgin Queen led not only to an erotics, but to a politics of the representation of the new lands. Hakluyt refuted reports of the barrenness of the land (although, referring to the Outer Banks, and speaking only of agriculture, his claim was incorrect) by connecting Virginia with Elizabeth, and insisting that neither could be barren; to suggest otherwise would constitute *lèse-majesté*.[11] However, in such a context the lover is much more often frustrated than satisfied; deferral rather than consummation defines this relationship. Just as Raleigh's endless courtship of the queen eventually came to naught, so the land may be expected to guard its treasures jealously. What disastrous consequences this attitude could have for actual colonists became clear in the misadventure of the Lost Colony.

### How to Lose a Colony

The "Lost Colony" refers to Sir Walter Raleigh's 1587 settlement on Roanoke Island, which was designated "lost" after Governor John White failed in 1590 to establish contact with the colonists. It had been preceded by an unsuccessful military outpost led by Ralph Lane, which left the second colony with far more debts than assets with respect to the local people. Although often said to be the first English colony in North America, it was predated not only by the earlier outpost, but by the colony founded by Sir Humphrey Gilbert, Raleigh's half-brother, in Newfoundland in 1583. However, owing to its status as one of the earliest English colonies, and, more particularly, to the enigmatic circumstances of its termination, the Lost Colony has been at the centre of a regional tradition of representation, one which has intensified since the end of the Civil War. I will examine several key themes drawn from the hundreds of narrative versions of the Lost Colony.

The documentary history of the Lost Colony is anything but straightforward, however. English interest in the Outer Banks of what is now North Carolina dates back to the 1560s. Looking for a base from which to harass Spanish treasure ships, the English were keenly interested in the central Atlantic coast of North America. Sir Walter Raleigh, exercising his royal charter, sent out scientific and information-seeking surveys to this region in the

1580s. In the mid-1580s, an early military colony at Roanoke foundered on poor relations with the local Algonquian Indians and inadequate provisions, due both to a failure to adequately supply the colony and the severe limitations of the local ecosystem to support agriculture.

Raleigh conceived of the colonization of Roanoke as a civilian and even humanitarian venture, but the military presence and the habits learned in the conquest of Ireland determined a pattern of interactions that doomed the first colony. Although the goal of scientific discovery was prominent, with the establishment of a "science center," such aspirations fell victim to the ingrained habits of conquest.[12] The commander of this first attempt, Ralph Lane, while searching for the treasure assumed to be in abundance, seized and killed a local chief, Wingina, for the trivial crime of the theft of a cup from the English baggage. Such acts contributed directly to the abandonment of the colony; the threat of retaliation by the local Indians appeared too great to remain.[13] This colony was given up in 1586 upon the arrival of a ship commanded by Sir Francis Drake; a resupply ship that arrived shortly thereafter left fifteen men behind.[14] These men, never seen again by their compatriots, were later found to have been murdered by Indians in retaliation for the murder of Wingina.

The second attempt to establish a colony, in 1587, was a well-financed venture that took into account the earlier problems. More colonists and more supplies were sent to Roanoke, and both aid from local friendly Indians and the prompt return of ships from England were promised. Women and children were included, and the early months of the colony saw the birth of the first English child, Virginia Dare, in their new world. Rather than military rule, a civilian system of government was established, modelled on the corporation. The idea of a civilian colony, well financed and provisioned, was indeed the correct strategy, as the later success at Jamestown proved.[15] Moreover, the corporation as organizing principle was to become quite common in later periods of exploration and settlement, in entities such as the Hudson's Bay Company. However, the Roanoke colony was neither large enough nor wealthy enough to survive unaided. In addition, it re-established itself on the poor soil of Roanoke Island, using the structures abandoned by the Lane colony, despite earlier plans to settle in the fresh territory of Chesapeake Bay.[16] These plans were abandoned because Chesapeake Bay and the rivers that fed into it provided deepwater access to the Spanish, who knew the coastline well. Thus, the colony might well have become a target and source of aid to the Spanish, rather than a secret toehold on the continent. Moreover, the Chesapeake was the seat of the powerful chief Powhatan, who exercised sovereign control over the entire region. Thus, the Lost Colony was intentionally sited in an area that was marginal. It was accessible only with great effort by small vessels (adding to the difficulty and uncertainty of resupply) and was poorly suited to provide year-round sustenance for a permanent population. Also, the already strained relations with local Indians were exacerbated by an act of murder in the very early days of the second colony.[17]

What is more, the ships did not return the next year: the Grand Armada of Spain forestalled any attempt to resupply the colony. Only after three years had passed was an incomplete and cursory look for the colony attempted by John White. The site had been abandoned, perhaps in some haste, and only the word CROATOAN, the name of a nearby island, was left behind, carved on a post. This was a signal, for the colonists had decided ahead of time that, should they be forced to flee, they would post their destination. Lacking was a cross, the pre-arranged sign of distress. However, due to the unlucky occurrence of a hurricane, no sustained attempt was made to search Croatoan (Hatteras) or to ask the friendly Natives living there for information. No more systematic surveys of the region were even attempted until scouts from the Jamestown Colony to the north were dispatched two decades later.[18]

What these scouts reported was the most likely scenario: that the colonists, under threat from hostile groups and not resupplied, had gone off to live with mainland groups that were part of the Powhatan Confederacy. One colonist, George Percy, reported seeing a boy with blond hair and light skin. An Indian scout, relied upon by William Strachey in his *History of Travel into Virginia Brittania,* more dubiously reported seeing European-style housing and other traces of an English cultural presence.[19] Although details of the reports are clearly fictional – it is unlikely that colonists would have been able to build two-storey stone houses of the sort mentioned, given the lack of surface stone in this area – the gist of the report is plausible.[20] David B. Quinn speculates that the colonists flourished until coming under the power of the great Powhatan, who massacred them and enslaved the survivors.[21] The survivors may or may not have been killed in later years, but the "lost" colonists probably found refuge and eventually mixed with the mainland Indian populations. Several groups in North Carolina, most notably the Lumbee Indians, have claimed at one time to be the descendants of this mixed population.[22] This single question regarding the fate of the colonists has spurred numerous conjectures, many quite fanciful. For the most part, they attempt to demonstrate continuity between the colonists and a living community in eastern North Carolina, and are usually written and published by members of that community.[23]

### Performance and Paradox

It has frequently been noted that the image of the Indian in American and European thought clusters around two, contradictory, poles: the Noble Savage and the bloodthirsty savage. The lineaments of this paradox are complex, and can be traced to pre-modern European cosmologies, as well as

Enlightenment philosophers, most notably Denis Diderot.[24] This paradox, reinforced by the pragmatics of first contact, in which extreme hopes and fears are projected onto real persons, determined the course of events in many contact situations. From the time of Columbus, colonial agents employed two representational strategies, often simultaneously, to categorize the other. One was to ethnicize the two poles, by positing a manichaean opposition between good and bad groups. Columbus used the names "Arawak" and "Carib" to describe these aspects, believing them to denote real ethnic groups, a mistake repeated by generations of historians.[25] To a certain degree, this strategy was pursued by the leaders of the Roanoke colonies, who were keen to separate out the "friendly" chiefs and their polities from the "unfriendly" ones, although the degree of friendliness displayed by chiefs was generally conditioned by their prior experiences with the English. (Moreover, the pragmatics of the situation tended to produce a more nuanced reading of each side by the other, one which becomes superseded by more dualistic rhetorical models.) Another strategy was to locate the paradox within the character of all Indians, to portray them as in constant struggle between the noble and savage dimensions of their natures. Each strategy, although politically and psychologically unrealistic, opens up its own dramatic possibilities. The first strategy lends itself to rather straightforward heroic plot lines, in which all the action is external; the latter turns on a more complex, and we might say modern, internal drama of conflict and doubt. I have termed this general matrix including both strategies a "poetics of ambiguity."

The poetics of ambiguity is nowhere better displayed than in the Lost Colony narrative as it has been expressed in hundreds of versions ranging from the scholarly to the demotic. Many iterations, including Paul Green's 1937 "symphonic drama" *The Lost Colony,* invoke distinctions between friendly and unfriendly Indians, led by the characters Manteo and Wanchese, who are based on real historical actors.[26] However, the fact of the colony's mysterious end reduces the figure of the Indian generally from historical actor to perfectly ambiguous symbol. The complexities of motivation and action are either simplified in manichaean terms or are mystified, and thus removed from rational calculation. Indeed, in some versions, Manteo, the friendly chief, becomes hostile after the murder of several of his kinsmen in the early days of the colony. Just as the essence of poetic language is its ambiguity, so the literary Indian finds its apotheosis in a historical ellipsis, pregnant with indeterminacy.

That this ambiguity is more than a simple reflection of a gap in the historical record is clear in the symbolic uses to which the figure of the Indian in the Lost Colony has been put. Beginning in the late nineteenth century, literary productions on the Lost Colony theme flourished. The burden of nearly all of these poems, plays, and novels was to establish a charter myth for the society that arose from early English colonization (although not, of course, from the Lost Colony itself). The ambiguity of the Indian is essential to this rhetorical project. On the one hand, the Indian, as Aboriginal inhabitant, possessed prior rights to the land. Unlike Columbus, who symbolically "emptied" the land in finding it devoid of Christian inhabitants, the English were forced by circumstance and disposition to deal with the Indians. Despite the rhetorical shading, descriptions of the land and its inhabitants were much more empirically grounded than were those of Columbus. What that information suggested was that these people would necessarily play some role in future developments. The doctrine of *terra nullius*, "empty land," was difficult to apply in the face of a settled agricultural society with a political organization similar to that of Europe before the rise of absolute monarchy.[27] The coastal Algonquians were organized into semi-autonomous villages, each headed by a *werowance*, or "peace chief." These werowances may have been tributaries of a paramount regional chief, such as the famous Powhatan, and yet had some voice in the larger polity through a council of chiefs. Thus, the early European colonists were more likely to think of the Indians as rivals than as subordinates or slaves.[28] The upshot of this is that the Indian must be complicit in the historical transition from an Aboriginal to a Euro-American society.

On the other hand, the savage (and especially non-Christian) nature of the Indian ensures his forfeiture of both land and social priority. One common theme of most Lost Colony literature is evolutionary progress, which is, by definition, incompatible with savagery. Thus, even the "friendly" Indians, who are seen as more open to the possibilities of civilization, are forced to admit their own obsolescence. This is the tack taken by Paul Green in his epic play *The Lost Colony*.[29] Clearly, this is a retrospective reading of the past. In the sixteenth century, colonists and their leaders viewed the Indians as potential enemies or allies to be intimidated or courted, but not as remnants of a past world that would soon evaporate. If they believed in their own inevitable superiority, it was due to their possession of the "true religion" rather than for technological innovations such as firearms (which at this early point proved inferior to bows and arrows). Instead, the inexorability of evolutionary supersedence and the topos of the "Vanishing Indian" are very much products of the nineteenth century in American history: a time when white society was itself undergoing rapid change.[30] Paul Green's play is as much about the painful transition from an agrarian to an industrial society as it is about the Lost Colony itself. Nevertheless, the trope of inevitable loss and change allowed modern readers and audiences to incorporate the events of the Lost Colony into their own individual and collective history. As I have suggested, the Lost Colony, however tenuous its connection to modern North Carolina society, becomes appropriated as a charter myth of that society.

## The White Doe

Narratives of the Lost Colony by their very nature deal with historical transformations. They are what Raymond Fogelson has called "epitomizing events," narrative constructions in which gradual diachronic processes are telescoped into poetic unities of time and place.[31] The Lost Colony epitomizes the world-shattering transition between an entirely indigenous society and one in which Europeans are significant political and social actors, although not yet dominant ones. The narrative of the White Doe appears as part of a larger epic poem written by Sallie Southall Cotten and published in 1901.[32] In this highly popular poem, subtitled "The Fate of Virginia Dare, an Indian Legend," the essential issue is extracting the first English child born in America from an ambiguous and untenable position. The use of an "Indian" style of narrative is astute, in that it overcomes two problems. First, the lack of information about the Lost Colony and Virginia Dare lends itself to a mythological genre, which proclaims itself to be anti-history, and thus free from the strictures of mainstream Western discourse about the past. Second, the use of authentic and ersatz Indian narrative elements in the framework of an epic poem suggests the very sort of hybridity the author is asserting. Thus, the history of North Carolina from the Lost Colony onward is characterized by the poetics of epic poetry, heroic and teleological. Yet, within that march of history and contributing to it in important ways is the undercurrent of Indian themes, which provide precisely the sort of magical realism *avant la lettre* necessary to move from the failure of the Roanoke colony to a society based on the ideology of English colonization.

Cotten modelled her work, and her title, on Wordsworth's *The White Doe of Rylstone,* a lengthy poem published in 1815 that deals similarly with the question of historical memory and the legacy of violent events. However, Cotten limited the reflective romanticism of Wordsworth largely to decorative touches; the essence of her poem is much closer to heroic epic than to Wordsworthian introspection. American writers, especially Longfellow, Hawthorne, and Cooper, provided more direct influences, particularly in the use of Indian and ethnohistorical material. Cooper's invention of the "pseudo-Indian" (e.g., Leatherstocking), a character who possesses positive Indian traits of closeness to nature, but is unsullied by actual Indian ancestry, is an important precedent for Cotten's Virginia Dare, who would remain virginally aloof from her pursuers.

The central ideological problem, especially for those in the nineteenth and early twentieth century, was, not to put too fine a point on it, sex. The greatest horror of the time was "miscegenation," the intermixing of races, prototypically between a white woman and a darker man (although, in reality, it was quite common and much more likely to result from the union of white men and darker mistresses). By this rigid logic, signalled most obviously by the whiteness of the doe, the Lost Colony could not possibly have mixed with the Indian population; therefore, it must have been well and truly lost, must indeed have disappeared off the face of the earth. This was in fact the line taken by many narratives, which had the colonists being massacred by Indians or kidnapped by the Spanish. However, such an outcome was not adequate for one purpose: the establishment of an originary English presence. This required the survival, in some sense, of the colony. Certain groups, such as the Lumbee, believed in a physical, genealogical continuity. However, for the delicate sensibilities of white Victorian North Carolina, this was not possible. Instead, a vague "spiritual" survival is suggested.

The significance of an originary English presence for North Carolinians of this period cannot be overstated. Most importantly, it provided a charter for the rigid caste society that arose in the nineteenth century. This separated, most obviously, the three "races," whites, blacks, and Indians (who, except for the eastern Cherokee, were officially believed to have disappeared from the state). Equally significant, however, was the establishment of social priority, in a literal sense, among white North Carolinians. The early English presence in the eastern part of the state legitimized the tidewater elite, who were, in theory, of pure English descent.[33] In contradistinction, the interior was perceived as populated by Scotch-Irish, Moravians, Germans, and others of peasant stock.[34] The reality was, of course, much more complex. However, the elite based their claims largely on their purported English connection. In the antebellum period, this connection was represented in a thousand ways, from the style of clothing and houses to the invention of aristocratic genealogies. After the war, this pretense was increasingly difficult to maintain, until by the depression of the 1890s it became only a memory. At the same time, claims to aristocratic status increased, as its signs became less material and more symbolic: small mementos, coats of arms, and, above all, stories.[35]

It is in this context that we can analyze Cotten's poem. For though it does not make a specific genealogical claim, for the reasons cited above, it does make a generic claim of English aristocratic presence at the very founding of European America. Virginia Dare was no aristocrat: her maternal grandfather, John White, was a craftsman who was given the formal status of "gentleman" in order to satisfy the cultural expectations for a colonial governor. However, Virginia Dare is shown to be an aristocrat in the much more important, to the Victorians, category of sexual conduct.

The plot of this section of the poem is roughly this: Virginia Dare has moved with her family from the colony to the village of Manteo, a friendly chief, on the mainland. She has grown to maidenhood, and is, of course, radiantly beautiful. She is "fair" in both senses of the word, with "tresses ... in which sunbeams lingered" and eyes of "limpid blueness."[36] She is also accounted wise on the basis of her rudimentary knowledge of Christianity. (The other colonists are not mentioned at this point, as she seems to be the only carrier of this legacy.) Naturally, such a presence stirs up trouble among the men of the community. Four, in particular, are involved: Wingina and Wanchese, chiefs; Okisko, a "brave"; and Chico, an old sorcerer. Of the four, only Wingina and Wanchese were historical figures. Wingina was a werowance who had assisted the first colony, but later became hostile to the English. Although the English killed him in 1586, in retaliation for the theft of a cup, Cotten resurrected him for the occasion. Wanchese was, along with Manteo, one of the two chiefs taken to the court in London. To the dismay of the English, neither displayed the expected attitude of awe, and Wanchese subsequently became hostile to the English.[37]

The two chiefs are motivated by hostility to the whites, but the fictional characters are motivated by love of Virginia Dare, or, as she is known by this point, "Winona." This opposition is crosscut by nobility versus deviousness. That is, Okisko is a young man who may properly and openly love Winona, but Chico is an aged sorcerer whose love is illegitimate and hidden. Similarly, Wanchese is an open enemy of the whites, but Wingina is devious, using false friendship, trickery, and sorcery to destroy the colony. In this way, the permutations of the Indian character are presented in a two-by-two square. If we wished to construct a formal analysis of this semiotic space, it would be quite easy to do using a Greimassian square.[38] At its top left corner would be the noble friendly Indian (Okisko); the ignoble friendly Indian (Chico) would be at the top right. The noble unfriendly (Wanchese) would be at bottom left, and the ignoble unfriendly (Wingina) at bottom right.

In the poem, each member of this quartet plays a role in the transformation of Winona the fair maiden into the White Doe. "Brave Okisko," a stand-in for all "the young braves of the nation / thrilled with love for fair Winona," waits in vain for his ardour to be returned. Meanwhile, crafty old Chico attempts to woo her with tales of his past feats – a guarantee of failure if ever there was one! Tired of polite rejection, Chico lures her into a canoe by promising to take her to Roanoke, a place he describes as hanging with fruit, in an ironic reprise of the colonizing propaganda that led to the establishment of the Lost Colony. Fair Winona accompanies the sorcerer, unaware that he has secreted magically treated pearls – pearls being significantly the only item of value the colonists actually found at Roanoke – which he has made into a necklace. He presents her with the necklace, endowed with a complex magical spell, which she wears. The magic of the necklace does not take effect until she returns to land, at which point she is transformed into a white doe, lithe and sprightly. Subsequently, many hunters try to kill her, but she proves uncatchable. Eventually, word gets out that she is in fact the fair maiden transformed, information which sets another chain of events creakily into action.

Okisko consults a different sorcerer, who gives him a magic arrow. With this, he has the power to release Winona from the spell and, by implication, to win her heart. Wingina, pretending to believe that the White Doe is merely a deer, calls together all the men of his tribe, urging them to kill it. "Her white skin shall be my mantle / Her white meat shall serve for feasting," is Wingina's refrain, clearly a reference to cannibalism, the diacritic of savagery. The hunters pursue her, with the two ablest, Wanchese and Okisko, leading the way. Wanchese, not knowing the identity of the White Doe, carries with him a silver arrow given to him in England. He and Okisko catch the White Doe in the clearing of the old fort. Both shoot simultaneously and their arrows pierce her heart. Okisko's arrives slightly sooner, so the White Doe is transformed back into Winona, just before dying. With her dying words, she tells Okisko to "remember" her, while her body presents a tableau of Christian symbols. The arrows form a cross on her breast, which is taken by all as an omen. Her heart's blood dries up a magical spring, but also gives rise to a vigorous shooting vine (in another version identified as the vine of the scuppernong grape, which later generations used to make a very sweet wine).[39]

The author, in the poem's final section, helpfully gives the symbolic correspondences of arrow, spring, and vine. The arrow, "fatal to all sorcery / Was the gleaming light of Progress," which doused the spring of magic,

> And the tiny shoot with leaflets, by the sunlight warmed to life
> Was the Vine of Civilization in the wilderness of strife;
> With no friendly hand to tend it, yet it grew midst slight and wrong,
> Taking root in other places, growing green, and broad, and strong.

What is a bad habit in poetry – burdening the reader with a literal rendition of its own symbols – is the essence of ideology. As Frederic Jameson, interpreting Greimas, remarks, ideology is inherently self-interpreting, alternating between narrative and abstract formulations.[40]

What is significant about this late-Victorian tearjerker is not that it is unique, like a great work of art, but rather that it is entirely typical, filled with the platitudes of the day. The ideological work done here is quite interesting, for it establishes an orthodoxy that was to prevail for most of the twentieth century. Of course, it reflects its own time much more than it does the late sixteenth century, its purported subject matter. The 1890s in the American South was a very interesting period, one which was undergoing a transformation similar to that which Frederic Jameson has suggested for late capitalism.[41] Rather than representing the last gasps of Fordist industrial capitalism, "The White Doe" expresses the last gasps of plantation agrarianism. The signs of aristocracy slip free from the material base, becoming primarily narrative in nature. In a sense, the Cotten poem and other contemporary treatments of the Lost Colony are exercises in the symbolic capital of racial, rather than family, aristocracy. The claim of social priority for those of English descent – which, by then, most white North Carolinians could claim – was a readily available substitute for the increasingly outmoded and unsupportable claims to family status. This coincided with emerging notions of white racial solidarity in the face of perceived threats from African Americans, and, to a lesser degree, from northern capitalists. The figure of the Indian is an essential element in this matrix, not because of its active presence on the scene – indeed, it was mistakenly believed to have entirely disappeared from the tidewater South – but because of its medial quality.

Historically, the figure of the Indian mediates between a wilderness that is viewed alternately as colonized or edenic and savage. In fact, the qualities attributed to the landscape were illusory. To the degree that Roanoke was bountiful, it was already inhabited; to the degree that it was virginal, it was barren. A central paradox of the Lost Colony is that the earliest discourse upon it, by Hariot and, especially, Barlowe, represented an inversion of this reality: for them, Roanoke was bountiful and empty, virginal and fertile. This leads to a second paradox, that the colony failed to colonize this space; it was unsuccessful in mapping and controlling the landscape – what a colony is intended to do – to the point that it becomes "lost" in that very landscape.

This seemingly insurmountable problem is overcome in the story of the White Doe, with its foreshadowing of a civilization that would grow like, and alongside, cultivated plants. Slightly later, purportedly scholarly, versions of the Lost Colony narrative connect the vine of the Cotten poem to the growing of scuppernong wine grapes – a diacritic of civilization in the colonial context that goes back at least to Tacitus.[42] The White Doe herself is similarly pregnant with significance, although perhaps not a significance the author was conscious of. Although they were not traded much among tribes, deerskins and, to a lesser degree, meat, were valued commodities which constituted the main item of Indian-white exchange in the early colonial South. Entire networks of exchange were established between whites and Indian groups to supply a transatlantic trade that amounted to four hundred tons of dressed hides in 1764.[43] This marked a critical juncture in the historical process of the anglicization of the South. Indians were no longer a threat to colonization, but rather active partners in the creation of fortunes that would give rise to the new world in which they themselves would be marginalized.

The Indian is an essential figure in this transition, symbolically as well as materially. Past connection with Indians, who were presumed to have vanished by the nineteenth century, validated claims to social priority derived from presumptive descent from colonists. This produces a quality that I call (ab)originality, a status elliptically dependent upon Indians. For instance, visitors to the North Carolina Archives branch at Manteo, near the Lost Colony site, most frequently attempt to trace descent from the Lost Colonists. Although this would necessarily require many generations of Indian and mixed-race ancestors as well, these people identify themselves as white and specifically as Anglo-Carolinian. The narratives surrounding the Lost Colony, such as Cotten's "The White Doe," make the colony semiotically available for such purposes. Despite the implicit likelihood of "miscegenation," the Lost Colony narrative can become a charter for racial and ethnic hierarchy.

"The White Doe" unconsciously ties into that very literary tradition which gave rise to the project of colonization in the first place. Virginia Dare is the archetypal maiden, for whom men harboured desires both pure and impure. The deferral of their claims, through death, allows her purity to remain unsullied, although, by a rhetorical sleight of hand, her reproductive capacity is harnessed to the cause of civilization. It is precisely the separation of sexuality from reproduction that allows contemporary Anglo-Carolinians to imagine themselves as at once descended from the Lost Colonists and "untainted" by miscegenation. This is parallel to the process that Kristeva identifies as sublimation of the "defiling" sexuality of the mother, replaced by claims of bodily and group purity.[44] Thus, the purity and priority of the group may be paradoxically ensured by the sublimated sexuality of the race-mother.

### Conclusion: A Paradoxical Lost Colony

The Lost Colony is semiotically productive precisely because it rests on a set of paradoxes. Charles Nuckolls has argued that paradox is the productive nucleus of any cultural tradition.[45] This may be true, but it is certainly the case that paradox underlies ideology. Here, the contradiction between colonization and the state of being lost, between (ab)originality and racial hierarchy, ensures the continued productivity of Lost Colony narratives, even in the face of rapid social change. Indeed, periods such as the turn of the last century and the present era are particularly fertile ground for the genesis of new narrative formations. The increased interest in the Lost Colony, as demonstrated by a succession of recent popular works published in France, the United States, and England, is due in part to the easy availability of primary and secondary documents published during the quadricentenary of the 1980s, but perhaps even more to the paradoxical qualities of the narrative tradition, which invite symbolic treatment and speak to contemporary audiences.[46]

Within the state, interest in the Lost Colony has increased markedly during the post-quadricentenary period. Scholarly and amateur publications on the topic have been common.[47] Fort Raleigh National Historic Site has seen an increase in visitors. Commercial history-themed development has arisen in the form of the Roanoke Island Festival Park. Although far behind nearby Williamsburg and the James River sites in Virginia as regards tourist development, Roanoke has nevertheless been expanding rapidly, both in terms of numbers of visitors and the range of activities available for them, which now includes on-site historical re-enactments.[48] This development may be seen against the context of rapid social and technological change in North Carolina during the 1990s. The population of the state grew rapidly from 6.6 to 8.2 million (an increase of nearly 25 percent), much of the growth coming from migration. Charlotte became a national banking capital, Wilmington became a significant filmmaking locale, and the "Triangle" area became a major centre for high-tech industry and pharmaceuticals. Perhaps most notable was the remarkable increase in the Hispanic population, which rose from 1.2 percent to 4.7 percent of the larger population.[49]

One function of the Lost Colony as a representational field is to provide ready-made symbols of identity. As the actual population of the state changes rapidly, the need for symbolic anchors of the notion of "Tarheelness" increases. More broadly, the economic, technological, and cultural changes loosely termed "postmodernism" have been highly favourable for the production of narratives that relate to history and identity. Although Jean-François Lyotard may well have been correct in arguing for the end of "master narratives," their eclipse has given rise to a multiplicity of specific narratives that define communities and link them to historical events and horizons.[50] This may be viewed in terms of the construction of place, of local versus global. As Arjun Appadurai has stated the problem, it is one of producing and reproducing locality – reterritorializing – in the face of a world that is increasingly "deterritorialized," in Deleuze and Guattari's apt turn of phrase.[51] The conflict between local and global itself destabilizes the very community that might be assumed to ground local discourse. The influx of a Hispanic, primarily Mexican, population, along with a wider variety of ethnicities and national origins than were ever known in "modern" North Carolina society, combined with the outmigration of native Tarheels, have broken the inherent connection between the physical and imagined communities.[52] That imagined community (which we can signify by the term "Tarheel") is in fact dependent upon historical narrative for its very existence. This situation is not, however, entirely new. In the late nineteenth and early twentieth centuries, populations were displaced by the war, Reconstruction, industrialization, and even the rise of transportation and tourism.[53]

Recall that the ur-text of Tarheel displacement and longing for identity, Thomas Wolfe's *Look Homeward, Angel,* was published in 1929. Indeed, much of the narrative production on the Lost Colony, such as Cotten's "White Doe," similarly attempts to "re-place" Tarheel society, often via England and the notion of an "English nation."[54]

Indeed, we might say that the idea of such a nation has always been a fiction removed from the daily realities of life. The existence of non-white, non-English ethnic groups has a made such a notion fantastical. In one of the few writings on the Lost Colony to explicitly address race, Collier Cobb attempts to rescue the notions of both (ab)originality and racial purity. Discounting claims by Spanish settlements Santa Fe and St. Augustine to represent the first "white" presence in the territory of the United States, he says that "it has always been the usual thing for men of the Latin race to marry women of the lands they conquered." By contrast, "The Britisher brought his wife with him. How fortunate for North Carolina and for the greater part of North America that this is true!" Cobb is ambivalent on the idea of intermarriage between the Lost Colonists and Indians; he supports the claims of the Lumbee that their ancestors were white, but he thinks it more likely that they were "sailors." At the same time, he suggests that the "bankers" or "watermen" of the coast "are like to the men of Devonshire even to this day; and in their manners, customs, and speech may be found much to suggest the England of the Virgin Queen." Indeed, he goes on to say, tellingly, "that not a county of England had so large a proportion of its citizens of British origin as did middle and eastern North Carolina, if you omit the descendants of African slaves."[55] Thus, if one can somehow reconcile the idea of English repugnance at ethnic exogamy with the continuity of a tiny ill-equipped population, and, of course, ignore the presence of blacks, then eastern North Carolina may be seen as a sort of beacon of Anglo-Saxon civilization, more so even than late-imperial Albion herself!

One reason that so few Lost Colony writings explicitly address race is that such arguments are, on the level of logic and history, untenable. However, the poetic logic in which something may be simultaneously true and not true allows for such possibilities (see Chapter 1, this volume). The poetics of ambiguity present in the Indian characters condense the paradoxes of this entire narrative field, which turn on issues of race and (ab)originality, and the tension between the two. What may be naively and simply put as an empirical question – What was the fate of the Lost Colony? – is merely the first step into a labyrinth of ambiguity, in which questions of historical identity, "national" character, and group privilege may be broached.

# 7
# Stories from the Margins: Toward a More Inclusive British Columbia Historiography
*Wendy Wickwire*

During the first decades of the twentieth century, British Columbia became the site of a major social scientific research project. Anthropologist Franz Boas (1858-1942) was the driving force behind much of this work. Concerned that the indigenous cultures of this region would not survive the onslaught of westernization, Boas established a rigorous field research program aimed at ethnographic rescue. He envisaged the published monograph as the key to cultural preservation. Armed with sufficient field data, he was confident that he could produce textual portraits of the traditional cultures that would outlive the cultures themselves. That many of his so-called informants were horsepackers, miners, cannery workers, missionary assistants, and construction labourers several generations removed from his imagined pristine contact point did not deter him. Over the course of a few decades, he and his associates produced thousands of pages of written text framed against the backdrop of a Golden Age.

Stories formed the core of Boas' ethnographic legacy. With his focus on the deep past, however, these were not stories of the present or the recent historical past, that is, accounts of epidemics, floods, encounters with missionaries and government agents, and conflicts with miners and others. These were specialized stories set in the deep pre-contact past – so-called legends, folktales, myths – about the creation of the world and its first inhabitants.

The monographs produced from this work have attracted a large following, especially among folklorists, anthropologists, and historians. It is only recently that scholars have begun to analyze them critically.[1] Charles Briggs and Richard Bauman have taken the lead with an essay on Boas and the construction of modernity, charging that Boas' preference for "the more canonical genres of putatively authentic folk expression" is a natural extension of his Germanic education in "the philological program of Herder and Grimms."[2] A critical element in his text-making project, they suggest, "is that the social opposition between the traditional and modern worlds that it sought to construct was sustained by texts whose rootedness in modernist discursive practices and interests was suppressed in favor of producing an aura of authenticity and verisimilitude."[3] Joanne Fiske makes a similar point. "Ironically, in the long term," she notes, "Boas hardened notions of oral tradition as exotic narrative and laid foundations for its later reification and reinvention by neotraditionalists and professional observers who likewise treated cultural performances and exotic tales as inflexible over time."[4]

I confronted this problem directly when I embarked on my first large ethnographic project in the late 1970s. My focus was an elderly storyteller, Harry Robinson, a member of the Lower Similkameen Indian Band, a branch of the larger Salishan-speaking Okanagan Nation of south-central British Columbia. I met Harry in mid-August 1977, at his home near the town of Hedley in the Similkameen Valley. I was with friends who had invited him to accompany us to the Omak Stampede in Washington State just south of the border. As it was uncomfortably hot, Harry suggested that we spend the night at his house before heading to Omak.

Shortly after dinner, someone asked Robinson a simple question about a local landmark that prompted him to tell a long Coyote story which continued well into the evening. Intrigued by the story, I returned whenever I could to hear more. Before long, I was immersed in an oral history project that spanned thirteen years until Robinson's death in 1990 at age ninety.

In preparation for this project, I studied the published narrative collections for the region, reading everything from Boas to the most recently released material.[5] I emerged from this literature review well steeped in timeless ancestral tales – "How Turtle Got His Tail," "Why Spider Has Such Long Legs," "The Boy Fostered by Bears," "Skunk Takes Revenge," "Frog and Turtle Race," "The Origin of the Black Bear" – but unclear about how if at all these fit together, or what their intended messages might be. Except in the post-1970 collections, such stories included little about the identities of individual storytellers. I could therefore draw few conclusions about larger contextual issues, such as the role of gender, geographical location, or individual artistry in shaping particular stories. Nevertheless, the mere fact of surveying them gave me a feeling of preparedness for this project.

Or so I thought, until Robinson began recounting two stories with little connection to those I had encountered in the published records. Surprisingly, the first was an origin story that explained *my* beginnings as well as his.[6] The narrative featured a pair of male twins charged by God to undertake a series of important tasks related to the creation of the earth and the dispersion of its human inhabitants. The older twin performed his duties exactly as instructed. But the younger twin did the opposite, following his own plan and devising a clever alibi to conceal his disobedience. By the end of the story, Robinson had declared the older twin to be the first ancestor of the Okanagans and the younger one to be the first ancestor of the whites. Robinson's second story chronicled an appearance of God at Lytton to warn the people there (a young boy and his grandmother) about the arrival of white strangers who would settle the country and cause great social and physical upheaval.[7] (The two stories will be discussed in detail below.)

Because I had encountered so few references to whites or any other post-contact details among the published "myths/legends" I had surveyed, I hastily concluded that these two stories must be cultural anomalies. The theoretical literature on the subject seemed to support this view. Claude Lévi-Strauss, for example, one of the leading scholars of myth at the time, had delineated world cultures as "cold" (mythic Natives who resist any form of change) or "hot" (historical westerners who thrive on constant and irreversible change). Because I was working in what Lévi-Strauss would have classified as a "cold" zone, it followed that I should find mainly timeless, ahistorical narratives among the storytellers living there.[8]

But this was not the case. Although some of Robinson's stories – "Coyote Tricks Owl," "Coyote Plays a Dirty Trick," and "The Flood," for example – fit the classic atemporal mythic genre, the majority did not. In fact, Robinson seemed just as comfortable telling historical narratives set in real time as he was telling so-called mythical narratives set in the deep past.[9] If analyzed in Lévi-Straussian terms, then, this repertoire was actually more "hot" than "cold."

As is typical of storytellers from this region, Robinson rarely gave reasons for telling particular narratives; his choices appeared to me to be spontaneous.[10] It was only when he became seriously ill toward the end of our project that I began to doubt this. Fearing that the project might be drawing to an end, he cautioned me to "take a listen to these [tapes] a few times and think about it, to these stories and what I tell you now. Compare them. See if you can see something more about it. Kind of plain, but it's pretty hard to tell you for you to know right now. Takes time. And then you will see ... That's all. No more stories. Do you understand?"[11]

His comments suggested to me that he may have selected and ordered his stories more carefully than I realized. I reflected on how passionately he had launched our project with his stories about whites and how quickly I had dismissed these as anomalies. Perhaps I had missed something important here. What if these stories were, in fact, central to the larger project?

Throughout the past decade, a broadly based argument has emerged for the need for a stronger indigenous voice in mainstream historiography. Despite this concern, however, there has been little concrete movement in this direction. As Julie Cruikshank writes, "Native Americans' views of their own history remain rare in scholarly literature."[12] This chapter addresses this problem. It suggests that our historiography has been slow to incorporate a strong indigenous perspective because of its dependence on an ethnographic archive that is largely devoid of cultural context. The majority of stories in the archive have been stripped of tellers' identities and community affiliations. If historians are truly serious about incorporating indigenous histories into the mainstream record, they must recognize the limitations of the archives and begin to move instead toward fuller and more dynamic sources such as living storytellers.[13] Richard Bauman, who has been arguing for more than two decades for the need to consider "context," writes: "My concern has been to go beyond a conception of oral literature as disembodied superorganic stuff and to view it contextually and ethnographically, in order to discover the individual, social and cultural factors that give it shape and meaning in the context of social life."[14]

The stories of Harry Robinson offer a fresh starting point for such contextualization. Unlike their counterparts in the early collections, they rarely lose touch with the present, even when invoking the deep past. And they are not bothered by messiness, that is, uneven chronology, gaping holes and gaps, and large temporal leaps forward and backward. In fact, they seem to thrive on such fluidity and seeming disorderliness. Africanist scholar Carolyn Hamilton urges us to pay attention to the fluid and disorderly zones in oral tradition, for they often harbour important indigenous historiographies, "the very things conventionally deemed to be historians' 'sources.'"[15] Relying on the direction of Bauman, Briggs, Hamilton, Cruikshank, and others, this chapter forays into such zones.

**Storyteller as Source**
When I met Robinson during that summer of 1977, our two worlds were very different. Not only were we nearly fifty years removed in age, but we came from opposite ends of the continent. I was a white middle-class female from Nova Scotia with academic objectives in mind, and he was a recently retired rancher of Okanagan descent pursuing a serious interest in storytelling. Robinson had been raised by his mother, Arcell, and her parents, Louise and Joseph Newhmkn, at the small village of Chopaka in the Similkameen Valley. His father, James Robinson, an Okanagan of mixed ancestry, had abandoned Arcell before Robinson was born. Like most young men growing up during the first decades of this century in the Similkameen Valley, Robinson was immersed in the ranching life – taming horses, herding and running cattle, fencing, haying, and participating in rodeos. At age thirteen, he attended the local day school at Cawston. Frustrated by the twelve-mile return trip to school, however, Robinson quit after five months to pursue full-time ranchwork. In 1924, Robinson married a widow, Matilda Johnny, and joined her in running a large ranch until her death in 1971. They had no children.[16]

Although Robinson was attracted to storytelling as a child, he did not begin to hone his narrative skills until later in life when a serious hip injury immobilized him. Suddenly, as he explains it, he had time for serious reflection:

> I forget. I don't care for it and I forget. But the older I get, seems to come back on me. Supposin' if the radio, you could see the picture goin' by. Something like that, I could see, like, and remember. Older I get. Maybe God's thought that I should get back and remember so I can tell.[17]

In a way, storytelling filled the gap created by the loss of ranchwork. By the time I met him, Robinson had a well-established reputation for telling stories for days without stopping. As he explained it, "I can go for twenty-one hours or more when I get started, because this is my job. I'm a storyteller."[18] Robinson had learned most of his stories from his grandmother Louise, who looked after him while his mother worked. The arrangement was reciprocal, however, because Robinson's grandmother was blind and needed his assistance. During their many hours together, Louise told her grandson stories. Robinson also credited numerous others for his storytelling ability: John Ashnola, who was in his nineties when he was struck with the 1918 flu, and Mary Narcisse, who was close to one hundred when she died in 1944.

The setting for Robinson's storytelling was the front room of his bungalow. At a small arborite table precisely laid out with his pens, paper, scissors, knives, rulers, cigarettes, and ashtray, Robinson felt at ease. He usually initiated a story after dinner. Except for pauses to smoke, he spoke without interruption for several hours at a time. His only prop was a continuous series of striking hand gestures, indeed, a whole hand language that told the story almost as a mutual dance. He stopped when he noticed that my eyelids were drooping, usually around midnight or later. I rarely interrupted while stories were in progress. He told whatever he felt like telling and my tape recorder appeared not to bother him. Other than instructing me to turn it off during a smoke break, he made little reference to the machine.

Over the years, increasing numbers of his listeners could not understand Okanagan, so Robinson eventually told all of his stories in English, a translation process that he had made consciously to keep his stories alive. He regarded our recording project, especially when it evolved into a book project, as a serious undertaking. He wanted his stories well circulated, both in the Aboriginal and non-Aboriginal communities: "Is not to be hidden," he wrote to me on 27 January 1986. "It is to be showed in all Province in Canada and United States. That is when it come to be a book."

## Narratives about Whites

Stories of Old Coyote dominate the published narrative collections from south-central British Columbia, with most focusing on his travels, transformations, and eventual banishment. Few convey much about his origins. Titles such as "Coyote Steals Fire" and "Coyote Digs Roots" are typical.[19] Robinson took a different approach. His concern from the outset of our project was to explain Coyote's *beginnings* – where and how he came into being – and his impact on the flow of *post*-contact history. One of the stories Robinson narrated to me opens at a time when there is nothing but darkness, water, and a being he calls "God."[20] God begins to think about the need for light, land, and people, and suddenly these appear:

> God made the sun.
> I said he made the sun,
>     but he didn't use any hammer or any knife or anything
>         to make the sun.
> Just on his thought.
> He just think should be sun so he could see.
> He just think and it happened that way.
> Then after that and he could see.
> All water.
> Nothing but water.
>
> No trees.
> No nothing but sun way up high in the sky.
>
> And God think should be land.
> And if it was land, there should be people in the land.
> Be better.
>
> So after, he think,
>     "I go down and get near to this water
>         and see what I'll do."
> And he came down on the air.

With these thoughts, three rose bushes burst through the surface of the water. God plucks six leaves from each bush and places them on the surface of the water. As he ponders where he will stand, the small leaves become large leaves, "big enough for six men to stand on." God stands on one of the leaves and plucks four blossoms from the bush:

He take one and put it where he was standing.
And he take another one and another one.
Picked up four.
Leaves was just round,
   kind of round like that.
And there should be four.
But one of this four is doubled.
It's doubled like that.
Seems to be like that, you know.
It's doubled, but you could still see the side.
But in another way it looks like four.
But one of them is doubled and that makes five.

God pauses for a moment to consider how he will deal with the double blossom:

This one that's doubled,
That could be the twin,
   can be called twin.
In another way he's two.
But in another way he's one because he's double.
But these others are separate.
All right.
Figure that out and he say,
   "All right, you guys, get up.
      Come alive."

They all get up.
And when they get up
   they five men because this is double.
And that become two when they get up.
But they twin.
And that's the *SHA-ma* [white] and that's the Indian
These twin, they brothers.

Finding himself in the company of five men standing on leaves, God turns to the eldest and asks him to dive into the water:

"We want the ground.
We want the dirt.
But maybe you dive into the water.
Dive in and down you go as far as you can go.

And feel around.
You might happen to touch something.
If you do, try to hold 'em.
Try to get some.
Then you come back."

This man dutifully dives into the water but emerges empty-handed: "No, there is nothing I can find." So God asks the second and third men to perform the task. They too return with nothing. He then instructs the older twin to undertake the dive:

So he went down and he happen to scratch something.
And he come back.
And he caught a very little small grain.
About this size.
It's very little.
He got that,
   and it got stuck under the fingernails.
He feel around and he got 'em stuck in there.
And he didn't know,
   but he got 'em stuck under the fingernail.
That's the older from the twin.

So he come out and he said,
   "No, I didn't find anything."

Although God knows that the older twin has what he is looking for, he withholds this information until the younger twin completes his dive:

For the younger one just to be satisfied,
   let him go down.
He's not going to find nothing.
But just to be satisfied,
   so he wouldn't be jealous.

When the younger twin returns to the surface with nothing, God turns to the older twin and declares him the victor:

You got 'em.
You find 'em.

The older twin replies, "No."

"Yeah, you find 'em.
You did.
You find 'em.
Let's see your hand."
He says,
    "Put your hand this way like that."

God looks at the older twin's hand and pulls the "little grain" from his fingernail. He then drops it into the latter's palm. It was "a little wee stone, a little grain, a rock, just small." He explains its significance:

"All right, that's going to be the Earth.
That's going to be the world.
And kinda close your hand like that."
And told him not to drop it.
"Keep it on your hand
    but kinda close your hand."

When the older twin closes his hand, "the first thing he know, he holding more like a ball." God tells him to "put it down this place where we're standing." As he does this, suddenly "there was the Earth instead of leaves." And God and the five men were standing on it. "And they could see quite a ways."

God now explains to the first three people that he is going to "throw" each one of them "in the air ... for a long ways." He tells them that "wherever you landed at anywhere and that's where you going to be. That's going to be your land." He gives each man a document that is essential to his survival: "it will tell you what you going to do from the time you landed in there till the end of the world." After throwing the first three to three corners of the world, God decides to take a four-day break before deciding what to do with the twins. Before departing, he gives them some important instructions:

"Now you seen your brothers gone,
    the other one and the other one.
But you're two going to stay right here
    till I go back to where I come.
And stay over there for three, four days.
Four days.
Then I come back.
And you guys going to stay right here.
When I come back I can tell you
    what you going to be and what you going to do.

And this paper you supposed to have.
But there's only one.
But you guys are two.
You are twin.
And I put this paper here.
I put it down in the land right here.
When I come back,
   I can tell you what you going to do.
And we open up this letter.
And I'll judge both of you."

God then places "the paper on the ground" and disappears. Finding himself alone with his older twin brother, the younger twin begins to worry about his future:

"This paper, he's going to give 'em to my friend
   because he's the older one.
He's going to get the paper, not me.
And he's going to be the boss.
And not me.
But I take this paper and I hide 'em.
And when he [God] come he can ask and we can tell 'em
   'We don't know.
   Wind blow.
   It mighta blow away.'"

While his brother is out of sight, the younger twin snatches the paper and hides it under his clothes. On his return, God questions the twins about the missing paper. The older twin responds truthfully that he doesn't know where it went. The younger twin offers a story, hoping that God will believe it: "we walked around and we run and we play. We musta' hit that stone with our feet and slide off from the paper. Then the wind was blowing and the wind blowed it. Could be." But God knows that he is telling "a lie."

And that younger one, now today, that's the white man.
And the older one, that's me [Robinson].
That's the Indian.
And that's why the white man
   they can tell a lie more than the Indian.

Having repossessed the paper, God instructs the younger twin to run and jump over a large body of water. Not surprisingly, the younger twin, the white twin if you like, is distressed about his predicament. But God does not leave him empty-handed. Before banishing him, he gives him the stolen "paper," noting that it will help him return to his place of origin. "But not right away. A long time from now. You going to have a heck of a time. You're going to lose a lot of people ... But you still going to make it." This is all figurative, of course. God is referring here to generations of descendants of the younger twin. God tells the younger twin, his descendants will "stay in this place till the end of the world." But "*this* one [God points to the older twin] is going to stay here in this place. That's *his* land."

Before banishing the younger twin, God makes him promise that when his descendants encounter the descendants of the older twin they will promise to "show [them] what's on that paper" – the stolen written document.

With the younger twin out of the picture, Robinson began filling in the details of the older twin, underscoring the nature of his own relationship to the latter: "The older one, that's me. That's the Indian." He portrayed him as a powerful "half coyote and half Indian" figure who transformed the landscape to its current form. Until Coyote meets an old man (God, in disguise) whom he challenges to move a mountain, Coyote has few restrictions on his activities. Annoyed by Coyote's inflated sense of power, however, God eventually strips him of his special abilities and banishes him by boat to a distant place. "Just like he put him in jail," notes Robinson.

This story, in Robinson's view, explains many things; for example, why a large ocean separates the original home territory of whites from Indians, why whites derive their power from writing and paper, why Indians rely on oral tradition, and why "the white man can tell a lie more than the Indian." According to Robinson, "it's begin to do that from that till today." It also explains why "now, if the white man tell a lie, it don't seems to be so bad. But if the Indian tells a lie, that's *really* bad."[21]

God, meanwhile, continued to oversee the full sweep of history, making occasional appearances, usually in times of crisis. He turned up at Lytton, for instance, many years before the arrival of whites, and this is where the second of the two stories begins.[22] Disguised as an old man, God's mission at Lytton was twofold: to alleviate a situation of starvation and to reiterate what he had told the younger twin at the beginning of time – that "white-skinned" people would arrive some day to "live here for all time." After teaching a boy and his grandmother new methods of procuring food, he explained how these newcomers will transform the land. Their "hayfields" and "gardens," he noted, will create a patchwork appearance. He told people at Lytton, as he had told the older twin previously, that they would not lose their land to these newcomers: "This island supposed to be for the Indians," God explained. As a testament to his word, he left behind a patchwork blanket that turned to stone on his departure. Robinson knew it as the "spotted rock."[23]

At this point, the two stories converge. As Robinson explained it, the younger twin's descendants eventually reached the older twin's homeland, where they cleared and tilled the land, giving it a patchwork appearance as God had forewarned. In many respects, however, they did not behave as God had instructed. Instead of following the rules laid out in God's "paper," for example, the newcomers seized Indian land, established their own forms of governance, and "scared" and "killed" its inhabitants. Angered by this deviation from his plan, God snatched Coyote out of seclusion and instructed him to meet with the king of England. Coyote made his way to England where he outlined the details "king to king." The king responded that he was not prepared for a war with "Coyote's children." Coyote was elated: "Okay that will be your word from now until the end of the world." Together, Coyote and the king worked out an agreement, which the king promised to turn into a book. "When you are finished all the writing," Coyote explained, "that'll be the Indian Law."[24]

According to Robinson's story, it took a century and several monarchs to bring the book to fruition. Titled *The Black and White* to reflect its dual authorship – Coyote (black) and the king (white) – there were four copies. One remained in England with the queen; the others, at her instruction, were hand-delivered to Ottawa, Winnipeg, and Victoria where they are to be shown to Indians as soon as they could read. "That is now," notes Robinson. "But before this time they hide it. They never show the Indians unless they ask."

Robinson undoubtedly had many reasons for launching our project with these stories. Not only did they establish our shared beginnings but they also explained our differences, such as why my culture was dependent on paper and literacy, and his on orality and spirituality. These stories also provided a necessary backdrop to the later stories, which centred on serious antagonisms between "Indians" and "whites." To understand them fully, he believed, I needed to know that they began with a simple "white" lie that spawned two contrasting forms of power and knowledge – one derived from nature and the other derived from paper and writing. "You know," he explained, "God put the Indians in the head, in the heart for the things to know. [T]he white people, they got the paper ... [T]here is a lot of these white people ... they think that we don't know anything till the white people come."[25] Robinson's stories would challenge this perception.

## Toward a More Contextualized Oral Tradition

As noted above, indigenous stories about whites are rare in the British Columbia ethnographic archive. In the few cases where whites appear in stories, they do so in the context of unpublished field notes or in the margins of the mainstream published collections. Because early collectors were intrigued by stories of first encounters between whites and Aboriginal peoples, they often took note of these. It is not surprising, therefore, that the scholarly debate on Aboriginal historical consciousness has concentrated mainly on issues of first encounter.[26]

Although the studies of early contact narratives are useful, they have not generated any significant insights beyond the rather obvious notion that indigenous peoples carried stories about first encounters with whites into this century. The fragmentary nature of the documentation and an array of complex editorial and translation issues have hindered their usefulness as serious historical sources. Other factors – for example, not knowing the identity of the narrators, or how to interpret the mythologized accounts – have also obscured their value. Some of the stories, such as those of the Nlaka'pamux of south-central British Columbia, present explorer Simon Fraser and his crew as spiritual transformers returning from the deep past.[27] It is not surprising that many traditional historians have had difficulty taking such accounts seriously.

The Harry Robinson material overcomes some of these problems by offering scholars a broader framework for understanding such stories. As with many "contact narratives" in the ethnographic archive, Robinson's accounts have mythological associations but they also have a context. Knowing, for instance, that neither he nor his storytelling tradition supported fictional accounts (indeed, the very concept was a foreign one) opens new possibilities for the interpretation of myth. Rather than being viewed as fictional embellishments or imaginative reworkings, as they might be in a Western context, instances where myth and history merge (such as when Coyote travels to Britain to meet with the reigning monarch) can be taken as serious reflections on the past.

Among scholars of oral narrative tradition, there is a growing interest in accounts that blend history and myth. For more than a decade, anthropologists Jonathan D. Hill, Terence Turner, Emilienne Ireland, and others have been systematically studying indigenous histories in South America.[28] They suggest that history and myth be analyzed as "complementary and mutually informing" genres. Ireland, who focuses on white man stories among the Waura people of South America, has found, for example, that myth "can transform the very perception of reality not only in the sense of rewriting the history of specific events in the past, but in the sense of making statements about the present and the future as well." Through their myths about conflict with white man, the Waura took "a historic tragedy of monstrous proportions and transformed it into an affirmation of their own moral values, and of their destiny to survive as a people."[29]

Robinson's story about the legacy of the younger twin fits this pattern. Unlike the dominant historical narratives of our culture, Robinson's is not a tragic account of cultural demise. His Indians are never passive victims of white actions. Rather, his is a story of success and survival against huge odds. His account characterizes Indians in a positive light – as a select group that were given this land by their creator along with a form of knowledge that would enable them to survive. They were never in the dark. Rather, they knew about the impending arrival of whites. Their ancestor, Coyote, will show up some day to put things right, just as he did in the old days. Whites, on the other hand, are presented negatively – a banished people who colonized this country through fraudulence associated with their assigned and alienated (literally) form of knowledge. Their most characteristic cultural trait is their inability to share. They are, and always will be, according to the story, visitors in this land.

Viewed against this backdrop, Robinson's stories, both traditional and historical, illustrate opposing manifestations of human nature, one derived from Coyote, and the other from my first ancestor. His story of Coyote's ability to overcome death echoes similar stories of the "power" of "Indians" in recent times to move freely through the realms of life and death. Just as Coyote could summon Fox to revive him after death, so too could Indian doctors summon smooth stumps, running water, and other sources to cure their friends and family members. Just as God could foretell the transformation of the landscape by agriculture, "Indians" in historical times could foretell the alteration of their territory by a network of highways. Robinson's origin story asserts an innate connection to their "God-given" territory through accounts of hunters saved by wolverines and grizzly bears.[30]

As descendants of the younger twin, whites represent the opposite. They are the source of continuous conflict, from the beginning of time to the present day. In story after story, whites reveal themselves to be masters of the arts of theft and deception. The story of George Jim, an Okanagan man abducted from prison in the 1880s while serving a seven-year sentence for manslaughter, plays out in full detail the saga of the younger twin. Jim is taken to England (the homeland of the younger twin), where he is held captive for years. Meanwhile, the prison officials notify Jim's family that he has died in jail. When the family asks for his body, the prison sends them the body of a Chinese man. The story chronicles a long string of such deception.[31]

As in the origin story, the main source of white power is material – "paper" (or literacy). Through his narratives, Robinson illustrates how his community resisted the new legal order, as in the case of George Jim, where a community works together to maintain his hiding place as search parties comb the area for their "wanted man," or, in another instance, when a community suppresses the confession of one of its members, a woman who murdered a white man for attacking her as she travelled alone on a trail.[32] Such stories are meaningful on their own but when set against the backdrop of Robinson's origin story and the Lytton prophecy account, they explain more fully the roots of the contradictions of contemporary life. More important, they offer a rationale for the existence of two "competing form[s] of historical consciousness."[33]

## Academic Narratives and Living History

Many scholars would situate Robinson's stories about the origin of "whites" and God's appearance at Lytton in the larger context of a religious movement active in the region in the mid-nineteenth century. Leslie Spier was the first to draw serious attention to this movement and its "prophet dance" ritual in 1935. Through a careful survey of the ethnographic sources available at the time, Spier identified a broad range of fragmentary data about prophets who had died and returned to life carrying special messages about the impending end of the world and the coming of "Whites."[34]

With its focus on Europeans and quasi-Christian ritual – that is, references to God, Heaven, epidemics, new technology and subsistence patterns – Spier's work on prophecy offered a refreshing change from the strictly ahistorical focus of the earlier Boasians. In the end, though, it failed to realize the full potential of the historical narrative by framing its research questions on the past, rather than the present. From Spier in the 1930s to Wayne Suttles and others more recently, the emphasis has been on understanding prophecy narratives in the context of *initial* "contact" with whites.[35] The main issue driving the work, for example, was whether nineteenth-century Columbia Plateau prophets and prophecies had indigenous or early post-contact origins. Spier had argued that the movement had indigenous roots, but later scholars, such as David Aberle, Wayne Suttles, and Deward Walker, saw it as a product of early relations between Aboriginals and Europeans. Christopher Miller, who offers one of the more current perspectives on the debate, supports their position.[36]

The academic debate has further complicated our understanding of prophecy by relying mainly on the early ethnographic archive for its source material, thus framing prophecy as an artifact of the past – a tradition that died out in the mid- to late 1880s.

Robin Ridington was among the first to shift the prophecy debate into the present. Drawing on extended field research among the Dunne-za in northeastern British Columbia, he revealed that the prophecy movement was still being maintained, not just by living prophets, but through their stories of the earlier prophets' "trails to heaven."[37] In her work with Athapaskan storytellers in western subarctic communities near the upper Yukon River in the 1970s and 1980s, Julie Cruikshank noted a similar pattern. The prophets may have died out but the "narratives *about* prophets continue to be told."[38] Both Robinson's origin story and his "Prophecy at Lytton" build on these findings by presenting the prophecy narrative tradition as alive in southern British Columbia.

And Robinson's case is not isolated. In my fieldwork throughout the larger region in the 1980s and early 1990s, I encountered many individuals who were eager to tell prophecy stories. Their view was that their ancestors had known about the arrival of the *SHA-ma* (white) people well before it occurred. According to Louie Phillips of Lytton, there were individuals who were known for their ability to look into the future. Such people could "tell all what's going to happen before it happens." Phillips recalled the words of one: "Not very long from now these people that's coming in here, from their country into our country ... [they're] going to look different from what we are now and who we are. It's going to look different when those white people come here. Say they look like us, only they're White."[39] Annie York of Spuzzum explained similarly that "in the beginning before the first Whites came, the Indians have their own religion. *Shpeentlum*, his wife, she went into trance. She died for three or four days, and when she returned to this life, she was taught prayers to use, and ... she foretold everything that was coming ahead ... even the airplanes, cars, electric stoves, what they're going to look like."[40]

Hilda Austin of Lytton recalled the comments of "Willie Munroe's great-grandmother [,who] really knows what's going to happen in the future":

> Our dishes are going to rattle. And we never had any dishes before. Our fire is going to be covered up ... She really knows, this old lady, what's going to happen in the future. She already knows. She told us that this was going to come one day. These people going to come from another world, from overseas I guess. Everything that she seen already what she's been doing, it's going to be different when these people come from another world, another country.[41]

Although the storylines of these narratives may not coincide exactly with those of Robinson's, they highlight some of the same issues – that contemporary oral tradition from the region is premised on the view that Indians knew about whites and the changes they would incur, well before their actual arrival. The prominence that Robinson and his colleagues gave to such prophecy narratives suggests that the academic debate needs to expand its focus to include this living perspective. As Cruikshank notes, "It is the retrospective consideration of prophecy stories as routine explanation for contemporary events that interests me here."[42]

### New Readings of Old Texts

In addition to expanding the academic debate on prophecy, Robinson's stories also enable us to read both the archival and contemporary collections of so-called myths and legends through a broader lens. For example, just as Robinson introduced himself to me by telling a story about God's encounter with a boy and his grandmother at Lytton, the Nlaka'pamux storytellers at Lytton introduced themselves to Boas in 1888 with a similar story entitled "Der Knabe und die Sonne" (The Boy and the Sun).[43] Boas, who recorded the story in the local church in the presence of the resident missionary, was disappointed with the results, and noted this in his journal: "The people have been Christians for a long time and that stands very much in my way. I hear very little about olden times."[44] Nevertheless, he took down this story and published it seven years later as a traditional "legend" of the "Ntlakyampamuq."[45] Knowing the context for Robinson's story, however, one wonders whether the Lytton storytellers in 1888 told Boas this story about the Sun Man, who "descended from the sky" to trade his bow for a fur coat from a boy and his grandmother, to convey more contemporary issues, just as Robinson did for me.[46]

Boas later edited and published three versions of the same story collected by James Teit.[47] According to the latter, Sun offers "many fine presents," including cooler weather, bows and arrows, and a goat-hair robe in exchange for the patchwork blanket. In Robinson's story, the visitor (God) exchanges new forms of prayer, new fishing and hunting techniques, and news of the impending arrival of whites in return for the patchwork blanket.

Unlike the early accounts, Robinson's incorporates quasi-Christian language: "I am the God. I'm the Father," the visitor tells the boy and his grandmother. "I come from Heaven." It also draws the story into the present by explaining the arrival of whites who would transform the landscape. But Robinson's version carries an even more current message. As he explains, the main thrust of God's statement that day in Lytton was to assert that, despite the white presence on Indian territory, land would never be transferred. "They going to live here with you. But this is *your* place," God told the boy and his grandmother.[48] Thus, Robinson presents the story as confirmation of Aboriginal sovereignty. He assigns the story even more tangible relevance by including a segment about his search for the "spotted rock" – the patchwork blanket that had turned to stone when God departed from Lytton on that day. God left behind this spotted rock to serve as a permanent marker of his important exchange.

These tellings and retellings of "The Boy and the Sun" stories raise a range of compelling questions. Could the "Sun" of the Boas and Teit accounts be related to Robinson's God? Could Boas, without realizing it, have mistaken a contemporary, even quasi-Christianized, story for a traditional "legend"? Is the forewarning about whites in Robinson's story specific to contemporary tellings? Or did Boas overlook (or eliminate) such details to maintain cultural "purity"?[49]

The few accounts of "whites" that exist in the archival collections shed some light on these questions. Teit, for example, gathered several Nlaka'pamux stories of the first whites (Simon Fraser and his crew) who passed through Nlaka'pamux territory in 1808. They reveal that when the Nlaka'pamux encountered whites, they gave them names that were drawn, for the most part, from the skyworld. For example, they called Fraser "Sun," and his crew-members "Moon," "Morning-Star," and "Coyote."[50] Although two accounts attribute the name Sun to "some kind of shining emblem he [Fraser] wore on his hat or cap, which resembled the symbol of the Sun," there may be a larger significance to the name.

When one follows images of the "Sun" through the ethnographic archive, the latter emerges as a figure with close associations to whiteness, both literal and figurative. He is a manlike figure linked to an upper world/skyworld – or a place "where dead people go." He also has close ties to Lytton. Teit, for example, noted in one story that Sun was "formerly ... a great chief who lived at Lytton." Sun could move back and forth between this world and an upper world.[51] More significant in the archival accounts are the similarities between Sun and a chiefly figure known variously as Old One, Old Man, Great Chief, Big Chief, Father Mystery, and Great Mystery, who also lived in an "upper world" and was seen descending to this world "on a cloud." Like Robinson's "God," this "great chief" was credited in some accounts with the creation of people; and he was the source of special messages – about epidemics, whites, new technology, the end of the world, and so forth.

There was some debate about the identity of this chiefly figure. Upon first encountering him, Teit concluded that he was the equivalent of the Christian God. By 1898, however, he had changed his view on this: "I am inclined to think that he is a personage belonging to their ancient mythology and not the God of the Whites." Later, it would appear, he returned to his original view, writing that Great Chief, or Old Man, "is God." Christine Quintasket (pen name, Mourning Dove), an Okanagan woman who also collected "traditional" stories during Teit's time, stressed that her people believed in "the great spirit chief [long] before they ever heard of Christianity." Yet Walter Cline, who undertook ethnographic fieldwork among the Okanagon in north-central Washington State in 1930, was convinced that this figure was a Christian import.[52]

When examined against the backdrop of Robinson's story, however, the key questions raised by "God," "Old One," "Creator," and "Sun" may not concern their association with whiteness. Sun was obviously white and bright. Old One, or Great Chief, appears in the early accounts as a human-looking man with a light complexion and a long white beard. He had close connections to Coyote, who was also described as "a man of very light complexion who could speak all languages." "Moon" too was "formerly a handsome white-faced Indian." The Nlaka'pamux at Lytton may have named Fraser and his crew Sun, Moon, Morning-Star, and even Coyote because of this. Some contemporary elders claim that their ancestors believed Fraser to be the "Son of the Sun." Others, such as Louie Phillips of Lytton, claimed that his ancestors believed that Fraser was "Jesus Christ."[53]

## Reading the Past through the Present

Drawing on fragmentary and inconclusive evidence, one could easily conclude that the religious world view of the Aboriginal peoples of south-central British Columbia was (and is) premised on a belief in an omnipresent Creator figure, not unlike the Christian God. For example, Robinson's reference to "God"/"Big Chief" can be interpreted as such. When one takes into consideration the string of stories about Sun, Old One, Big Chief, Son of the Sun, and even Louie Phillip's Christ, however, one can see that the issue is not so transparent.

What may be key here is not *who* the figure is but *how* he has been invoked over the years. The following description of a "great chief," recorded by Teit, is a good case in point. In isolation, it could be read, even dismissed, as just another Christianized narrative. Set within the context of Robinson's stories about the origin of whites, however, it can be seen as part of a larger narrative that has deep roots. Published in 1917 in a collection of "traditional" stories, it is unusual for its first-person voice and its mention of a nineteenth-century chief by name:

> The great chief led us to this country, and placed us in it to occupy it, multiply in it, and be happy. He gave us a rich country, with plenty in it for us to eat. He did not give this country to the whites or anyone else ... We know about our origin ... Our traditions tell us that even in mythological times our ancestors lived here ... This is why our chief Cexpe'ntlEm, in talking to the whites (in 1858) told them they had entered his house and were now his guests. He asked them to treat his children as brothers, and they would share the same fire. He did not know that they would afterwards treat his people as strangers and inferiors, and steal their land and food from them.[54]

When this story is combined with others, such as those collected by Walter Cline in 1930 for the southern Okanagan, it takes on larger significance. One of Cline's interviewees, David Isaac, described "God" as a "white chief" who declared: "White men like himself would come into the region, take the best lands from the Indians, exterminate the game, bring fatal diseases, and introduce railways, automobiles and airplanes. The land would dry up and the Indians would finally pass away ... The White chief was believed in long before the Whites came. He had created everything, and to him all

good people went when they died. Sometimes people saw him in trances."
Cline recorded a similar account from an "informant" named Suszen. Like
Isaac, Suszen claimed that when "God created the world, ... he took away
one land from the top and put it to one side for the Indians-to-be. God took
the laws with the Indian land and left the other land without laws. Then
God built an ocean to separate these lands: one land was for the Indians,
another for the white people. Indians did not need books because they knew
things in their minds that they learned from the creatures."[55]

These accounts of Indians, whites, and God resonate fully with Robinson's
account. In addition, they demonstrate the value of contemporary stories
and highlight the problems of analyzing these against the backdrop of an
essentialized, abstract Christian God. To assume that the chiefly figure at
the centre of these stories is the Christian God is to miss the point that
these storytellers may be trying to convey – that their world and that of
their "white" counterparts are inherently different.

Another approach is to consider instances where God was invoked outside of the ethnographic archive, for example in the public hearings of the
McKenna-McBride Royal Commission on Indian Affairs (1913-14). This commission provided chiefs throughout British Columbia an opportunity to air
their concerns about land and other issues. The transcripts from these hearings are among the few surviving documents that represent direct first-hand
voices of Aboriginal people. They reveal that the chiefs frequently invoked
"God" in their statements. Chief Daniel of Siska-Skuppa Band, for example,
told the commissioners on 16 November 1914 that "God made you and I
out of the same flesh ... When God made the world he expected us all to
share and share alike ... God is my father and your father ... The Queen is
our guardian – The Queen represents us just like a setting hen with a flock
of chickens." A Nlaka'pamux man named Patrick explained the following
day that "God Almighty put me here ... [He] gave us the birds and animals
for our food ... and he went back from here and went back to his own home
in heaven; and before God left he never meant to have any gaols or police-
men to restrict us." Chief Paul Heena spoke on 18 November: "I would like
to have the things that were given to us originally by the Lord ... You know
that God created this in the beginning and that is why the white people say
[stay?] to the west and to the north."[56]

By the end of the hearings, the commissioners must surely have concluded that they had witnessed, if nothing else, the culmination of a successful Christian missionary campaign. Many academics would probably
draw similar conclusions. But when these early stories are combined with
those of Harry Robinson and others collected by James Teit and Walter Cline,
they place this chiefly figure on an entirely different plane that probably
included, for example, God's testimony at Lytton and Coyote's meetings
with the king.

## Conclusion

In his northwest coast field journals and personal correspondence, Franz Boas expressed frustration at having to listen to what he considered to be mere "nonsense." His objective, after all, was to record the more authentic "myth cycles." But even when, on 12 October 1886, he encountered what he considered an authentic traditional story such as "The Birth of the Raven," he could not easily classify it. Immediately after recording this story on 12 October 1886, he noted in his journal: "It is especially curious that myth cycles do not seem to be alike among the different tribes speaking the same language."[57]

These are just a few of the problems that Boas encountered in his efforts to compile and classify the "authentic" oral traditions of the northwest coast. Judith Berman suggests that Boas may have had a conceptual handicap that prevented him from "arriving at deeper insights into the myths he collected." She illustrates her point with a study of Boas' analysis of a Kwakw'ala herring myth: "Boas's problem with this story was that he understood the words but not what was being said. The truth about the origin of herring is bound up in word play and metaphor, as well as conceptual concepts which Boas never, to the end of his life, seemed to compass ... Boas suffered from a kind of conceptual tone-deafness, an insensitivity to the categories and interconnections of Kwagul culture."[58] Similarly, David Murray has highlighted the problems associated with Boas' preoccupation with *communal* cultural expression. "The stress on the communal rather than on the individual, on system rather than single instance," he writes, "allowed Western 'developed' people to see the power of culture rather than the individual ... [I]n stressing their total integration and unity and ignoring or suppressing the cultural 'impurities' and acculturations, [they] marked those cultures off and reinforced the standard view of them as wholly 'other.'"[59]

This chapter builds on the perspectives advocated by Berman and Murray by arguing that, just as we cannot make sense of the old narrative collections in the Boasian ethnographic archive without considering their ideological underpinnings, we also cannot fully appreciate more recent Aboriginal oral tradition without understanding how profoundly that tradition has been shaped by the Boasian research paradigm. In his search for the purest expressions of communal "myth," Boas failed to take note of impure individual cultural expressions. Although he left us with a tangible record of what he considered to be authentic stories, he did not provide us with many concrete examples of stories he rejected as inauthentic. One wonders whether some of these may have been similar to the stories I initially dismissed as anomalies – accounts of the origin of whites and Coyote's travels to England.

This chapter has highlighted the benefits of undertaking intensive work with living Aboriginal historians. In addition to providing rare examples of the "contested ways people invoke the past to talk about the present and the present to talk about the past," such communicative experiences force us to question the composition of the mainstream records.[60] Why do some stories gain immediate entry while others are rejected? Contemporary research with living storytellers can also begin to break down the sharp lines that we have drawn between myth and history and demonstrate the value of paying attention to what Carolyn Hamilton calls the "fluid" zones in oral tradition. As Michael Harkin suggests, living Aboriginal oral histories often operate at the "highest and most meaningful level" of "real" history – the point where "historical narrative and a bounded social group merge to create a collective historical consciousness."[61] At the very least, this chapter is intended to infuse new life into a BC historiography that to date has paid little attention to Aboriginal interpretations of the past.

# 8

# When the White *Kawau* Flies

*Judith Binney*

Aue! Ko Hine-ruarangi ra!

Alas! It is indeed Hine-ruarangi![1]

This chapter examines some narratives of contact told in Te Urewera, the mountainous heart of the central North Island of Aotearoa New Zealand. These stories originate in Maori ways of seeing and depicting their world. They convey morals and express cultural values; many are stories of warning. The accounts are preserved in memory not so much as a record of past times but as a tool by which to act in the present, and in the future.[2] They carry a "plereomatic" view of history, one whereby contemporary events are understood through earlier predictive words and remembered narratives.[3] As Julie Cruikshank's studies from the Yukon showed, prophecy narratives "orthodoxly" provide imaginative frameworks for "explaining" the unexpected.[4] Those from the Urewera similarly stitch the past to the present, and to a predicted future, where fulfillment may be found.

The stories that I have chosen to retell are about encounters with Europeans at crucial stages in a long history of contact, exchange, and conflict. They belong to a framework of thought that draws upon the ancestral world of Maori, where the guiding presence of the ancestors *(tīpuna)* may be manifest in dreams, and where portents *(tohu)* in the natural world can suggest hidden destinies. They are also built on a scaffolding of knowledge that derives from a profound internalization of the Christian scriptures, adopted by Maori to explain many of their historical experiences in the nineteenth century. The narratives that I have selected stretch across time in their originating historical contexts and in their changing import. By the act of retelling them, I am "imposing" an ordering upon them that is my own. But that is the nature of writing history.

Oral accounts change as they are told in differing contexts, and in front of differing audiences. The stories are rewrought, even as the narrator insists

on the accuracy of their transmission. When they are told in altered contexts, new implications and meanings spring from "old vessels." That is
because they are the vehicles by which people find ways of connecting
diverse periods of time and unforeseen events.[5] It follows that multiple interpretations co-exist, and (as this chapter demonstrates) that many oral
stories remain "pre-eminently open-ended."[6] In retelling these narratives
from the Urewera, I do not intend to suggest that they represent a past that
is closed.

The pre-eminent tribe of the Urewera is Ngai Tuhoe, and the stories told
here are, for the large part, their oral narratives. The accounts stretch in
time from the "musket" wars in the 1820s to the first Tuhoe land sales within
their "Rohe Potae" (Encircling Borders) in 1910. The chapter covers a period
of ninety years, thus, a long "encounter" narrative. It looks at the tribe who
is considered to have been the most isolated of all Maori groups. It therefore
may seem to be a particularly perverse site for telling "stories of encounter,"
but the choice is a deliberate one.

The coastal tribes, such as the people from the East Coast of the North
Island, where James Cook made his first landfall in Aotearoa New Zealand
in October 1769, possess a number of predictive narratives "anticipating"
the arrival of the Europeans. One version tells of the "Pākerewhā," a "made-
up" word of ominous portent. This coined term was (probably) an intentional play on the Maori name for Europeans, Pakeha, which images their
paleness and is recorded in common use by 1815, and the word *rewha,* referring to the new diseases associated with the arrival of trading ships. In
this narrative, the prophet Toiroa, who died in July 1867, anticipated the
coming of people with red and white skins like the earthworm, *titipa.* He
made images of the strange clothes that they would wear, and the vessels in
which they would travel. His famous song of predictive portent, "Tiwha
tiwha te pō" (Dark, Dark Is the Night), is carefully dated 1766 (three years
before Cook's arrival) in a Maori manuscript from the nineteenth century.[7]

Although Tuhoe were relatively isolated from Europeans in the early nineteenth century, their communication networks with other Maori tribes were
extensive. European missionaries (Anglican and French Roman Catholic)
first entered their lands in the early 1840s. Neither missionary group stayed
for long. Tuhoe's acquisition of literacy in Maori, together with their grasp
of the Bible, was largely self-taught, as the missionaries noted. Effectively,
Tuhoe created their own "class leaders" during the 1840s and early 1850s.
In 1866, they experienced their first European military invasion and land
confiscation; they were then repeatedly invaded between 1869 and 1872 (see
Map 2). After the wars were over, in 1872, they defined and controlled their
borders, named the Rohe Potae. Then, in 1896, they won legislative protection for the Urewera as a self-governing tribal district; this was unique. It was
established after the outbreak of a "small war" in 1895,[8] Tuhoe's unsuccessful

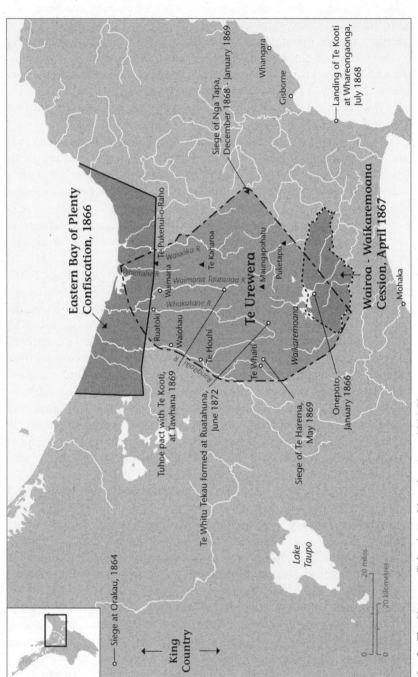

**Eastern Bay of Plenty Confiscation, 1866**

Siege of Nga Tapa, December 1868 – January 1869

Landing of Te Kooti at Whareongaonga, July 1868

Whangara

Gisborne

Te Pukenui-o-Raho

Waiotahe R

Te Kaharoa

Waioaka R

Maungapohatu

Waimana

Waimana Tauranga R

Puketapu

**Te Urewera**

Whakatane R

Ruatoki

Waiohau

*Waikaremoana*

Mohaka

Te Houhi

**Wairoa - Waikaremoana Cession, April 1867**

Tuhoe pact with Te Kooti, at Tawhana 1869

Te Whaiti

Onepoto, January 1866

Te Whitu Tekau formed at Ruatahuna, June 1872

Siege of Te Harema, May 1869

Siege at Orakau, 1864

**King Country**

*Lake Taupo*

20 miles

20 kilometres

0

0

*Map 2*   The Urewera: Tuhoe's world under siege, 1866-72

effort to prevent the government construction of a "strategic" highway through the Urewera. (This road, linking Te Whaiti, Ruatahuna, and Waikare-moana, remains the only road through the Urewera.) Another outcome of the "small war" was the arrival of Elsdon Best, as quartermaster for the roadworkers, in 1895. He would become the author of the greatest tribal history written in the country, *Tuhoe*. Compiled in the late 1890s, written mostly between 1906 and 1907, and published ultimately in 1925, Best's work provides early versions of some of the oral stories recounted today.[9]

Tuhoe stories bring various perspectives to the theme of encounter. Their earliest narratives of "encounter" describe news from afar. They begin with their contact with other Maori groups who have acquired goods and knowl-edge from the pale-skinned strangers. They reveal a dawning awareness of the presence of Europeans and their animals in the north. However, the narratives focus initially on changes in relationships between indigenous groups; they are concerned with changes in Maori relations. By the 1830s, Tuhoe, renowned for their proverbial saying "Tūhoe moumou tangata ki te pō" (stating their willingness to send men to their deaths), were becoming involved in concerted efforts to negotiate peace settlements between the tribes. New stories emerged around this theme. But the mid-century colo-nial wars brought bitter fighting, as Tuhoe were driven to defend their lands from invasion. After the fighting was over, narratives of peace re-emerged. The "encounter" stories were, however, soon rewoven to address the prob-lems of illicit or manipulated land sales.

One major continuing narrative is identified in this chapter. It is the search for a sanctuary, or more literally a shelter *(tāwharau)* for Tuhoe, which com-menced in the inter-tribal wars in the 1820s. The theme is recreated in the predictive versions of the story of the "Hokowitu,"[10] or "Te Whitu Tekau," Tuhoe's "Council of Seventy."[11] At a political level, this was the governing council of Tuhoe, formed at the end of the colonial wars in 1872. However, the narratives concerning the Seventy – in their many variations – are, as will be shown, invariably told as unfinished tales. The Tuhoe stories recounted to me – almost a century after Best's work – had purposes that became clearer as they reappeared in the new context of awareness of the imminent hear-ings on Tuhoe's land grievances before the Waitangi Tribunal. The tribunal is a commission of inquiry with authority to examine grievances between Maori and the Crown (that is, the government) since the 1840 signing of the Treaty of Waitangi with the British.[12] The hearings for the Urewera dis-trict began in November 2003, and the last claimants' hearing took place at Maungapohatu in February 2005.[13] In these claims, Tuhoe are seeking repa-rations for past injustices, including the 1866 confiscation of land by the government.

All the narratives told in this chapter have been reworked and recast as they have been brought into the present by generations of storytellers. They carry messages, overt and hidden. They are parables for the times in which they are told; they stand, simultaneously, as mnemonics to the past. They proclaim and warn; they chastise and they remember. The narratives recount loss; but they bear seeds of hope. They are stories about confronting vast changes wrought by others. They examine other systems of knowledge in the world, and other forms of power that were either imposed upon Tuhoe or were seemingly negotiated in good faith, but violated. The narratives step aside from quotidian affairs as they seek resolutions. They are essentially stories for the survivors – and for successive generations – to remember, to interpret, and to re-enact with new intent, according to their times.

## War and Peace

For readers who may find difficulties with the unfamiliar names, I remind them of the famous dialogue between the anthropologist E. Evans-Pritchard and a Sudanese visitor to his tent:

Cuol:  I am Cuol. What is your name?
E-P:    My name is Pritchard.
Cuol:  What is your father's name?
E-P:    My father's name is also Pritchard.
Cuol:  No, that cannot be true. You cannot have the same name as your father.[14]

Tuhoe first learnt of *"kuri waha tangata"* (man-bearing dogs) when the Tuhoe chief Te Maitaranui (Te Rangiaho) visited the Bay of Islands, on the northeast coast, in about 1820.[15] This was the time of the foundation of the first mission stations, and the story locates Tuhoe's awareness of the significance of the European-introduced horses – and simultaneously their distance from them. The other vital piece of knowledge with which Te Maitaranui returned was an awareness of guns. He was soon followed by the Bay of Islands' *hapū* (tribal groups), armed with muskets: they struck at Tuhoe in about 1822. Everyone fled inland for shelter. The story remembers, however, that the Bay of Islands' leader, Pomare I, heard at Ruatoki the crowing of a rooster that he himself had given to Te Maitaranui during his visit. Hearing the alien cock, Pomare curtailed his assault, reading the call as a tohu, an omen. He sought out Te Maitaranui, who had taken refuge at Maungapohatu, Tuhoe's sacred mountain.[16] The peace made between Tuhoe and Pomare in 1822 is always attributed to Te Maitaranui. To commemorate their peacemaking, a walking stick was made with a rooster carved on its handle. Much later, the stick was presented to the government by the Tuhoe elder Te Makarini (Tamarau Waiari).[17] This narrative is the earliest recorded story among Tuhoe of *"te ao hurihuri,"* the world turned upside down. To recall the language of the Andean encounter with the Spanish in the sixteenth century, it is a story of *pachacuti,* "the world turned over." For Tuhoe, the first changes occur in the Maori world.

Although Te Maitaranui's contemporary, the famous Tuhoe chief Te Ngahuru, proudly refused to use the musket,[18] others quickly sought out the new weapons. Some travelled to other parts of the country to get arms. By the 1830s, Tuhoe were equipped and involved in extensive raids on other tribal groups in the central North Island. It is from the years of internecine fighting of the mid-1830s that the emblematic narrative, which was to be reworked successively over time, emerges: the story of Paora Kiingi I (Paora Te Au) (Te Tawai), who decided to cease the fighting.

As the senior grandson of Tuhoe's pre-eminent leader *(ariki),* Te Umuariki, Paora Kiingi assembled a large military expedition to avenge his grandfather's death, which had occurred in battle in about 1829 at Whangara (on the East Coast). All the tribes of the migratory ancestral canoe, the Mataatua, assembled and cooperated in building a huge canoe out of *tōtara* wood from the Huiarau ranges in the Urewera. But the war canoe did not leave the mouth of the Whakatane River. At the feast held on the coast, just before the war party was due to depart, Paora Kiingi aborted the expedition. Instead, he journeyed himself to create *te tatau pounamu* (the greenstone door of peace), a binding covenant,[19] with the people of the East Coast. The famous proverb *(whakataukī)* "'Kia tāwharautia a Mātaatua'* – Let Mātaatua be sheltered,"[20] urging the need for sanctuary, and always attributed to Paora Kiingi I, stemmed from this unprecedented occasion.[21] The peace he forged is known as Te Here-o-Te Marama (The Binding of the Light); he commemorated it by constructing a carved meeting-house for the new era, built as a shelter for Mataatua's people in Te Waimana Valley. Paora Kiingi repeated his commitment to peace in his *ohākī* (dying speech), when he reminded Tuhoe to seek not war but shelter for themselves.[22] As the Tuhoe elder John Ru Tahuri observed when we spoke together in 1998, Paora Kiingi's decision was "the beginning of that *tāwharau* [shelter]; all the others came afterwards, in support of what Paora had said."[23]

The proverb (whakataukī), which reminds Tuhoe that their identity is carried within their migration canoe Mataatua, re-emphasized their need for unity. The Mataatua canoe is the ancestral canoe of most of the eastern Bay of Plenty tribes, notably Ngati Awa, as well as for Tuhoe. Thus, the whakataukī reminded the people of the need for a broader unity when faced with external threat. This saying became Tuhoe's guiding principle, one that would be denied, recalled, and confirmed during Tuhoe's experiences with Europeans in the nineteenth century.

In 1864, Ngati Maniapoto of upper Waikato, who were a mainstay of the Kiingitanga (Maori King movement), called for assistance to stop the invasion of their tribal lands by troops, and the accompanying government proclamation of land confiscation. Tuhoe were not allied with the Kiingitanga. But they called a meeting at Ruatahuna to consider whether to give military assistance to Waikato. The major spokesman for support was Piripi Te Heuheu from Maungapohatu. Among those who opposed was Te Whenuanui I, the younger son of Te Umuariki. Both men had been among those who had assembled for the East Coast expedition in about 1829. The debate, therefore, turned around the whakataukī.[24]

Te Whenuanui argued for peace, urging that the bulk of the Urewera men must stay at home, because "the fighting is coming near to us."[25] But he also talked about helping to contain the fight in Waikato, northwest of the Urewera. As John Tahuri commented, Te Whenuanui recognized that "if the war did escalate they could be in real trouble with their lands, too."[26] The majority, however, remained firmly on the side of defence within their boundaries. Tutakangahau, one of the senior chiefs from Maungapohatu, recollected later that most of the leaders had urged, "'Let Mātaatua be sheltered.' The fire [of war] is burning on the island."[27] Their decision was to protect their borders, not to travel to war.

Another factor, however, was introduced into the discussions by Piripi Te Heuheu. There was a commitment Tuhoe had made in 1856, when, in a ceremony of unity held at Pukawa on Lake Taupo, they (along with other tribes) had tied a flax rope – theirs being named for their ancestral mountain, Maungapohatu – to a giant central post, which was named for the host's mountain, Tongariro. The tying of the mountains had taken place at the first assembly (of several) that led to the formation of the Kiingitanga in 1858. Now, the hosts at Pukawa, Ngati Tuwharetoa, were giving their support to Maniapoto's resistance, and Piripi argued that Tuhoe were also obligated by their compact.[28] Piripi was making a political statement of the need to defend the whole island, as the lands of Waikato and Maniapoto had been militarily invaded.

The third factor that came into the debate was the much earlier pact of equals, which Tuhoe oral accounts recall. This was forged between Te Purewa from Maungapohatu and Peehi Tukorehu of Ngati Maniapoto during the fighting of the 1820s. This arose from an invading expedition led by Tukorehu to Ruatahuna; the oral narratives record the story in the form of a personal duel fought between the two men when Tukorehu demanded right of passage. Their *mana* (power) proving equal in the drawn contest, each pledged to assist the other if he needed help in the future. It was this pact between Tuhoe and Maniapoto, as John Tahuri recalled, that finally underpinned the decision to send some men to assist Maniapoto in 1864.[29]

The decision was a disaster for Tuhoe. At the siege of Orakau, after fifty-six hours of continuous fighting, the defending forces were defeated. One Tuhoe survivor described how they returned to Ruatahuna: "When we left the defences we did so in a body, chiefs, fighting men, women and young people. The soldiers almost surrounded us and many of our people were slain, and many wounded ... We had one horse, also badly wounded, with us, and those most severely wounded took it in turns to ride it. That was how we returned home."[30] In fact, Tuhoe had sent only a few fighters (a party of about fifty, including eight women) with Piripi Te Heuheu. But Te Whenuanui had regretted his initial decision, and had gone with his daughter to join the fighting party. Now he returned, wounded, his daughter killed, to be greeted with reproaches and abuse. The widows of Ruatahuna put on their most torn and ragged garments, and they sang the famous *waiata* (song) that they composed for him, "Manawa Wera" (Burning Heart), a hostile welcome.[31] He had lost the cream of Tuhoe.

Thus, from 1864, the whakataukī acquired new force. But war came into the Urewera when the district was invaded for the first time by "booted feet," in 1866. Land confiscation followed. Tuhoe first resisted by guerrilla strategies, but the scale of the Urewera fighting widened significantly after 1869, when Tuhoe gave their support to a second cause, the protection of the military leader and prophet Te Kooti Arikirangi. Te Kooti is central to several of the narratives in this chapter, and therefore needs a brief introduction. He belonged to the Rongowhakaata tribe from the East Coast, and became the religious leader for the people of the Urewera after he took refuge among them. He had earlier been sent into exile on Chatham Island, where he developed a new faith, based in the scriptures, that became known as Ringatu (The Upraised Hand). In June 1868, Te Kooti escaped from the island, leading three hundred former prisoners (many of them women and children), and after bitter pursuit, fled to the Urewera mountains.[32] These spiralling conflicts ended only when Te Whenuanui, after he surrendered in 1870, negotiated with the government's agents for the Urewera to become an autonomous zone controlled by its chiefs. In exchange, Tuhoe reluctantly joined in the final abortive search in the Urewera for Te Kooti, apparently betraying him. But he eluded them all, and successfully reached the shelter of Ngati Maniapoto and the King Country in May 1872.

It is from this time that the whakataukī re-emerged historically as the constant guiding principle for Tuhoe as they struggled to uphold this negotiated autonomy. From 1872, their lands were known as the Rohe Potae, the Encircling Boundaries of Tuhoe. In this year, Tuhoe formed their protective union, Te Whitu Tekau, the Council of Seventy, and in so doing they drew on a number of interwoven principles, or models. One was the ohākī, or dying speech, of Paora Kiingi I. Another was the seventy elders of Israel, drawn from the book of Exodus. The third model was the conceptual "round number" judged appropriate for undertaking any great task in the Maori world, "Hokowhitu."

The Union of 1872 was also known as the Union of Mataatua, because of the shared principle of descent from the migration canoe. The genealogical links between the Mataatua canoe tribes extend beyond the Tuhoe tribe, and an attempt was clearly being made to establish a collective agreement across the several tribes. They invoked the Union as their tāwharau (shelter). In so doing, they invoked the words of Paora Kiingi.

Letters to the government proclaimed a Union of the "70" chiefs of Te Urewera, whose task was, as Te Whenuanui said, "to carry on the work of this bird of peace and quietness."[33] Almost certainly, the chiefs identified themselves with the seventy leaders of Israel to whom God gave "the spirit" when he lifted it from Moses. The chiefs became the "prophets," or those with foresight,[34] as they set themselves apart from Te Kooti, who had stood as Moses to them, and whom they had driven from the Urewera. In 1872, a "line" of Armed Constabulary posts was established by the government along the western edge of the Urewera "to prevent Te Kooti from coming out of the King Country and getting back into the Urewera."[35] Tuhoe messengers and orderlies, also paid by the government under the agreement with the chiefs, were part of this military effort.

Tuhoe's "Council of Seventy" was never a literal number. Its purpose is best depicted in Tuhoe's song of challenge *(pātere)* called "Ko Ranginui," which was probably composed in the 1880s. The aim of Te Whitu Tekau was to reverse the curse *(te ūpokokohua)* of confiscation that had fallen upon their lands through the decision of Piripi Te Heuheu to fight at Orakau. The song is sung today by Tuhoe as a *waiata tangi*, a lament for their lost land:

> Te raupatu taku whenua toka, te raupatu taku whenua tangata
> Ko Te Kaharoa, ko Pukenui-o-Raho, Waiputatawa
> Kokou-matua tomokia te whare Te Whitu Tekau
> Whakaea i te hahani o te raupatu
> Te urunga tū, te urunga tapu, te mauri tū
> Te mauri tapu, Te Whitu Tekau.

> The confiscation of my own land, the confiscation of land of my people,
> Te Kaharoa, Pukenui-o-Raho, Waiputatawa,[36]
> Anointed elders, enter the house of Te Whitu Tekau
> To rebut the false allegations for the seizure,
> The refuge, the sacred pillow, the life force,
> The sacred life force, Te Whitu Tekau.[37]

After Te Kooti's pardon in 1883, when he became (ostensibly) free to travel, Tuhoe invited him to return to the Urewera. He immediately warned them that their "Union of Seventy" was insufficient, or "incomplete." This new narrative appeared in a number of contexts, all of which touch on land disputes in the 1880s and 1890s. The version that follows is a prediction recorded at a meeting during Te Kooti's visit in 1892, when a surveying conflict developed at Ruatoki. There, Tuhoe pleaded with him to help them stop the troubles afflicting the people and the land "within the Shelter of Mataatua" *("*ki roto i te Tawharau o Mataatua"), "that is the Seventy" ("kia 70 tekau nga Tangata"). As the records for this Ruatoki meeting note, Te Kooti replied, "It [the number seventy] was an Omen, an Odd number, a widow [a solitary branch left behind on a tree], but when it comes into being, at that point, let the number [of people] assembled to lead concerning the difficulties be 80. Let Te Hurinui [Apanui] be the Guardian" ("He Aitua he Tawhara he pouaru hoki – engari kia toopu, na ka whakaekea ki te 80 hei whakahaere mo nga raruraru. Ko Te Hurinui hei Tiaki.")

The records then added that "the planning was put under oath by Te Kooti. He stood up and tied his belt to the main post of that house." ("A oatitia iho e Te Kooti taua whakahaere. Tu ana ia herea ana e ia tona tatua maurea ki te pou tokomanawa o taua whare.")[38] In this dramatic manner, Te Kooti tied the Mataatua canoe tribes and the meeting-house Awanui-a-Rangi (where the event occurred) as one with himself. The house and the named leader, Te Hurinui, belonged to Ngati Awa, the coastal people of Whakatane, where the great war canoe had been stopped by Paora Kiingi. Te Kooti gave them all a new directive: to become the Eighty.

This narrative is one of the seminal stories about Te Kooti. There are now as many versions as there are elaborations of its meaning. What – or who – are the additional ten? Robert (Boy) Biddle explained in 1987,

> Te Kooti decided that seventy was an uneven number. He said, "No. You make it even. We'll take it to Eighty. I'll give you ten." From that day to this, nobody knows what the ten is. It was a way to stop Tuhoe closing the door. The ten he put on so it could never be closed again to anybody. We term it, *"He taha wairua tērā"* [that spiritual aspect]. It's just to keep it open, available to any person. So it could never be closed to anybody. It's open all the time.[39]

In this telling, the narrative of the Eighty is intentionally left unfinished. It thereby allows for a multiplicity of ways in which to fulfill Te Kooti's demand. The open-ended nature of the narrative explains the actions of Te Kooti's successor from within Tuhoe, Rua Kenana Hepetipa, who called himself Moses and Messiah, the Maori brother of Christ: in June 1906, he took "Eighty" chiefs of Tuhoe on a pilgrimage to Gisborne, Te Kooti's place of birth.

Rua's was a ritualized journey. He intended to claim Te Kooti's mana (authority), and to recover Aotearoa from King Edward VII. Among the chiefs who went with Rua was Te Hurinui, the aristocratic chief of Ngati Awa, whom Te Kooti had asked to become "Guardian" of the new Union. Like Tuhoe, Ngati Awa trace their descent from the Mataatua canoe, but their political relationships with Tuhoe were (and are) ambivalent. In 1906, both Rua and Te Hurinui were trying to complete the tasks set by Te Kooti of establishing unity and recovering Maori autonomy; neither quest is understood to have been achieved.

The notion of tāwharau, the "sheltering" of Mataatua, has underpinned many narratives. At first, they urged the need to end the inter-tribal wars that created forced migration in many parts of the North Island to escape the marauding parties. The Tuhoe accounts and songs then recall the conflicts that began at Orakau in 1864. They remember the errors of judgment by Piripi Te Heuheu and the young Te Whenuanui I, who learned not to export war. Forced to negotiate with the government in 1871, Te Whenuanui became the prime creator of Te Whitu Tekau. The policies of the Seventy rested on maintaining the principle of peace.

Te Whitu Tekau became the governing council of Tuhoe for the later nineteenth century. Its leaders, notably Kereru Te Pukenui, along with Te Whenuanui II (Te Haka), negotiated Tuhoe's agreement with the government that set up the Urewera District Native Reserve in 1896. They hoped, and expected, that the Rohe Potae of Tuhoe would be internally self-governing, as the Urewera District Native Reserve Act appeared to promise. When the premier, Richard Seddon, introduced it into Parliament, he stated that it was in fulfillment of the original agreement made in 1871 with Te Whenuanui I and Kereru to bring an end to the fighting.[40] Tuhoe's leaders, during their concurrent negotiations with Seddon, emphasized the idea of the law *(te ture)* as their new shelter. But Tuhoe were betrayed by legal chicanery. And so, within a decade, the quest to create the Eighty was reborn under Rua's leadership.

### Miraculous Escapes

The war period in the Urewera spawned other oral accounts. I choose one among the many which tell of "miraculous" escapes. It is the narrative of the two horses of Te Kooti: one black, one white, two of the four horses of the Apocalypse. The story of the black horse is rarely told, for this horse brings death by famine, and its rider bears the scales of judgment in his hand.[41]

John Ihe, a Tuhoe elder, narrated the story in 1983:

He [Te Kooti] had two horses: one black and one white one. The black one is the bad one. That's why they get two ... The black one, he only takes the saddle, and himself to get on that horse. Nothing else to get on that horse. Oh, very *tapu* [sacred] that. Nobody allowed to get on that horse – the black one, no!

*Question:* Why is the black horse "bad"?

*John:* It's very hard to explain; it's like tapu, church: when he comes out in this world, when Jesus gives him those things. But the black one is the one at the back – way at the back, when they go to war. You've got this special fellow to lead that horse. They sing out at the back, "Keep him well away!" You've got to keep him away from the horse with the pack saddle, the food and all sorts. Got to keep him way at the back! No one can ride that black horse except Te Kooti. Never! If you rode that horse, then finish! For everybody.

That horse is to keep the fellows getting shot at the back. If anybody shooting [at] you, that horse is at the back. If he goes at the front – oh boy – everybody get killed at the back!

Of course, he's got the white horse at the front. The white horse takes some of Te Kooti's stuff. The black horse, he never takes anything. The white horse he's got Te Kooti's walking stick and all his gears. Of course, they walk. He doesn't ride that horse.[42]

In this narrative, the white and the black horse move as a pair, commanded by Te Kooti. They are each other's reverse images: "That's why they get two," as John put it. Te Kooti's followers, guided by the white horse and protected at the rear by the black, passed under a great waterfall and eluded the military hunting them.

In other narratives, the white horse is that on which Te Kooti repeatedly escaped government pursuit in the Urewera. These are the stories of the great white horse – *"te hōiho mā wairua,"* the horse with spiritual powers[43] – which bore him away from impossible military situations, for Te Kooti was a fighter who was never captured in war. The most famous version is Te Kooti's escape from the terrible siege of Nga Tapa, on the eastern edge of the Urewera, in January 1869. There, some say, the white horse leapt with him from a cliff that no goat could climb. In some versions, the white horse is called Pokai Whenua, Travel the Land; in others, he is Te Awhitiki, emphasizing his procreative strength, and in yet others again he is called Te Panerua, for the horse passes like the northeast wind across the land at night.

The narratives of Te Kooti's white horse, which begin with the siege at Nga Tapa, continue into the post-war period. They commenced at this time not only as explanation for the apparently inexplicable, the bold escape from an encircling siege army of seven hundred men. They commenced because there *was* an actual horse – one solitary horse – seized in a lightning military raid in December 1868, and which Te Kooti rode, as he had been severely wounded in the foot. This horse was noted in a military report.[44] In April 1869, a second white horse – also newly stolen – that Te Kooti rode during his assault on Mohaka, Hawke's Bay, was similarly observed and re-membered.[45] The powerful myth-narratives sprang from these literal origins,[46] and the horse was transformed into the quintessential image of freedom.

The white horse in the book of Revelation was one imaginative source for the myth-narrative, for it bears the conqueror, saviour, and judge: "And I saw heaven opened, and behold a white horse; and he that sat upon him was called Faithful and True, and in righteousness he doth judge and make war ... And he was clothed with a vesture dipped in blood: and his name is called The Word of God."[47] In times of war, the scriptural account confirms the justice of the cause of the man who rides the white horse. The narrative was consciously extended by Rua, who claimed to be Te Kooti's predicted successor. Rua's horse is specifically stated in oral accounts to have been Te Kooti's white horse, although now its name became Te Ia, the White Crest of the Wave. Te Ia and Rua were photographed in about 1906,[48] the time when the white horse brought Rua to Gisborne on his quest to reclaim Maori "sovereignty," or the "kingship." In such manner, earlier narratives were re-enacted by those who recounted them. They were given newly construed meanings for their times, and they repeatedly shaped human action.

### Stories about the Land

Another clustering of accounts, which are also reworked in different versions, arose from Tuhoe's first encounters with early land surveyors and the Native Land Court. One powerful story concerns the fraudulent purchase of seven thousand acres belonging to Ngati Haka and Patuheuheu, two hapū (tribal groups) of Tuhoe. It arose from the failure of a Tuhoe committee, a chosen Council of Twelve (possibly following the twelve apostles)[49] to mediate with a European, Harry Burt, who claimed to have bought the land, Waiohau, from its owners. In January 1886, the Twelve met Burt at Te Houhi (the main settlement of Waiohau) in an effort to persuade him to accept a thousand acres as sufficient to meet his claims. Te Kooti came to Te Houhi to help mediate, for he was a friend of Burt, and Burt himself had been a friend of Te Houhi's chief. But, adopting the pseudonym Hare Rauparaha as a disguise (and simultaneously claiming an invented relationship with the celebrated Ngati Toa chief Te Rauparaha), Burt illegally took the case to the Native Land Court. There, exploiting his position as a licensed court interpreter, he successfully acquired the title for two Maori cohorts from whom he purchased it (placing it, however, in his European wife's name). It was from this calculated fraud that the extended narrative of "Te Umutaoroa" (The Earth Oven of Long Cooking) sprang. The failure of mediation and the violation of friendship brought forth a sequence of new predictions.

The earliest version is simple enough. As Burt himself observed, when he attempted, in 1887, to defend his acquisition of title, the original owners said that "Te Kooti has told us that Burts money will be like a rotten pit of potatoes. He (Te Kooti) had named Waiohau Block 'Umuta[o]roa' and Burt will never get it."[50] The failure of a parliamentary inquiry in 1889 to restore the title to the original owners, despite finding in their favour, ensured that the narrative would shift to another form of resolution both more potent and more distant. In 1892, Te Kooti predicted,

Te kupu ki te Umutaoroa – Te Houhi
Ka taona e ahau tenei hangi ma taku tamaiti e hura.
Tenei mea te hangi, ko nga kai o roto hei ora mo te tangata.

The word concerning Te Umutaoroa – Te Houhi
I am preparing this *hāngi* (earth oven) for my child to unearth.
The food inside this hāngi will be for the salvation of the people.[51]

For Burt, however, Te Kooti predicted the earth oven would contain only "raw" and putrefying food: the greatest insult possible from host to guest, and the marker of the end of all reciprocity. For its rightful owners, however, the "long steaming" of the hāngi was predicted to provide – at a future date – the "cooked" sustenance of life.

The narrative of the Eighty (told above) is linked at Waiohau with the saga of their lost land. In 1999, Hieke Tupe, then eighty-one years old, remembered the story this way. Te Kooti came to Te Houhi and warned them to seek their tāwharau in unity:

"Tuhoe, tāwharautia koe" – "Tuhoe, unite as one."
"But we have," they objected.
Te Kooti asked, "How many are you?"
"We are Seventy," they replied.
"He aituā kehe," he said. "It's a bad omen, an unlucky number, an uneven number. I will give you ten, to make it eighty."
We still ask, "What is that ten? Is it the ten commandments?"[52]

The story of the Eighty is again left unfinished. So, too, is a later narrative in which Te Umutaoroa became the place of pilgrimage for each of the claimants who sought to establish that he was Te Kooti's predicted successor. As Boy Biddle told the story in 1983,

Up where the Aniwhenua dam is now, it used to be dry land before ... Te Kooti was there, he slept at this particular *pā* [Te Houhi], and where he did sleep, he said to them in the morning, "I had a dream last night: the valley of the Rangitaiki here was just dense fog, right from the top of it to the other side of it." He said, "I couldn't see through this fog, so the place where I slept, it will be known as Te Umutaoroa." That's a hāngi – it would be perpetually in that form until this person came and uncovered it.

So this place became quite a gathering place for these false Christs, false prophets. They rush up there! Well, Wi Raepuku [who made the trek in

1922] went up there, and he was going to exhume this thing, and find out what was in it. Well, to be quite truthful there was nothing there, it's just bare ground there. So it's a symbolic thing; it was not an actual hāngi. And the only result he got out of it, he broke the wheel off his buggy – so he couldn't get back! He had to ride the horse that was towing the buggy, and leave the buggy behind! Of course, Tuhoe said to him, "Well, that's what you get for dabbling in things you don't understand!" ... We've had others since that time, go up there.[53]

Te Umutaoroa has become an unfulfilled quest-narrative. It is unfulfilled because the land is lost; indeed, it is now drowned beneath the waters of a hydro-electric dam, built in 1980. Little islands dot the lake where Te Umutaoroa once was. Once again new meanings are being wrought from this changed landscape.

The people of Te Houhi were expelled from their settlement in 1907. They received some small compensation in land from the government and, in 1920, formal recognition that their original title was lost through fraud on the part of Burt. Their land claim was presented before the Waitangi Tribunal in 2004 in the hope of a better resolution. But Te Kooti's quest-narrative has acquired an autonomous life. It is no longer tied to its origins, a land fraud carried out by a trickster who had once been Te Kooti's friend.[54] It has been transformed to possess vastly extended meanings concerning his successor, the one who is to complete the quest, the Messiah for his times.

For Ngati Whare, the tribe living on the western edge of the Urewera, the pressures placed on their land were similar, and began as soon as the wars ended. However, instead of an individual act of fraud, they faced insistent efforts by the government's land-purchasing agents. From 1873, the government claimed (by deed of proclamation) a sole right of purchase along the southwest borders of the Urewera. A policy was developed of acquiring "liens" (or proclaimed "interests") on the land, enabling it to purchase without competition. In June 1884, Te Kooti returned to Te Whaitinui, the central community of Ngati Whare. He came to Murumurunga *marae* (communal area) to open the meeting-house the people had built there in his honour. Famously, his horse shied and Te Kooti saw the inverted carved figure of the lizard on the central pole of the front porch, its wide mouth turned down to devour the land. He predicted,

Kainga katoatia a ko te paepae o te whare nei ki roto [ka] kati tonu hei huihuinga mo nga morehu.

[It will be completely consumed, and only the threshold of this house inside will remain as the meeting place for the survivors.][55]

The narrative for the house, which Te Kooti named Eripitana, was that it should become *"te tapu o ngā tapu"* (the holy of holies).[56] This led to its abandonment, out of fear. The name "Eripitana" is glossalalia (speaking in tongues) standing as a mnemonic to the scriptural promise of Isaiah 11:11, that the remnant of the people, *"ngā mōrehu,"* would be saved.[57] Although the original house fell derelict, its successor, bearing the same name, stands proudly at Murumurunga. The tapu has been successfully lifted from it.

The warning for the land, however, was one of loss. Te Kooti's vision was presaged by the sudden appearance of the white cormorant *(kawau),* reputed to live in the "Great Canyon" that gives Te Whaitinui its name.[58] Hine-ruarangi is an ancestral bird of ill-omen. In the narratives, she is the daughter of Toi, the founder of Te Whaitinui-a-Toi (to give the place its full name):

> When Te Kooti was here, he saw Hine flying over the vale of Te Whaiti. His word came forth: "These lands, and the people thereof, shall fall before the white man. His *mana* shall be over both. His lines (survey) shall disembowel the land!"
> We asked: "What is the token?"
> He replied: "The sign of the fatal *kawau,* the sign of the daughter of Toi, who ever warns her descendants of evil to come."[59]

Hine-ruarangi is the guardian of Te Whaiti. In this narrative, recorded by Best at the time of the construction of the road from Te Whaiti to Ruatahuna, her lineage is traced to Toi (Toi-kairakau, Toi-Eater of Wood), the ancestor of the earliest arrivals in the Urewera, who predated the Mataatua canoe immigrants. She belongs to the land; her appearance is an omen, he tohu. As a *white* cormorant, she is a fearsome exception to the norm. So too is the call of the stranger-cockerel, heard at other times and other places – at Ruatoki in 1822 and during the Passion of Christ. Animistic guardians inhabit oral accounts when the world is out of joint.

The narrative obliquely recalls the arrival of the first government surveyors at Te Whaiti, in 1885. In June, J.C. Blythe, who intended to make the road survey, was stopped at Te Whaiti. Although he was ultimately permitted to travel (with an escort) as far as Ruatahuna, he was not allowed to take any measurement nor survey for the planned road.[60] In the following year, he returned with Percy Smith, then assistant surveyor-general, and at a large and "formal" meeting with Tuhoe and Ngati Whare leaders, the two men were told that the road would not be permitted. Te Makarini (Tamarau Waiari) was a spokesman for Te Whitu Tekau in opposition to the road. At the end, Smith shouted that the road "would go on in spite of them," and left rudely.[61] Nine years later, Smith organized for Best to go to the Urewera with the government roadworkers. He was sent, in part, to record Tuhoe's history.

The narrative of Hine-ruarangi anticipates survey disputes, as well as the road dispute, which would continue. Together, the surveys would slice the land into pieces. In her study of early nineteenth-century surveying in New Zealand, Giselle Byrnes has depicted surveyors' activities as "political texts."[62] Robert Ellis' contemporary paintings of Rakaumangamanga, the mountain that guards his wife's family land in the Bay of Islands, similarly traces survey lines and trig points across a dismembered landscape as lines of conquest. The first government survey report for the Urewera, written by Percy Smith in 1896, adopted the language of conquest to depict its newly completed mapping efforts: "Thus the last area of any size in the North Island has become subject to the ruling process of triangulation."[63] Surveying lines, all that busy activity of pencil and rubber and subdivisions, as a later government land purchase agent in the Urewera revealingly put it,[64] cut through Tuhoe's control of their land.

The first land sales inside the Rohe Potae were made to the government in 1910. The 1896 Urewera District Native Reserve Act had created a sole right of land purchase for the government, with the consent of Tuhoe's "General Committee." This committee, set up under the act, was not formed until 1909, and was not willing to sell land. It wanted instead to have fixed-term leases, which had been forbidden under the act. In 1909, the Liberal government decided to use Rua as a lever to break open Tuhoe's opposition to selling land. This decision was taken by two Maori leaders within Parliament, James Carroll, then minister of Native Affairs, and Apirana Ngata. John Tahuri, who was the son of one of Rua's wives, described in 1998 how Rua was persuaded to agree:

> After Timi Kara [James Carroll] and Apirana [Ngata] failed to get him to sell land, they invited him down to Wellington in 1909. Did you know about that? And he went down. They did something – nobody knows what they did to him there, but they did something with him because he changed his stance.
>
> When he came back he called a big meeting at Maungapohatu with his followers. He said, "Sell the land; the land doesn't belong to us. We're just tenants in common." And he started to look back to scriptures. He said, "The day will come when all those lands will go back to those very original people who was given land by God right from the beginning." This is what he was telling his people. He said, "It won't happen now, but ... it will happen." He made reference to a certain part of the Old Testament to prove his point.
>
> "All right," he said. "Even us, on this little country." He said, "Sell the land. That's why I am saying to you, sell the land and make use of the money from the government from the Bank of New Zealand." There is a walata [song] about it. It said, the time will come. He said, "Get their money,

the Bank of New Zealand, and use it – because the day will come," he said, "those lands will come back to us." Well, because of that, they gave the mandate to sell.[65]

There were, however, hidden thorns in Rua's advice. He had taken the refrain "Get their money, the Bank of New Zealand" from a famous song composed for Tuhoe by Te Kooti, which he had sung in February 1891 at the opening of Te Whai-a-Te Motu (The Pursuit across the Island), their great meeting-house. This house, located at Mataatua marae, Ruatahuna, and named in memory of Te Kooti's flight from government forces, had been initiated by Te Whenuanui I, who had done most of the carving himself. He had built it to commemorate Paora Kiingi's words, *"He tāwharau te Mātaatua."*[66] The house would be "the shelter for Mataatua."

But at the opening, Te Kooti sang, with sarcasm, "Get, go get the money belonging to the Governor at the Bank of New Zealand" ("Tikina, tikina ra te moni a te Kawana kei te peeke o Niu Tireni"). He warned of consequential losses for the poor, who would be stranded, lamenting for the land, while the chiefs lived in *"nga whare tiketike"* ("the stately houses").[67] He prophesied that the meeting-house would become merely a centre for gambling, and as Tahuri commented, "Right up till the twenties they were still gambling in there. Te Kooti predicted all that."[68]

John Tahuri's narrative draws on a complex history of hope and betrayals. First, it reminds us that the two major Maori leaders of "economic modernization," Carroll and Ngata, were responsible for Tuhoe's reluctant agreement to sell significant portions of their land to the government in 1910. Second, it hints at some hidden pressure brought to bear on Rua. That can only have been an "unspoken" threat to apply the Tohunga Suppression Act, passed in 1907 with the express intention of curtailing Rua's practices as a faith healer *(tohunga)*. The act could be applied only by order of the Native Affairs minister, Carroll; curiously, it was never used against Rua. Third, the narrative explains the way in which Rua persuaded the people at Maungapohatu to agree to sell land. It asks, implicitly, was Rua's assertion that the land would return to Maori simply part of a fraud or was it a promise given in good faith, one that, some day, might be fulfilled? As Tahuri said, laughing, "It's just a waiting game, really. Whether it will ever happen ..."[69] Finally, it serves to remind listeners of the ambiguity of Te Kooti's predictions for Tuhoe. The account remains open-ended; the story is, again, not finished.

## Conclusion

The narratives on which I have drawn are mostly contemporary stories, recorded orally in the 1980s and 1990s. The narrators were all fluent Maori speakers; their competence in English was widely varied. Some, such as John

Tahuri and Boy Biddle, were well aware of written histories. They not only knew Best's *Tuhoe* (almost every Tuhoe household owns a copy), but also more recent work, notably the co-authored photographic history of Rua, *Mihaia,* which drew extensively on oral interviews with Rua's children and other Tuhoe, and which has been consistently in print since 1979. Two anthropologists also worked with Tuhoe during the 1970s and 1980s: Peter Webster and Jeffrey Sissons, both of whom have, in different ways, studied Rua and the community to which he belonged.[70] Some of Tuhoe's leaders have themselves become academics, teaching in various departments in the New Zealand universities.[71] Their primary concern as Tuhoe, however, is the urgency of the task of ensuring continued transmission of Tuhoe historical and cultural knowledge *(mātauranga)* within the tribe.

I met the elders quoted here in varied contexts. The recordings were made, with their permission, for three different books and a further essay.[72] They were made always with the intention of narrating their understanding of the matter under discussion, and the stories emerged spontaneously. The dialogue with the late John Tahuri is among the most recent, and it was made because he wanted to be recorded. His historical knowledge was influenced by published works. However, he was *primarily* informed by the living oral world that he inhabited, and by the many nineteenth-century Tuhoe *whakapapa* (genealogical) books and other manuscripts, of which he was a guardian. Most Maori elders today have similar wellsprings for their knowledge. They draw on local oral knowledge and a wide variety of other sources in both English and Maori.

In most Maori oral accounts, the mana of the group to whom the narrator belongs moulds his or her perceptions of the past. The narratives do not tell a chronological history, nor do they consider other groups' interpretations of events. There is no agreement on the stories, let alone their interpretations, or their outcomes. They are neither valid nor invalid, historically. But they can be seen to arise from specific, and sometimes identifiable, historical contexts.

Scriptural references in stories that originated with a specific land loss, such as Te Houhi and Maungapohatu, feed on the promise of restitution of the "original" lost land, "Canaan." John Tahuri's historical awareness of other peoples had expanded since he first heard the stories told to him by his elders in the 1920s. He discussed, as a gloss to his narrative in 1998, the political decolonizations that had occurred since the Second World War, starting with the independence of India. With South Africa's recovery of majority rule, he added, "that completes the black continent. It's only them, Australia, and our little country [left]. Well, who knows, maybe the fulfillment of what the scripture had for mankind ..."[73] The explanatory power of the scriptural stories lies in the promises of restitution for both land and authority that exist in those texts, and the promise of a unique relationship with God.

In the Urewera, the flight of Hine-ruarangi is feared still. She watches and warns, for she is the omen of dislocation and change. She belongs to the ancestral world of Aotearoa, and her appearances are like those of the *wak'a,* the guardian ancestors of the Andean mountains, who are predicted to "turn the world over" again. In Aotearoa, co-existing forms of mana and knowledge are acknowledged: ancestral, scriptural, and "modern" knowledge systems all inform the telling of history in Maori communities. The oral narratives of the Maori world remain plereomatic in their structures because their inner purpose is to find resolutions to the Maori situation as a colonized people.

# 9

# The Interpreter as Contact Point: Avoiding Collisions in Tlingit America

*Richard Dauenhauer and Nora Marks Dauenhauer*

The key to the stories of first contacts between Europeans and indigenous peoples is communication. How did contacts occur between cultures so different that there could be no common notion even of reality, not to mention a common language? In the very first contacts, pantomime and gesture and gift were the ambiguous initial efforts to exchange meaning. Over time, gestures became sign languages, which were eclipsed by the slowly evolving ability of a few individuals to speak or understand a common language.

The emergence of interpreters was obviously critical. They became the contact point between the two cultures through which more complex dialogues could occur, differences could be explained, and conflicts smoothed over. Their linguistic and diplomatic abilities were clearly essential to trade and other processes such as evangelization and colonization.

Perhaps even more important, these translators became the bottleneck or filter through which knowledge of one culture was passed to the other. In many situations only one translator was available, and thus all communication was dependent on his or her agenda and positioning. Lewis Hyde reminds us that "We may sometimes assume that a translation provides a window onto the original, but just as often, as Derek Walcott says, 'to translate is to betray.'" Translators enter a space in between the two communities. They may earn their wages from one side or the other, but some always come from existing in the space in between.[1]

Yet scholars of the contact process have not paid much attention to the individuals who performed the role of linking cultures, in spite of what seems to be their critical position. In most cases, the translator was a Native wife, a captive, or the offspring of intercultural marriages: the Creole, Metis, or mixed blood. These interpreters existed on the margins of Native and colonial society, rarely stepping into the historical limelight, often unnamed in the histories that depended so much on their skills. We do not know, in most cases, how quickly or slowly the ability to converse developed, or how numerous were individuals on either side who could act as interpreters.

Tlingit America enables us to gain insight into the process of contact because we can look at the individuals who were in fact the physical and communicative links between immigrants and Natives, would-be colonizers and successful resistors of colonization. Thanks to the corporate nature of the Russian attempt to colonize what became southeastern Alaska, a comparative wealth of correspondence documents the ambiguous roles of translators. What emerges is that, in the century and a quarter of Russian contacts and colonization, only a handful of Tlingit or Creoles learned enough Russian to effectively translate, and no Russians learned enough Tlingit. These few people were the conduit for all the official communication between Russians and Tlingit, and for much of the informal communication as well. They were the eyes and ears through which Russia tried to understand America (or at least a part of it). Even more problematic for the Russians, the very people on whom they had to rely to communicate with the Tlingit were not Russians; in fact, some were captives taken from the Tlingit. Their loyalties were always suspect.

For over two centuries, the Tlingit Indians of Southeast Alaska have experienced ongoing and evolving contact with three colonial powers: Russia, Britain, and the United States. Of these, the Russian contact was the earliest, starting from 1741 and becoming most intense between the 1790s and 1867, the time period on which this chapter focuses. British contact, short but crucial, concentrated in the southern Tlingit area around the present-day town of Wrangell. It began in 1839, when the Hudson's Bay Company (HBC) leased the territory, as well as hunting and trading rights, from the Russian-American Company (RAC). The lease was renewed until Russia sold Alaska to the United States in 1867.[2] The Russian American period of Alaska history, little known in general, remains a highly specialized area of academic research among historians.[3]

Here, we focus on the lives and times of three Tlingit men – Dmitrii Larionov, Kalistrat Gedeonov, and Niktopolian Gedeonov – who were that conduit between cultures, the main interpreters upon whom the RAC relied for more than thirty critical years, 1821 to 1855. We look at the circumstances of their birth, the violent events that led them to learn Russian, how and why they became interpreters for the Russians, and the roles they played as linguistic, cultural, social, political, and diplomatic mediators and counsellors. Their daily activities as recorded in the RAC correspondence are played out in two different but overlapping contexts: the larger, international history of the northwest coast, involving rivalries among the major colonial powers in fur-trading enterprises largely driven by the Chinese market; and Tlingit domestic history, involving relationships among the various clans which were played out in agendas concerning trade, hunting rights, war, peace, and kinship.

Before we do that, however, it is necessary to provide the context for their remarkable careers and positions between two cultures. The popular image of the Russian American period is often a stereotype of nasty, inept Russians brutalizing helpless Native people, except for the proud, fierce, and warlike Tlingit, who lurk namelessly and facelessly in ambush, waiting to destroy the unwary colonists who cower in their forts, afraid to venture out. There is some truth behind each stereotype, but the real social dynamics of the period are far more complex, and must be gleaned from what remains of the paper trail. The correspondence of the RAC, a treasure trove of information about daily life in Russian America, serves as the primary contact narrative for this chapter.[4]

Combining this new archival resource with our own personal ethnographic fieldwork of the past thirty years, we are able for the first time to put Tlingit names and personalities into the published record of the period, trace the careers of several Tlingit individuals who had contact of one kind or another with the RAC, flesh out and give a face to the indigenous side of the history, and create a narrative of contact out of the archival records.[5]

The routine correspondence of the RAC reminds us that the colony was multi-lingual and multi-ethnic. Languages spoken in Southeast Alaska in the course of daily business included Russian, Tlingit, Swedish, Finnish, German, English, Unangan Aleut, Alutiiq (Kodiak "Aleut"), and sometimes also Eyak and Tanaina Athabaskan. Although the popular image claims otherwise, there were few ethnic Russians in Russian America. Several governors were Finns, there was a Finnish Lutheran church in Sitka, and at one point an estimated 40 to 60 percent of the workforce was Kamchadal. Creoles (defined here as children of Alaska Native mothers and Russian fathers) and Aleuts comprised much of middle management.

The correspondence especially reveals the extent to which the colonial management knew that it must, and in fact did, rely heavily on its Tlingit interpreters as counsellors and mediators in a range of sensitive and potentially explosive situations. They were interpreters of culture as well as language in the multi-ethnic society of Russian America. Nonetheless, managers also felt the need for caution, as they did not completely trust the Tlingit, including their own translators upon whom they had to rely in avoiding collisions.

Throughout the half century covered here, the Russians remained vigilant and nervous regarding the possibility of armed conflict with the Tlingit. The encounters at Sitka of 1802 and 1804, and at Yakutat in 1805 were fresh in their memories. In 1802, the Tlingit destroyed the Russian fort at Sitka; in 1804 the Russians recaptured Sitka. In 1805, the Tlingit destroyed the Russian post at Yakutat. In 1806 and 1807, the Russians retaliated. A communication of 23 August 1851 warns that the Kake Tlingit were still so little pacified that they did not hesitate to attack European ships.[6] In 1802, the Kake Tlingit had been allies in a sequence of coordinated attacks on Russian positions from Kake to Yakutat, as part of the Sitka revolt; nearly fifty years later, the threat of attack still remained.

Interpreters seem to have been in very short supply, and the RAC valued its most talented ones. Tlingit interpreters were rare because the Russians had relatively little close contact with the Tlingit, which was not the case with the Unangan and Kodiak Aleuts, where there was longer integration and substantial bilingualism. The Tlingit retained a degree of de facto sovereignty, for the Russians had very little influence, even in Sitka, over their language, culture, and economy. This independence continued for about twenty years into the American period, when it began to erode. The Russians did not have the offensive military strength to subdue the Tlingit; therefore, they depended almost entirely on vigilant defence, and on diplomacy and mutually beneficial trade agreements to build good community relations and minimize the danger of major revolt or attack, or minor harassment of hunting parties. They continually negotiated very carefully with the Tlingit for purchase of fur, timber, food, and various other items, for establishing trading posts and forts (especially in the Stikine area, near what is now Wrangell), and for exploration of coal deposits (as near the village of Kake).

The Tlingit interpreters were indispensable in preserving this domestic tranquility, and not only between the Russians and Tlingit: they also worked to make or keep peace among Tlingit clans, attempting to prevent vendetta and war. In addition, they acted as advocates for their people, helping negotiate equitable contracts, investigating a shooting and a murder, and in more dramatic episodes, rescuing people from slavery or from torture and execution as witches.

The lives and careers of our three interpreters all begin at Yakutat, Alaska, and are linked by the revolt of August 1805 and subsequent events. At the end of the eighteenth century, the Russians were expanding into Southeast Alaska, which Chirikov had first sighted in 1741. In 1788, Izmailov and Bocharov visited Lituya Bay, just south of Yakutat. Both contacts generated narratives: Chirikov's shore party was attacked and the survivors wrote about it, creating the Tlingit debut in Western contact literature; the Lituya Bay first contact story entered Tlingit oral literature in several complementary variants.[7] In 1796 and 1799, the Russians established colonies at Yakutat and Sitka.

### "The Sitka Interpreter Dmitrii"
Dmitrii Stepanovich Larionov (ca. 1805-47), junior Tlingit interpreter for the Russian-American Company, enters and departs the published paper trail as a footnote. As far as we know, this is limited to the sole asterisk and

reference crediting "the Sitka interpreter Dmitrii" for his help with *Remarks about the Kolosh and Kodiak Languages,* published by Ioann Veniaminov (St. Innocent) in 1846.[8] But, through the RAC correspondence, we are able to identify the person footnoted and can begin to flesh out his life and career to a considerable extent.

Dmitrii enters the archival records in a letter of 21 January 1821 from Chief Manager M.I. Murav'ev to the Main Office (CS 2/38:179v). This describes how a Tlingit man and woman, accompanied by a boy whose father was "the Russian Larionov," had fled to the Sitka fort because the Tlingit intended to sacrifice them. This event had occurred during the administration of Murav'ev's predecessor (unnamed, but presumably S.I. Yanovskii, the son-in-law of Aleksandr Baranov, chief manager of the Russian-American company until 1818; Yanovskii was in charge between 1818 and 1820). Some years before, in 1805, when the Tlingit captured Yakutat, they had taken the boy and his mother prisoner. Although this had been known for a long time, ransoming or exchanging the boy had proved impossible. When the Tlingit discovered that the refugees were at the fort, they asked for their return, but Murav'ev would not yield them up. Instead, he sent the Tlingit couple to Kodiak. He reported that Dmitrii, then fifteen years old, spoke not a word of Russian but that his white face and striking resemblance to his brother indicated his origins. (Dmitrii had two half-brothers by his father and a Russian or Kodiak wife, and a full sister, Pelageia.) Concluding that hiding him from the Tlingit was a useless exercise, Murav'ev sent him to live with his brother. By 1822, Dmitrii had gone to sea.

The RAC correspondence is often laconic in its references to persons because the writers could generally assume that the recipients were already familiar with the context. From a variety of other sources and research, we can supply Dmitrii's background, known or assumed in 1821. Dmitrii Stepanovich Larionov (ca. 1805-47) was a Creole, the son of a Russian father and a Tlingit mother. All evidence confirms the explicit identification of the Dmitrii of the RAC correspondence as the son of Stepan Larionov, commander of the Russian settlement at Yakutat, killed there when the Tlingit captured the post in August 1805. A letter of 24 September 1805 from Ivan Repin to Baranov reports, "Our enemies, the native workers, and part of the Yakutat natives have massacred all the Russians and our late chief Stepan ... Larionov. All were slain, to the last man. Only the children of the Russians were spared."[9] Repin's letter puts the massacre's date at about 20 August, and adds that ten Chugach and Kodiak Natives who were out berry picking also survived, and escaped by *baidarka* (an Aleut two- or three-hatched kayak).

We can speculate at great length regarding the details of Dmitrii's life between 1805 and 1821, but cannot confirm them at present. The record for the adult Dmitrii resumes a year after his 1821 appearance with a 28 February 1822 (CS 3/156:93) Main Office reply to Murav'ev, approving his action in purchasing the Tlingit couple and Larionov, the son of a Russian, who were to be sacrificed by their Tlingit masters. Larionov was to be numbered among the Creoles. In April 1822, Dmitrii Larionov is listed as a sailor on the galiot *Rumiantsov* (CS 3/108:26). By all accounts, Dmitrii was a valued and often-rewarded employee. Several memos of the 1820s document his raises and bonuses.

Dmitrii Larionov next appears in the company records in a 30 March 1835 (CS 12/28:19v) letter from Chief Manager Wrangell to Ensign Kuznetsov, commander of the schooner *Chilkat*. The letter, describing strategies in a volatile political situation, directs that the Tlingit interpreter Larionov was to be taken to the St. Dionysius redoubt (stockade), and that the Tlingit interpreter Gedeon was to be brought to Sitka. This is the first explicit reference to Dmitrii's role as an interpreter, and also the first correspondence in which Dmitrii and fellow interpreter Gedeon (Niktopolian Gedeonov) both appear. Dmitrii's name features in two other documents of the same date: a passport document listing Dmitrii Larionov and his wife, Anna, as passengers on the schooner *Chilkat*, and a memo to the manager of Redoubt St. Dionysius duplicating the content of the Kuznetsov letter regarding trading strategies and confirming that Larionov was being sent to replace Gedeon as interpreter.

Dmitrii and Anna apparently stayed at Redoubt St. Dionysius (now Wrangell) for two years, but they did not seem pleased with the assignment. Dmitrii asked to be released from company service. Chief Manager Kupreianov responded in a memo of 23 March 1836 (CS 13/60:40v) to manager Moskvitinov that he wanted Dmitrii to remain in company service with a salary increase of seventy-five rubles. The couple remained in Redoubt St. Dionysius but Anna asked to visit Sitka. In a memo of 19 March 1837 (CS 14/31:35), Kupreianov remarked that it was extremely difficult for vessels to transport passengers from one place to another solely to see their relatives, and that the request of the wife of interpreter Larionov to come to Sitka was therefore denied. Elsewhere in the same memo, the governor ordered manager Ignatii Andreianov to stop watering down the rum for the Tlingit so that they would not be dissatisfied; they had been accustomed to receiving full-strength rum.

Dmitrii is next mentioned in a 21 October 1837 memo (CS 15/346:4v) from Wrangell to Fleet Lieutenant Zarembo, informing him that the priest of the local church, Ioann Veniaminov, was being sent to perform his duties at Redoubt St. Dionysius. When done, he was to return on Zarembo's vessel. If Zarembo received this order after he had left the redoubt, he was to return there to pick up the priest and also interpreter Larionov, who was at the redoubt. Interpreter Gedeonov, who had proven unworthy to occupy a position on Kupreianov's staff, was being sent to the redoubt to replace Larionov.

A memo of 30 June 1838 to the local office granted a fifty-ruble bonus to Dmitrii Larionov for zealous fulfillment of the duties of Tlingit interpreter. Larionov is also mentioned in memos of 1841 and 1842, discussed below in the section focusing on themes and activities in the RAC correspondence.

The final entry for Dmitrii Larionov is a memo of 12 May 1847 (CS 28/ 399:82v) from Chief Manager Teben'kov to the Main Office, reporting his death and describing the problem of finding good interpreters to replace him, a subject addressed below.

### Niktopolian Gedeonov and Kalistrat Gedeonov

The stories of Kalistrat and Niktopolian Gedeonov begin with the 1806 hostage-taking raid on Yakutat ordered by Baranov in retaliation for the Tlingit revolt of 1805, in which Dmitrii Larionov's father was killed. There are contradictions and complications in the published historical record beyond the scope of this chapter, but the essential fact is that two teenaged Tlingit boys were among those taken hostage by the Russians in this raid. Kiril T. Khlebnikov writes that in 1806, "Baranov had sent the American Captain Campbell, who seized the main Chilkhat [Chilkat] toen [*toyon,* leader] Asik, who controlled Yakutat, taken two of his tribesmen [*"plemiannikov"* in the 1835 Russian original] as hostages, and ransomed out of captivity an Aleut and his wife." The story continues in an endnote: "The hostages were taken to Kad'iak [Kodiak] where, at their own wish they were baptized and given the names Kalistrat and Gedeon. They married there and had children. Later transferred to Sitka, they received a salary and later served as interpreters with the Kolosh [Tlingit]. Kalistrat died in 1832 but Gedeon survived and is now chief interpreter."[10]

The Hieromonk (priest-monk) Gideon (also spelled "Gedeon"), describing the school at Kodiak in a 26 May 1807 letter to Baranov, identified five Tlingit hostages and gave their Tlingit names and ages. He noted that the school enrolment was up to a hundred students "including even the Tlingit hostages, who have willingly embraced our Greco-Russian Orthodox faith on the 23rd of November of the same year 1806."[11]

Gideon was the godfather for the five young men, each of whom took Gedeonov as his family name; from this point, five Gedeons, or Gedeonovs, two of whom were Niktopolian and Kalistrat, enter the paper trail. From Gideon, we learn that Niktopolian's Tlingit name was Tygike; we have not been able to identify or confirm this name. Kalistrat is also known as Nikostrat, and his Tlingit name is given as L'kaina. In modern Tlingit spelling, this is Lḵeináa; most elders whom we have consulted confirm that this name is of the Raven moiety and L'uknax̱.ádi clan. If this correct (and if

Khlebnikov's understanding of the term "tribesmen" refers to clan and kin, not just to community), then Niktopolian and the leader Asik are also probably of the same clan, and both young men may be his actual biological nephews as well as his clan nephews according to Tlingit social structure. This is extrapolation based on a common denominator but it would make sense for the Russians to take high-ranking people as hostages. Knowing the clan membership of the Gedeonovs would in turn help us determine their probable political and diplomatic alliances among the various communities and clans. Our field research on this is inconclusive at present.

Currently, we know of no reference to either Niktopolian or Kalistrat Gedeonov from between 1806, the time of their arrival in Kodiak, and 1821, although some may turn up as research continues. Niktopolian began working for salary in Kodiak in 1821, and Kalistrat followed suit in Sitka in 1822. In the spring of 1828, Niktopolian, too, was transferred to Sitka, and that fall he went back to Kodiak to fetch his family to join him at his new permanent duty station in Sitka.

Kalistrat and Niktopolian Gedeonov are easily confused by persons using the RAC correspondence for the first time; this is due to the fact that, in situations where it was clear which Gedeonov was meant, writers commonly did not mention their first names. Before 1828, the only interpreter named Gedeon, or Gedeonov, at the Kodiak office was Niktopolian; likewise, the only one at the Sitka office was Kalistrat. This explains why, in these early years, when writing to the Kodiak and Sitka offices, the chief manager might simply refer to the "interpreter Gedeon" without specifying further. After 1828, when both Gedeonovs were in Sitka, the chief manager was generally very careful to distinguish between them by using their first names.

Kalistrat (Nikostrat, or Lḵeináa) Gedeonov was born ca. 1788 in Yakutat. Hired by Chief Manager M.I. Murav'ev on 5 December 1822, he worked with the RAC for ten years. Out of respect for his long and reliable service, his debt to the company was cancelled and he received salary increases and bonuses almost every year. He died on 17 April 1832.

Niktopolian (Tygike) Gedeonov, born ca. 1792 in Yakutat, died in Sitka on 27 July 1855, aged sixty-three. He was hired by Chief Manager Murav'ev on 31 July 1821 and served until his death in 1855. His death record says that he died of "old age" and was buried near the Tlingit Trinity Church in Sitka. The documentation for his nearly thirty-five years of company employment lists numerous raises, bonuses, and commendations for service. In 1849, he was awarded an imperial silver medal for his many years of constant devotion and zeal. He was not the only Tlingit interpreter, but numerous references mention him as the best. For example, in June 1834, realizing that Niktopolian was indispensable in the critical RAC negotiations with the Stikine Tlingit, Chief Manager Etolin was forced to withdraw him from a northbound exploration mission and send him south as quickly as possible because the substitute was not adequate (CS 11/7:425v and 426).

## Themes and Activities in the Correspondence

Finding skilled interpreters was an ongoing problem for the RAC. In a letter of 12 May 1847 (CS 28/399:82v), Chief Manager Teben'kov noted the death of Dmitrii Larionov and the difficulty of replacing him. With the death of Larionov, junior interpreter of the Tlingit language, all dealings with the Tlingit were referred to senior interpreter Niktopolian Gedeonov. Although he was very well disposed toward the Russians, Gedeonov was also advanced in years and this obliged Teben'kov to think about having such necessary people as interpreters in reserve. Tlingit Pavel Kuchke-ke-ke was on salary to replace Larionov, but his knowledge of the Russian language was very limited and thus he could not take Gedeonov's place. From the company's Tlingit toyon Kukhkan, Teben'kov requested two of his relatives, a grandson and a nephew, and sent them to Aian (in the Russian far east) to learn Russian. He asked the commander of Aian port to give this matter his attention and to return these young Tlingit men to Sitka after two years. He assigned pay of three hundred rubles per year to each and charged it to Sitka office expenses. We have assumed that Teben'kov's Kukhkan (Kooxx'aan in modern orthography) was the husband of Dmitrii Larionov's sister Pelageia and therefore his brother-in-law. Through this connection, we know that Larionov and his Tlingit mother were of the Eagle moiety, since Kooxx'aan is a name used by the Kiks.ádi clan of the Raven moiety, and people were required to marry into the opposite moiety.

Four years later, in August 1851, another reference is made to Niktopolian's advancing years; the interpreter Pavel, presumably the Kuchke-ke-ke mentioned earlier, had been assigned to help him. The report noted that Pavel was considered a Kake Tlingit by birth.

Several letters address the shortage of interpreters following the death of Niktopolian. One, of 10 June 1858 (CS 39/318:124v), notes that a Tlingit boy named Sakhlia was being sent to Aian for two years to learn the Russian language. The Sitka office was to outfit him properly with shoes and clothing for the trip, and up to three hundred rubles per year were prescribed for his support. It is too early in our research to be certain, but this Sakhlia may possibly be the ancestor of the Sheakley family, whose oral history records an ancestor who went to Russia, and whose name may be an anglicization of the Tlingit name. He is not listed in the Sitka confessional lists of the 1860s.

The next day, on 11 June 1858 (CS 39/334:130v-131), Chief Manager Voevodski informed Main Office regarding the interpreters who remained at the port of Sitka after the death of Tlingit interpreter Gedeonov: these included Mariia Kabachakova, the two junior interpreters Pavel Kuchkeke (sic), who was poorly skilled, and Gavrilo Kategan (or Kategak?), who had studied at Aian port and who was a relative of the local toyon Mikhail Kukhkan. This is presumably the grandson or nephew mentioned in the letter of 12 May 1847. Due to old age, Mariia Kabachakova had gone blind and could not carry out her former duties; Pavel Kuchkeke had left service. Therefore, Voevodski arranged with toyon Mikhail Kukhkan that Sakhlia, then fifteen, would be sent to Aian; he asked the assistance of the commander of Aian port in training the boy in the Russian language over the course of two years. In March 1861 (CS 43/188:58-59), Chief Manager Furuhjelm asked the Aian office to return Sakhlia, who had been in Aian since 1858.[12]

The interpreters were involved in a range of diplomatic activities. These included community relations, in which the Russians tried to establish friendly and mutually beneficial trade relations with the Tlingit. Kalistrat and Niktopolian Gedeonov, who were also advocates for Tlingit interests, helped defuse potentially volatile or exploitative situations on a day-to-day basis.

In December 1825, Kalistrat Gedeonov investigated the shooting of a local Tlingit by a sentry. The Tlingit claimed they were night-fishing for herring at the stream mouth by the fort; the sentry thought they were attacking.

In August 1847, Niktopolian investigated the murder of a Tlingit man (CS 28/602:256). Part diplomat and part detective, he gathered evidence, and found and questioned witnesses. The nearest court that could handle such a criminal offence was in Yakutsk, in central Siberia, and the accused could not be sent there until next spring. In the meantime, Chief Manager Teben'kov transferred the accused to Kodiak.

In a report of 12 May 1847 (CS 28/370:57v) to the Main Office, Teben'kov credited Niktopolian for success in rescuing victims who were about to be killed as slave sacrifices or accused witches.

A long and detailed letter of 9 August 1851 (CS 32/615:445) from Chief Manager Rozenberg to the Sitka office describes the role of Niktopolian Gedeonov in explaining and negotiating contracts. In this case, company agent Peter Stepanovich Kostromitinov had asked permission to take two young Sitka women as servants with his family to California. One of them was a free Tlingit woman named Avdot'ia Shanakhtuchun. Great care was taken to spell out the obligations of both parties, and to prevent any kind of exploitation of the women.

Many letters deal with the role of the Tlingit interpreters in one of the major company activities, sea otter hunting. These letters give us an idea of what was involved in outfitting the hunts, and what inter-ethnic tensions existed among the Russians, Aleuts, and Tlingit. Kalistrat was assigned as interpreter on a hunt in Yakutat and Lituya Bay in spring and summer 1832. The hunt lasted for four months and involved thirty baidarkas based from a mother ship. Kalistrat was given a comfortable three-hatch baidarka. Many

Tlingit names are mentioned in the letters; the Russians, involved in a delicate balance of giving gifts to the leaders while remaining vigilant, did not entirely trust them. In exchange for Russian offers of friendship, the leaders agreed that their people would neither hinder the Aleuts while they hunted nor harass them in their night camps.

Dmitrii Larionov appears in a long memo of 22 March 1841 (CS 20/56:64) from Chief Manager Etolin to the Russian skipper Lindenberg, dealing with the political and multi-ethnic complications of sea otter hunting in the Yakutat area. The details, involving interaction among the Tlingit, Eyak, and Aleuts (probably Unangan as well as Kodiak Alutiit), are beyond our scope but illustrate the social dynamics that lie at the heart of the interpreter's role as cultural as well as linguistic translator, as mediator, counsellor, and peacemaker. One instruction was that the hunting party should always be accompanied by interpreter Larionov.

Various orders and reports over the years show how the Russians tried to establish friendly and mutually beneficial trade relations with the Tlingit. These letters include detailed descriptions of trade items and the names of many Tlingit individuals who received gifts, including boats and clothing. On 16 May 1834 (CS 11/309:294), Chief Manager Wrangell ordered an exploratory schooner voyage north along Chatham Strait and Lynn Canal with instructions to barter for furs as opportunities arose, in Angoon and Icy Strait. He also directed the expedition to locate the largest settlements and the coastal Tlingit trade routes, to discern their relationships to the interior, to learn everything possible about the rivers, the fur-bearing animals, and the Tlingit seasonal use of various sites in the area, and to determine if and when the Tlingit wished a company trading vessel to visit them.

It appears that the richest village in the Lynn Canal area was that of the Tlingit Kaagwaantaan leader Aanaxoots, who often visited Sitka and whom Wrangell knew personally. Forewarned of the arrival of the company schooner, he had promised to send a good pilot to meet it. Thus, the expedition was instructed to try to reach Aanaxoots' village and to treat him well. Assigned to the schooner was interpreter Niktopolian Gedeonov, who, Wrangell noted, would be useful not only in conversing with and questioning the Tlingit, but also in trade.

A succession of general managers directed staff to be friendly with the Tlingit, but to continue taking precautions against attack; they were also to receive daily intelligence reports on Tlingit activities from the interpreters. The 1841 and 1842 instructions from Chief Manager Etolin to Lieutenant Bartram, his next in command, are illustrative of this. In both years, before embarking on his inspection tours (which covered the distance from Atka, the Aleutian and Pribylov Islands, Kodiak, to Fort Ross, California), Etolin left instructions for Bartram that ranged from routine housekeeping to using "prudent caution" when foreign vessels visited port to making scientific observations of the magnetic needle and of tides. Bartram was also to keep abreast of all dealings with the Tlingit; to this end, he was to order interpreters Larionov and Gedeonov to report daily, morning and evening, regarding what was new among the Tlingit. He was to try to keep peace with the Tlingit, to prevent the company's people from quarrelling with them, especially on holidays, and to ensure that only a few people were permitted to leave the fort at one time. In 1841, warning Bartram that the Tlingit leaders would probably invite themselves as guests, Etolin permitted him to regale them with rum, etc., at company expense, per the accepted custom; but in 1842, though Bartram could still entertain them at company expense, he was not to regale them with rum (CS 20/439:341v, for 1841, and CS 21/439:341v, for 20 June 1842).

Thus, forty years after the events of 1802, the Russians were still apprehensive concerning the possibility of Tlingit attack, and justifiably so. The Tlingit remained economically, socially, and politically independent of the Russians; Tlingit actions were not always predictable to the Russians, who never completely understood their internal politics, agendas, and alliances. The Tlingit-Russian relationship was clearly an uneasy truce. This was compounded by the ever-present threat posed by British and American expansion, a sense of danger that increased with the Crimean War (1853-56).

Multi-ethnic and multi-national tensions and anxieties persisted among the Russians, Tlingit, Aleuts, and British and American traders. Treachery, real or imagined, is a recurring theme. The theme of Tlingit treachery thwarted by constant vigilance and good intelligence appears often in the correspondence. In two brief, enigmatic memos of 4 June 1832, one to Fleet Lieutenant Teben'kov and the other to his second-in-command, Khlebnikov, Wrangell reacted to news of a crisis received from sources in Yakutat. He informed Teben'kov and Khlebnikov that he would leave immediately for Yakutat, taking Niktopolian Gedeonov with him, and would send him back to Sitka with whatever information he himself had gathered in Yakutat. If an envelope arrived addressed to Wrangell, Khlebnikov was to unseal it and act according to its content. From Wrangell's subsequent report of 31 October 1832 (CS 9/480:389, Wrangell to the Main Office), we can infer that the emergency described above involved a Tlingit plot to attack the hunting party at sea, but that the attempt was thwarted and the scheme came to nothing. The expedition ended to the satisfaction of the Aleuts and Tlingit alike. Wrangell rewarded certain of the toyons.

A letter of 31 March 1839 from Kupreianov to the manager of Redoubt St. Dionysius, Ignatii Andreianov, refers to another instance in which a Tlingit threat was nullified. Andreianov had reported that the Stikine Tlingit had averted the evil intentions of the Kake Tlingit who arrived at the redoubt during the previous summer. In his letter, Kupreianov directed Andreianov to thank them in his name, regale the participants at company expense, and promise them some distinction when he himself arrived at Stikine (CS 17/72:73). This thwarting by the "friendly Indians" was probably part of an ongoing pattern of rivalry. Keeping the Russians in control (in preference to the HBC) fit the Stikines' agenda of protecting their own trade monopoly with the interior.

In such situations, the role of the interpreter is not always entirely clear. Even Niktopolian, consistently rewarded with bonuses and promotions, so praised for merit and success in preserving domestic tranquility, so repeatedly cited as indispensable, as at Stikine in the winter of 1834-35 (CS 11/7:426; CS 11/8:430; CS 11/11:433), came under suspicion at times. He seems to have fallen in and out of company management's good graces.

This process appears to begin in the mid-1830s. In the spring of 1835, Gedeonov was transferred to Sitka, and Dmitrii Larionov replaced him at Stikine (CS 12/28:19v; CS 12/30:23). Gedeonov was apparently based in Sitka from 1835 to fall 1837, but on 21 October 1837 he was ordered back to Stikine, with the comment that he had proven unworthy to occupy a position on Kupreianov's staff (CS 15/436:4v). On the same date, parallel orders were sent to the manager of Redoubt St. Dionysius (CS 15/437:5) and to the Sitka office (CS 15/442:8v). Gedeonov's transfer may have resulted from a personality conflict with Kupreianov, but it is safer not to speculate, as the paper trail is ambiguous.

By 31 March 1839, there seems to have been some reconciliation. Kupreianov wrote to the manager of Redoubt St. Dionysius, Ignatii Andreianov, that at the request of the interpreter Gedeonov, his son, Ivan, a minor, had been placed in the Sitka school at company expense. For such a boon, Kupreianov hoped that Gedeonov would try to serve the company honestly and conscientiously, seeing his children well established in his old age (CS 17/72:73). Subsequent references to Ivan Gedeonov in the correspondence document his rise and promising career as a naval officer. Unfortunately, he died young.

In a 9 July 1839 letter to Andreianov, Kupreianov recounted a rumour that the Yakutat Tlingit leader Chagu (Aleksandr), who claimed close kinship with interpreter Gedeonov, intended to liberate him from the Russians. Suspecting that Gedeonov probably knew of and agreed to this plan, Kupreianov directed Andreianov to warn him regarding the consequences of such cooperation. Should Chagu's attempt succeed, not only Gedeonov, but his whole clan and tribe would find the company a severe judge, one that punished such deeds whenever and wherever they occurred, and had every means to retrieve him from the Tlingit for correction (CS 17/416:395v).

## Larionov and Veniaminov

Dmitrii Larionov is the only RAC interpreter specifically identified with assisting in linguistic research and translation of religious materials. As noted above, Dmitrii first came to our attention as a footnote in the Tlingit-language work published by Ioann Veniaminov. This priest, mentioned in the routine RAC correspondence of the 1830s, would in time become renowned for his work in evangelism, theology, ethnology, and linguistics. Elevated as Bishop of Alaska, with the monastic name of Innocent, he eventually became Metropolitan of Moscow and was ultimately canonized by the Russian Orthodox Church as St. Innocent. Part of Veniaminov's success in the ethnographic and linguistic research he conducted during his relatively short stay in Sitka must be attributed to his interpreters, especially Dmitrii. We still know very little about their brief working relationship (which is not the case for Veniaminov's much longer collaboration with his Aleut helper Ivan Pan'kov, which resulted in brilliant publications in Aleut). It is interesting to consider the overlapping careers of Veniaminov and the man he identified as "the Sitka interpreter Dmitrii," because this further narrows the time during which the two men could have worked together. Veniaminov, born in 1797, was about eight years older than Dmitrii, born ca. 1805. During his first stay in Sitka, Veniaminov was in his late thirties and early forties; Dmitrii was in his early thirties. The chronology can be summarized as follows:

- 1834-35. Veniaminov maintained no significant contact with the Tlingit community at large. Dmitrii was presumably in Sitka, but this is not documented. In March 1835, Dmitrii was transferred to Redoubt St. Dionysius for two years.
- 1836. Veniaminov began to make contact with the Tlingit community. Presumably, his interpreter was Niktopolian Gedeonov. Veniaminov took a summer trip to Fort Ross.
- 1837. After an October trip to Redoubt St. Dionysius, Veniaminov returned to Sitka with Dmitrii Larionov. Niktopolian Gedeonov was transferred to the redoubt.

Therefore, Veniaminov and Dmitrii had one full year together in Sitka before Veniaminov's departure for Russia in November 1838. Veniaminov's Tlingit work was still in its relative infancy when he left the field for duties in Siberia.[13] We can only speculate what might have happened in the history of Tlingit literacy, literature, and theology had a sustained creative working relationship between Ioann Veniaminov and Dmitrii Larionov been possible. As brief as it was, perhaps Dmitrii's most important legacy was his fieldwork with Veniaminov, which left us some of the earliest written documentation of the Tlingit language.

## Stikine

The RAC correspondence records more than twenty years of involvement of Larionov and the Gedeonovs with the Stikine Tlingit, where Russian interests and anxieties were manifold.[14] Beyond the constant threat of conflict between the Tlingit and Russians, there were ongoing feuds among the Tlingit clans. At one time or another, the Stikine Tlingit were at war with Sitka, Kake, and Chilkat. Both the Russians and the British remained neutral in these conflicts, and attempted to negotiate peace. War disrupted trade; neutral as well as warring Tlingit were reluctant to travel for fear of attack or being caught in crossfire. The war between Sitka and Stikine lasted for over twenty years, with ongoing reprisals. Peace was officially made only in the twentieth century.

To their distrust of the Tlingit, the Russians added apprehension concerning the British presence. Their policy regarding the British was complex and changing: in 1834, their desire was to prevent them from sailing up the Stikine (CS 11/310:301), but in 1837, their policy seemed to be not to hinder them (CS 15/439:5v). Disputes between the rival RAC and HBC were resolved in 1839, when the Russians leased the Stikine fort and trading franchise to the HBC. In June 1840, they surrendered Redoubt St. Dionysius to the HBC, who renewed the lease until 1867, when Russia sold Alaska to the United States. The lease weathered the Crimean War (during which the RAC and HBC territories remained neutral) and major shakeups in both companies.

The British presence in the Stikine area for almost a generation before the sale of Alaska had both a short- and a long-range impact on the Tlingit. No one at the British fort spoke Tlingit; much of the time there was no interpreter, and about half of the workforce was Hawaiian. Several Tlingit mutinies occurred in the late 1840s, and the Russians found themselves acting as mediators between the British and the Tlingit.[15] Eventually, the British phased out their trading posts from Fort Vancouver on the Columbia to the Taku and Stikine in Southeast Alaska, finding it easier to consolidate in Victoria and send trading ships. The Tlingit often ignored the ships, preferring to remain free agents, trading with whomever they wished, voyaging to Victoria when they felt like trading, and playing the Russians and British against each other for the best price. But the Stikine Tlingit were also in a bind when the British pulled out: they were at war with all other surrounding Tlingit, and they needed the Russians as a source of European goods.

For all their efforts in the Stikine, however, the Russians' influence seems more significant in its absence than in its presence. The addition of the Stikine area to the British sphere of influence was to have a long-term impact on Tlingit culture. The southern Tlingit were increasingly oriented to Victoria and to English-language and Anglo-American culture, in contrast to the central and northern Tlingit, who remained Russian-oriented until 1867. We agree with Laura F. Klein's thesis that the British influence from

1840 to 1867 was crucial in shaping the development of Tlingit culture in the late nineteenth and early twentieth centuries. She argues that exposing the Stikine Tlingit to Anglo-American language and culture through trade and intermarriage equated to a process of "demystifying" them,[16] much as occurred for the interpreters described here through their experiences with Russian language and culture.

Unlike the Americans, neither the Russians nor the British were interested in changing the Tlingit, as they wished to trade with them, not to pacify or "civilize" them.[17] Thus, the traditional Tlingit lifestyle, language, and cultural patterns remained largely undisrupted. In the 1880s, however, Wrangell became the centre of the expanding American Presbyterian missionary effort; this, in combination with the gold rush and increasing interference in Tlingit lives by settlers and administrators, resulted in the collapse of the Tlingit monopoly on commerce and their subsequent loss of socio-political independence. It is significant that many of the Tlingit leaders of the late nineteenth and early twentieth centuries came from families that had bilingual and bicultural exposure to Anglo-Americans, including intermarriage, during the pre-transfer generation.[18] In contrast, the Russian linguistic and socio-political track became a dead end in the new order. After the 1880s, the Russian legacy, because of its recognition of Tlingit language and culture, appealed increasingly to the conservative members of Tlingit society, whereas the progressives were oriented to English-language education and the Presbyterian Church.[19] The subjects of our study had all died by 1867, and we have traced no living descendants at present, although we would expect some among the Tlingit and Kodiak Alutiit. The survival of Russian Orthodox spirituality in Alaska Native culture is another matter entirely, but lies beyond the scope of this chapter.[20]

As Frances Karttunen points out,[21] incompetent and unwilling interpreters did not last long, but the successful ones were able to live in two worlds. They were unconventional people who became bridges between their own indigenous world and another new and unfamiliar one. Perhaps "liminal" is a better word than "marginal" to describe these people who operate at the boundaries of two worlds. Like many of Karttunen's examples, our subjects are either Creole (Larionov) or Tlingit captives (the Gedeonovs). All three married Kodiak Aleut (Alutiit) women and had successful careers with the RAC. It is also interesting to speculate regarding the home language of all three interpreters: was it Russian as a common second language, did either parent speak his or her first language to the children, and did either spouse speak the other's language? To what extent were Larionov and the Gedeonovs trilingual, speaking Alutiiq as well as Tlingit and Russian?

Famous Tlingit men such as Katlian and Shakes have long been recognized and praised. We are pleased that through the RAC correspondence on day-to-day affairs we can begin to sketch in the names, faces, and personalities of hitherto unknown and unsung Tlingit people who were at the same time ordinary and extraordinary. These are not stereotypes of unseen, anonymous Indians lurking in ambush, but Tlingit individuals professionally involved in the daily affairs of business, diplomacy, and public relations, helping the Tlingit in Russian America and Russians in Tlingit America meet each other with a minimum of collision.

# Notes

## Introduction: Myth Understandings

1 Cartier believed that Asia was not far to the west when he was blocked in 1534 by the Lachine rapids, as they came to be known after René-Robert Cavelier de La Salle, a fur trader and discoverer of the Mississippi Delta, travelled west, in 1669, believing he could find a short-cut to China. The naming of the rapids as "La Chine," meaning China, is a derisive reference to La Salle's attempt. R. Douglas, *Meaning of Canadian City Names* (Ottawa: F.A. Acland, 1922); Robert McGee, *The Arctic Voyages of Martin Frobisher: An Elizabethan Venture* (Montreal and Kingston: McGill-Queen's University Press, 2001).

2 Peter Hulme, *Colonial Encounters: Europe and the Native Caribbean, 1492-1797* (London and New York: Methuen, 1986), 18, 21; Jonathan Hart, "Images of the Native in Renaissance Encounter Narratives," *ARIEL* 25, 4 (1994): 55-76.

3 Hulme, *Colonial Encounters*, 271, notes that the three "monstrous races" most prominent in Columbus' journal are first mentioned in Homer's *Iliad* (Amazons, 3.189, 6.186) and Herodotus' *Histories* (Anthropophagi, 4.18; Cynocephali, 4.191; Amazons, 4.110-17); for an introduction to Polo bibliography, see John Critchley, *Marco Polo's Book* (Aldershot, GB: Variorum, 1992).

4 It is not likely that the blind poet Homer saw the Amazons "with his own eyes."

5 Rachel Dogget, *New World of Wonders: European Images of the Americas, 1492-1900* (Washington, DC: Folger Shakespeare Library, 1992); Stephen Greenblatt, *Marvelous Possessions: The Wonder of the New World* (Chicago: University of Chicago Press, 1991); E.H. Gombrich, *Art and Illusion: A Study in the Psychology of Pictorial Representation* (London: Phaidon, 1968).

6 From the west, see R.T. Callaghan, "The Use of Simulation Models to Estimate Frequency and Location of Japanese Edo Period Wrecks along the Canadian Pacific Coast," *Canadian Journal of Archaeology* 27 (2003): 74-94; from the east, see the intriguing DNA evidence in Theodore G. Schurr, "Mitochondrial DNA and the Peopling of the New World," *American Scientist* 88 (May-June 2000): 246-53.

7 See, for example, the anthology of contact stories by Julia Blackburn, *The White Men: The First Responses of Aboriginal Peoples to the White Man* (London: Orbis, 1979).

8 Julie Cruikshank, "Oral Tradition and Oral History: Reviewing Some Issues," *Canadian Historical Review* 75, 3 (1994): 412; John Sutton Lutz, "What Connected at Contact? Comparing Aboriginal and European Contact Narratives from the Pacific Coast" (paper presented to the Canadian Historical Association Conference, Quebec City, May 2001).

9 Mary Louise Pratt, *Imperial Eyes: Travel Writing and Transculturation* (London: Routledge, 1992).

10 R.G. Collingwood, *The Idea of History* (1946; repr., New York and London: Oxford University Press, 1956).

11 Natalie Zemon Davis, "Polarities, Hybridities: What Strategies for Decentring?" in *Decentring the Renaissance: Canada and Europe in Multidisciplinary Perspective, 1500-1700*, eds. Germaine Warkentin and Carolyn Podruchney (Toronto: University of Toronto Press, 2001), 21-31. She notes these strategies are not mutually exclusive.

12 The meeting, held at a retreat centre north of Victoria, British Columbia, was the centrepiece of a larger colloquium called "Worlds in Collision: Critically Analyzing Aboriginal and European Contact Narratives," hosted by the Centre for Studies in Religion and Society at the University of Victoria in February 2002. The chapters here were much enriched by the other presentations and questions from the colloquium.

13 E.H. Carr, quoted in Greg Dening, *Performances* (Chicago/Melbourne: University of Chicago Press/Melbourne University Press, 1996), 72.

14 Mikhail Bakhtin, *The Dialogic Imagination: Four Essays by M.M. Bakhtin*, ed. Michael Holquist, trans. Caryl Emmerson and Michael Holquist (Austin: University of Texas, 1996).

15 Stephen Greenblatt, *Marvelous Possessions,* 119; Denning, *Performances;* Nicholas Thomas, *Entangled Objects: Exchange, Material Culture and Colonialism in the Pacific* (Cambridge, MA: Harvard University Press, 1991).

16 See, especially, I.S. MacLaren, "Exploration/Travel Literature and the Evolution of the Author," *International Journal of Canadian Studies* 5 (Spring 1992): 39-68.

17 L.G. Moses, "Performative Traditions in American Indian History," in *A Companion to American Indian History,* eds. Philip Deloria and Neil Salisbury (Malden, MA: Blackwell, 2002), 194.

18 Quoted in Terence Turner, "Ethno-ethnohistory: Myth and History in Native South American Representations of Contact with Western Society," in *Rethinking History and Myth: Indigenous South American Perspectives on the Past,* ed. Jonathan D. Hill (Urbana: University of Illinois Press, 1988), 253.

19 Dening, *Performances,* 74; Richard White calls these "creative and expedient misunderstandings," in *The Middle Ground: Indians, Empires and Republics in the Great Lakes Region, 1650-1815* (Cambridge: Cambridge University Press, 1991), x.

20 Greenblatt, *Marvelous Possessions,* 145.

21 Lewis Hyde, *Trickster Makes This World: Mischief, Myth and Art* (New York: Farrar, Straus, and Giroux, 1998), 264, 300; Eric Hinderaker, "Translation and Cultural Brokerage," in *A Companion to American Indian History,* eds. Deloria and Salisbury, 357-75.

22 Hyde, *Trickster Makes This World,* 299; see also the similar Lushootseed story told in 1923 by Chief William Shelton at Tulalip, recorded in Vi Hilbert, *Haboo: Native American Stories from Puget Sound* (Seattle: University of Washington Press, 1985).

23 Dening, *Performances,* 45, 167.

24 The classic statement is Homi Bhabha, "Signs Taken for Wonders: Questions of Ambivalence and Authority under a Tree outside Delhi, May 1817," in *Europe and Its Others: Proceedings of the Essex Conference on the Sociology of Literature,* eds. Francis Barker et al. (Colchester, GB: University of Essex, 1985), 89-106; Roland Barthes, quoted in D. Porter, *Haunted Journeys: Desire and Transgression in European Travel Writing* (Princeton: Princeton University Press, 1991), 6-7.

25 Bernard Smith, *European Vision and the South Pacific, 1768-1850: A Study in the History of Art and Ideas* (Oxford: Clarendon Press, 1960).

26 We can see this in the determinants of success or failure in the French settlements along the St. Lawrence, the British settlements in Massachusetts and Virginia, and the Spanish settlements along the Florida coast: J.E. Kicza, "First Contacts," in *A Companion to American Indian History,* eds. Deloria and Salisbury, 27-45.

27 Jonathan D. Hill, "Myth and History," in *Rethinking History and Myth,* ed. Hill, 6; M. Holden, "Making All the Crooked Ways Straight: The Satirical Portrait of Whites in Coast Salish Folklore," *Journal of American Folklore* 89 (1976): 271-93.

28 Pratt, *Imperial Eyes,* 15-37.

29 Thomas King, *The Truth about Stories: A Native Narrative* (Toronto: Anansi, 2003), 9.

30 Hill, "Myth and History," 14-15; Michel Foucault, *History of Sexuality,* vol. 2, *Uses of Pleasure* (New York: Vintage, 1977), 9.

### Chapter 1: Close Encounters of the First Kind

1 Marshall McLuhan, *The Gutenberg Galaxy* (Toronto: University of Toronto Press, 1962), 50.

2 These stories are from a keynote address given by Barre Toelken at the Alaska Conference on Native Arts in America; a revised version was published in Suzi Jones, ed., *Native Arts Issues* (Anchorage; Alaska State Council on the Arts, 1982), 8-13. My quotations are taken from his address.

3  Cassirer uses this term throughout *Language and Myth* (New York: Dover, 1944).
4  I first read about "not ants, but ants" in an essay by Scott Momaday, who identified the individual only as a friend. Larry Evers said he thought it might be Barre Toelken, who confirmed to me that it was indeed his story.
5  Umberto Eco's sly remark about lying is in his *Theory of Semiotics* (Bloomington: Indiana University Press, 1976), 7.
6  Wilde's essay was gathered together with some others and published by Wilde in a book titled *Intentions* (London: James R. Osgood, McIlvaine and co., 1891)
7  The definition of infinity has several sources. I heard it from my mother; and Eli Maor attributes it to an unidentified schoolboy in *To Infinity and Beyond: A Cultural History of the Infinite* (Princeton, NJ: Princeton University Press, 1991).
8  E.L. Doctorow made his remark in an interview. Joachim Fiebach, "Dimensions of Theatricality in Africa," *Research in African Literature* 30, 4 (Winter 1999): 187-201. Paul Veyne, *Did the Greeks Believe in Their Myths?* trans. Paula Wissing (Chicago: University of Chicago Press, 1988).
9  Lewis Hyde, *Trickster Makes This World: Mischief, Myth and Art* (New York: Farrar, Straus and Giroux, 1998), 209.
10  Judge McEachern's comments are recorded in the transcripts of the *Delgamuukw* trial (1987-91), finally decided (in favour of the plaintiffs) by the Supreme Court of Canada on 11 December 1997. *BC Studies* devoted a special issue to the trial and judgment; and a book of excerpts, cartoons, and commentary from the trial was compiled by Don Monet and Skanu'u (Ardythe Wilson), *Colonialism on Trial: Indigenous Land Claims and the Gitksan and Wet'suwet'en Sovereignty Case* (Philadelphia: New Society, 1992). Leslie Pinder wrote a powerful monograph titled *The Carriers of No: After the Land Claims Trial* (Vancouver: Lazara Press, 1991), and Dara Culhane a scholarly study, *The Pleasure of the Crown: Anthropology, Law and First Nations* (Burnaby, BC: Talonbooks, 1998).
11  *The Educated Imagination* is the title of a book by Frye (from his Massey Lectures) published by the Canadian Broadcasting Corporation in 1963.
12  Frye's comment is from his Notebooks for 1946-48, first published in the *Northrop Frye Newsletter* 8, 2 (Fall, 2000): 3; McEachern's comments are recorded in the transcripts of the *Delgamuukw* trial (1987-91).
13  The remarks by Halldor Laxness are from "What Was Before the Saga: A Jubilee Discourse," published in the *American Scandinavian Review* (1974).
14  The phrase "seeing with an innocent eye" is adapted from John Ruskin's discussion of the "innocence of the eye" in *The Elements of Drawing* (1856), elaborated by E.H. Gombrich in *Art and Illusion: A Study in the Psychology of Pictorial Representation* (London: Phaidon, 1968).
15  The story of Mediik was told during the *Delgamuukw* trial. A version of the story can be found in Walter Wright and Will Robinson, *Men of Medeek* (Kitimat, BC: Northern Sentinel Press, 1962).

## Chapter 2: First Contact as a Spiritual Performance

1  Juan Perez, "Diaro," 19-20 July 1774, in Herbert Beals, ed. and trans., *Juan Perez on the Northwest Coast: Six Documents of His Expedition in 1774* (Portland: Oregon Historical Society, 1989), 77.
2  I am excluding the Russian contacts in what is now Alaska, which followed a different trajectory.
3  Estebán José Martinez, "Diaro," 20-21 July, in Beals, *Juan Perez*, 101.
4  Greg Dening, *Performances* (Chicago/Melbourne: University of Chicago Press/Melbourne University Press, 1996), 108-9; I am indebted to this work of Dening's for the suggestion of these encounters as "performance pieces." Readers familiar with Judith Butler's work will see the potential to push "performance" in the sense I am using here, to "performative subversions" where Native and newcomer are created through their interaction. I have not done this here but develop this idea with respect to racial identities in "Making Race in British Columbia: Power, Race and the Importance of Place," in *Power and Place in the North American West*, eds. Richard White and John Findlay (Seattle: University of Washington Press, 1999), 61-86; for Butler's work, see *Gender Trouble: Feminism and the Subversion of Identity* (New York and London: Routledge, 1999).

5 Admittedly, the word "spiritual" fits imperfectly, since the distinction between the spiritual and non-spiritual world probably did not exist in indigenous thinking, nor would it have for many Europeans at the time; it is an approximation, referring to the more "immaterial" features of their world views. Although located on the northeastern shore of the Pacific Ocean, ethnographic convention calls this cultural area the Pacific Northwest, indicating its relationship to the United States of America.

6 The phrase in quotes is from Terence Turner, "Ethno-ethnohistory: Myth and History in Native South American Representations of Contact with Western Society," in *Rethinking History and Myth: Indigenous South American Perspectives on the Past,* ed. Jonathan D. Hill (Urbana: University of Illinois Press, 1988), 239. See also the discussion of "contact zone" on p. 4, this volume.

7 Mikhail Bakhtin, in Tzvetan Todorov, *Mikhail Bakhtin: The Dialogical Principle,* trans. Wlad Godzich, vol. 13 of *Theory and History of Literature* (Minneapolis: University of Minnesota, 1984), 109.

8 Jonathan D. Hill, "Myth and History," in *Rethinking History and Myth,* ed. Hill, 6.

9 A regional example is E.O.S. Scholefield, *British Columbia from the Earliest Times to the Present* (Vancouver: S.S. Clarke, 1914).

10 Henry Reynolds, *The Other Side of the Frontier: An Interpretation of the Aboriginal Response to the Invasion and Settlement of Australia* (Townsville, Australia: James Cook University, 1981); K.R. Howe, *The Loyalty Islands: A History of Culture Contacts, 1840-1900* (Honolulu: University Press of Hawaii, 1977); Robin Fisher, *Contact and Conflict: Indian European Relations in British Columbia, 1774-1890* (1977; repr., Vancouver: UBC Press, 1992); Bruce Trigger, "Early Responses to European Contact: Romantic versus Rationalistic Interpretations," *Journal of American History* 77, 4 (March 1991): 1195-1215.

11 Hill, "Myth and History," 2.

12 Marshall Sahlins, *Historical Metaphors and Mythical Realities: Structure in the Early History of the Sandwich Islands Kingdom* (Ann Arbor: University of Michigan Press, 1981); Gananath Obeyesekere, *The Apotheosis of Captain Cook: European Mythmaking in the Pacific* (Princeton, NJ: Princeton University Press, 1992). Evaluations of this debate can be found in Robert Borofsky, "Cook, Lono, Obeyesekere, and Sahlins," *Current Anthropology* 38, 2 (1997): 255-82; Dening, *Performances;* and Nicholas Thomas, "Partial Texts: Representation, Colonialism and Agency in Pacific History," *Journal of Pacific History* 25, 2 (1990): 139-58.

13 Other examples would be Christopher Miller and George R. Hammell, "A New Perspective on Indian-White Contact: Cultural Symbols and Colonial Trade," *Journal of American History* 73, 2 (September 1986): 311-28; Gerald Sider, "When Parrots Learn to Talk and Why They Can't: Domination, Deception and Self-Deception in Indian-White Relations," *Comparative Studies in Society and History* 29 (1987): 3-23.

14 Marius Barbeau Papers, B234, file 12, Canadian Museum of Civilization, Ottawa, quoted in Robert Galois, ed., *A Voyage to the North West Side of America: The Journals of James Colnett, 1786-89* (Vancouver: UBC Press, 2004), 269-70.

15 American Philosophical Society, Boas Papers, Microfilm Reel 3, No. 35, William Beynon, 1939, quoted in Galois, *A Voyage to the North West,* 270-72.

16 There are no good overviews of regional spiritual worlds, but some recent studies have focused on individual Aboriginal groups. See Jay Miller, *Lushootseed Culture and the Shamanic Odyssey: An Anchored Radiance* (Lincoln: University of Nebraska Press, 1999); Crisca Bierwert, *Brushed by Cedar, Living by the River: Coast Salish Figures of Power* (Tucson: University of Arizona Press, 1999); for the Nuu-chah-nulth, see Philip Drucker, *The Northern and Central Nootkan Tribes,* Bureau of Ethnology Bulletin 144 (Washington, DC: Smithsonian Institution, 1951).

17 See, for an example, John J. Cove and George F. MacDonald, eds., *Tsimshian Narratives, Collected by Marius Barbeau and William Beynon* (Ottawa: Canadian Museum of Civilization, 1987).

18 There are, of course, good reasons why so little attention has been paid to Aboriginal contact narratives: they are difficult to find, and their content, usually linked to the spiritual, is difficult to interpret. There are also important methodological issues relating to

translation, feedback, editorial insertions, and general attempts to yank the chain of gullible anthropologists. One technique to reduce the idiosyncratic and external influences is to compare a large collection of accounts, and to this end I am drawing from a collection of nearly two hundred. See John Sutton Lutz, "What Connected at Contact? Comparing Aboriginal and European Contact Narratives from the Pacific Coast" (paper presented to the Canadian Historical Association Conference, Quebec City, May 2001).

19 C.M. Tate, interviewed by J.S. Matthews, *Early Vancouver: Narratives of Pioneers of Vancouver, B.C.,* vol. 2 (Vancouver, 1933), 306; G.M. Sproat, *Scenes and Studies of Savage Life* (London: Smith, Elder, 1868), 139-42.

20 Scholefield, *British Columbia from the Earliest Times,* 82; the story of the copper canoe is from José Mariano Moziño, *Noticias de Nutka: An Account of Nootka Sound in 1792,* trans. I.H.W. Engstrand (Seattle: University of Washington Press, 1991), 61.

21 Malachat Peter to Mrs. Mary Amos, Add MSS 870, box 2, vol. 23, Philip Drucker Field Notes, British Columbia Archives, Victoria, BC. Drucker notes that modern Nuu-chah-nulth speak of four deities, the Above Chief, Horizon Chief, Land Chief, and Undersea Chief.

22 King Journal in J.C. Beaglehole, ed., *The Journals of Captain James Cook on His Voyages of Discovery* (Rochester, NY: Boydell Press, 1999), appendix 3, 1394-95. Spelling from original.

23 In Matthews, *Early Vancouver,* 2:49.

24 Louis Miranda and Philip Joe, "How the Squamish Remember George Vancouver," in *From Maps to Metaphors: The Pacific World of George Vancouver,* eds. Robin Fisher and Hugh Johnston (Vancouver: UBC Press, 1993), 3-5.

25 Three versions of a Tlingit encounter with Jean-François de La Pérouse are in Nora Marks Dauenhauer and Richard Dauenhauer, eds., *Haa Shuká, Our Ancestors: Tlingit Oral Narratives* (Seattle: University of Washington Press, 1987), 293-309, 434-42; Franz Boas, *Chinook Texts* (Washington, DC: Smithsonian Institution Bureau of Ethnology, 1894), 275-78; Wendy Wickwire, "To See Ourselves as the Other's Other: Nlaka'pamux Contact Narratives," *Canadian Historical Review* 75, 1 (1994): 1-20.

26 Thomas F. McIlwraith, *Bella Coola Indians* (Toronto: University of Toronto Press, 1948), 56; Catharine McClellan, "Indian Stories about the First Whites in Northwestern North America," in *Ethnohistory in Southwestern Alaska and Southern Yukon: Method and Content,* ed. Margaret Lantis (Lexington: University Press of Kentucky, 1970), 103-33; William Beynon, in Marius Barbeau Fieldnotes, MS-2101, Reel A1415, B-F9.0.15, British Columbia Archives; personal communication from Bill Poser, 2002.

27 See James Teit, *The Shuswap,* vol. 2 of *The Jesup North Pacific Expedition,* ed. Franz Boas. Memoir of the American Museum of Natural History (New York: G.E. Stechert, 1909), 451.

28 Anthony Pagden, *European Encounters with the New World: From Renaissance to Romanticism* (London and New Haven: Yale University, 1993), 24.

29 Quoted in Herbert Beals, ed. and trans., *For Honor and Country: The Diary of Bruno de Hezeta* (Portland: Oregon Historical Society, 1985), 30.

30 Definition of motet from Oxford English Dictionary, http://dictionary.oed.com; Crespi quoted in George Butler Griffin, ed., *The California Coast: A Bilingual Edition of Documents from the Sutro Collection* (Norman: University of Oklahoma Press, 1969), 229.

31 Quoted in John Kendrick, *The Men with Wooden Feet* (Toronto: NC Press, 1986), 17-18; these acts of possession have been analyzed by Patricia Seed, *Ceremonies of Possession in Europe's Conquest of the New World, 1492-1690* (Cambridge, MA: Cambridge University Press, 1995).

32 R.S. Sugirtharajah, "Biblical Studies after the Empire: From a Colonial to a Postcolonial Mode of Interpretation," in *The Postcolonial Bible,* ed. R.S. Sugirtharajah (Sheffield: Sheffield Academic Press, 1998), 103. Thanks to Harold Coward for this reference.

33 Ibid.

34 Proverbs 25:2.

35 "The Instructions" to James Cook, quoted in Beaglehole, *The Journals of Captain James Cook,* ccxxiii; the Spanish instructions enjoined Perez, de Hezeta, Quadra, and others to treat the Aboriginal people "affectionately," with no force to be used against them except in self-defence. See Beals, *For Honor,* 31, 78.

36  Reginald Horsman, *Race and Manifest Destiny: The Origins of American Racial Anglo-Saxonism* (Cambridge: Harvard University Press, 1981); Audrey Smedley, *Race in North America* (Boulder, CO: Westview Press, 1993), 41-71.

37  The fact that a world view has a spiritual component does not necessarily imply that it will be peaceful. Everything depends on the local configuration of spirituality. Examples of aggressive spirituality would be the sixteenth- and seventeenth-century Spanish approaches to the indigenous peoples of Latin America or the Hawaiian interpretation of Cook.

38  Beals, *For Honor*, 77-78.

39  Kenneth Owens, ed., *The Wreck of the Sv. Nikolai: Two Narratives of the First Russian Expedition to the Oregon Country 1808-1810* (Portland: Western Imprints, 1985), 69-73.

40  Albert Regan, "Some Traditions of West Coast Indians" *Proceedings of the Utah Academy of Sciences* 86 (1934): 73-93.

41  Leland Donald, *Aboriginal Slavery on the Northwest Coast of North America* (Berkeley: University of California Press, 1997). In explaining his justification for not exacting reprisals on the Quinault, de Hezeta wrote of the practical difficulties of a punitive expedition but also referred to the instructions he had: "not to give offense" to the indigenous people "except in the case of the need for self defense," which had passed. The spirituality of the Europeans here helped prevent a round of reprisals. Beals, *For Honor*, 78.

42  Marilyn Bennett, *Indian Fishing and Its Cultural Importance in the Fraser River System* (Vancouver: Fisheries Service, Department of the Environment, Canada, and the Union of BC Indian Chiefs, ca. 1973), 24.

43  Incidentally, I have found no indication that the Europeans were aware of the cause of their pleasant reception or that they attempted to play up their association with the spirit world. On the contrary, they took pains to describe to Aboriginal people, with the limited means they had to communicate, just where Europeans had come from: "Boston Land" or "King George Land." However, subsequent Europeans, including fur traders and especially missionaries, used Aboriginal beliefs regarding the link to the supernatural to manipulate Aboriginal people.

44  Trigger, "Early Responses."

45  For the persistence of these eighteenth-century ideas into the twenty-first century, see Thomas Flanagan, *Our Home or Native Land?* (Montreal and Kingston: McGill-Queen's University Press, 2000); for a critique of the European myth of the lazy Indian, see John Sutton Lutz, *Makuk and the Myth of the Lazy Indian: Aboriginal Work and Welfare in British Columbia* (Vancouver: UBC Press, forthcoming in 2007).

46  See, for example, the Okanagan story told by Harry Robinson, in ch. 7 of this volume.

47  Dening, *Performances*, 78; R. Cole Harris, *The Resettlement of British Columbia: Essays on Colonialism and Geographical Change* (Vancouver: UBC Press, 1997); Frances Densmore, *Music of the Indians of British Columbia* (New York: Da Capo Press, 1972).

48  See Chamberlin, ch. 1, this volume.

49  Drucker, *Northern and Central Nootkan Tribes*, 144, 452.

50  Marius Barbeau fieldnotes, MS-2101, Reel A1415, British Columbia Archives, 908-13, 1199-1202, 1219.

51  Michael Harkin, *The Heiltsuks: Dialogues of Culture and History on the Northwest Coast* (Lincoln: University of Nebraska Press, 1997); Brett Christopher, *Positioning the Missionary: John Booth Good and the Confluence of Cultures in Nineteenth-Century British Columbia* (Vancouver: UBC Press, 2000); Sergei Kan, *Memory Eternal: Tlingit Culture and Russian Orthodox Christianity through Two Centuries* (Seattle: University of Washington Press, 1999).

52  The best discussion of the transformation of meaning in intercultural exchange is in Nicholas Thomas, *Entangled Objects: Exchange, Material Culture and Colonialism in the Pacific* (Cambridge, MA: Harvard University Press, 1991).

53  Moziño, *Noticias*, xxix, 66; the story about the axe is recorded for the Haida in W.H. Collison, *In the Wake of the War Canoe* (London: Seeley, Service, 1915), 120; the same story, told of the Tsimshian, appears in Marius Barbeau fieldnotes, MS-2101, Reel A415, British Columbia Archives, 908-9; Horatio Hale, ed., "The 'Jargon' or Trade-Language of Oregon," in *Ethnography and Philology*, vol. 6 of Charles Wilkes, *Narrative of the United States Exploring Expedition. During the years 1838, 1839, 1840, 1841, 1842*, 5 vols. and atlas

(1844; repr., Ridgewood, NJ: Gregg Press, 1968); for Chinese coins as part of northwest coast ceremonial objects, see Grant Keddie, "The Question of Asiatic Objects on the North Pacific Coast of America: Historic or Prehistoric?" *Contributions to Human History* 3 (March 1990): 1-26.

54 Diamond Jenness, *The Faith of a Coast Salish Indian*, ed. Wilson Duff, British Columbia Museum Memoirs in Anthropology, no. 3 (Victoria: British Columbia Provincial Museum Department of Education, 1955); Irving Goldman, "The Alkatcho Carrier of British Columbia," in *Acculturation in Seven American Indian Tribes*, ed. R. Linton (Gloucester, MA: Peter Smith, 1963), 375; Catharine McClellan, *My Old People Say: An Ethnographic Survey of Southern Yukon Territory* (Ottawa: National Museum of Man, 1975), 6.

55 Hill, "Myth and History," 6; Turner, "Ethno-ethnohistory," 235-36.

### Chapter 3: Reflections on Indigenous History and Memory

1 R.G. Collingwood, *The Idea Of History* (New York and London: Oxford University Press, 1956). See, in particular, pt. 5, "Epilegomena," 205-334.

2 Dominick LaCapra, "Rethinking Intellectual History and Reading Texts," *History and Theory* 19, 3 (1980): 247.

3 Dominick LaCapra, "History, Language, and Reading: Waiting for Crillon," *American Historical Review* 100, 3 (June 1995): 803.

4 Clifford Geertz, "Thick Descriptions: Toward an Interpretive Theory of Culture," in *The Interpretation of Cultures*, ed. Geertz (New York: Basic Books, 1973), 13.

5 In case my efforts were too opaque, this paragraph is meant, among other things, to indicate my intellectual debt to and respect for the writings of Mary Louise Pratt, Wendy Wickwire, Julie Cruikshank, Richard White, Arthur Ray, Elizabeth Vibert, Wayne Suttles, Clifford Geertz, and Marshall Sahlins. I owe other debts to the host of Aboriginal elders and intellectuals who have shared their knowledge with me (as well as those who have already passed away but saw fit to share aspects of their knowledge in forms, such as cassette tapes and anthropologists' archived field notes, that could be accessed by subsequent generations). Without these generous people, the discussion presented here would have been impossible. In particular I am indebted to Archie Charles, Pierre Ayessick, Jimmie Charlie, Patrick Charlie, Bill Pat-Charlie, George Chehalis, Andy Commodore, Amy Cooper, Edna Douglas, Sam Douglas, Rosaleen George, Matilda Gutierrez, Albert "Sonny" McHalsie, Herb Joe, Robert Joe, Albert Louie, Vi Hilbert, Hugh Kelly, Edmund Lorenzetto, Old Pierre, Clarence Pennier, Hank Pennier, Nancy Phillips, Gwen Point, Steven Point, Wes Sam, Robert Thomas, and Amy Victor. I am also indebted to the inspirational scholarship of Homer Barnett, Criska Bierwert, Brian Dippie, Wilson Duff, Sally Snyder, R. Cole Harris, Charles Hill-Tout, Bruce Miller, Jay Miller, and Dianne Newell. My understanding of Coast Salish history and culture has also been influenced by, and benefited from, conversations with Mark Ebert, Bruce Miller, Michael Kew, Gordon Mohs, David Schaepe, and Brian Thom. For their helpful comments on earlier drafts of this chapter, I am grateful to Sonny McHalsie, Jim Miller, M. Teresa Carlson, and Ken Coates. Any errors of fact or interpretation are mine alone.

6 From an indigenous perspective, 1846 is rather meaningless as a definition of contact. It represents a political and administrative change in European imperialism, but little direct difference in Aboriginal people's lives. In that year, following the division of what had previously been the jointly claimed US/British Oregon Territory, Britain assumed unilateral sovereignty over what is now British Columbia.

7 I refer primarily to my own recent and ongoing experience as an expert witness in Aboriginal rights litigation, as well as observations I made between 1992 and 2001 while I acted as historian and advisor to the Stó:lō Nation, which is engaged in contemporary treaty negotiations.

8 See, for example, the discussion of the second violation late-Victorian-era Canadian women underwent at the hands of the courts when they attempted to accuse men of rape, only to find that they and their way of viewing situations were put of trial instead of the rapist. Karen Dubinsky, *Improper Advances: Rape and Heterosexual Conflict in Ontario, 1880-1920* (Chicago: University of Chicago Press, 1993).

9   Wayne Suttles, "Private Knowledge, Morality, and Social Class among the Coast Salish," in *Coast Salish Essays*, ed. Wayne Suttles (1972; repr., Vancouver: Talonbooks, 1987), 6. The Coast Salish consultants with whom I have worked have described and defined matters of class and status in largely identical terms.

10   I am indebted to Bruce Miller for suggesting this term to explain the role of prominent men who, through some remarkable act, establish themselves and their descendants as supra-family leaders of particular settlement or tribal collectives.

11   See, for example, the accounts of Swaneset's travels as described by Old Pierre in Diamond Jenness, *Faith of a Coast Salish Indian*, ed. Wilson Duff, British Columbia Museum Memoirs in Anthropology, no. 3 (Victoria: British Columbia Provincial Museum Department of Education, 1955).

12   I develop this last point in much greater detail in "The Power of Place, the Problem of Time" (PhD diss., Department of History, University of British Columbia, 2003).

13   I am indebted to John Sutton Lutz for suggesting the term "history wars" as a way to describe the historically based conflicts in Coast Salish society.

14   Although it is helpful to conceive of people as sources of history and historical legitimacy (vis-à-vis the role of the written text in Western society), perhaps it would be more accurate to say that within Coast Salish society, people, that is, certain properly trained people, are regarded more as conduits of history.

15   The most common Central Coast Salish term for the Creator is Chíchelh Siyá:m (literally, respected wealthy leader up above), but this term, as Wayne Suttles has shown, was probably derived from Chinook Jargon and introduced by missionaries. See Wayne Suttles, ed., *Katzie Ethnographic Notes*, British Columbia Provincial Museum Memoirs in Anthropology, no. 2 (Victoria: British Columbia Provincial Museum, 1955), 6; Wayne Suttles, "The Plateau Prophet Dance among the Coast Salish," in *Coast Salish Essays*, ed. Suttles, 164, 178, 185-87; Jenness, *Faith of a Coast Salish Indian*, 88; Wilson Duff, The Upper Stalo, British Columbia Provincial Museum Memoirs in Anthropology, no. 1 (Victoria: British Columbia Provincial Museum, 1952), 119-20. The earlier, and I believe more indigenous, concept of the Creator is captured in the now obsolete term Scha-us (literally "Great First"). The earliest discussion of the term Scha-us, and an account of how missionaries sought to replace this word and aspects of the ideas informing its meaning, can be found in the papers of an early Hudson's Bay Company employee (and husband of a Coast Salish woman), J.W. McKay. See his "Indian Tribes, Correspondence 1881, regarding Festivals, Traditions etc.," Add MSS 1917, J.W. McKay Papers, British Columbia Archives, Victoria, BC.

16   Rosaleen George and Elizabeth Herrling, personal communication on a number of occasions between 1995 and 2001.

17   In their language, this was expressed as "Xólhmet te mekw stam s'i:wes te selsila:lh chet." Rosaleen George and Elizabeth Herrling, interviewed by Sonny McHalsie, 16 November 2002.

18   Jenness, *Faith of a Coast Salish Indian*, 77.

19   Ibid., 78.

20   Popularly known among many non-Natives as Bigfoot.

21   As Wayne Suttles has documented, the Coast Salish draw no meaningful distinction between the reality of what westerners might regard as natural and supernatural animals. A sasquatch is just as real to Coast Salish people as a bear, though it is recognized to be of a different nature. See Wayne Suttles, "On the Cultural Track of the Sasquatch," in *Coast Salish Essays*, ed. Suttles, 73-99.

22   I did not tape-record this sqwelqwel. Rather, the dialogue presented here is based on notes I made of the story following the dinner. The words are those of the original speaker as best as I can remember them.

23   Spirits are more active at night than in the day. Fires and smoke are portals through which ancestral spirits can observe and communicate with the living.

24   Suttles, "Private Knowledge," 3-14.

25   Fisher's critique is contained in a special issue of *BC Studies* which was dedicated to assessing McEachern's decision. Scholarly appraisal was as critical of the chief justice's improper use and interpretation of historical evidence and methodologies as of his dismissal of anthropology and oral history. Robin Fisher, "Judging History: Reflections on the Reasons

for Judgment in *Delgamuukw v. B.C."* in "Anthropology and History in the Courts (the Gitksan and Wet'suwet'en Case)," ed. Bruce G. Miller, special issue, *BC Studies* 95 (Autumn 1992): 43-54.

26 See Charles Hill-Tout, "Ethnological Studies of the Mainland Halkomelem, a Division of the Salish of British Columbia," *72nd Report of the British Association for the Advancement of Science for 1902* (London, 1903), 416-41. Also Sally Snyder, "Skagit Society and Its Existential Basis: An Ethnofolkloristic Reconstruction" (PhD diss., Department of Anthropology, University of Washington, 1964). Hill-Tout and other early ethnographers recorded that historical experts were able to trace their genealogy back seven or eight generations at most, a feat they considered highly remarkable. Sally Snyder, in commenting on this fact and its continuance among the Coast Salish people she consulted in the 1960s, speculated that perhaps the Coast Salish concept of history was cyclical, beginning anew every eight generations, and that as a result it was culturally impossible for there to be a history that predated eight generations. This is an interesting idea that requires further research and contemplation. Somewhat supporting it is the fact that the Halkomelem language has distinctive kin words for people removed up to seven generations in either direction from the speaker. That is, there is a word for great-great-great-great-grandparent as well as great-great-great-great-grandchild. Significantly, the terms are the same for each of these relations. The important thing is not whether one is a descendant or an ancestor, but rather, how far removed one is from the person who is speaking.

27 I have chosen not to name the Aboriginal people who provided me with critiques of John Doe's historical narratives. I want people to focus on the issues associated with the indigenous presentation and critique of historical accounts, and not the personalities involved in this particular case. It is important to explain, however, that the discussion and quotes in the preceding paragraphs come from four different Aboriginal people who were among the nine elders and cultural experts I interviewed in the early and mid-1990s as I tried to learn more about John Doe's narratives. One was a middle-aged man who had been designated by the political leadership as a cultural authority and spokesperson. The second was a respected spiritual leader involved in both the winter dance and the masked dance. The third was a prominent senior politician. The fourth was a widely respected female elder and fluent Halq'eméylem speaker who was also a member of John Doe's extended family.

28 Neither shaman nor recognized tribal historians ever fully reveal the details of their knowledge to anyone except their acolytes, unless they absolutely have to do so in the context of discrediting a competing narrative. To take such a step would not only weaken the spiritual integrity of the information, but, as John Doe implied, provide one's rivals with valuable material that could be used against one's own family or community. For example, a shaman would not reveal the sacred incantations used to effect a cure, just as a historian would provide his audience only with those aspects of a genealogical record that would enhance the family's claim. Knowledge of a great-aunt who had been captured, made a slave, and then ransomed, for example, might be withheld lest other families with competing claims to hereditary prerogatives should use such information to discredit the first family's honour, thereby weakening its claim.

29 Franz Boas, "Indian Tribes of the Lower Fraser River," in *64th Report of the British Association for the Advancement of Science for 1894* (London: British Association for the Advancement of Science, 1894), 454-63.

30 "A Map of America between the latitudes 40 and 70 North and Longitudes 80 and 150 west Exhibiting the Principal Trading Stations of the North West Company" (drawn by David Thompson, but uncredited), NMC 6763, Library and Archives Canada, Ottawa.

31 See, for example, "Charcoal Sketch by C.O. Phillips," 18 November 1858, CM A1571, British Columbia Archives, and "Sketch of Part of British Columbia," by Lieut. R.C. Mayne, R.N., of H.M.S. Plumper, 1859, CM 3371, British Columbia Archives.

32 W.K. Lamb, ed., *Simon Fraser: Letters and Journals, 1806-1808* (Toronto: MacMillan, 1960), 100.

33 Sonny McHalsie, personal communication, 1994.

34 As a young pubescent girl, Matilda Gutierrez (now an elder) was brought to the site of the scratch marks by two elderly men and made to sit where X̱á:ls had sat as he did battle. She

was told the story of X̱á:ls and then instructed to remain sitting, alone, on that spot through-out the night. She was to "think about X̱á:ls and what he did." She was beginning her training as someone responsible for learning and ultimately communicating the stories of X̱á:ls to the next generation.

35  Lamb, *Simon Fraser,* 88.

36  Wendy Wickwire, "To See Ourselves as the Other's Other: Nlaka'pamux Contact Narra-tives," *Canadian Historical Review* 75, 1 (March 1994): 1-20.

37  C.F. Newcombe. "Story of First White Man," as told by Pierre Ayessick, ca. 1894. Tran-scribed from notes in C.F. Newcombe Papers, A01763, 44, 11, 18j, British Columbia Ar-chives, Victoria.

38  Thomas Crosby, *Among the An-ko-me-nums; or Flathead Tribes of Indians of the Pacific Coast* (Toronto: William Briggs, 1907), 185-86.

39  See Sonny McHalsie et al., "Making the World Right through Transformations," in *A Stó:lō Coast Salish Historical Atlas,* ed. Keith Thor Carlson (Vancouver: Douglas and McIntyre, 2001), 6-7.

40  For a lively debate over this subject as it applies in the Hawaiian context, see Gananath Obeyesekere, *The Apotheosis of Captain Cook: European Mythmaking in the Pacific* (Princeton: Princeton University Press, 1992), and Marshall Sahlins, *How Natives Think: About Captain Cook for Example* (Chicago: University of Chicago Press, 1995).

41  Wayne Suttles, "Central Coast Salish," in *Handbook of North American Indians,* vol. 7, *The Northwest Coast,* ed. Wayne Suttles (Washington, DC: Smithsonian Institution, 1990), 466.

42  Jan Vansina, *Oral Tradition as History* (Madison: University of Wisconsin Press, 1985).

43  Julie Cruikshank in collaboration with Angela Sidney, Kitty Smith, and Annie Ned, *Life Lived Like a Story: Life Stories of Three Yukon Native Elders* (Lincoln: University of Nebraska Press, 1990); Julie Cruikshank, *The Social Life of Stories: Narrative and Knowledge in the Yukon Territory* (Lincoln/Vancouver: University of Nebraska Press/UBC Press, 1998).

44  Once again, I have chosen not to identify this person so as to keep the focus on the issues rather than particular personalities.

45  Snyder, "Skagit Society," 21-22.

46  Jenness, *Faith of a Coast Salish Indian;* see, in particular, ch. 3, "Man and Nature," 35-40. Significantly, Old Pierre's historical information is generally accepted as legitimate by con-temporary Coast Salish people in a way that John Doe's is not, primarily, it seems, because Old Pierre was specially trained and because he carefully cited to his audiences who had provided him with his information.

47  As an illegitimate child, this elder had lived year-round in a residential school, and there-fore did not have opportunities to acquire information directly from high-status members of his extended family.

48  Collingwood, *The Idea of History,* 256.

49  Ibid., 252.

50  Mary Carruthers, *The Book of Memory: A Study of Memory in Medieval Culture* (Cambridge: Cambridge University Press, 1990), 4.

51  Dell Hymes, *"Now I Know Only so Far": Essays in Ethnopoetics* (Lincoln and London: Univer-sity of Nebraska, 2003), 8-10.

## Chapter 4: Poking Fun

1  Catharine McClellan, "Indian Stories about the First Whites in Northwestern North America," in *Ethnohistory in Southwestern Alaska and Southern Yukon: Method and Content,* ed. Margaret Lantis (Lexington: University Press of Kentucky, 1970), 103-33; Julie Cruik-shank, *The Social Life of Stories: Narrative and Knowledge in the Yukon Territory* (Lincoln/ Vancouver: University of Nebraska Press/UBC Press, 1998); Peter Nabokov, "Native Views of History," in *The Cambridge History of the Native Peoples of the Americas,* eds. Bruce Trigger and Wilcomb Washburn (Cambridge: Cambridge University Press, 1996), 1-59; Keith Thor Carlson, ch. 3, this volume.

2  Cruikshank, *The Social Life of Stories;* Robin Ridington, *Little Bit Know Something: Stories in a Language of Anthropology* (Vancouver and Toronto: Douglas and McIntyre, 1990); Wendy

Wickwire, *Nature Power: In the Spirit of an Okanagan Storyteller* (Vancouver/Seattle: Douglas and McIntyre/University of Washington Press, 1992).

3 Patrick Moore and Angela Wheelock, *Wolverine Myths and Visions: Dene Traditions from Northern Alberta* (Lincoln: University of Nebraska Press, 1990).

4 Cruikshank, *The Social Life of Stories;* Wendy Wickwire, ch. 7, this volume; Carlson, ch. 3, this volume.

5 The name of this story, "Tés Ní'ā 'Standing Walking Stick [Mountain],'" refers to a high mountain east of Pelly Lakes where a Kaska shaman who was offended by white traders planted his walking stick and ascended into heaven.

6 See, for example, Nabokov, "Native Views of History," 13; Frederica de Laguna, *The Story of a Tlingit Community: A Problem in the Relationship between Archaeological, Ethnological, and Historical Methods*, Bureau of American Ethnology Bulletin 172 (Washington, DC: Smithsonian Institution, 1990), 202.

7 George Thornton Emmons, "Native Account of the Meeting between La Perouse and the Tlingit," *American Anthropologist* 13, 2 (1911): 294-98; McClellan, "Indian Stories about the First Whites"; George Blondin, "When the First White People Came," in his *When the World Was New: Stories of the Sahtu Dene* (Yellowknife: Outcrop Publishers, 1990), 98-99; Kitty Smith, "The First Time They Knew *K'och'en*, Whiteman," in *Our Voices: Native Stories of Alaska and the Yukon*, eds. James Rupert and John Bernet (Toronto: University of Toronto Press, 2001), 223-27.

8 This story was recorded with Mida Donnessey at a 1999 language workshop at Simpson Creek, Yukon, and was written in Kaska and translated into English by Leda Jules and Pat Moore (manuscript in possession of Pat Moore). Liza Magun, "The First Time We Saw White People," trans. William Atkinson and Pat Moore, in *Dene Gudeji: Kaska Narratives*, ed. Pat Moore (Whitehorse: Kaska Tribal Council, 1999), 430-43; Alfred Caesar, "The First White People" (manuscript translation in possession of Pat Moore, 1999).

9 This story was recorded with Mary Charlie in 1995 at her home in Ross River, Yukon, and was written in Kaska and translated into English by Pat Moore and Leda Jules. For the published version, see Mary Charlie, "Tés Ní'ā," trans. Leda Jules and Pat Moore, in *Dene Gudeji: Kaska Narratives*, ed. Pat Moore (Whitehorse: Kaska Tribal Council, 1999), 246-67.

10 John Rae to George Simpson, 29 July 1850, Manuscript B. 200/b/15-29, Fort Simpson Correspondence Book, Hudson's Bay Company Archives, Provincial Archives of Manitoba, Winnipeg, Manitoba.

11 The old man ascended into heaven.

12 Robert Campbell, *Two Journals of Robert Campbell 1808 to 1853* (1853 manuscript; repr., Seattle: Shorey Bookstore, 1967), 43, 50.

13 Cruikshank, *The Social Life of Stories*, 122

14 Complete Kaska texts and translations of stories from both genres are presented in Patrick Moore, "Point of View in Kaska Historical Narrative" (PhD diss., Indiana University, 2002).

15 Alfred Caesar, "The First White People" (manuscript translation in the possession of Pat Moore, 1999).

16 Keith Basso, *Portraits of "The Whiteman": Linguistic Play and Cultural Symbols among the Western Apache* (Cambridge: Cambridge University Press, 1979).

17 Ibid., 16.

18 Ibid.

19 Robert Cochran, "'What Courage!': Romanian 'Our Leader' Jokes," *Journal of American Folklore* 102, 405 (1989): 259.

20 Geneva Smitherman, *Talkin That Talk: Language, Culture, and Education in African America* (London and New York: Routledge, 2000), 225.

21 Mikhail Bakhtin, *The Dialogic Imagination: Four Essays*, ed. Michael Holquist (Austin: University of Texas Press, 1981).

22 Michael Harkin, *The Heiltsuks: Dialogues of Culture and History on the Northwest Coast* (Lincoln and London: University of Nebraska Press, 1997), 62.

23 Mary Charlie, "*Destl'edemā* (Squirrel Woman)," in *Dene Gudeji*, ed. Moore, 185-245.

24 Charles Briggs and Richard Bauman, "Genre, Intertextuality, and Social Power," *Journal of Linguistic Anthropology* 2, 2 (1992): 131-72.

25   Mikhail Bakhtin, "The Problem of Speech Genres," in *Speech Genres and Other Late Essays,* eds. Caryl Emerson and Michael Holquist (Austin: University of Texas Press, 1986); Briggs and Bauman, "Genre, Intertextuality, and Social Power"; Trudier Harris, "Genre," *Journal of American Folklore* 108, 403 (1995): 509-27.

26   Julia Kristeva, *Desire in Language,* trans. Leon Roudiez (New York: Columbia University Press, 1980).

27   Briggs and Bauman, "Genre, Intertextuality, and Social Power," 146.

28   This story was recorded at a language workshop with Kaska elders in Ross River, and was written in Kaska and translated into English by Pat Moore and Leda Jules (manuscript in possession of Pat Moore, 1999).

29   Amos Dick, "Warfare at Lūge Lē" (manuscript English translation in possession of Pat Moore, 1999).

30   Robert Campbell to John Lewes, 25 July 1843 and 3 October 1843, Manuscript B. 200/c/1, Fort Simpson Correspondence Inward, Hudson's Bay Company Archives, Provincial Museum of Manitoba, Winnipeg. Robert Campbell to John Lewes, 3 October 1843.

31   Julie Cruikshank has suggested that this reference to eight years may also reflect a traditional theme that actions which are completed in cycles of eight (eight days, eight years) result in good fortune (personal communication, 12 April 2002).

32   Liza Magun, "The First Time We Saw White People," trans. William Atkinson and Pat Moore, in *Dene Gudeji,* ed. Moore, 432.

33   Remarkably, later writers attributed the Pelly Banks cannibalism to the Natives, not the traders. Robert Coutts, for instance, says, "In the early winter of 1849, while [Robert] Campbell was at Fort Selkirk, the post burned down, leaving the staff destitute. Two of the men died of starvation that winter and some of the Indians resorted to cannibalism to save themselves." Robert Coutts, *Yukon Places and Names* (Sidney, BC: Gray's Publishing, 1980), 209. His description, like those of other historians, is based on their interpretation of the following ambiguous passage in *Two Journals of Robert Campbell:* "the two men Forbisher and Debois died of starvation and several of the Indians around and pitiably sad to relate, some of the poor wretches had been driven by their unspeakable sufferings to commit some acts of cannibalism." Campbell, *Two Journals,* 90. Coutts and others interpreted "poor wretches" as referring to Native people, probably due to their own stereotypes that Natives, not the traders, would engage in cannibalism.

34   Briggs and Bauman, "Genre, Intertextuality, and Social Power."

35   McClellan, "Indian Stories about the First Whites," 125.

36   Briggs and Bauman, "Genre, Intertextuality, and Social Power."

**Chapter 5: Herbert Spencer, Paul Kane, and the Making of "The Chinook"**

1   I am grateful to Tracy Pelland for his assistance with some of the research for this chapter.

2   Paul Kane [?], *Wanderings of an Artist among the Indians of North America from Canada to Vancouver's Island and Oregon through the Hudson's Bay Company's Territory and back again* (London: Longman, Brown, Green, Longmans, and Roberts, 1859). Subsequent references to this book will depend on this edition and be signified by the date of publication (1859). Translations of the first edition appeared in French (Paris, 1861), German (Leipzig, 1862), and Danish (Copenhagen, 1863). The most frequently consulted edition of the work is J. Russell Harper, ed., *Paul Kane's Frontier. Including "Wanderings of an Artist among the Indians of North America,"* edited with a bibliographical introduction and a catalogue raisonné (Austin/Toronto: University of Texas Press/University of Toronto Press, 1971). Subsequent references to this edition appear with the publication date (1971). The only edition currently in print is *Wanderings of an Artist among the Indians of North America,* ed. John W. Garvin, introd. Lawrence Burpee (Toronto: Radisson Society, 1925; facs. repr., Mineola, NY: Dover, 1996). References to this edition are designated by (1996). Because the other English-language edition of *Wanderings,* introd. J.G. MacGregor (Edmonton: M.G. Hurtig, 1968) is a facsimile of the Radisson Society edition, the (1996) page references are accurate for it, as well.

3   Mary Louise Pratt, *Imperial Eyes: Travel Writing and Transculturation* (New York: Routledge, 1992).

4 See, for example, Ramsay Cook, ed. and introd., *The Voyages of Jacques Cartier* (Toronto: University of Toronto Press, 1993), xix.

5 William J. Kerby, *The Catholic Encyclopedia*, vol. 14 (New York: Robert Appleton, 1912), s.v. "Sociology," online ed. (2003), http://www.newadvent.org/cathen/14115a.htm.

6 Alexander Maryanski and Jonathan H. Turner, *Encyclopedia of Sociology*, eds. Edgar F. Borgatta and Rhonda J.V. Montgomery, 5 vols. (New York: Macmillan, 2000), s.v. "Functionalism and Structuralism."

7 Ibid.

8 Herbert Spencer, "Provincial Preface," in *North and South American Races. Compiled by Professor* [David] *Duncan* (New York: D. Appleton, 1878), pt. 6 of Herbert Spencer, *Descriptive Sociology; or, Groups of Sociological Facts, Classified and Arranged by Herbert Spencer. Compiled and Abstracted by David Duncan ... Richard Scheppig ... and James Collier*, 15 pts. (London: Williams and Norgate, 1873-1919), [i] (hereafter, *Descriptive Sociology*).

9 J. Michael Armer and John Katsillis, *Encyclopedia of Sociology*, s.v. "Modernization Theory."

10 Susan R. Pitchford, *Encyclopedia of Sociology*, s.v. "Race."

11 Kathryn Hamer, "Kane, Paul," *The Oxford Companion to Canadian Literature*, gen. ed. William Toye (Toronto: Oxford University Press, 1983), 403; 2nd ed., gen. eds. Eugene Benson and William Toye (Toronto: Oxford University Press, 1997), 588.

12 That is, Harper, *Paul Kane's Frontier*.

13 The seven-cent stamp, issued 11 August 1971, bore a reproduction of the Art Gallery of Ontario's copy of Kane's oil-on-canvas painting, *Indian Encampment on Lake Huron*, c. 1845-58, 48.3 x 73.7 cm, AGO 2121, the original of which is held by the Royal Ontario Museum, 45.7 x 73.7 cm, ROM 912.1.8. The catalogue raisonné in Harper, *Paul Kane's Frontier* lists these as III-19 and III-18, respectively (p. 273).

14 *Visions from the Wilderness: The Art of Paul Kane*, 60 min., prod. and dir. John Bessai, ed. Joan Prowse, distrib. McNabb and Connolly (Toronto: CineFocus Canada, 2001); for related websites, see CineFocus Canada, "Visions from the Wilderness: The Art of Paul Kane" (2002), http://www.paulkane.ca/php/index.php; and CineFocus Canada, "New Media" (2006), http://www.cinefocus.com/index.php.

15 Paul Kane, Field Notes 1846-1848, 11.85/5, Stark Museum of Art, Orange, Texas; Portrait Log and Landscape Log 1846-1848, and Field Notes 1845, 11.85/4, Stark Museum of Art. The field notes 1846-48 have been published in Paul Kane, "'I came to rite thare portraits': Paul Kane's Journal of His Western Travels, 1846-1848," ed. I.S. MacLaren, *American Art Journal* 21, 2 (Spring 1989): 6-88. The portrait log (but not the landscape log) was published in revised and abridged form in Harper, *Paul Kane's Frontier*, appendix 2, 315-17.

16 Draft manuscript of *Wanderings of an Artist*, 4 vols.: 17 June 1845-July 1846, 11.85/2A; 9 May 1846-6 September 1848, 11.85/2B; 6 October 1846-12 September 1848, 11.85/2C; 17 June 1845-30 November 1845, 11.85/3, Stark Museum of Art.

17 On Speke, see David Finkelstein, "'Unravelling Speke': The Blackwoods and the Construction of John Hanning Speke as Author in His *Journal of the Discovery of the Source of the Nile*," *Bibliotheck* 18 (1992-93): 40-57; and David Finkelstein, "Breaking the Thread: The Authorial Reinvention of John Hanning Speke in His *Journal of the Discovery of the Source of the Nile*," *Text* 9 (1997): 280-96. On Hearne, Mackenzie, and Cook, see I.S. MacLaren, "Samuel Hearne's Accounts of the Massacre at Bloody Fall, 17 July 1771," *ARIEL: A Review of International English Literature* 22, 1 (January 1991): 25-51; I.S. MacLaren, "Notes on Samuel Hearne's *Journey* from a Bibliographical Perspective," *Papers/Cahiers of the Bibliographical Society of Canada* 31, 2 (Fall 1993): 21-45; I.S. MacLaren, "Alexander Mackenzie and the Landscapes of Commerce," *Studies in Canadian Literature* 7 (1982): 141-50; and I.S. MacLaren, "Exploration/Travel Literature and the Evolution of the Author," *International Journal of Canadian Studies* 5 (Spring 1992): 39-68. The case of Jacques Cartier (1491-1557) is notorious. Assessing the confusion of the textual representations of contact during Cartier's voyages, Marcel Trudel has concluded that "the problem persists in its entirety." "Cartier, Jacques," *Dictionary of Canadian Biography*, ed. George W. Brown (Toronto: University of Toronto Press, 1966), 1:171. Few realize that, for Cartier's voyages, no known manuscript writings exist in the hand of the "discoverer" of Canada. Meanwhile, in the view of one of his modern editors, the nineteenth century essentially invented Cartier, supplying the Dominion of

Canada and, later, French Canadian nationalism with a heroic figure because of "la nécessité politique"; thereby did the narratives of his three voyages necessarily and largely unproblematically assume the status of foundational texts for a history and a culture. Michel Bideaux, ed., *Jacques Cartier: Relations* (Montreal: Les Presses de l'Université de Montréal, 1986), 9.

18  *Wanderings* (1859), 178; (1971), 92; (1996), 121.

19  The article appeared three times under the same title before the March 1859 publication of the book: Paul Kane, "The Chinook Indians," *Canadian Journal: A Repertory of Industry, Science, and Art; and a Record of the Proceedings of the Canadian Institute* 3, 12 (July 1855): 273-79; *Daily British Colonist*, 6 August 1855, [1-2]; 7 August 1855, [1-2]; 8 August 1855, [1-2]; and 9 August 1855, [1]; and *Canadian Journal of Industry, Science, and Art: Conducted by the Editing Committee of the Canadian Institute*, n.s., 2, 7 (January 1857): 11-30. The reprint in the *Daily Colonist* differed only in incidental ways from the first version, and, although it claims to have been "revised," the third version does not differ from the previous two. The *Daily Colonist* version has been republished, in Thomas Vaughan, ed., *Paul Kane: The Columbia Wanderer* (Portland, OR: Oregon Historical Society, 1971), 20-51.

20  Draft manuscript of *Wanderings*, 11.85/3, [38].

21  Portrait Log, 11.85/4, [67a]-[70a].

22  See Harper, *Paul Kane's Frontier*, catalogue raisonné IV-418, 299.

23  Samuel Parker, *Journal of an Exploring Tour beyond the Rocky Mountains, under the Direction of the A.B.C.F.M. performed in the Years 1835, '36, and '37* (Ithaca, NY: privately printed, 1838), 252.

24  This alteration, which puts the persona of Kane closer to the narrated event, anticipates the book's handling (in chapter 21) of the massacre in late November 1847 of Narcissa and Marcus Whitman at their mission near modern Walla Walla, in southeastern Washington State. Kane had stayed with the Whitmans in July 1847 but by the time of the massacre he was hundreds of kilometres to the north, across the Rockies and up on the Athabasca River at Fort Assiniboine, north of Fort Edmonton. In the book's account of the massacre, Kane is situated at Fort Colvile (near modern Colville, Washington), far closer to the action of Indian barbarity and atrocity. Obviously, then, the field notes contain no reference to the missionaries' deaths. (Indeed, Kane could have travelled as far east as Toronto in 1848 before hearing of the massacre, although word of it might have reached him during the winter of 1847-48 while he was at Fort Edmonton, Fort Pitt, and Rocky Mountain House.) Analysis of the effect of this narrative alteration is provided in Bessai and Prowse's documentary, *Visions from the Wilderness* (see n. 14, above).

25  "The Chinook Indians," *Canadian Journal* (July 1855): 277; (January 1857): 24; *Daily Colonist*, 8 August 1855, [2]; Vaughan, *Paul Kane*, 41; *Wanderings* (1859), 178; (1971), 92; (1996), 121.

26  *Descriptive Sociology*, 6:33.

27  Another example of the reliance of *Wanderings* on published sources for its "eyewitness" authority appears in the appendix to the first edition, which bears the title "Census of Indian Tribes inhabiting the North-west Coast of America, for the year 1846." In fact, Kane did not arrive in the area until the end of 1846, crossing the mountains in November and arriving at the Hudson's Bay Company post, Fort Vancouver, only in December. *Wanderings* gives no indication that anyone other than Kane compiled this four-page census. However, the census that appeared in 1859 as the appendix to *Wanderings* is in fact based on a wider and earlier one compiled by the Hudson's Bay Company beginning in 1835. The complete version appeared in print for the first time in 1855, four years before the publication of *Wanderings*, as table 1, "Indian Tribes of the Pacific Coast," in Henry Rowe Schoolcraft, dir., *History of the North American Indians*, 6 vols., pt. 5, *Information respecting the History, Condition and Prospects of the Indian Tribes of the United States* (Philadelphia: J.B. Lippincott, 1855), 487-89.

   Schoolcraft's spellings occasionally diverge markedly from those in *Wanderings*. Nonetheless, both versions probably originate from James Douglas, "Statistics of the Northwest Coast of America," MS B 40 D72.5, fols. 138-40, James Douglas Diary, British Columbia Archives, Victoria, BC, cited in Robert Boyd, *The Coming of the Spirit of Pestilence: Introduced Infectious Diseases and Population Decline among Northwest Coast Indians, 1774-1874*

(Vancouver/Seattle: UBC Press/University of Washington Press, 1999), 348. More curious is the fact that the census pertains to peoples whom *Wanderings* does not describe and in whose lands Kane did not travel: "Nass," "Chimseyans," "Skeena," "Hootsinoo," "Stekini," "Port Stuart," "Queen Charlotte's Island," and so forth. *Wanderings* (1859), 458-61; (1971) and (1996) lack this appendix. Schoolcraft's table 2, "Indian Population of Washington Territory," and table 3, "Tribes of Oregon Territory," would have been more logical candidates for inclusion in *Wanderings*. Schoolcraft, *History*, 5:490-91, 492-93. Such additions and alterations at the publication stage of *Wanderings* suggest that it, like the travel genre more generally, amounts at points to a miscellany rather than a traveller's eyewitness journal, placing on view the epistemologies (such as a census) and the ideological, political, and economic aims of the traveller or explorer's culture, and, if only implicitly, embodying the contradictions arising from the coming together of those aims with the epistemologies and interests of the cultures whom the traveller or explorer is "discovering." See Bruce Greenfield, "The Problem of the Discoverer's Authority in Lewis and Clark's *History*," in *Macropolitics of Nineteenth-Century Literature: Nationalism, Exoticism, Imperialism,* eds. Jonathan Arac and Harriet Ritvo (Philadelphia: University of Pennsylvania Press, 1991), 12-35.

More accurate data for 1846 may be found in the census generated by Henry James Warre (1819-98), an English lieutenant in the 14th Regiment, and Mervin Vavasour (1821-66), a Canadian lieutenant in the Royal Engineers. In 1845, a year before Kane's arrival, they had journeyed west with Hudson's Bay Company brigades in the guise, as HBC inland governor Sir George Simpson put it, of private gentlemen travelling "for the pleasure of field sports and scientific pursuits." Joseph Schafer, ed., "Documents Relative to Warre and Vavasour's Military Reconnoissance [sic] in Oregon in 1845-6," *Oregon Historical Quarterly* 10 (1909): 35. In fact, they were appointed to reconnoitre the Oregon crisis and take stock of the challenges involved for Britain in defending the territory. (The Oregon Treaty had reached Washington on 6 June 1846, well before they filed their report.) Their census was printed for the first time in 1848 in R[obert]. M[ontgomery]. Martin, *The Hudson's Bay Territories and Vancouver's Island, with an Exposition of the Chartered Rights, Conduct, and Policy of the Honorable Hudson's Bay Corporation* (1848; repr., London: T. and W. Boone, 1849), 80-82, cited in E.E. Rich, ed., *The Letters of John McLoughlin from Fort Vancouver to the Governor and Committee: Third Series, 1844-46,* introd. W. Kaye Lamb, Champlain Society, Hudson's Bay Company Record Series, vol. 7 (London: Champlain Society, 1944), 71n.

28  Other aspects of Kane's art and writing pertinent to this essay, including the discrepancy between field sketches and studio oil paintings, have been discussed by I.S. MacLaren in the following: "Exploration/Travel Literature"; "The Metamorphosis of Travellers into Authors: The Case of Paul Kane," in *Critical Issues in Editing Exploration Texts. Papers given at the Twenty-eighth Conference on Editorial Problems, University of Toronto, 6-7 November 1992,* ed. Germaine Warkentin (Toronto: University of Toronto Press, 1995), 67-107; "Paul Kane Goes South: The Sale of the Family's Collection of Field Sketches," *Journal of Canadian Studies* 32, 2 (Summer 1997): 22-47; and "Cultured Wilderness in Jasper National Park," *Journal of Canadian Studies* 34, 3 (Fall 1999): 7-58.

29  David Beers Quinn, *North America from Earliest Discovery to First Settlements: The Norse Voyages to 1612* (New York: Harper and Row, 1977), 546.

30  For examples of Manners and Customs sketches of the Chinook published before Kane's narrative, see Ross Cox, *Adventures on the Columbia River, including the Narrative of a Residence of Six Years on the Western Side of the Rocky Mountains, among various Tribes of Indians hitherto unknown: together with a Journey across the American Continent,* 2 vols. (London: Henry Colburn and Richard Bentley, 1831), 1:111-12, 301-36; 2:133-35; and Parker, *Journal,* 178-85, 242-52.

31  *Wanderings* (1859), 173; (1971), 91; (1996), 118.

32  The misuse of the name "Flathead" to refer to the Chinook offers one inconclusive clue that a fur trader named Peter Skene Ogden (1794-1854), who met and befriended Kane at Fort Vancouver, and corresponded with him after his departure, did *not* involve himself directly in the writing of the draft manuscript of *Wanderings:* it was the Flathead whom the anonymous author of a book long attributed to Ogden, *Traits of American Indian Life and*

*Character. By a Fur Trader* (London: Smith, Elder, 1853), judged the best Native North Americans. His use of the name is an accurate one: "If the author can be said to have any preference for one of these swarthy clans before another, it is possibly for the chivalrous 'Flatheads,' who 'have never been known to shed the blood of a white man,' and are as brave in war as the 'Crows' and 'Blackfeet,' their hereditary enemies" (iv). For attributions of this book to Ogden, see T[hompson]. C[oit]. Elliott, "Peter Skene Ogden, Fur Trader," *Oregon Historical Quarterly* 11 (1910): 268; Frederick William Howay, "Authorship of *Traits of Indian Life*," *Oregon Historical Quarterly* 35 (1934): 42-49; and Douglas S. Watson, Preface to *Traits of American Indian Life and Character* (San Francisco: Grabhorn, 1933; facs. repr. of 1933 ed., New York: AMS, 1972). Ogden died five years before *Wanderings* was published. On his influence on Kane, see I.S. MacLaren, "'Caledonian Suttee'? An Anatomy of Carrier Cremation Cruelty in the Historical Record," *BC Studies* 149 (Spring 2006): 13-18, 22.

33 "Annual Report of the Council, 1855," *Canadian Journal: A Repertory of Industry, Science, and Art; and a Record of the Proceedings of the Canadian Institute* 3, 17 (December 1855): 398.

34 "Fifteenth Ordinary Meeting – March 31st, 1855," *Canadian Journal: A Repertory of Industry, Science, and Art; and a Record of the Proceedings of the Canadian Institute* 3, 10 (May 1855): 243. For more on the relation between Kane and Allan, see MacLaren, "Paul Kane Goes South," 23-25.

35 "Fifteenth Ordinary Meeting"; "The Chinook Indians," *Canadian Journal* (July 1855): 273.

36 "The handwritten Minutes [of the institute] make it clear that the lecturer was G.W. Allan. There is no evidence that Kane was even present." Conrad E. Heidenreich, "Report to the Royal Canadian Institute on the Identification of the Paul Kane Picture Owned by the R.C.I. (May 11, 1995)" (typescript, 9 pages, 11 figs., Royal Canadian Institute, Toronto, 11 May 1995).

37 Paul Kane, "Notes of a Sojourn among the Half-Breeds, Hudson's Bay Company's Territory, Red River," *Canadian Journal of Industry, Science, and Art: Conducted by the Editing Committee of the Canadian Institute*, n.s., 1, 2 (February 1856): 128-38; and "Notes of Travel among the Walla-Walla Indians," *Canadian Journal of Industry, Science, and Art: Conducted by the Editing Committee of the Canadian Institute*, n.s., 1, 5 (September 1856): 417-24.

38 "Annual Report of the Council, 1855," 399.

39 "Fourteenth Ordinary Meeting – 5th April, 1856," *Canadian Journal of Industry, Science, and Art: Conducted by the Editing Committee of the Canadian Institute*, n.s., 1, 4 (July 1856): 405.

40 *Wanderings* (1859), 171; (1971), 91; (1996), 117.

41 Draft manuscript, 11.85/2C, [28].

42 William Fraser Tolmie, "History of Puget Sound and the Northwest Coast ... Victoria 1878" (manuscript, 60 pages, Bancroft Library, University of California, Berkeley), 31.

43 Michael Silverstein, personal communication, 18 March 1999.

44 [Nicholas Biddle], *History of the Expedition under the Command of Captains Lewis and Clark, to the Sources of the Missouri, thence across the Rocky Mountains and down the River Columbia to the Pacific Ocean. Performed during the Years 1804-5-6. By Order of the United States*, [ed. Paul Allen,] 2 vols. (Philadelphia: Bradford and Inskeep, 1814), 2:45.

45 Ibid., 2:48. See also Gary Moulton, ed., *The Journals of the Lewis and Clark Expedition*, 13 vols. (Lincoln: University of Nebraska Press, 1983-2001), 5:353n.

46 David H. French and Kathrine S. French, "Wasco, Wishram, and Cascades," in *Plateau*, ed. Deward Walker Jr., vol. 12 of *Handbook of North American Indians*, gen. ed. William C. Sturtevant (Washington, DC: Smithsonian Institution, 1998), 375.

47 Silverstein, personal communication, 18 March 1999.

48 I am indebted to Robert Boyd for this possible explanation (personal communication, 8 April 2002).

49 George C. Shaw, *The Chinook Jargon and How to Use It; a Complete and Exhaustive Lexicon of the Oldest Trade Language of the American Continent* (Seattle: Rainier Printing, 1909), 64. For *qitsutxwa* and *chùtxwa*, see David D. Robertson, "Paul Kane on 'Katchutequa,'" 21 August 2003, http://listserv.linguistlist.org/cgi-bin/wa?A2=ind0308c&L=chinook&D=1&F=P&S= &P=475. For *chùtxwa*, Robertson (personal communication, 25 January 2006) refers to Henry B. Zenk and Tony A. Johnson, *Chinúk-Wawa: Kákwa ntsayka úlman tílixam àaska munk-kəmtəks ntsáyka/As Our Elders Teach Us to Speak It* (Grand Ronde, OR: Confederated Tribes of

the Community of Grand Ronde, 2003). A good example of the repulsion expressed by the published persona of Kane occurs in the book's description of the Chinook language as the reason for the need to invent Chinook Jargon: "I would willingly give a specimen of the barbarous language of this people, were it possible to represent by any combination of our alphabet the horrible, harsh, spluttering sounds which proceed from their throats, apparently unguided either by the tongue or lip. It is so difficult to acquire a mastery of their language that none have been able to attain it, except those who have been born among them. They have, however, by their intercourse with the English and French traders, succeeded in amalgamating, after a fashion, some words of each of these tongues with their own, and forming a sort of patois, barbarous enough certainly, but still sufficient to enable them to communicate with the traders. This patois I was enabled after some short time to acquire, and could converse with most of the chiefs with tolerable ease." *Wanderings* (1859), 182-83; (1971), 93; (1996), 125.

50  See Percy G. Adams, *Travel Literature and the Evolution of the Novel* (Lexington: University Press of Kentucky, 1983).

51  *Wanderings* (1859), 183; (1971), 93; (1996), 125; *Descriptive Sociology*, 6:23.

52  Draft manuscript, 11.85/3, [73].

53  "The Chinook Indians," *Canadian Journal* (July 1855): 274; (January 1857): 14; *Daily Colonist*, 7 August 1855, [1]; Vaughan, *Paul Kane*, 27.

54  W[illiam]. Wilks and H.R. Hutchinson, eds., *Journal Kept by David Douglas during His Travels in North America 1823-1827* (London: W. Wesley and Son, for the Royal Horticultural Society, 1914), 138.

55  The Chinook Jargon word to which "The Chinook Indians" and *Wanderings* refer is given, for example, as *"klahāwēam"* in Horatio Hale, ed., *Ethnography and Philology*, vol. 6 of Charles Wilkes, *Narrative of the United States Exploring Expedition. During the years 1838, 1839, 1840, 1841, 1842*, 5 vols. and atlas (1844; repr., Philadelphia/London: Lea and Blanchard/Whittaker/Wiley and Putnam, 1845; facs. repr., Ridgewood, NJ: Gregg Press, 1968), 638. It appears as "Kla-howya" in Schoolcraft, *History*, 5:549. In 1909, George Shaw spelled it as Kla-how-ya and glossed it as "the ordinary salutation at meeting or parting" in his *Chinook Jargon* (10). Modern linguistic studies suggest that the Chinook word is "LaXayam," which means both the salutation and the adjective for "poor." (Here, the letter "L" stands for the voiceless lateral fricative which is written as an "à" in the standard Americanist alphabet. The sound is basically the same as the Welsh "ll." The letter "X," representing a sound described as a voiceless uvular fricative, is probably not far from the back "ch" in a German word such as "ach" or "Bach" [I am indebted to Henry Zenk for this clarification].) When LaXayam is used as a salutation meaning "How are you?" or "How do you do?" its pronunciation sufficiently resembles the sound of the English question addressed to Clark (perhaps the US explorer William Clark [1770-1838] or the North West Company and Astorian fur trader John Clarke [1781-1853]) to give warrant to this "folk etymology" adduced in *Wanderings*.

Although no earlier published instance of "Clark, how are you?" has yet come to light, its 1859 appearance in *Wanderings* spawned its own legacy. Wording in Isaac Taylor's reference source, *Words and Places* (London: Macmillan, 1864), appears to have depended on the text of *Wanderings*: "At Fort Vancouver, the medium of intercourse is a curious Lingua Franca, composed of Canadian-French, English, Iroquois, Cree, Hawaian [sic], and Chinese." Taylor continues in a footnote: "Wilson, *Pre-historic Man*, vol. ii, p. 431. An American is called *Boston*, and the ordinary salutation is *Clakhohahyah*, which is explained by the fact that the Indians, frequently hearing a trader named Clark, long resident in the Fort, addressed by his companions in the village, '*Clark*, how are you?' imagined that this sentence was the correct English form of salutation" (401n). The source adduced by Taylor is the book by Kane's academic friend in Toronto, Sir Daniel Wilson, *Prehistoric Man: Researches into the Origin of Civilisation in the Old and the New World*, 2 vols. (Cambridge and London: Macmillan, 1862). A recent publication has remarked that Wilson "was partly responsible for the appearance of such books as Paul Kane's *Wanderings of an Artist*." Heather Murray, "Daniel Wilson as Littérateur: English Professor, Critic, and Poet," in *Thinking with Both Hands: Sir Daniel Wilson in the Old World and the New*, ed. Elizabeth Hulse (Toronto:

University of Toronto Press, 1999), 222. Wilson wrote an extensive review of *Wanderings* in 1859 as well as Kane's obituary: "D.W.," Review of *Wanderings of an Artist, Canadian Journal of Industry, Science, and Art: Conducted by the Editing Committee of the Canadian Institute,* n.s., 4, 21 (May 1859): 186-94; "D.W.," "Paul Kane, the Canadian Artist," *Canadian Journal of Industry, Science, and Art: Conducted by the Editing Committee of the Canadian Institute,* n.s., 13, 73 (May 1871): 66-72. He rehearses the "Clark" anecdote in *Prehistoric Man,* and indicates that Kane told him that "by means of it [Chinook Jargon] he soon learned to converse with the chiefs of most of the tribes around Fort Vancouver with tolerable ease" (2:431). The spelling of the salutation in Wilson's book is that found in *Wanderings*: "*Clak-hoh-ah-yah*" (Wilson, 2:430). Wilson goes on (2:432) to quote Hale (644), thereby completing the circle of references.

The "Clark, how are you?" identification persists, most recently in the Internet version of *Brewer's Dictionary of Phrase and Fable* (New York: Bartleby.Com, 2000), http://www.bartleby.com/81/3626.html. However, although its "Clak-ho-har'yah" entry cites Taylor's book as its source, the spelling of the word differs from his, as it does from Wilson's and the versions attributed to Kane. In 1924, missionary Jean Marie Raphaël Le Jeune (1855-1930) reproduced the folk etymology in his own work, though whether he had heard it himself or read it in *Wanderings* is unknown. He wrote that "Kla'hoyam" means "how d'ie do?" and that "Klahowyam, is said to have derived from 'Well, Clarke, how are you?'" Le Jeune, *Chinook Rudiments* (Kamloops, BC: n.p., 1924), 12, 10. I am indebted to Henry Zenk (personal communication, 20 May 2002) for drawing my attention to this reference, quoted in Samuel V. Johnson, "Chinook Jargon: A Computer Assisted Analysis of Variation in an American Indian Pidgin" (PhD diss., University of Kansas, 1978), 388.

56  *Wanderings* (1859), 187; (1971), 94; (1996), 128; *Descriptive Sociology,* 6:27.
57  For example, a separate entry, "Chinook olives," referring exclusively to *Wanderings,* occurs in Frederick Webb Hodge, ed., *Handbook of American Indians North of Mexico,* Smithsonian Institution Bureau of American Ethnology Bulletin 30, 2 pts. (Washington, DC: Government Printing Office, 1912), 1:275.
58  In her advocacy of the use of urine as plant fertilizer, Carol Steinfeld details an array of historical uses of urine for religious, culinary, hygienic, therapeutic, agricultural, and other purposes. Steinfeld, *Liquid Gold: The Lure and Logic of Using Urine to Grow Plants* (Dartington, UK/Sheffield, VT: Green Books/Green Frigate Books, 2004). She notes that "urine is usually sterile in healthy populations" (3-4), and that it comprises "95 percent water, with some salts and urea" (23), this last being "a recognized antibacterial, antifungal, and antiviral agent" (25). She claims that "human urine has been used as a health tonic and cure throughout recorded history, and most likely long before" (23). For her book's related website, see http://www.liquidgoldbook.com (2006). See also D.A. Bainbridge, "Quercus, a Multipurpose Tree for Temperate Climates," *International Tree Crops Journal* 3 (1986): 291-98. Bainbridge describes the widespread use of acorns as a food source but his mention of the admixture of them with urine is confined to a reference to the passage in *Wanderings* (293).
59  John G. Bourke, comp., *Scatalogic Rites of all Nations. A Dissertation upon the Employment of Excrementitious Remedial Agents in Religion, Therapeutics, Divination, Witchcraft, Love-Philters, etc., in all Parts of the Globe* (Washington, DC: W.H. Lowdermilk, 1891), 32, 29. Without mentioning Chinook olives or *Wanderings,* two contemporary authors who discuss various uses of urine refer their readers to Bourke's work. See Steinfeld, *Liquid Gold,* v. She in turn is indebted to Paul Spinrad, *The RE/Search Guide to Bodily Functions* (San Francisco: RE/Search Publications, 1994), 126, who notes that Sigmund Freud wrote a foreword to the German translation of *Scatologic Rites,* published in 1913.
60  John G. Bourke, comp., *Compilation of Notes and Memoranda bearing upon the Use of Human Ordure and Human Urine in Rites of a Religious or Semi-Religious Character among various Nations* (Washington, DC, 1888), 21; *Scatalogic Rites,* 38.
61  Draft manuscript, 11.85/2C, [30-31].
62  Draft manuscript, 11.85/2C, [31]; "The Chinook Indians," *Canadian Journal* (July 1855): 275; (January 1857): 19; *Daily Colonist,* 7 August 1855, [2]; Vaughan, *Paul Kane,* 33. Had it been included in *Wanderings,* the passage would appear at about (1859), 187; (1971), 94; (1996), 128.

63 Draft manuscript, 11.85/2C, [31-32]; "The Chinook Indians," *Canadian Journal* (July 1855): 275-76; (January 1857): 19; *Daily Colonist*, 7 August 1855, [2]; Vaughan, *Paul Kane*, 33-35.
64 *Wanderings* (1859), 189-90; (1971), 95; (1996), 129-30; *Descriptive Sociology*, 6:25.
65 *Wanderings* (1859), 216; (1971), 101; (1996), 149; *Descriptive Sociology*, 6:33.

**Chapter 6: Performing Paradox**
Research for this paper was made possible by a fellowship from the National Endowment for the Humanities.

1 David Beers Quinn and Alison Quinn, eds., *The First Colonists: Documents on the Planting of the First English Settlement in North America, 1584-1590* (Raleigh: North Carolina Department of Cultural Resources, 1982), iv.
2 Robert D. Arner, *The Lost Colony in Literature* (Raleigh: North Carolina Department of Cultural Resources, 1982).
3 Marshall Sahlins, *Historical Metaphors and Mythical Realities: Structure in the Early History of the Sandwich Islands Kingdom* (Ann Arbor: University of Michigan Press, 1981).
4 Greg Dening, *Performances* (Chicago: University of Chicago Press, 1996).
5 Michael Harkin, "History, Narrative, and Temporality: Examples from the Northwest Coast," *Ethnohistory* 35 (1988): 99-130. See William Powell, *Paradise Preserved: A History of the Roanoke Island Historical Association* (Chapel Hill: University of North Carolina Press, 1965).
6 Mary Fuller, "Images of English Origins in Newfoundland and Roanoke," in *Decentring the Renaissance: Canada and Europe in Multidisciplinary Perspective, 1500-1700*, eds. Germain Warkentin and Carolyn Podruchny (Toronto: University of Toronto Press, 2001), 141-58.
7 John Donne, *Poems of John Donne*, ed. E.K. Chambers, vol. 1 (London: Lawrence and Bullen, 1896), 148-50.
8 Fuller, "Images of English Origins," 141-58. This opposition between utilitarian and non-utilitarian colonies suggested by Fuller does not accord precisely with reality, as precious metals were sought for in Canada, and the agricultural productivity of Roanoke was an important factor in its location; nonetheless, it does represent an important trope of colonization.
9 Arthur Barlowe, "Arthur Barlowe's Narrative of the 1584 Voyage," in *The First Colonists: Documents*, eds. Quinn and Quinn, 2.
10 Mary Fuller, "Raleigh's Fugitive Gold: Reference and Deferral in *The Discovery of Guiana*," in *New World Encounters*, ed. Stephen Greenblatt (Berkeley: University of California Press, 1993), 218-40.
11 Jeffrey Knapp, "Elizabethan Tobacco," in *New World Encounters*, ed. Greenblatt, 284-85.
12 Ivor Noel Hume, "Roanoke Island: America's First Science Center," *Journal of the Colonial Williamsburg Foundation* 16, 3 (1994): 14-28.
13 Karen Ordahl Kupperman, *Roanoke: The Abandoned Colony* (Savage, MD: Rowman and Littlefield, 1994); Michael Oberg, "Gods and Men: The Meeting of Indian and White Worlds on the Carolina Outer Banks, 1584-1586," *North Carolina Historical Review* 86 (1999): 367-90.
14 Walter Biggs et al., "A Summary and True Discourse of Francis Drake's West Indian Voyage (extract)," in *The First Colonists: Documents*, eds. Quinn and Quinn, 77-81.
15 Kupperman, *Roanoke: The Abandoned Colony*, 107.
16 Richard Hakluyt, *Explorations, Descriptions, and Attempted Settlements of Carolina, 1584-1590*, ed. David L. Corbitt (Raleigh: North Carolina Department of Archives and History, 1948), 99.
17 Kupperman, *Roanoke: The Abandoned Colony*, 117; Lee Miller, *Roanoke* (New York: Arcade Publishing, 2000).
18 Kupperman, *Roanoke: The Abandoned Colony*, 131-33.
19 Ibid., 137-38; David Beers Quinn, *The Lost Colonists: Their Fortune and Probable Fate* (Raleigh: North Carolina Department of Cultural Resources, 1984).
20 But see Thomas C. Parramore, "The 'Lost Colony' Found: A Documentary Perspective," *North Carolina Historical Review* 78 (2001): 167-83.
21 Quinn, *The Lost Colonists: Their Fortune*.
22 Karen Blu, *The Lumbee Problem: The Making of an American Indian People* (New York: Cambridge University Press, 1980).

23  Josiah Bailey, "Was the Lost Colony Really Lost? Some in Cartaret County Tell a Different Version of John White's Historic Expedition," *Our State* 58, 9 (1991): 12-14; Lew Barton, *The Most Ironic Story in American History: An Authoritative, Documented History of the Lumbee Indians of North Carolina* (Pembroke, NC: Lew Barton, 1967); A.D. Dart, "Raleigh's Lost Colony," *Southern Workman*, August 1913, 445-46; Alexander Hume Ford, "The Finding of Raleigh's Lost Colony," *Appleton's Magazine* (July 1907): 22-31; C.K. Howe, *Solving the Riddle of the Lost Colony* (Beaufort, NC: C.K. Howe, 1947); Hamilton McMillan, *The Lost Colony Found: An Historical Sketch of the Discovery of the Croatan Indians* (Lumberton, NC: Robeson Job Print, n.d.); Albert F. Pate, *The Search for Johnny Chevin: Being a Poetic Quest out of the Most Ancient Records and Oldest Oral Traditions for the Descendants of Sir Walter Raleigh's "Lost Colony"* (Pikeville, NC: Albert F. Pate, 1991).

24  Robert Berkhofer, *The White Man's Indian: Images of the American Indian from Columbus to the Present* (New York: Alfred A. Knopf, 1978); Philip Deloria, *Playing Indian* (New Haven: Yale University Press, 1998); Denis Diderot, *Supplement au Voyage de Bougainville ou Dialogue entre A et B* (1772; repr., Paris: Livre de Poche, 1972).

25  Peter Hulme, *Colonial Encounters: Europe and the Native Caribbean, 1492-1797* (London and New York: Methuen, 1986), 73-78.

26  The Paul Green play, *The Lost Colony*, written and originally staged in 1937, is still produced for a summer season each year in Manteo, NC, adjacent to Fort Raleigh National Historic Site. A "symphonic drama," it was the first in-situ, outdoor historical drama (as opposed to a pageant) in the United States. Its plot is based on imagined historical events involving the primary Indian characters Wanchese and Manteo, and English figures such as Raleigh, John White, and Ananias Dare. For Green, the Lost Colony represented the establishment of an egalitarian, liberal English society on American soil, the nobility of which would be betrayed by those who came later. See Laurence G. Avery, *A Paul Green Reader* (Chapel Hill: University of North Carolina Press, 1998), 11-12.

27  Stephen Greenblatt, *Marvelous Possessions: The Wonder of the New World* (Chicago: University of Chicago Press, 1991), 60-61; Thomas Hariot, "A brief and true report on the new found land of Virginia," in *The Lost Colonists: Documents,* eds. Quinn and Quinn, 46-76; Dale L. Hutchinson et al., eds., *Foraging, Farming, and Coastal Biocultural Adaptation in Late Prehistoric North Carolina* (Gainesville: University Press of Florida, 2002). The coastal Algonquians appear to have pursued a mixed economy, including some foraging and, especially, fishing, as was to be expected. This entailed some seasonal movement. The people of the coast were certainly more mobile and had a more diverse resource base than did groups to the west and north. However, this observation does not contradict the notion that this was a settled agricultural society, a point brought home clearly by John White's depiction of coastal Algonquian society.

28  Fred Gleach, *Powhatan's World and Colonial Virginia: A Conflict of Cultures* (Lincoln: University of Nebraska Press, 1997); Helen Rountree, *Pocahontas's People: The Powhatan Indians of Virginia through Four Centuries* (Norman: University of Oklahoma Press, 1990).

29  Laurence G. Avery, *A Paul Green Reader* (Chapel Hill: University of North Carolina Press, 1998), 125-26.

30  Deloria, *Playing Indian,* 64-65, 73-77.

31  Raymond Fogelson, "Who Were the Ani-Kutani? An Excursion into Cherokee Historical Thought," *Ethnohistory* 31 (1984): 255-63.

32  Sallie Southall Cotten, "The White Doe: The Fate of Virginia Dare, an Indian Legend," in *England and Roanoke: A Collection of Poems, 1585-1987,* eds. William S. Powell and Virginia Powell (1901; repr., Raleigh: North Carolina Department of Cultural Resources, 1988), 126-53. The almost immediate influence of Cotten's poem can be seen in the work of another published poet, Benjamin Sledd, who uses the image of the white doe in his poem "The Vision of the Milk-White Doe," published in 1902.

33  Collier Cobb, "Early English Survivals on Hatteras Island," in *The North Carolina Booklet* 14, 2 (1914): 91-99. The well-known University of North Carolina geologist Collier Cobb adds a further twist to the idea of an Elizabethan presence on the Outer Banks: shipwrecks, some as early as 1558, deposited English sailors, so that a Creole population was well established by the time of the Lost Colony. Surely, such a community would have been noted by Harriot or White!

34  W.J. Cash, *The Mind of the South* (New York: Vintage, 1991), 5-10.

35  Ibid., 124, 158-62.

36  Cotten, "The White Doe," 135.

37  Kupperman, *Roanoke: The Abandoned Colony*, 115-17.

38  Algirdas J. Greimas, *On Meaning: Selected Writings on Semiotic Theory* (Minneapolis: University of Minnesota Press, 1987), 63-84.

39  Cotten's own refined background is evident in her frequent use of classical allusion. The pursuit of a woman as prey who upon capture is transformed into a plant is reminiscent of the myth of Daphne. A common trope for virginity in Victorian times, Daphne represents the idea of a possession always deferred, and so is appropriate in the context of the Lost Colony.

40  Frederic Jameson, "Foreword," in *On Meaning: Selected Writings*, xiii-xiv.

41  Frederic Jameson, *Postmodernism: Or, the Cultural Logic of Late Capitalism* (Durham, NC: Duke University Press, 1993).

42  Ford, "The Finding of Raleigh's Lost Colony," 22-31. The belief that the scuppernong grape and its possibilities for vinification were discovered by the Lost Colonists is central to the theory that the Lumbee are their descendants. The Lumbee, like other communities in eastern North Carolina, traditionally made sweet wine from the scuppernong grape. The connection was still significant in the popular imagination in the early to mid twentieth century. The first commercial wine produced in the United States, immediately upon the repeal of prohibition, was called Virginia Dare, and made from scuppernong grapes (http://www.winereviewonline.com/wine_lore.cfm; Raymond Fogelson personal communication 2004).

43  James Axtell, *The Indians' New South: Cultural Change in the Colonial Southeast* (Baton Rouge: Louisiana State University Press, 1997).

44  Julia Kristeva, *Powers of Horror: An Essay on Abjection*, trans. Leon S. Roudiez (New York: Columbia University Press, 1982).

45  Charles Nuckolls, *Culture: A Problem That Cannot Be Solved* (Madison: University of Wisconsin Press, 1998).

46  Marc Chénetier, *La Perte de l'Amérique: Archéologie d'un amour* (Paris: Belin, 2000); Miller, *Roanoke;* Giles Milton, *Big Chief Elizabeth: How England's Adventurers Gambled and Won the New World* (London: Sceptre, 2000). One should not discount the significance of the quadricentenary. Providing a wealth of primary and scholarly texts, mainly through the aegis of the North Carolina state government, it undoubtedly spurred popular interest in the Lost Colony. During the 1960s, it should be recalled, the Civil War became a remarkable growth industry, producing both scholarship and touristic experiences (as well as hobbyists, re-enactors, and similar phenomena). This was also, of course, linked to the events of the 1960s, especially the civil rights movement.

47  Bailey, "Was the Lost Colony Really Lost?"; Parramore, "The 'Lost Colony' Found"; Pate, *The Search for Johnny Chevin*.

48  See Richard Handler and Eric Gable, *The New History in an Old Museum: Creating the Past in Colonial Williamsburg* (Durham, NC: Duke University Press, 1997).

49  US Bureau of the Census, 2000 Census, North Carolina Summary File 1.

50  Jean-François Lyotard, *The Postmodern Condition: A Report on Knowledge* (Minneapolis: University of Minnesota Press, 1984).

51  Arjun Appadurai, *Modernity at Large: Cultural Dimensions of Globalization* (Minneapolis: University of Minnesota Press, 1996), 188; Gilles Deleuze and Félix Guattari, *A Thousand Plateaus: Capitalism and Schizophrenia*, trans. Brian Massumi (Minneapolis: University of Minnesota Press, 1987). See also Akhil Gupta and James Ferguson, *Anthropological Locations: Boundaries and Grounds of a Field Science* (Berkeley: University of California Press, 1997).

52  Benedict Anderson, *Imagined Communities: Reflections on the Origin and Spread of Nationalism* (New York: Verso, 1983).

53  C. Vann Woodward, *The Burden of Southern History* (New York: New American Library, 1968), 3-25.

54  Inglis Fletcher, "The Elizabethan Background of North Carolina," *DAR Magazine,* March 1952: 274-78; J.W. Higginson, "An English Nation," *Harper's,* April 1883, 707-10.

55  Collier Cobb, "Race and Rehabilitation" (address before the Roanoke Colony Memorial Association at Old Fort Raleigh, Roanoke Island, North Carolina, Virginia Dare Day, 18 August 1923), 2-3.

### Chapter 7: Stories from the Margins

A version of this chapter appeared in the *Journal of American Folklore*, 118, 70 (Fall 2005). Copyright 2005 by the Board of Trustees of the University of Illinois. Used with permission of the University of Illinois Press.

1  See, for example, James Clifford, *The Predicament of Culture: Twentieth-Century Ethnography, Literature, and Art* (Cambridge: Harvard University Press, 1988); David Murray, *Forked Tongues: Speech, Writing and Representation in North American Indian Texts* (Bloomington: Indiana University Press, 1991); Michael Harkin, "Past Presence: Conceptions of History in Northwest Coast Studies," *Arctic Anthropology* 33, 2 (1996): 1-15; Michael Harkin, "(Dis)pleasures of the Text: Boasian Ethnology on the Central Northwest Coast," in *Gateways: Exploring the Legacy of the Jesup North Pacific Expedition, 1897-1902,* eds. Igor Krupnik and William W. Fitzhugh (Washington, DC: Smithsonian Institution, 2001), 93-105; Charles Briggs and Richard Bauman, "'The Foundation of All Future Researches': Franz Boas, George Hunt, Native American Texts, and the Construction of Modernity," *American Quarterly* 51, 3 (1999): 479-527; Judith Berman, "*The Culture as It Appears to the Indian Himself:* Boas, George Hunt, and the Methods of Ethnography," in *Volkgeist as Method and Ethic: Essays on Boasian Ethnography and the German Anthropological Tradition,* ed. George W. Stocking Jr. (Madison: University of Wisconsin Press, 1996), 215-56; Arnold Krupat, *Ethnocriticism: Ethnography, History, Literature* (Berkeley: University of California Press, 1992); Michael Elliott, *The Culture Concept: Writing and Difference in the Age of Realism* (Minneapolis: University of Minnesota Press, 2002); Rosalind Morris, *New Worlds from Fragments: Film Ethnography, and the Representation of Northwest Coast Cultures* (Boulder: Westview Press, 1994); and Christopher Bracken, *The Potlatch Papers: A Colonial Case Study* (Chicago: University of Chicago Press, 1997).

2  Briggs and Bauman, "'The Foundation of All Future Researches,'" 504. For a more detailed analysis of the influences of the Germanic intellectual tradition on Boas' anthropology, see Matti Bunzl, "Franz Boas and the Humboldtian Tradition: From *Volkgeist* and *National-charakter* to an Anthropological Concept of Culture," in *Volkgeist as Method and Ethic,* ed. Stocking, 17-78.

3  Briggs and Bauman, "'The Foundation of All Future Researches,'" 504.

4  Joanne Fiske, "From Customary Law to Oral Traditions: Discursive Formation of Plural Legalisms in Northern British Columbia, 1857-1993," *BC Studies* 115-16 (Autumn–Winter 1997-98): 284.

5  My literature review included Franz Boas, "Indianische Sagen von Nord-pacifischen Küste Amerikas," in *Donerabdruck aus den Verhandlungen der Berliner Gesellschaft fur Anthropologie, Ethnologie and Urgeschichte, 1891 bis 1895* (Berlin: A. Asher, 1895); James Teit, "Traditions of the Thompson River Indians of British Columbia," in *Memoirs of the American Folk-Lore Society,* ed. Franz Boas (London: Houghton, Mifflin, 1898), 203-416; James Teit, *Mythology of the Thompson Indians,* ed. Franz Boas, Memoir of the American Museum of Natural History, vol. 8, pt. 2 (New York: G.E. Stechert, 1912); Franz Boas, ed., *Folk-Tales of Salishan and Sahaptin Tribes,* collected by James Teit, Marion K. Gould, Livingston Farrand, and Herbert Spinden (New York: G.E. Stechert, 1917), 1-201; Leslie Spier, ed., *The Sinkaietk or Southern Okanagon of Washington,* General Series in Anthropology, no. 6 (Menasha, WI: George Banta, 1938); and Mourning Dove, *Coyote Stories,* ed. Heister Dean (1933; repr., Lincoln: University of Nebraska Press, 1990); Randy Bouchard and Dorothy Kennedy, "Lillooet Stories," *Sound Heritage* 6, 1 (1977): 1-78. Later, I added Dorothy Kennedy and Randy Bouchard, *Shuswap Stories* (Vancouver: CommCept Publishing, 1979), and Darwin Hanna and Mamie Henry, eds., *Our Tellings: Interior Salish Stories of the Nlha7kápmx People* (Vancouver: UBC Press, 1995).

6  Robinson told me this story on 29 August 1979 at his home in Hedley, BC, during our first formal recording session. A verbatim transcript appears in Wendy Wickwire, ed., *Write It on Your Heart: The Epic World of an Okanagan Storyteller* (Vancouver: Talonbooks and Theytus, 1989), 31-52.

7 Robinson told me this story on 20 September 1980 at his home in Hedley. A verbatim transcript appears in ibid., 168-97.

8 Claude Lévi-Strauss, *The Savage Mind* (Chicago: University of Chicago Press, 1966). Since the late 1980s, the structuralist separation of history and myth has been the subject of critical debate. See, for example, the chapters in Jonathan D. Hill, ed., *Rethinking History and Myth: Indigenous South American Perspectives on the Past* (Urbana: University of Illinois Press, 1988).

9 See, for example, "Captive in an English Circus" and "To Hell and Back," in Wickwire, *Write It on Your Heart,* 244-66, 267-81; and "Rainbow at Night" and "Go Get Susan, See What She Can Do," in Wendy Wickwire, *Nature Power: In the Spirit of an Okanagan Storyteller* (Vancouver/Seattle: Douglas and McIntyre/University of Washington Press, 1992; Vancouver: Talonbooks, 2004), 44-52, 123-47.

10 Because Robinson knew that many visitors preferred to hear the old "legends" and "myths," he may have assumed in the early stages of our acquaintance that I too would be most interested in these. As the project unfolded, however, he took charge and told whatever stories he felt like telling. Throughout our work together, especially in 1982, I questioned him fairly systematically about notions of spirituality. His response to such questions was to tell a series of stories about "power." I published some of these in Wickwire, *Nature Power.*

11 From transcripts of audiotaped interviews conducted between 1977 and 1991 (in the author's possession).

12 Julie Cruikshank, *The Social Life of Stories: Narrative and Knowledge in the Yukon Territory* (Lincoln/Vancouver: University of Nebraska Press/UBC Press, 1998), 119.

13 For excellent examples of contextual analysis, see Richard Bauman, *Story, Performance, and Event: Contextual Studies or Oral Narrative* (New York: Cambridge University Press, 1986); Joel Sherzer, *Speech Play and Verbal Art* (Austin: University of Texas, 2002); Richard Bauman and Charles Briggs, *Voices of Modernity: Language Ideologies and the Politics of Inequality* (New York: Cambridge University Press, 2003).

14 Bauman, *Story, Performance, and Event,* 2.

15 Carolyn Hamilton, "*Living by Fluidity:* Oral Histories, Material Custodies and the Politics of Archiving," in *Refiguring the Archive,* eds. Carolyn Hamilton et al. (Amsterdam: Kluwer Academic Publishers, 2002), 226.

16 Wickwire, *Write It on Your Heart,* 11-13.

17 Interview by author, 16 April 1984.

18 Interview with author, 15 April 1984.

19 See, for example, "Coyote Tales," in Boas, *Folk-Tales,* 1-13; and Mourning Dove, *Coyote Stories.*

20 What follows are excerpts from the audiotaped version of this story that I recorded in November 1980 at Robinson's home. As noted above, I had recorded a shortened version of the story on 29 August 1979, during our first formal recording session. A verbatim transcript of this story appears in Wickwire, *Write It on Your Heart,* 31-52. All quotations used here are taken from the 1980 account.

21 Wickwire, *Write It on Your Heart,* 119-22, 46.

22 Robinson told me this story in full on 20 September 1980 at Hedley. It is transcribed in full in Wickwire, *Write It on Your Heart,* 168-97.

23 Wickwire, *Write It on Your Heart,* 186-87.

24 Interview by author, 20 November 1980.

25 Wickwire, *Nature Power,* 23.

26 See, for example, Michael Harkin, "History, Narrative, and Temporality: Examples from the Northwest Coast," *Ethnohistory* 35, 2 (1998): 99-130; Wendy Wickwire, "To See Ourselves as the Other's Other: Nlaka'pamux Contact Narratives," *Canadian Historical Review* 75, 1 (March 1994): 1-20; Cruikshank, *The Social Life of Stories;* Catharine McClellan, "Indian Stories about the First Whites in Northwestern North America," in *Ethnohistory in Southwestern Alaska and Southern Yukon: Method and Content,* ed. Margaret Lantis (Lexington: University Press of Kentucky, 1970), 103-33; and Elizabeth Vibert, "'The Natives Were Strong to Live': Plague, Prophecy and Prelude to the Encounter," in *Traders' Tales: Narratives of Cultural Encounters in the Columbia Plateau, 1807-1846* (Norman: University of Oklahoma Press, 1997), 50-83.

27  Wickwire, "To See Ourselves"; for a Coast Salish variant of this story, see p. 61 of the present volume.
28  See Jonathan D. Hill, "Myth and History," 1-17; Terence Turner, "Ethno-ethnohistory: Myth and History in Native South American Representations of Contact with Western Society," 235-81; and Emilienne Ireland, "Cerebral Savage: The Whiteman as Symbol of Cleverness and Savagery in Waura Myth," 157-73, all in *Rethinking History and Myth,* ed. Hill.
29  Turner, "Ethno-ethnohistory," 237; Ireland, "Cerebral Savage," 172.
30  For more on this, see Wickwire, *Write It on Your Heart,* 75-85; Wickwire, *Nature Power,* 240-47.
31  Wickwire, *Write It on Your Heart,* 244-82.
32  Wendy Wickwire, ed., *Living By Stories: A Journey of Landscape and Memory* (Vancouver: Talonbooks, 2005), 148-51.
33  Cruikshank, *The Social Life of Stories,* 137.
34  Leslie Spier, *The Prophet Dance of the Northwest and Its Derivatives: The Source of the Ghost Dance,* General Series in Anthropology, no. 1 (Menasha, WI: George Banta, 1935).
35  Wayne Suttles, "The Plateau Prophet Dance among the Coast Salish," *Southwest Journal of Anthropology* 6, 4 (1966): 352-96; David Aberle, "The Prophet Dance and Reactions to White Contact," *Southwestern Journal of Anthropology* 15 (1959): 74-83; Deward Walker, "New Light on the Prophet Dance Controversy," *Ethnohistory* 16 (1969): 245-55.
36  Christopher Miller, *Prophetic Worlds: Indians and Whites on the Columbia Plateau* (New Brunswick, NJ: Rutgers University Press, 1985).
37  Robin Ridington, *Swan People: A Study of the Dunne-za Prophet Dance,* Canadian Ethnology Service Mercury Series, no. 38 (Ottawa: National Museums of Canada, 1978), and *Trail to Heaven: Knowledge and Narrative in a Northern Community* (Toronto: Douglas and McIntyre, 1988).
38  Cruikshank, *The Social Life of Stories,* 117.
39  Louie Phillips, personal communication, 10 March 1991.
40  Interview with Annie York, 31 May 1985.
41  Interview with Hilda Austin, 8 April 1991.
42  Cruikshank, *The Social Life of Stories,* 117.
43  Boas, "Indianische Sagen," 17. Marianne Boelscher-Ignace and Ashley Hilliard provided the English translation of this story.
44  Quoted in Ronald Rohner, comp. and ed., *The Ethnography of Franz Boas: Letters and Diaries of Franz Boas Written on the Northwest Coast from 1886 to 1931* (Chicago: University of Chicago Press, 1969), 100.
45  Boas, "Indianische Sagen," 17.
46  For a more detailed analysis of this story, see Wendy Wickwire, "Prophecy at Lytton," in *Voices from Four Directions: Contemporary Translations of the Native Literatures of North America,* ed. Brian Swann (Lincoln: University of Nebraska Press, 2004), 134-70.
47  Teit, "Traditions," 52; Teit, *Mythology,* 231; Boas, *Folk-Tales,* 35.
48  Wickwire, *Write It on Your Heart,* 185, 187 (emphasis added).
49  A comparison of Teit's field notes to Boas' final edited version suggests that Boas occasionally applied a heavy editorial hand before publishing the stories he received from Teit. In the case of the NkékaumstEm story about the boy and his grandmother, Teit's fieldnotes listed "a gun" among the various items that Sun traded. Teit Fieldnotes, ed. Franz Boas, Anthropology Archives, American Museum of Natural History, New York City, n.d. Yet when Boas edited the story for publication, he eliminated the word "gun" from the list of items that Sun traded for the skin robe. Boas, *Folk-Tales,* 43.
50  Teit, *Mythology,* 416; Boas, *Folk-Tales* 64.
51  Teit, *Mythology,* 415, 320-21; Teit, "Traditions," 54.
52  Teit, *Mythology,* 326; Teit, "Traditions," 109; Teit, *Mythology,* 226; Mourning Dove, *Coyote Stories,* 17; Spier, *The Sinkaietk,* 167.
53  Teit, "Traditions," 52; Teit, *Mythology,* 397; Teit, "Traditions," 91; Hanna and Henry, *Our Tellings,* 124; Wickwire, "To See Ourselves," 13-16.
54  Boas, *Folk-Tales,* 49-50.
55  Walter Cline, in Spier, *The Sinkaietk,* 176, 177.

56 Evidence, 17/11/14, Evidence, 17/11/14, and Evidence, 18/11/14, Canada, Royal Commission on Indian Affairs for the Province of British Columbia (McKenna-McBride Commission), Evidence, 1913-14, British Columbia Archives, Victoria, BC.
57 Quoted in Rohner, *The Ethnography of Franz Boas*, 38.
58 Judith Berman, "Oolachan-Woman's Robe: Fish, Blankets, Masks and Meaning in Boas' Kwakw'ala Texts," in *On the Translation of Native American Literatures*, ed. Brian Swann (Washington, DC: Smithsonian Institution Press, 1992), 126.
59 Murray, *Forked Tongues*, 99.
60 Cruikshank, *The Social Life of Stories*, 23.
61 Michael Harkin, "History, Narrative, and Temporality," 101.

**Chapter 8: When the White *Kawau* Flies**
I would like to acknowledge helpful comments on an earlier version of this chapter, presented at the colloquium "Worlds in Collision" at the University of Victoria, British Columbia, especially those of Wendy Wickwire and Ted Chamberlin. I am also grateful to the editor, John Lutz, for his additional suggestions.
N.B. The macron (diacritic) marks the long vowel in Maori words. Proper names and place names are not marked in this chapter, and they are variously spelled in source materials.
1 From Elsdon Best, *Tuhoe: The Children of the Mist*, 2 vols. (1925; repr., 3rd ed., Wellington, NZ: A.H. and A.W. Reed for the Polynesian Society, 1977), 1:149. The narrative of the albino *kawau* (cormorant), Hine-ruarangi, is discussed below.
2 See Rosaleen Howard-Malverde, *The Speaking of History: "Willapaakushayki" or Quechua Ways of Telling the Past* (London: Institute of Latin American Studies, 1990), 3-4.
3 I have examined "pleromatic history" and Maori narratives in a previous essay, "Myth and Explanation in the Ringatū Tradition: Some Aspects of the Leadership of Te Kooti Arikirangi Te Turuki and Rua Kēnana Hepetipa," *Journal of the Polynesian Society* 93, 4 (December 1984): 345-98.
4 Julie Cruikshank, *The Social Life of Stories: Narrative and Knowledge in the Yukon Territory* (Lincoln/Vancouver: University of Nebraska Press/UBC Press, 1998), 2-3, 40, 118, 135.
5 Gavin Smith, "'He holds him with his glittering eye': Intellectuals and the Re-covering of the Past," in *Memory at the Margins: Essays in Anthropology and World History*, eds. Gavin Smith, June Nash, and Dolores Waldenstrom Stanley (Victoria, BC: World History Caucus, University of Victoria, 1995), 11.
6 Ibid., 22.
7 The song text, and accompanying narrative, is in Judith Binney, *Redemption Songs: A Life of the Nineteenth-Century Maori Leader Te Kooti Arikirangi Te Turuki* (1995; repr., Honolulu/Melbourne: University of Hawaii Press/University of Melbourne Press, 1997), 11-12.
8 So named by Apirana Ngata, in *New Zealand Parliamentary Debates* (NZPD), "Second Reading of the Urewera District Native Reserve Amendment Bill, debate," 148 (1909), 1388.
9 The narratives in *Tuhoe* were recorded in a number of different contexts: told to Best personally; narrated in the Native Land Court; and told to the first Urewera Commission (1899-1902), which was set up to establish land blocks within the Urewera District Native Reserve. Best acted as secretary of the commission in its early years.
10 Thus named in Robert Price's 1874 account of the council's early formation, *Through the Uriwera Country* (Napier: Daily Telegraph Office, 1891), 45. Hokowhitu is a band or complement of men. Translated literally, the term means 140 (20 times 7) men.
11 Te Whitu Tekau may be translated as either 10 or 20 times 7. All references to the council in English were to the "Seventy." I suggest that the number "seventy" had scriptural associations, discussed below. It was not to be interpreted as a literal number.
12 The Waitangi Tribunal was given retrospective powers of inquiry by statute in December 1985. The treaty signed at Waitangi on 6 February 1840 created New Zealand as a British colony. The Maori text of the treaty, which bears the vast majority of the five hundred signatures collected during 1840, simultaneously recognized *"te tino rangatiratanga"* (the fullness of chieftainship) and Maori rights as British citizens.
13 The Waitangi Tribunal has yet to report on the Urewera claims.

14 And much more followed. Quoted in Greg Dening, *Performances* (Chicago/Melbourne: University of Chicago Press/Melbourne University Press, 1996), 193-94.

15 Narrative told by Hemi Kopu, Tuhoe elder of Ruatoki, to Best, in *Tuhoe*, 1:557.

16 Ibid., 531-33. Best was quoting "a native account," but here did not identify the narrator.

17 From a transcript of dialogues between the Tuhoe elder Horopapera Tatu and Jeffrey Sissons in 1977-78, in Sissons, *Te Waimana: The Spring of Mana* (Dunedin: University of Otago Press, 1991), 279. Horopapera Tatu died in 1978.

18 J. Wharehuia Milroy, "Te Ngahuru," *Dictionary of New Zealand Biography (DNZB)* (Wellington, NZ: Allen and Unwin/Department of Internal Affairs, 1990), 1:474. As a Tuhoe elder (as well as an academic), Milroy drew on his oral knowledge.

19 "The greenstone door" (a lintel, or threshold of peace) entered into colonial fiction as the title of a novel by William Satchell concerning the New Zealand wars, published in 1914.

20 Best cited it in *Tuhoe*, 1:494, but ridiculed the associated narrative of peace.

21 Oral Source (OS): Tuhoe elder John Ru Tahuri, Rotorua, 23-24 March 1998, tape 1b. Dialogue with Judith Binney and Robert Wiri. John Tahuri died in April 2005.

22 Best, *Tuhoe*, 1:493-94.

23 OS: John Tahuri, 23-24 March 1998, tape 1b.

24 Best, *Tuhoe*, 1:566-67.

25 Ibid., 567.

26 OS: John Tahuri, 23-24 March 1998, tape 1a.

27 Tutakangahau, talking with Best. Tutakangahau was one of Best's main informants. Best, *Tuhoe*, 1:567.

28 Pou Temara, "Te Whenuanui," *DNZB*, 2:529. Temara, like Milroy, writes with personal knowledge as Tuhoe. He is also an academic.

29 OS: John Tahuri, 23-24 March 1998, tape 1a. The expedition led by Tukorehu is mentioned in Best, *Tuhoe*, 1:181. The narrative of the duel, and the consequential pact, was also told by Hirini Melbourne (a Tuhoe and an academic until his untimely death in 2003) in his biography of Te Purewa, *DNZB*, 1:485.

30 Paitini Wi Tapeka, 1906, narrated (and translated) in Best, *Tuhoe*, 1:574-75. Paitini's brother, Paora, was killed at Orakau. Piripi Te Heuheu and his wife Mere also died there.

31 Ibid., 576.

32 For a brief biography, see Judith Binney, "Te Kooti Arikirangi Te Turuki," *Oxford Dictionary of National Biography,* vol. 54 (Oxford: Oxford University Press, 2004).

33 Te Whenuanui and all the tribe to the government, 9 June 1872, *Appendices to the Journal of the House of Representatives (AJHR)* (1872), F-3A, 29. (No Maori original.)

34 Exodus 24:1, 9-10; Numbers 11:16, 24-25.

35 S. Percy Smith, "Reminiscences," 1916, 124, MSS 281, box 1, Auckland Museum, Auckland, NZ. The "King Country" refers to the tribal lands of Ngati Maniapoto, who were by then also sheltering the Maori king in exile. Percy Smith was surveyor-general, and was responsible for the decision to force through the Urewera road in 1895. He was also, equally importantly, the founder of the Polynesian Society in 1892, whose purpose was to record Polynesian history and traditions.

36 The song refers here to three mountains in the eastern Bay of Plenty. Te Kaharoa is on the eastern edge of the modern Urewera district, overlooking the land block Tahora No. 2: its inclusion in the waiata was a reference to the unauthorized survey and loss of much of Tahora No. 2 in 1887-89. Te Pukenui-o-Raho, which stands immediately south of the 1866 confiscation line where it crosses the Waiotahe River, is a recurring oral reference marker for that confiscation. Both mountains are marked on Map 2. Waiputatawa mountain (and trig station) lies four miles due north of Pukenui-o-Raho, inside the confiscated block. These three "boundary markers" *(pou rāhui)* are pointers to major nineteenth-century land losses for Tuhoe in the eastern Bay of Plenty.

37 "Ko Ranginui," recorded by Tuhitaare, a Tuhoe *tohunga* (expert). Text by courtesy of Taiarahia Black, Tuhitaare's great-grandson; translation by courtesy of Tama Nikora of Tuhoe. In the song, "the curse" (ūpokokohua) of confiscation is attributed to Piripi Te Heuheu's decision to go to Orakau, Maniapoto's place: "te ūpokokohua Te Urewera / Whakarewa ko Piripi Te Heuheu / Ki Orākau ko Maniapoto."

38 Records of a meeting at Ruatoki, 17 March 1892, Robert Biddle MSS, trans. Hineira Woodard and J. Wharehuia Milroy (private collection), 5:131. This collection was collated by Robert Biddle, secretary of the Haahi Ringatu (Ringatu Church), in 1927. Biddle was the first secretary of the church, which was registered in 1929, thirty-six years after Te Kooti's death.

39 OS: Robert (Boy) Biddle, Kutarere, 15 October 1987, tape 3b. Boy Biddle was his father's successor as secretary of the Haahi Ringatu. Boy Biddle was a leading elder within Tuhoe until his death in 1996.

40 NZPD, "Urewera District Native Reserve Act, introduced," 96 (1896), 166 (Richard Seddon).

41 Revelation 6:5.

42 OS: John Ihe, Waiotahe, 28 January 1983, tape 1a.

43 OS: Ned (Mokopuna) Brown, Mangatu, 14 February 1982, tape 1b.

44 J.C. Richmond to Colonel T. Haultain, 19 December 1868, Army Defence (AD) 1/1868/5014, Archives New Zealand, Wellington, NZ (NAW).

45 The details are in Binney, *Redemption Songs*, 161, 593n56.

46 In Poverty Bay (Turanganui) and East Coast farms today, white horses are seen with unusual frequency: perhaps they are descendants of early farming and military stock.

47 Revelation 19:11-13.

48 Photographs reproduced in Judith Binney, Gillian Chaplin, and Craig Wallace, *Mihaia: The Prophet Rua Kenana and his Community at Maungapohatu* (1979; repr., 4th ed., Auckland: Auckland University Press, 2005), 24, 28.

49 Twelve is a "sacred" number, or a number of power, in the Ringatu faith. The holy day is the twelfth of each month.

50 H.R. Burt, signed statement, 10 December 1887, Maori Affairs (MA) 1/1920/218/1, NAW (also copied in Wai 212 E4, vol. 2, p. 65, Waitangi Tribunal).

51 "The Prediction of One to Follow," MSS collated by Te Haahi o Te Kooti Rikirangi, Frank Davis, Dossier 10:10, restricted conditions of access, Alexander Turnbull Library (ATL), Wellington, NZ. This volume contains sayings and texts pertaining to Te Kooti compiled by Te Haahi o Te Kooti Rikirangi, a separately registered branch of the Ringatu faith.

52 OS: Hieke Tupe, Waiohau, 26 November 1999.

53 OS: Boy Biddle, Kutarere, 5 March 1983, tape 2a.

54 This aspect, and many more details of the fraud, are discussed in Judith Binney, "Te Umutaoroa: The Earth Oven of Long Cooking," in *Histories, Power and Loss: Uses of the Past – A New Zealand Commentary*, eds. Andrew Sharp and Paul McHugh (Wellington, NZ: Bridget Williams Books, 2001), 147-64.

55 Biddle MSS, 5:5. Trans. Jane McRae.

56 Rangiruru, Ngati Whare elder of Te Whaiti, quoted in S.M. Mead, ed., "Three Carved Houses at Te Whaiti: Part III, Eripitana" (research dossier, Anthropology Department, University of Auckland, 1970), 3.

57 See Binney, *Redemption Songs*, 326.

58 Robert Wiri discusses its history in "The Prophecies of the Great Canyon of Toi: A History of Te Whāiti-nui-a-Toi in the Western Urewera Mountains of New Zealand" (PhD diss., University of Auckland, 2001). He considers the story of Hine-ruarangi on pages 6, 239-40.

59 Best, *Tuhoe*, 1:149-50. Best lived at Te Whaiti in 1895-96, and this story is his translation (and gloss) of a narrative he was told at that time.

60 J.C. Blythe, "Report of Expedition 2-11 June 1885," *AJHR* (1885), C-1A, 32.

61 S. Percy Smith, 9 March 1886, Diary, MS-1985; Smith, Notebook 1883-90, MS-2023, ATL.

62 Giselle Byrnes, "Inventing New Zealand: Surveying, Science, and the Construction of Cultural Space, 1840s-1890s" (PhD diss., University of Auckland, 1995), 16. Revised and published as *Boundary Markers* (Wellington, NZ: Bridget Williams Books, 2001).

63 S. Percy Smith, "Annual Report on Department of Lands and Survey," *AJHR* (1896), C-1, xi. The first topographical map of the Urewera is set alongside this statement.

64 W.H. Bowler to Native Department, 15 March 1920, MA 1/1910/28/10, NAW.

65 OS: John Tahuri, 23-24 March 1998, tape 5a.

66 Ibid., tape 1b.

67 The full song text is quoted in Binney, *Redemption Songs*, 448.

68  OS: John Tahuri, 23-24 March 1998, tape 1b.
69  Ibid., tape 5a.
70  Binney, Chaplin, and Wallace, *Mihaia;* Peter Webster, *Rua and the Maori Millennium* (Wellington, NZ: Victoria University Press, 1979); Sissons, *Te Waimana.*
71  Such as the late John Rangihau, Wharehuia Milroy, the late Hirini Melbourne, Pou Temara, Taiarahia Black, Hineira Woodard, and Robert Wiri.
72  Binney, Chaplin, and Wallace, *Mihaia;* Judith Binney and Gillian Chaplin, *Ngā Mōrehu: The Survivors* (1986; repr., 3rd ed., Auckland: Auckland University Press, 2004); Binney, *Redemption Songs;* Binney, "Te Umutaoroa."
73  OS: John Tahuri, 23-24 March 1998, tape 5a.

### Chapter 9: The Interpreter as Contact Point

1  Lewis Hyde, *Trickster Makes This World: Mischief, Myth, and Art* (New York: Farrar, Straus, and Giroux, 1998), 264.
2  This lease and its impact are little known and appreciated. See, especially, Laura F. Klein, "Demystifying the Opposition: The Hudson's Bay Company and the Tlingit," *Arctic Anthropology* 24, 1 (1987): 101-14.
3  Much of the primary archival material is in Russian manuscript, and often in Russia itself, where many of the archives were classified and closed during the Soviet era. Thanks especially to the labours of Richard A. Pierce, his colleagues, and the Limestone Press, many of the important primary documents and books of and about the period are steadily becoming available in English translation. In this regard, we also thank Lydia T. Black and Sergei Kan for their contributions to the field in general, and to this chapter in particular. Their work is referenced elsewhere. Kan's most recent work, and that most relevant to our topic, is his research of the life and times of the Tlingit-Creole interpreter Ivan Zhukov (1825-86): "Bilingual/Bicultural Interpreters and Informants of the Jesup Expedition Era," in *Constructing Cultures Then and Now: Celebrating Franz Boas and the Jesup North Pacific Expedition,* eds. Laurel Kendall and Igor Krupnik, Circumpolar Anthropology, no. 4 (Washington, DC: Smithsonian Institution Press, 2003), 185-97. Zhukov's material, which appears under the spelling "Shukoff," was used extensively by George Thornton Emmons and is cited in his *The Tlingit Indians,* ed. Frederica de Laguna (New York, Seattle, and London: University of Washington Press and the American Museum of Natural History, 1991). Kan, "Bilingual/Bicultural" also discusses the well-known Sitka interpreter George Kostromitinov (1854-1915). An excellent Russian treatment is A.V. Grinev, *Indejtsy Tlinkity v Period Russkoj Ameriki 1741-1867* (Novosibirsk: Nauka, 1991), which contains over twenty pages of previously unpublished archival documents, gives detailed accounts of Russian-Tlingit relations, including the Sitka and Yakutat revolts, and mentions many Tlingit individuals by name. An English-language translation was produced by Richard L. Bland and Katarina G. Solovjova, *The Tlingit Indians in Russian America 1741-1867* (Lincoln, NB: University of Nebraska Press, 2005).
4  We are indebted to Katherine L. Arndt for calling our attention to this resource and for subsequently guiding us to it and through it, generously sharing her unpublished English summaries of relevant letters; we also thank her for her additional research, checking the interpreters and their families in the various Russian Orthodox Church records from 1797 to 1879.
5  Due to restrictions on length, many important topics, such as Tlingit names and genealogies, remain beyond the scope of this chapter. In an ongoing research project, we are attempting to decipher the Russian spellings of Tlingit names, re-elicit or otherwise confirm these names with community elders, and thereby identify their clan affiliation according to Tlingit social structure. This will shed new light on socio-political dynamics behind events mentioned in the RAC correspondence, especially regarding trading relations and alliances in clan wars and intrigues involving the company. We must also omit the extended family information found in church records (by Katherine Arndt, and generously shared with us). In several places, we also avoid discussion of the complexities and contradictions in the historical record, both written and oral. We hope to expand on these and other topics at a later date.

6 *Russian-American Company Records [Sent]. 1818-67 Correspondence of the Governors General, Communications Sent,* 47 vols. (Washington, DC: US National Archives, 1818-67), CS 32/ 643:485v. The citation format used here refers to the US National Archives microfilm of *Communications Sent* (CS) volume/the number: and the folio. Thus, CS 32/643:485v is vol. 32 of *Correspondence Sent,* no. 643, folio 485 (verso). The lack of a "v" after the number automatically indicates a recto. Originals are at the US National Archives, Washington, DC, and microfilm copies are at various sites, including the Alaska State Historical Library in Juneau. Correspondence descriptions are from the English summaries compiled by Katherine L. Arndt (personal communication, 1997-2002). Also, unless otherwise noted, book references in this chapter are to published English translations. For this chapter, it was necessary to confirm and cite the Russian original of only one book passage, and none of the RAC correspondence.

7 For a review of these encounters, see Nora Marks Dauenhauer and Richard Dauenhauer, eds., *Haa Shuká, Our Ancestors: Tlingit Oral Narratives* (Seattle: University of Washington Press, 1987), 434-40.

8 Ioann Veniaminov, *Zamechaniia o Koloshenskom i Kadiakskom Iazykakh* (St. Petersburg: Imperial Academy of Sciences, 1846).

9 P.A. Tikhmenev, *A History of the Russian American Company,* vol. 2, *Documents,* eds. Richard A. Pierce and Alton S. Donnelly, trans. Dmitri Krenov (Kingston: Limestone Press, 1979), 151. Space does not permit further discussion of the 1805 revolt, a complex story with rich Tlingit oral and Western written traditions. For Tlingit oral accounts recorded in 1949-50, see Frederica de Laguna, *Under Mount Saint Elias: The History and Culture of the Yakutat Tlingit* (Washington, DC: Smithsonian Institution Press, 1972), 173-76, 234-36, 259-61. See also Richard A. Pierce, *Russian America: A Biographical Dictionary* (Fairbanks and Kingston: Limestone Press, 1990), 295.

10 Kiril T. Khlebnikov, *Baranov: Chief Manager of the Russian Colonies in America,* ed. Richard A. Pierce, trans. Colin Bearne (Fairbanks and Kingston: Limestone Press, 1973), 67-68, 124. "Tribesmen" is a critical word, and it accurately translates the original Russian "Plemiannikov." See Kiril T. Khlebnikov, *Zhizneopisanie Aleksandra Andreevicha Baranova, Glavnago Pravitelia Rossiiskikh Kolonii v Amerike* (St. Petersburg: V Morskoi Tipografii, 1835), 119. Among her valuable comments on earlier drafts of this chapter, Dr. Lydia T. Black noted that "plemiannik is a nephew; tribesman is soplemennik; the origin of both words is from plemia (tribe) but plemiannik implies not only co-tribesman but also a kinsman."

11 Hieromonk Gideon, *The Round the World Voyage of Hieromonk Gideon 1803-1809,* trans. with an introduction and notes by Lydia T. Black (Fairbanks and Kingston: Limestone Press, 1989), 109.

12 Other Tlingit interpreters are identified in the paper trail, but space limitations prevent us from documenting them. In October 1805, Georg Heinrich von Langsdorff described a Tlingit woman interpreter whom we assume was the wife of Plotnikov, a survivor of the 1802 Sitka attack. In 1818, Chief Manager Hagemeister mentioned three interpreters: a woman named Domna, a Tlingit hostage named Nikolai, and Paraskovia, the wife of the fur hunter Sokolov. RAC correspondence of 16 May 1834 mentions another Nikolai, who was not satisfactory.

13 We have evaluated Veniaminov's work in Richard Dauenhauer and Nora Marks Dauenhauer, "Ioann Veniaminov as Linguist and Folklorist: Tlingit Language and Folklore" (paper presented at the Veniaminov Bicentennial Conference "Ioann Veniaminov in Alaska and Siberia and his Contribution to Arctic Social Science," University of Alaska-Fairbanks, 5-7 December 1997).

14 Space restrictions prevent our going into any detail on this. See Katherine L. Arndt, "Russian Relations with the Stikine Tlingit, 1833-1867," *Alaska History* 3, 1 (Spring 1988): 27-43; Jonathan Dean, "'Their Nature and Qualities Remain Unchanged': Russian Occupation and Tlingit Resistance, 1802-1867," *Alaska History* 9, 1 (Spring 1994): 1-17; Klein, "Demystifying the Opposition."

15 Klein, "Demystifying the Opposition," 104.

16 Ibid.

17  See Richard L. Dauenhauer, *Conflicting Visions in Alaskan Education* ([Fairbanks]: University of Alaska Veniaminov Bicentennial Project; repr., Juneau: Tlingit Readers, 2004).

18  See Nora Marks Dauenhauer and Richard Dauenhauer, eds., *Haa Ḵusteeyí, Our Culture: Tlingit Life Stories* (Seattle: University of Washington Press, 1994), especially the biographies of Matilda Paul Tamaree, William Paul, Andrew Hope, and the founders of the Alaska Native Brotherhood.

19  See Sergei Kan, *Memory Eternal: Tlingit Culture and Russian Orthodox Christianity through Two Centuries* (Seattle: University of Washington Press, 1999). See also the introduction to Dauenhauer and Dauenhauer, *Haa Ḵusteeyí, Our Culture*, 42-103.

20  See Kan, *Memory Eternal;* S.A. Mousalimas, *From Mask to Icon: Transformation in the Arctic* (Brookline, MA: Holy Cross Orthodox Press, 2003); Michael J. Oleska, *Orthodox Alaska: A Theology of Mission* (Crestwood, NY: St. Vladimir's Seminary Press, 1992); Michael J. Oleska, ed., *Alaskan Missionary Spirituality* (New York and Mahwah, NJ: Paulist Press, 1987); and Andrei A. Znamenski, *Shamanism and Christianity: Native Encounters with Russian Orthodox Missions in Siberia and Alaska, 1820-1917* (Westport, CN: Greenwood Press, 1999).

21  Frances Karttunen, *Between Worlds: Interpreters, Guides, and Survivors* (New Brunswick, NJ: Rutgers University Press, 1994), xi-xiv.

# Bibliography

Aberle, David. "The Prophet Dance and Reactions to White Contact." *Southwestern Journal of Anthropology* 15 (1959): 74-83.

Adams, Percy G. *Travel Literature and the Evolution of the Novel.* Lexington: University Press of Kentucky, 1983.

Anderson, Benedict. *Imagined Communities: Reflections on the Origin and Spread of Nationalism.* New York: Verso, 1983.

Appadurai, Arjun. *Modernity at Large: Cultural Dimensions of Globalization.* Minneapolis: University of Minnesota Press, 1996.

*Appendices to the Journal of the House of Representatives (AJHR)*, F-3A. Wellington, NZ: Government Printer, 1872.

*Appendices to the Journal of the House of Representatives (AJHR)*, C-1A. Wellington, NZ: Government Printer, 1885.

*Appendices to the Journal of the House of Representatives (AJHR)*, C-1. Wellington, NZ: Government Printer, 1896.

Armer, J. Michael, and John Katsillis. *Encyclopedia of Sociology,* edited by Edgar F. Borgatta and Rhonda J.V. Montgomery. 5 vols. New York: Macmillan, 2000. s.v. "Modernization Theory."

Arndt, Katherine L. "Russian Relations with the Stikine Tlingit, 1833-1867." *Alaska History* 3, 1 (Spring 1988): 27-43.

Arner, Robert D. *The Lost Colony in Literature.* Raleigh: North Carolina Department of Cultural Resources, 1982.

Avery, Laurence G. *A Paul Green Reader.* Chapel Hill: University of North Carolina Press, 1998.

Axtell, James. *The Indians' New South: Cultural Change in the Colonial Southeast.* Baton Rouge: Louisiana State University Press, 1997.

Bailey, Josiah. "Was the Lost Colony Really Lost? Some in Cartaret County Tell a Different Version of John White's Historic Expedition." *Our State* 58, 9 (1991): 12-14.

Bainbridge, D.A. "Quercus, a Multipurpose Tree for Temperate Climates." *International Tree Crops Journal* 3 (1986): 291-98.

Bakhtin, Mikhail. *The Dialogic Imagination: Four Essays by M.M. Bakhtin,* edited by Michael Holquist, translated by Caryl Emmerson and Michael Holquist. Austin: University of Texas, 1996.

–. "The Problem of Speech Genres." In *Speech Genres and Other Late Essays,* edited by Caryl Emerson and Michael Holquist, translated by Vern McGee. 60-102. Austin: University of Texas Press, 1986.

Barbeau, Marius. Field Notes. British Columbia Archives, Victoria, BC.

Barlowe, Arthur. "Arthur Barlowe's Narrative of the 1584 Voyage." In *The First Colonists: Documents on the Planting of the First English Settlement in North America, 1584-1590,* edited by David B. Quinn and Alison M. Quinn, 1-12. Raleigh: North Carolina Department of Cultural Resources, Division of Archives and History, 1982.

Barton, Lew. *The Most Ironic Story in American History: An Authoritative, Documented History of the Lumbee Indians of North Carolina.* Pembroke, NC: Lew Barton, 1967.

Basso, Keith. *Portraits of "The Whiteman": Linguistic Play and Cultural Symbols among the Western Apache.* Cambridge: Cambridge University Press, 1979.

Bauman, Richard. *Story, Performance, and Event: Contextual Studies of Oral Narrative.* New York: Cambridge University Press, 1986.

Bauman, Richard, and Charles Briggs. *Voices of Modernity: Language Ideologies and the Politics of Inequality.* New York: Cambridge University Press, 2003.

Beaglehole, J.C., ed. *The Journals of Captain James Cook on His Voyages of Discovery.* Rochester, NY: Boydell Press, 1999.

Beals, Herbert, ed. and trans. *For Honor and Country: The Diary of Bruno de Hezeta.* Portland: Oregon Historical Society, 1985.

–. *Juan Perez on the Northwest Coast: Six Documents of His Expedition in 1774.* Portland: Oregon Historical Society, 1989.

Bennett, Marilyn. *Indian Fishing and Its Cultural Importance in the Fraser River System.* Vancouver: Fisheries Service, Department of the Environment, Canada, and the Union of BC Indian Chiefs, ca. 1973.

Berkhofer, Robert. *The White Man's Indian: Images of the American Indian from Columbus to the Present.* New York: Alfred A. Knopf, 1978.

Berman, Judith. *"The Culture as It Appears to the Indian Himself:* Boas, George Hunt, and the Methods of Ethnography." In *Volkgeist as Method and Ethic: Essays on Boasian Ethnography and the German Anthropological Tradition,* edited by George W. Stocking Jr., 215-56. Madison: University of Wisconsin Press, 1996.

–. "Oolachan-Woman's Robe: Fish, Blankets, Masks and Meaning in Boas' Kwakw'ala Texts." In *On the Translation of Native American Literatures,* edited by Brian Swann, 125-62. Washington, DC: Smithsonian Institution Press, 1992.

Best, Elsdon. *Tuhoe: The Children of the Mist.* 2 vols. 1925. Reprint, 3rd ed., Wellington, NZ: A.H. and A.W. Reed, for the Polynesian Society, 1977.

Beynon, William. Marius Barbeau Fieldnotes. British Columbia Archives, Victoria, BC.

Bideaux, Michel, ed. *Jacques Cartier: Relations.* Montreal: Les Presses de l'Université de Montréal, 1986.

Bierwert, Crisca. *Brushed by Cedar, Living by the River: Coast Salish Figures of Power.* Tucson: University of Arizona Press, 1999.

Binney, Judith. "Myth and Explanation in the Ringatū Tradition: Some Aspects of the Leadership of Te Kooti Arikirangi Te Turuki and Rua Kēnana Hepetipa." *Journal of the Polynesian Society* 93, 4 (December 1984): 345-98.

–. *Redemption Songs: A Life of the Nineteenth-Century Maori Leader Te Kooti Arikirangi Te Turuki.* 1995. Reprint, Honolulu/Melbourne: University of Hawaii Press/University of Melbourne Press, 1997.

–. "Te Umutaoroa: The Earth Oven of Long Cooking." In *Histories, Power and Loss: Uses of the Past – A New Zealand Commentary,* edited by Andrew Sharp and Paul McHugh, 147-64. Wellington, NZ: Bridget Williams Books, 2001.

Binney, Judith, and Gillian Chaplin. *Ngā Mōrehu: The Survivors.* 1986. Reprint, 3rd ed., Auckland: Auckland University Press, 2004.

Binney, Judith, Gillian Chaplin, and Craig Wallace. *Mihaia: The Prophet Rua Kenana and His Community at Maungapohatu.* 1979. Reprint, 4th ed., Auckland: Auckland University Press, 2005.

Blondin, George. *When the World Was New: Stories of the Sahtu Dene.* Yellowknife: Outcrop Publishers, 1990.

Blu, Karen. *The Lumbee Problem: The Making of an American Indian People.* New York: Cambridge University Press, 1980.

Boas, Franz. *Chinook Texts.* Washington, DC: Smithsonian Institution Bureau of Ethnology, 1894.

–. "Indian Tribes of the Lower Fraser River." In *64th Report of the British Association for the Advancement of Science for 1894,* 454-63. London: British Association for the Advancement of Science, 1894.

–. "Indianische Sagen von Nord-pacifischen Küste Amerikas." In *Donerabdruck aus den Verhandlungen der Berliner Gesellschaft fur Anthropologie, Ethnologie and Urgeschichte, 1891 bis 1895.* Berlin: A. Asher, 1895.

–, ed. *Folk-Tales of Salishan and Sahaptin Tribes.* Collected by James Teit, Marion K. Gould, Livingston Farrand, and Herbert Spinden, 1-201. New York: G.E. Stechert, 1917.

Borofsky, Robert. "Cook, Lono, Obeyesekere, and Sahlins." *Current Anthropology* 38, 2 (1997): 255-82.

Bouchard, Randy, and Dorothy Kennedy. "Lillooet Stories." *Sound Heritage* 6, 1 (1977): 1-78.

–. *Shuswap Stories.* Vancouver: CommCept Publishing, 1979.

Bourke, John G., comp. *Compilation of Notes and Memoranda bearing upon the Use of Human Ordure and Human Urine in Rites of a Religious or Semi-Religious Character among various Nations.* Washington, DC, 1888.

–. *Scatalogic Rites of all Nations. A Dissertation upon the Employment of Excrementitious Remedial Agents in Religion, Therapeutics, Divination, Witchcraft, Love-Philters, etc., in all Parts of the Globe.* Washington, DC: W.H. Lowdermilk, 1891.

Boyd, Robert. *The Coming of the Spirit of Pestilence: Introduced Infectious Diseases and Population Decline among Northwest Coast Indians, 1774-1874.* Vancouver/Seattle: UBC Press/ University of Washington Press, 1999.

Bracken, Christopher. *The Potlatch Papers: A Colonial Case Study.* Chicago: University of Chicago Press, 1997.

Brewer, E. Cobham, ed. "Clak-ho-har'yah." In *Brewer's Dictionary of Phrase and Fable.* 1898. Rev. ed., New York: Bartleby.Com, 2000. http://www.bartleby.com/81/3626.html.

Briggs, Charles, and Richard Bauman. "'The Foundation of All Future Researches': Franz Boas, George Hunt, Native American Texts, and the Construction of Modernity." *American Quarterly* 51, 3 (1999): 479-527.

–. "Genre, Intertextuality, and Social Power." *Journal of Linguistic Anthropology* 2, 2 (1992): 131-72.

Bunzl, Matti. "Franz Boas and the Humboldtian Tradition: From *Volkgeist* and *National-charakter* to an Anthropological Concept of Culture." In *Volkgeist as Method and Ethic: Essays on Boasian Ethnography and the German Anthropological Tradition,* edited by George W. Stocking Jr., 17-78. Madison: University of Wisconsin Press, 1996.

Butler, Judith. *Gender Trouble: Feminism and the Subversion of Identity.* New York and London: Routledge, 1999.

Byrnes, Giselle. "Inventing New Zealand: Surveying, Science, and the Construction of Cultural Space, 1840s-1890s." PhD diss., University of Auckland, 1995. Revised and published as *Boundary Markers.* Wellington, NZ: Bridget Williams Books, 2001.

Caesar, Alfred. "The First White People." Manuscript translation in the possession of Patrick Moore, 1999.

Campbell, Robert. *Two Journals of Robert Campbell 1808 to 1853.* 1853 typescript. Reprint, Seattle: Shorey Bookstore, 1967.

Canada. Royal Commission on Indian Affairs for the Province of British Columbia (McKenna-McBride Commission). Evidence. 1913-14. British Columbia Archives, Victoria, BC.

Carruthers, Mary. *The Book of Memory: A Study of Memory in Medieval Culture.* Cambridge: Cambridge University Press, 1990.

Cash, W.J. *The Mind of the South.* New York: Vintage, 1991.

Cassirer, Ernst. *Language and Myth.* New york: Dover, 1944.

Charlie, Mary. "*Destl'edemā* (Squirrel Woman)," translated by Marie Skidmore, Leda Jules, William Atkinson, and Pat Moore. In *Dene Gudeji: Kaska Narratives,* edited by Pat Moore, 185-245. Whitehorse: Kaska Tribal Council, 1999.

–. "Tés Ní'ā," translated by Leda Jules and Pat Moore. In *Dene Gudeji: Kaska Narratives,* edited by Pat Moore, 246-67. Whitehorse: Kaska Tribal Council, 1999.

Chénetier, Marc. *La Perte de l'Amérique: Archéologie d'un amour.* Paris: Belin, 2000.

Christopher, Brett. *Positioning the Missionary: John Booth Good and the Confluence of Cultures in Nineteenth-Century British Columbia.* Vancouver: UBC Press, 2000.

Clifford, James. *The Predicament of Culture: Twentieth-Century Ethnography, Literature, and Art.* Cambridge: Harvard University Press, 1988.

Cobb, Collier. "Early English Survivals on Hatteras Island." *The North Carolina Booklet* 14, 2 (1914): 91-99

—. "Race and Rehabilitation." Address before the Roanoke Colony Memorial Association at Old Fort Raleigh, Roanoke Island, North Carolina, Virginia Dare Day, 18 August 1923.

Cochran, Robert. "'What Courage!': Romanian 'Our Leader' Jokes." *Journal of American Folklore* 102, 405 (1989): 259-74.

Collingwood, R.G. *The Idea of History.* New York and London: Oxford University Press, 1956.

Collison, W.H. *In the Wake of the War Canoe.* London: Seeley, Service, 1915.

Cook, Ramsay. "Donnacona Discovers Europe: Rereading Jacques Cartier's Voyages." Introduction to *The Voyages of Jacques Cartier,* edited by Ramsay Cook, ix-xli. Toronto: University of Toronto Press, 1993.

Cotten, Sallie Southall. "The White Doe: The Fate of Virginia Dare, an Indian Legend." In *England and Roanoke: A Collection of Poems, 1585-1987,* edited by William S. Powell and Virginia Powell, 126-53. 1901. Reprint, Raleigh: North Carolina Department of Cultural Resources, 1988.

Coutts, Robert. *Yukon Places and Names.* Sidney, BC: Gray's Publishing, 1980.

Cove, John J., and George F. MacDonald, eds. *Tsimshian Narratives, Collected by Marius Barbeau and William Beynon.* Ottawa: Canadian Museum of Civilization, 1987.

Cox, Ross. *Adventures on the Columbia River, including the Narrative of a Residence of Six Years on the Western Side of the Rocky Mountains, among various Tribes of Indians hitherto unknown: together with a Journey across the American Continent.* 2 vols. London: Henry Colburn and Richard Bentley, 1831.

Crosby, Thomas. *Among the An-ko-me-nums; or Flathead Tribes of Indians of the Pacific Coast.* Toronto: William Briggs, 1907.

Cruikshank, Julie. *The Social Life of Stories: Narrative and Knowledge in the Yukon Territory.* Lincoln/Vancouver: University of Nebraska Press/UBC Press, 1998.

Cruikshank, Julie, Angela Sidney, Kitty Smith, and Annie Ned. *Life Lived Like a Story: Life Stories of Three Yukon Native Elders.* Lincoln: University of Nebraska Press, 1990.

Culhane, Dara. *The Pleasure of the Crown: Anthropology, Law and First Nations.* Burnaby, BC: Talonbooks, 1998.

Dart, A.D. "Raleigh's Lost Colony." *Southern Workman,* August 1913, 445-46.

Dauenhauer, Nora Marks, and Richard Dauenhauer, eds. *Haa Ḵusteeyí, Our Culture: Tlingit Life Stories.* Seattle: University of Washington Press, 1994.

—. *Haa Shuká, Our Ancestors: Tlingit Oral Narratives.* Seattle: University of Washington Press, 1987.

—. "Ioann Veniaminov as Linguist and Folklorist: Tlingit Language and Folklore." Paper presented at the Veniaminov Bicentennial Conference "Ioann Veniaminov in Alaska and Siberia and his Contribution to Arctic Social Science," University of Alaska-Fairbanks, 5-7 December 1997.

Dauenhauer, Richard L. *Conflicting Visions in Alaskan Education.* [Fairbanks]: University of Alaska Veniaminov Bicentennial Project. Reprint, Juneau: Tlingit Readers, 2004.

Davis, Frank. Dossier, vol. 10. Alexander Turnbull Library, Wellington, NZ.

Davis, Natalie Zemon. "Polarities, Hybridities: What Strategies for Decentring?" In *Decentring the Renaissance: Canada and Europe in Multidisciplinary Perspective, 1500-1700,* edited by Germaine Warkentin and Carolyn Podruchney, 21-31. Toronto: University of Toronto Press, 2001.

de Laguna, Frederica. *The Story of a Tlingit Community: A Problem in the Relationship between Archaeological, Ethnological, and Historical Methods.* Bureau of American Ethnology Bulletin 172. Washington, DC: Smithsonian Institution, 1990.

–. *Under Mount Saint Elias: The History and Culture of the Yakutat Tlingit.* Washington, DC: Smithsonian Institution Press, 1972.

Dean, Jonathan. "'Their Nature and Qualities Remain Unchanged': Russian Occupation and Tlingit Resistance, 1802-1867." *Alaska History* 9, 1 (Spring 1994): 1-17.

Deleuze, Gilles, and Félix Guattari. *A Thousand Plateaus: Capitalism and Schizophrenia.* Translated by Brian Massumi. Minneapolis: University of Minnesota Press, 1987.

Deloria, Philip. *Playing Indian.* New Haven: Yale University Press, 1998.

Dening, Greg. *Performances.* Chicago/Melbourne: University of Chicago Press/Melbourne University Press, 1996.

Densmore, Frances. *Music of the Indians of British Columbia.* New York: Da Capo Press, 1972.

Dick, Amos. "Warfare at Lūge Lē." Manuscript English translation in possession of Patrick Moore, 1999.

Diderot, Denis. *Supplément au Voyage de Bougainville ou Dialogue entre A et B.* 1772. Reprint, Paris: Livre de Poche, 1972.

Donald, Leland. *Aboriginal Slavery on the Northwest Coast of North America.* Berkeley: University of California Press, 1997.

Donne, John. *Poems of John Donne.* Edited by E.K. Chambers. Vol. 1. London: Lawrence and Bullen, 1896.

Douglas, James. "Statistics of the Northwest Coast of America." MS B 40 D72.5, folders 138-40. James Douglas Diary. British Columbia Archives, Victoria, BC.

Douglas, R. *Meaning of Canadian City Names.* Ottawa: F.A. Acland, 1922.

Drucker, Philip. *The Northern and Central Nootkan Tribes.* Bureau of Ethnology Bulletin 144. Washington, DC: Smithsonian Institution, 1951.

"D.W." "Paul Kane, the Canadian Artist." *Canadian Journal of Industry, Science, and Art: Conducted by the Editing Committee of the Canadian Institute,* n.s., 13, 73 (May 1871): 66-72.

–. Review of *Wanderings of an Artist. Canadian Journal of Industry, Science, and Art: Conducted by the Editing Committee of the Canadian Institute,* n.s., 4, 21 (May 1859): 186-94.

Eco, Umberto. *Theory of Semiotics.* Bloomington: Indiana University Press, 1976.

Elliott, Michael. *The Culture Concept: Writing and Difference in the Age of Realism.* Minneapolis: University of Minnesota Press, 2002.

Elliott, T.C. "Peter Skene Ogden, Fur Trader." *Oregon Historical Quarterly* 11 (1910): 268.

Emmons, George Thornton. "Native Account of the Meeting between La Perouse and the Tlingit." *American Anthropologist* 13, 2 (1911): 294-98.

–. *The Tlingit Indians.* Edited by Frederica de Laguna. New York, Seattle, and London: University of Washington Press and the American Museum of Natural History, 1991.

Fiebach, Joachim. "Dimensions of Theatricality in Africa." *Research in African Literature* 30, 4 (Winter 1999): 186-201.

Finkelstein, David. "Breaking the Thread: The Authorial Reinvention of John Hanning Speke in His *Journal of the Discovery of the Source of the Nile.*" *Text* 9 (1997): 280-96.

–. "'Unravelling Speke': The Blackwoods and the Construction of John Hanning Speke as Author in His *Journal of the Discovery of the Source of the Nile.*" *Bibliotheck* 18 (1992-93): 40-57.

Fisher, Robin. *Contact and Conflict: Indian European Relations in British Columbia, 1774-1890.* 1977. Reprint, Vancouver: UBC Press, 1992.

–. "Judging History: Reflections on the *Reasons for Judgment* in *Delgamuukw v. B.C.*" In "Anthropology and History in the Courts (the Gitksan and Wet'suwet'en Case)," edited by Bruce G. Miller. Special issue, *BC Studies* 95 (Autumn 1992): 43-54.

Fiske, Joanne. "From Customary Law to Oral Traditions: Discursive Formation of Plural Legalisms in Northern British Columbia, 1857-1993." *BC Studies* 115-16 (Autumn-Winter 1997-98): 267-88.

Flanagan, Thomas. *Our Home or Native Land?* Montreal and Kingston: McGill-Queen's University Press, 2000.

Fletcher, Inglis. "The Elizabethan Background of North Carolina." *DAR Magazine,* March 1952, 274-78.

Fogelson, Raymond. "Who Were the Ani-Kutani? An Excursion into Cherokee Historical Thought." *Ethnohistory* 31 (1984): 255-63.

Ford, Alexander Hume. "The Finding of Raleigh's Lost Colony." *Appleton's Magazine,* July 1907, 22-31.

Fort Simpson Correspondence Inward. Hudson's Bay Company Archives, Provincial Museum of Manitoba, Winnipeg, Manitoba.

"Fourteenth Ordinary Meeting – 5th April, 1856." *Canadian Journal of Industry, Science, and Art: Conducted by the Editing Committee of the Canadian Institute,* n.s., 1, 4 (July 1856): 404-6.

French, David H., and Kathrine S. French. "Wasco, Wishram, and Cascades." In *Plateau,* edited by Deward Walker Jr., 360-77. Vol. 12 of *Handbook of North American Indians,* general editor William C. Sturtevant. Washington, DC: Smithsonian Institution, 1998.

Frye, Northrop. *The Educated Imagination.* Toronto: Canadian Broadcasting Corporation, 1963.

–. *Northrop Frye Newsletter* 8, 2 (Fall 2000): 3.

Fuller, Mary. "Images of English Origins in Newfoundland and Roanoke." In *Decentring the Renaissance: Canada and Europe in Multidisciplinary Perspective, 1500-1700,* edited by Germain Warkentin and Carolyn Podruchny, 141-58. Toronto: University of Toronto Press, 2001.

–. "Raleigh's Fugitive Gold: Reference and Deferral in *The Discovery of Guiana.*" In *New World Encounters,* edited by Stephen Greenblatt, 218-40. Berkeley: University of California Press, 1993.

Galois, Robert, ed. *A Voyage to the North West Side of America: The Journals of James Colnett, 1786-89.* Vancouver: UBC Press, 2004.

Geertz, Clifford. "Thick Descriptions: Toward an Interpretive Theory of Culture." In *The Interpretation of Cultures,* edited by Geertz. New York: Basic Books, 1973.

Gideon, Hieromonk. *The Round the World Voyage of Hieromonk Gideon 1803-1809.* Translated by Lydia T. Black. Fairbanks and Kingston: Limestone Press, 1989.

Gleach, Fred. *Powhatan's World and Colonial Virginia: A Conflict of Cultures.* Lincoln: University of Nebraska Press, 1997.

Goldman, Irving. "The Alkatcho Carrier of British Columbia." In *Acculturation in Seven American Indian Tribes,* edited by R. Linton, 333-89. Gloucester, MA: Peter Smith, 1963.

Gombrich, E.H. *Art and Illusion: A Study in the Psychology of Pictorial Representation.* London: Phaidon, 1968.

Greenblatt, Stephen. *Marvelous Possessions: The Wonder of the New World.* Chicago: University of Chicago Press, 1991.

Greenfield, Bruce. "The Problem of the Discoverer's Authority in Lewis and Clark's *History.*" In *Macropolitics of Nineteenth-Century Literature: Nationalism, Exoticism, Imperialism,* edited by Jonathan Arac and Harriet Ritvo, 12-35. Philadelphia: University of Pennsylvania Press, 1991.

Greimas, Algirdas J. *On Meaning: Selected Writings on Semiotic Theory.* Minneapolis: University of Minnesota Press, 1987.

Griffin, George Butler, ed. *The California Coast: A Bilingual Edition of Documents from the Sutro Collection.* Norman: University of Oklahoma Press, 1969.

Grinev, A.V. *Indejtsy Tlinkity v Period Russkoj Ameriki 1741-1867.* Novosibirsk: Nauka, 1991.

–. *The Tlingit Indians in Russian America, 1741-1867.* Translated by Richard L. Bland and Katarina G. Solovjova. Lincoln: University of Nebraska Press, 2005.

Gupta, Akhil, and James Ferguson. *Anthropological Locations: Boundaries and Grounds of a Field Science.* Berkeley: University of California Press, 1997.

Hakluyt, Richard. *Explorations, Descriptions, and Attempted Settlements of Carolina, 1584-1590.* Edited by David L. Corbitt. Raleigh: North Carolina Department of Archives and History, 1948.

Hale, Horatio, ed. *Ethnography and Philology.* Vol. 6 of Charles Wilkes, *Narrative of the United States Exploring Expedition. During the years 1838, 1839, 1840, 1841, 1842.* 5 vols. and atlas. 1844. Reprint, Philadelphia/London: Lea and Blanchard/Whittaker/Wiley and Putnam, 1845. Facsimile reprint, Ridgewood, NJ: Gregg Press, 1968.

Hamer, Kathryn. "Kane, Paul." *The Oxford Companion to Canadian Literature,* general editor William Toye, 403. Toronto: Oxford University Press, 1983; 2nd ed., general editors Eugene Benson and William Toye, 588. Toronto: Oxford University Press, 1997.

Hamilton, Carolyn. "*Living by Fluidity:* Oral Histories, Material Custodies and the Politics of Archiving." In *Refiguring the Archive,* edited by Carolyn Hamilton, Verne Harris, Jane Taylor, Michele Pickover, Graeme Reid, and Razia Saleh, 209-27. Amsterdam: Kluwer Academic Publishers, 2002.

Handler, Richard, and Eric Gable. *The New History in an Old Museum: Creating the Past in Colonial Williamsburg.* Durham, NC: Duke University Press, 1997.

Hanna, Darwin, and Mamie Henry, eds. *Our Tellings: Interior Salish Stories of the Nlha7kápmx People.* Vancouver: UBC Press, 1995.

Harkin, Michael. "(Dis)pleasures of the Text: Boasian Ethnology on the Central Northwest Coast." In *Gateways: Exploring the Legacy of the Jesup North Pacific Expedition, 1897-1902,* edited by Igor Krupnik and William W. Fitzhugh, 93-105. Washington, DC: Smithsonian Institution, 2001.

–. *The Heiltsuks: Dialogues of Culture and History on the Northwest Coast.* Lincoln and London: University of Nebraska Press, 1997.

–. "History, Narrative, and Temporality: Examples from the Northwest Coast." *Ethnohistory* 35, 2 (1988): 99-130.

–. "Past Presence: Conceptions of History in Northwest Coast Studies." *Arctic Anthropology* 33, 2 (1996): 1-15.

Harper, J. Russell, ed., with biographical introduction and a catalogue raisonné. *Paul Kane's Frontier. Including "Wanderings of an Artist among the Indians of North America."* Austin/Toronto: University of Texas Press/University of Toronto Press, 1971.

Hariot, Thomas. "A brief and true report on the new found land of Virginia." In *The First Colonists: Documents on the Planting of the First English Settlements in North America, 1584-1590,* edited by David B. Quinn and Alison M. Quinn, 46-76. Raleigh: North Carolina Department of Cultural Resources, Division of Archives and History, 1982.

Harris, R. Cole. *The Resettlement of British Columbia: Essays on Colonialism and Geographical Change.* Vancouver: UBC Press, 1997.

Harris, Trudier. "Genre." *Journal of American Folklore* 108, 403 (1995): 509-27.

Heidenreich, Conrad E. "Report to the Royal Canadian Institute on the Identification of the Paul Kane Picture Owned by the R.C.I. (May 11, 1995)." Typescript, 9 pp., 11 figs., Royal Canadian Institute, Toronto, 11 May 1995.

Higginson, J.W. "An English Nation." *Harper's,* April 1883, 707-10.

Hill, Jonathan D. "Myth and History." In *Rethinking History and Myth: Indigenous South American Perspectives on the Past,* edited by Jonathan D. Hill, 1-17. Urbana: University of Illinois Press, 1988.

–, ed. *Rethinking History and Myth: Indigenous South American Perspectives on the Past.* Urbana: University of Illinois Press, 1988.

Hill-Tout, Charles. "Ethnological Studies of the Mainland Halkolmelem, a Division of the Salish of British Columbia." *72nd Report of the British Association for the Advancement of Science for 1902,* 416-41. London, 1903.

*History of the Expedition under the Command of Captains Lewis and Clark, to the Sources of the Missouri, thence across the Rocky Mountains and down the River Columbia to the Pacific Ocean. Performed during the Years 1804-5-6. By Order of the Government of the United States.* [Edited by Paul Allen.] 2 vols. Philadelphia: Bradford and Inskeep, 1814.

Hodge, Frederick Webb, ed. *Handbook of American Indians North of Mexico.* Smithsonian Institution Bureau of American Ethnology Bulletin 30. 2 pts. Washington, DC: Government Printing Office, 1912.

Horsman, Reginald. *Race and Manifest Destiny: The Origins of American Racial Anglo-Saxonism.* Cambridge: Harvard University Press, 1981.

Howard-Malverde, Rosaleen. *The Speaking of History: "Willapaakushayki" or Quechua Ways of Telling the Past.* London: Institute of Latin American Studies, 1990.

Howay, Frederick William. "Authorship of *Traits of Indian Life.*" *Oregon Historical Quarterly* 35 (1934): 42-49.

Howe, C.K. *Solving the Riddle of the Lost Colony.* Beaufort, NC: C.K. Howe, 1947.

Howe, K.R. *The Loyalty Islands: A History of Culture Contacts, 1840-1900.* Honolulu: University Press of Hawaii, 1977.

Hulme, Peter. *Colonial Encounters: Europe and the Native Caribbean, 1492-1797.* London and New York: Methuen, 1986.

Hume, Ivor Noel. "Roanoke Island: America's First Science Center." *Journal of the Colonial Williamsburg Foundation* 16, 3 (1994): 14-28.

Hutchinson, Dale L., Ann Kakaliouras, Lynette Norr, and Mark Teaford. *Foraging, Farming, and Coastal Biocultural Adaptation in Late Prehistoric North Carolina.* Gainesville: University Press of Florida, 2002.

Hyde, Lewis. *Trickster Makes This World: Mischief, Myth, and Art.* New York: Farrar, Straus, and Giroux, 1998.

Hymes, Dell. *"Now I Know Only so Far": Essays in Ethnopoetics.* Lincoln and London: University of Nebraska Press, 2003.

Ireland, Emilienne. "Cerebral Savage: The Whiteman as Symbol of Cleverness and Savagery in Waura Myth." In *Rethinking History and Myth: Indigenous South American Perspectives on the Past,* edited by Jonathan D. Hill, 157-73. Urbana: University of Illinois Press, 1988.

Jameson, Frederic. "Foreword." In *On Meaning: Selected Writings on Semiotic Theory,* by Algirdas J. Greimas, xiii-xiv. Minneapolis: University of Minnesota Press, 1987.

–. *Postmodernism: Or, the Cultural Logic of Late Capitalism.* Durham, NC: Duke University Press, 1993.

Jenness, Diamond. *Faith of a Coast Salish Indian.* Edited by Wilson Duff. British Columbia Museum Memoirs in Anthropology, no. 3. Victoria: British Columbia Provincial Museum Department of Education, 1955.

Johnson, Samuel V. "Chinook Jargon: A Computer Assisted Analysis of Variation in an American Indian Pidgin." PhD diss., University of Kansas, 1978.

Kan, Sergei. "Bilingual/Bicultural Interpreters and Informants of the Jesup Expedition Era." In *Constructing Cultures Then and Now: Celebrating Franz Boas and the Jesup North Pacific Expedition,* edited by Laurel Kendall and Igor Krupnik, 185-97. Circumpolar Anthropology, no. 4. Washington, DC: Smithsonian Institution Press, 2003.

–. *Memory Eternal: Tlingit Culture and Russian Orthodox Christianity through Two Centuries.* Seattle: University of Washington Press, 1999.

Kane, Paul. "The Chinook Indians." *Canadian Journal of Industry, Science, and Art: Conducted by the Editing Committee of the Canadian Institute,* n.s., 2, 7 (January 1857): 11-30.

–. "The Chinook Indians." *Canadian Journal: A Repertory of Industry, Science, and Art; and a Record of the Proceedings of the Canadian Institute* 3, 12 (July 1855): 273-79.

–. "The Chinook Indians." *Daily British Colonist,* 6 August 1855, [1-2]; 7 August 1855, [1-2]; 8 August 1855, [1-2]; and 9 August 1855, [1].

–. Draft manuscript of *Wanderings of an Artist.* 4 vols.: 17 June 1845-July 1846, 11.85/2A; 9 May 1846-6 September 1848, 11.85/2B; 6 October 1846-12 September 1848, 11.85/2C; 17 June 1845-30 November 1845, 11.85/3. Stark Museum of Art, Orange, Texas.

–. Field Notes 1846-1848, 11.85/5. Stark Museum of Art, Orange, Texas.

–. "'I came to rite thare portraits': Paul Kane's Journal of His Western Travels, 1846-1848." Edited by I.S. MacLaren. *American Art Journal* 21, 2 (Spring 1989): 6-88.

–. "Notes of a Sojourn among the Half-Breeds, Hudson's Bay Company's Territory, Red River." *Canadian Journal of Industry, Science, and Art: Conducted by the Editing Committee of the Canadian Institute,* n.s., 1, 2 (February 1856): 128-38.

–. "Notes of Travel among the Walla-Walla Indians." *Canadian Journal of Industry, Science, and Art: Conducted by the Editing Committee of the Canadian Institute,* n.s., 1, 5 (September 1856): 417-24.

–. Portrait Log and Landscape Log 1846-1848, and Field Notes 1845, 11.85/4. Stark Museum of Art, Orange, Texas.

–. *Wanderings of an Artist among the Indians of North America.* Edited by John W. Garvin, introduction by Lawrence Burpee. Toronto: Radisson Society, 1925. Facsimile reprint, Mineola, NY: Dover, 1996.

–. *Wanderings of an Artist among the Indians of North America from Canada to Vancouver's Island and Oregon through the Hudson's Bay Company's Territory and back again.* London: Longman, Brown, Green, Longmans, and Roberts, 1859.

Karttunen, Frances. *Between Worlds: Interpreters, Guides, and Survivors.* New Brunswick, NJ: Rutgers University Press, 1994.

Keddie, Grant. "The Question of Asiatic Objects on the North Pacific Coast of America: Historic or Prehistoric?" *Contributions to Human History* 3 (March 1990): 1-26.

Kendrick, John. *The Men with Wooden Feet.* Toronto: NC Press, 1986.

Kerby, William J. *The Catholic Encyclopedia.* Vol. 14. New York: Robert Appleton, 1912. s.v. "Sociology." Online ed., 2003. http://www.newadvent.org/cathen/14115a.htm.

Khlebnikov, Kiril T. *Baranov: Chief Manager of the Russian Colonies in America.* Edited by Richard A. Pierce. Translated by Colin Bearne. Fairbanks and Kingston: Limestone Press, 1973.

–. *Zhizneopisanie Aleksandra Andreevicha Baranova, Glavnago Pravitelia Rossiiskikh Kolonii v Amerike.* St. Petersburg: V Morskoi Tipografii, 1835.

Klein, Laura F. "Demystifying the Opposition: The Hudson's Bay Company and the Tlingit." *Arctic Anthropology* 24, 1 (1987): 101-14

King, Thomas. *The Truth about Stories: A Native Narrative.* Toronto: Anansi, 2003.

Knapp, Jeffrey. "Elizabethan Tobacco." In *New World Encounters,* edited by Stephen Greenblatt, 272-311. Berkeley: University of California Press, 1993.

Kristeva, Julia. *Desire in Language.* Translated by Leon Roudiez. New York: Columbia University Press, 1980.

–. *Powers of Horror: An Essay on Abjection.* Translated by Leon S. Roudiez. New York: Columbia University Press, 1982.

Krupat, Arnold. *Ethnocriticism: Ethnography, History, Literature.* Berkeley: University of California Press, 1992.

Kupperman, Karen Ordahl. *Roanoke: The Abandoned Colony.* Savage, MD: Rowman and Littlefield, 1994.

LaCapra, Dominick. "History Language and Reading: Waiting for Crillon." *American Historical Review* 100, 3 (June 1995): 799-828 .

–. "Rethinking Intellectual History and Reading Texts." *History and Theory* 19, 3 (1980): 245-76.

Lamb, W.K., ed. *Simon Fraser: Letters and Journals, 1806-1808.* Toronto: MacMillan, 1960.

Laxness, Halldor. "What Was Before the Saga: A Jubilee Discourse." *American Scandinavian Review* (1974).

Le Jeune, Jean Marie Raphaël. *Chinook Rudiments.* Kamloops, BC: n.p., 1924.

Lévi-Strauss, Claude. *The Savage Mind.* Chicago: University of Chicago Press, 1966.

Lutz, John Sutton. "Making Race in British Columbia: Power, Race and the Importance of Place." In *Power and Place in the North American West,* edited by Richard White and John Findlay, 61-86. Seattle: University of Washington Press, 1999.

–. *Makuk: Aboriginal Work and Welfare in British Columbia.* Vancouver: UBC Press, forthcoming in 2007.

–. "What Connected at Contact? Comparing Aboriginal and European Contact Narratives from the Pacific Coast." Paper presented to the Canadian Historical Association Conference, Quebec City, May 2001.

Lyotard, Jean-François. *The Postmodern Condition: A Report on Knowledge.* Minneapolis: University of Minnesota Press, 1984.

McClellan, Catharine. "Indian Stories about the First Whites in Northwestern North America." In *Ethnohistory in Southwestern Alaska and Southern Yukon: Method and Content,* edited by Margaret Lantis, 103-33. Lexington: University Press of Kentucky, 1970.

–. *My Old People Say: An Ethnographic Survey of Southern Yukon Territory.* Ottawa: National Museum of Man, 1975.

McGee, Robert. *The Arctic Voyages of Martin Frobisher: An Elizabethan Venture.* Montreal and Kingston: McGill-Queen's University Press, 2001.

McHalsie, Sonny, David M. Shaepe, and Keith Thor Carlson. "Making the World Right through Transformations." In *A Stó:lō Coast Salish Historical Atlas,* ed. Keith Thor Carlson, 6-7. Vancouver: Douglas and McIntyre, 2001.

McIlwraith, Thomas F. *Bella Coola Indians.* Toronto: University of Toronto Press, 1948.

McKay, J.W. "Indian Tribes, Correspondence 1881, regarding Festivals, Traditions etc." Add Mss. 1917. J.W. McKay Papers. British Columbia Archives, Victoria, BC.

McKenna-McBride Royal Commission on Indian Affairs for British Columbia. Evidence. 1913-14. British Columbia Archives.

MacLaren, I.S. "Alexander Mackenzie and the Landscapes of Commerce." *Studies in Canadian Literature* 7 (1982): 141-50.

–. "'Caledonian Suttee'? An Anatomy of Carrier Cremation Cruelty." *BC Studies* 149 (Spring 2006): 3-37.

–. "Cultured Wilderness in Jasper National Park." *Journal of Canadian Studies* 34, 4 (Fall 1999): 7-58.

–. "Exploration/Travel Literature and the Evolution of the Author." *International Journal of Canadian Studies* 5 (Spring 1992): 39-68.

–. "The Metamorphosis of Travellers into Authors: The Case of Paul Kane." In *Critical Issues in Editing Exploration Texts. Papers Given at the Twenty-eighth Conference on Editorial Problems, University of Toronto, 6-7 November 1992*, edited by Germaine Warkentin, 67-107. Toronto: University of Toronto Press, 1995.

–. "Notes on Samuel Hearne's *Journey* from a Bibliographical Perspective." *Papers/Cahiers of the Bibliographical Society of Canada* 31, 2 (Fall 1993): 21-45.

–. "Paul Kane Goes South: The Sale of the Family's Collection of Field Sketches." *Journal of Canadian Studies* 32, 2 (Summer 1997): 22-47.

–. "Samuel Hearne's Accounts of the Massacre at Bloody Fall, 17 July 1771." *ARIEL: A Review of International English Literature* 22, 1 (January 1991): 25-51.

McLuhan, Marshall. *The Gutenberg Galaxy.* Toronto: University of Toronto Press, 1962.

McMillan, Hamilton. *The Lost Colony Found: An Historical Sketch of the Discovery of the Croatan Indians.* Lumberton, NC: Robeson Job Print, n.d.

Magun, Liza. "The First Time We Saw White People," translated by William Atkinson and Pat Moore. In *Dene Gudeji: Kaska Narratives*, edited by Pat Moore, 430-43. Whitehorse: Kaska Tribal Council, 1999.

Maor, Eli. *To Infinity and Beyond: A Cultural History of the Infinite.* Princeton, NJ: Princeton University Press, 1991.

Maori Affairs. Archives New Zealand, Wellington, NZ.

Martin, R.M. *The Hudson's Bay Territories and Vancouver's Island, with an Exposition of the Chartered Rights, Conduct, and Policy of the Honorable Hudson's Bay Corporation.* 1848. Reprint, London: T. and W. Boone, 1849.

Maryanski, Alexander, and Jonathan H. Turner. *Encyclopedia of Sociology,* edited by Edgar F. Borgatta and Rhonda J.V. Montgomery. 5 vols. New York: Macmillan, 2000. s.v. "Functionalism and Structuralism."

Matthews, J.S. *Early Vancouver: Narratives of Pioneers of Vancouver, B.C.* Vol. 2. Vancouver, 1933.

Mead, S.M., ed. "Three Carved Houses at Te Whaiti: Part III, Eripitana." Research dossier, Anthropology Department, University of Auckland, 1970.

Miller, Christopher. *Prophetic Worlds: Indians and Whites on the Columbia Plateau.* New Brunswick, NJ: Rutgers University Press, 1985.

Miller, Christopher, and George R. Hammell. "A New Perspective on Indian-White Contact: Cultural Symbols and Colonial Trade." *Journal of American History* 73, 2 (September 1986): 311-28.

Miller, Jay. *Lushootseed Culture and the Shamanic Odyssey: An Anchored Radiance.* Lincoln: University of Nebraska Press, 1999.

Miller, Lee. *Roanoke.* New York: Arcade Publishing, 2000.

Milton, Giles. *Big Chief Elizabeth: How England's Adventurers Gambled and Won the New World.* London: Sceptre, 2000.

Miranda, Louis, and Philip Joe. "How the Squamish Remember George Vancouver." In *From Maps to Metaphors: The Pacific World of George Vancouver,* edited by Robin Fisher and Hugh Johnston, 3-5. Vancouver: UBC Press, 1993.

Momaday, N. Scott. *House Made of Dawn.* New York: Harper and Row, 1968.

Moore, Patrick. "Point of View in Kaska Historical Narrative." PhD diss., Indiana University, 2002.

Moore, Patrick, and Angela Wheelock. *Wolverine Myths and Visions: Dene Traditions from Northern Alberta.* Lincoln: University of Nebraska Press, 1990.

Monet, Don, and Skanu'u (Ardythe Wilson). *Colonialism on Trial: Indigenous Land Claims and the Gitksan and Wet'suwet'en Sovereignty Case.* Philadelphia: New Society, 1992.

Morris, Rosalind. *New Worlds from Fragments: Film Ethnography, and the Representation of Northwest Coast Cultures.* Boulder: Westview Press, 1994.

Moulton, Gary, ed. *The Journals of the Lewis and Clark Expedition.* 13 vols. Lincoln: University of Nebraska Press, 1983-2001.

Mourning Dove. *Coyote Stories.* Edited by Heister Dean. 1933. Reprint, Lincoln: University of Nebraska Press, 1990.

Mousalimas, S.A. *From Mask to Icon: Transformation in the Arctic.* Brookline, MA: Holy Cross Orthodox Press, 2003.

Moziño, José Mariano. *Noticias de Nutka: An Account of Nootka Sound in 1792.* Translated by I.H.W. Engstrand. Seattle: University of Washington Press, 1991.

Murray, David. *Forked Tongues: Speech, Writing and Representation in North American Indian Texts.* Bloomington: Indiana University Press, 1991.

Murray, Heather. "Daniel Wilson as Littérateur: English Professor, Critic, and Poet." In *Thinking with Both Hands: Sir Daniel Wilson in the Old World and the New,* edited by Elizabeth Hulse, 211-33. Toronto: University of Toronto Press, 1999.

Nabokov, Peter. "Native Views of History." In *The Cambridge History of the Native Peoples of the Americas,* edited by Bruce Trigger and Wilcomb Washburn, 1-59. Cambridge: Cambridge University Press, 1996.

*New Zealand Parliamentary Debates.* 1896 and 1909.

"Northwest Chinookan Culture." *Central California Culture.* N.d. http://www.fourdir.com/ northwest_chinookan_culture.htm.

Nuckolls, Charles. *Culture: A Problem That Cannot Be Solved.* Madison: University of Wisconsin Press, 1998.

Oberg, Michael. "Gods and Men: The Meeting of Indian and White Worlds on the Carolina Outer Banks, 1584-1586." *North Carolina Historical Review* 86 (1999): 367-90.

Obeyesekere, Gananath. *The Apotheosis of Captain Cook: European Mythmaking in the Pacific.* Princeton: Princeton University Press, 1992.

[Ogden, Peter Skene]. *Traits of American Indian Life and Character. By a Fur Trader.* London: Smith, Elder, 1853.

Oleska, Michael J. *Orthodox Alaska: A Theology of Mission.* Crestwood, NY: St. Vladimir's Seminary Press, 1992.

–, ed. *Alaskan Missionary Spirituality.* New York and Mahwah, NJ: Paulist Press, 1987.

Owens, Kenneth, ed. *The Wreck of the Sv. Nikolai: Two Narratives of the First Russian Expedition to the Oregon Country 1808-1810.* Portland: Western Imprints, 1985.

Pagden, Anthony. *European Encounters with the New World: From Renaissance to Romanticism.* London and New Haven: Yale University Press, 1993.

Parker, Samuel. *Journal of an Exploring Tour beyond the Rocky Mountains, under the Direction of the A.B.C.F.M. performed in the Years 1835, '36, and '37.* Ithaca, NY: privately printed, 1838.

Parramore, Thomas C. "The 'Lost Colony' Found: A Documentary Perspective." *North Carolina Historical Review* 78, 1 (2001): 167-83.

Pate, Albert F. *The Search for Johnny Chevin: Being a Poetic Quest out of the Most Ancient Records and Oldest Oral Traditions for the Descendants of Sir Walter Raleigh's "Lost Colony."* Pikeville, NC: Albert F. Pate, 1991.

Phillips, C.O.J. "Charcoal Sketch by C.O. Phillips." 18 November 1858. British Columbia Archives, Victoria, BC.

Pierce, Richard A. *Russian America: A Biographical Dictionary.* Fairbanks and Kingston: Limestone Press, 1990.

Pinder, Leslie. *The Carriers of No: After the Land Claims Trial.* Vancouver: Lazara Press, 1991.

Pitchford, Susan R. *Encyclopedia of Sociology,* edited by Edgar F. Borgatta and Rhonda J.V. Montgomery. 5 vols. New York: Macmillan, 2000. s.v. "Race."

Powell, William. *Paradise Preserved: A History of the Roanoke Island Historical Association.* Chapel Hill: University of North Carolina Press, 1965.

Pratt, Mary Louise. *Imperial Eyes: Travel Writing and Transculturation.* New York: Routledge, 1992.

Price, Robert. *Through the Uriwera Country.* Napier: Daily Telegraph Office, 1891.

Quinn, David Beers. *The Lost Colonists: Their Fortune and Probable Fate.* Raleigh: North Carolina Department of Cultural Resources, 1984.

–. *North America from Earliest Discovery to First Settlements: The Norse Voyages to 1612.* New York: Harper and Row, 1977.

Quinn, David Beers, and Alison Quinn, eds. *The First Colonists: Documents on the Planting of the First English Settlement in North America, 1584-1590.* Raleigh: North Carolina Department of Cultural Resources, 1982.

Regan, Albert. "Some Traditions of West Coast Indians." In *Proceedings of the Utah Academy of Sciences* 86 (1934): 73-93.

Reynolds, Henry. *The Other Side of the Frontier: An Interpretation of the Aboriginal Response to the Invasion and Settlement of Australia.* Townsville, Australia: James Cook University, 1981.

Rich, E.E., ed. *The Letters of John McLoughlin from Fort Vancouver to the Governor and Committee: Third Series, 1844-46,* introduction by W. Kaye Lamb. Champlain Society, Hudson's Bay Company Record Series, vol. 7. London: Champlain Society, 1944.

Ridington, Robin. *Little Bit Know Something: Stories in a Language of Anthropology.* Vancouver and Toronto: Douglas and McIntyre, 1990.

–. *Swan People: A Study of the Dunne-za Prophet Dance.* Canadian Ethnology Service Mercury Series, no. 38. Ottawa: National Museums of Canada, 1978.

–. *Trail to Heaven: Knowledge and Narrative in a Northern Community.* Toronto: Douglas and McIntyre, 1988.

Robertson, David D. "Paul Kane on 'Katchutequa.'" 21 August 2003. http://listserv.linguistlist.org/cgi-bin/wa?A2=ind0308c&L=chinook&D=1&F=P&S=&P=475.

Robinson, Harry. Written correspondence with Wendy Wickwire (in the latter's possession).

Robinson, Will, and Walter Wright. *Men of Medeek.* Kitimat, BC: Printed by the Northern Sentinel Press, 1962.

Rohner, Ronald, comp. and ed. *The Ethnography of Franz Boas: Letters and Diaries of Franz Boas Written on the Northwest Coast from 1886 to 1931.* Chicago: University of Chicago Press, 1969.

Rountree, Helen. *Pocahontas's People: The Powhatan Indians of Virginia through Four Centuries.* Norman: University of Oklahoma Press, 1990.

Russian-American Company. *Russian-American Company Records [Sent]. 1818-67 Correspondence of the Governors General, Communications Sent.* 47 vols. Washington, DC: US National Archives, 1818-67.

Sahlins, Marshall. *Historical Metaphors and Mythical Realities: Structure in the Early History of the Sandwich Islands Kingdom.* Ann Arbor: University of Michigan Press, 1981.

–. *How Natives Think: About Captain Cook for Example.* Chicago: University of Chicago Press, 1995.

Schafer, Joseph, ed. "Documents Relative to Warre and Vavasour's Military Reconnoissance [sic] in Oregon in 1845-6." *Oregon Historical Quarterly* 10 (1909): 1-98.

Scholefield, E.O.S. *British Columbia from the Earliest Times to the Present.* Vancouver: S.S. Clarke, 1914.

Schoolcraft, Henry Rowe, dir. *History of the North American Indians.* 6 vols. Pt. 5, *Information respecting the History, Condition and Prospects of the Indian Tribes of the United States.* Philadelphia: J.B. Lippincott, 1855.

Seed, Patricia. *Ceremonies of Possession in Europe's Conquest of the New World, 1492-1690.* Cambridge, MA: Cambridge University Press, 1995.

Shaw, George C. *The Chinook Jargon and How to Use It; a Complete and Exhaustive Lexicon of the Oldest Trade Language of the American Continent.* Seattle: Rainier Printing, 1909.

Sherzer, Joel. *Speech Play and Verbal Art.* Austin: University of Texas, 2002.

Sider, Gerald. "When Parrots Learn to Talk and Why They Can't: Domination, Deception and Self-Deception in Indian-White Relations." *Comparative Studies in Society and History* 29 (1987): 3-23.

Sissons, Jeffrey. *Te Waimana: The Spring of Mana*. Dunedin: University of Otago Press, 1991.

Smedley, Audrey. *Race in North America*. Boulder, CO: Westview, 1993.

Smith, Gavin. "'He holds him with his glittering eye': Intellectuals and the Re-covering of the Past." In *Memory at the Margins: Essays in Anthropology and World History*, edited by Gavin Smith, June Nash, and Dolores Waldenstrom Stanley, 1-24. Victoria, BC: World History Caucus, University of Victoria, 1995.

Smith, Kitty. "The First Time They Knew *K'och'en*, Whiteman." In *Our Voices: Native Stories of Alaska and the Yukon*, edited by James Rupert and John Bernet, 223-27. Toronto: University of Toronto Press, 2001.

Smith, S. Percy. "Reminiscences." Auckland Museum, Auckland, NZ.

Smitherman, Geneva. *Talkin That Talk: Language, Culture, and Education in African America*. London and New York: Routledge, 2000.

Snyder, Sally. "Skagit Society and Its Existential Basis: An Ethnofolkloristic Reconstruction." PhD diss., Department of Anthropology, University of Washington, 1964.

Spencer, Herbert. *North and South American Races. Compiled by Professor* [David] *Duncan.* New York: D. Appleton, 1878. Pt. 6 of *Descriptive Sociology; or, Groups of Sociological Facts, Classified and Arranged by Herbert Spencer. Compiled and Abstracted by David Duncan ... Richard Scheppig ... and James Collier.* 15 pts. London: Williams and Norgate, 1873-1919.

Spier, Leslie. *The Prophet Dance of the Northwest and Its Derivatives: The Source of the Ghost Dance*. General Series in Anthropology, no. 1. Menasha, WI: George Banta, 1935.

–, ed. *The Sinkaietk or Southern Okanagon of Washington*. General Series in Anthropology, no. 6. Menasha, WI: George Banta, 1938.

Spinrad, Paul. *The RE/Search Guide to Bodily Functions*. San Francisco: RE/Search Publications, 1994.

Sproat, G.M. *Scenes and Studies of Savage Life*. London: Smith, Elder, 1868.

Steinfeld, Carol. *Liquid Gold: The Lure and Logic of Using Urine to Grow Plants*. Dartington, UK/Sheffield, VT: Green Books/Green Frigate Books, 2004.

Sugirtharajah, R.S. "Biblical Studies after the Empire: From a Colonial to a Postcolonial Mode of Interpretation." In *The Postcolonial Bible*, edited by R.S. Sugirtharajah. Sheffield: Sheffield Academic Press, 1998.

Suttles, Wayne. "Central Coast Salish." In *Handbook of North American Indians*. Vol. 7, *The Northwest Coast*, edited by Wayne Suttles, 453-75. Washington, DC: Smithsonian Institution, 1990.

–, ed. *Katzie Ethnographic Notes*. British Columbia Provincial Museum Memoirs in Anthropology, no. 2. Victoria: British Columbia Provincial Museum, 1955.

–. "The Plateau Prophet Dance among the Coast Salish." In *Coast Salish Essays*, edited by Wayne Suttles, 152-98. 1972. Reprint, Vancouver: Talonbooks, 1987.

–. "The Plateau Prophet Dance among the Coast Salish." *Southwest Journal of Anthropology* 6, 4 (1966): 352-96.

–. "Private Knowledge, Morality, and Social Classes among the Coast Salish." In *Coast Salish Essays*, edited by Wayne Suttles, 3-14. 1972. Reprint, Vancouver: Talon Books, 1987.

Taylor, Isaac. *Words and Places*. London: Macmillan, 1864.

Teit, James. *Mythology of the Thompson Indians*. Memoir of the American Museum of Natural History, vol. 8, pt. 2. New York: G.E. Stechert, 1912.

–. *The Shuswap*. Vol. 2 of *The Jesup North Pacific Expedition*, edited by Franz Boas. Memoir of the American Museum of Natural History. New York: G.E. Stechert, 1909.

–. Teit Fieldnotes. Anthropology Archives, American Museum of Natural History, New York City, n.d.

–. "Traditions of the Thompson River Indians of British Columbia." In *Memoirs of the American Folk-Lore Society*, edited by Franz Boas, 203-416. London: Houghton, Mifflin, 1898.

Thomas, Nicholas. *Entangled Objects: Exchange, Material Culture and Colonialism in the Pacific*. Cambridge, MA: Harvard University Press, 1991.

–. "Partial Texts: Representation, Colonialism and Agency in Pacific History." *Journal of Pacific History* 25, 2 (1990): 139-58.

Thompson, David (uncredited). "A Map of America between the Latitudes 40 and 70 North and Longitudes 80 and 150 West Exhibiting the Principal Trading Stations of the North West Company." Library and Archives Canada, Ottawa.

Tikhmenev, P.A. *A History of the Russian American Company.* Vol. 2, *Documents.* Edited by Richard A. Pierce and Alton S. Donnelly. Translated by Dmitri Krenov. Kingston: Limestone Press, 1979.

Todorov, Tzvetan. *Mikhail Bakhtin: The Dialogical Principle.* Translated by Wlad Godzich. Vol. 13, *Theory and History of Literature.* Minneapolis: University of Minnesota Press, 1984.

Tolmie, William Fraser. "History of Puget Sound and the Northwest Coast ... Victoria 1878." Manuscript. Bancroft Library, University of California, Berkeley.

Trigger, Bruce. "Early Responses to European Contact: Romantic versus Rationalistic Interpretations." *Journal of American History* 77, 4 (March 1991): 1195-1215.

Trudel, Marcel. "Cartier, Jacques." *Dictionary of Canadian Biography.* Vol. 1, edited by George W. Brown. Toronto: University of Toronto Press, 1966.

Turner, Terence. "Ethno-ethnohistory: Myth and History in Native South American Representations of Contact with Western Society." In *Rethinking History and Myth: Indigenous South American Perspectives on the Past,* edited by Jonathan D. Hill, 235-81. Urbana: University of Illinois Press, 1988.

US Bureau of the Census, 2000 Census, North Carolina Summary File 1.

Vancouver, George. *A Voyage of Discovery to the North Pacific Ocean and Round the World.* Edited by W. Kaye Lamb. London, 1798. Reprint, London: Hakluyt Society, 1984.

Vansina, Jan. *Oral Tradition as History.* Madison: University of Wisconsin Press, 1985.

Vaughan, Thomas, ed. *Paul Kane: The Columbia Wanderer.* Portland, OR: Oregon Historical Society, 1971.

Veniaminov, Ioann. *Zamechaniia o Koloshenskom i Kadiakskom Iazykakh.* St. Petersburg: Imperial Academy of Sciences, 1846.

Veyne, Paul. *Did the Greeks Believe in Their Myths?* Translated by Paula Wissing. Chicago: University of Chicago, 1988.

Vibert, Elizabeth. "'The Natives Were Strong to Live': Plague, Prophecy and Prelude to the Encounter." In *Traders' Tales: Narratives of Cultural Encounters in the Columbia Plateau, 1807-1846,* 50-83. Norman: University of Oklahoma Press, 1997.

*Visions from the Wilderness: The Art of Paul Kane.* Medium unknown. Produced and directed by John Bessai, edited by Joan Prowse, distributed by McNabb and Connolly. Toronto: CineFocus Canada, 2001.

Walker, Deward. "New Light on the Prophet Dance Controversy." *Ethnohistory* 16, 3 (1969): 245-55.

Warkentin, Germaine, and Carolyn Podruchney, eds. *Decentring the Renaissance: Canada and Europe in Multidisciplinary Perspective, 1500-1700.* Toronto: University of Toronto Press, 2001.

Watson, Douglas. Preface to *Traits of American Indian Life and Character,* by Peter Skene Ogden, v. 1853. Reprint, San Francisco: Grabhorn, 1933. Facsimile reprint of 1933 ed., New York: AMS, 1972.

Webster, Peter. *Rua and the Maori Millennium.* Wellington, NZ: Victoria University Press, 1979.

Wickwire, Wendy. "Prophecy at Lytton." In *Voices from Four Directions: Contemporary Translations of the Native Literatures of North America,* edited by Brian Swann, 134-70. Lincoln: University of Nebraska Press, 2004.

–. "To See Ourselves as the Other's Other: Nlaka'pamux Contact Narratives." *Canadian Historical Review* 75, 1 (March 1994): 1-20.

–, ed. *Living by Stories: A Journey of Landscape and Memory.* Vancouver: Talonbooks, 2005.

–, ed. *Nature Power: In the Spirit of an Okanagan Storyteller.* Vancouver/Seattle: Douglas and McIntyre/University of Washington Press, 1992; Vancouver: Talonbooks, 2004.

–, ed. *Write It on Your Heart: The Epic World of an Okanagan Storyteller.* Vancouver: Talonbooks and Theytus, 1989.

Wilde, Oscar. *Intentions*. London: James R. Osgood, McIlvaine and co., 1891.

Wilks, W[illiam], and H.R. Hutchinson, eds. *Journal Kept by David Douglas during His Travels in North America 1823-1827*. London: W. Wesley and Son, for the Royal Horticultural Society, 1914.

Wilson, Sir Daniel. *Prehistoric Man: Researches into the Origin of Civilisation in the Old and the New World*. 2 vols. Cambridge and London: Macmillan, 1862.

Wiri, Robert. "The Prophecies of the Great Canyon of Toi: A History of Te Whāiti-nui-a-Toi in the Western Urewera Mountains of New Zealand." PhD diss., University of Auckland, 2001.

Woodward, C. Vann. *The Burden of Southern History*. New York: New American Library, 1968.

Zenk, Henry B., and Tony A. Johnson. *Chinúk-Wawa: Kákwa ntsayka úlman tílixam łaska munk-kəmtəks ntsáyka/As Our Elders Teach Us to Speak It*. Grand Ronde, OR: Confederated Tribes of the Community of Grand Ronde, 2003.

Znamenski, Andrei A. *Shamanism and Christianity: Native Encounters with Russian Orthodox Missions in Siberia and Alaska, 1820-1917*. Westport, CN: Greenwood Press, 1999.

# Contributors

**Judith Binney**, Distinguished Companion of the New Zealand Order of Merit and Fellow of the Royal Society of New Zealand, is professor emerita of history at the University of Auckland, New Zealand. She is the author of a number of books and essays on aspects of Maori-European relations, notably *The Legacy of Guilt: A Life of Thomas Kendall* (2nd ed., 2005) and *Redemption Songs: A Life of the Nineteenth-Century Maori Leader Te Kooti Arikirangi Te Turuki* (1995 and 1997), which won the New Zealand Montana Book of the Year Award, 1996. She is co-author of the prize-winning *Ngā Mōrehu: The Survivors* (3rd ed., 2004) and *Mihaia: The Prophet Rua Kenana and His Community at Maungapohatu* (4th ed., 2005). She was co-editor and editor of the *New Zealand Journal of History,* 1987-2001.

**Keith Thor Carlson** is an associate professor in the History Department at the University of Saskatchewan where he teaches and conducts research in Aboriginal history and, in particular, the ethnohistory of the Pacific Northwest coast. He has authored or edited five books, including *A Stó:lō Coast Salish Historical Atlas* (2001) and, most recently, *Call Me Hank: A Sto:lo Man's Reflections on Logging, Living, and Growing Old* (2006). Carlson worked as historian and research coordinator for the Stó:lō Nation from 1992 through 2001, and much of his current research builds upon the relationships he developed with the Stó:lō community at that time.

**J. Edward Chamberlin** was born in Vancouver and educated at the Universities of British Columbia, Oxford, and Toronto. Since 1970, he has been on the faculty of the University of Toronto, where he is now university professor of English and comparative literature. He has been senior research associate with the Royal Commission on Aboriginal Peoples in Canada, as well as poetry editor of *Saturday Night,* and has worked extensively on Native land claims in Canada, the United States, Africa, and Australia. His books include *The Harrowing of Eden: White Attitudes towards Native Americans* (1975), *Ripe Was the Drowsy Hour: The Age of Oscar Wilde* (1977), *Come Back to Me My Language: Poetry and the West Indies* (1993), and *If This Is Your Land, Where Are Your Stories? Finding Common Ground* (2003). His latest book is *Horse: How the Horse Has Shaped Civilizations* (2006).

**Nora Marks Dauenhauer** was born (1927) in Juneau, Alaska, and was raised in Juneau and Hoonah, as well as on the family fishing boat and in seasonal subsistence sites around Icy Strait, Glacier Bay, and Cape Spencer. Her first language is Tlingit; she began to learn English when entering school at the age of eight. She has a BA in anthropology (Alaska Methodist University, 1976) and is internationally recognized for her fieldwork, transcription, translation, and explication of Tlingit oral literature. Her creative writing has been widely published and anthologized, and her Raven plays have been performed internationally, including at the Kennedy Center in Washington, DC. Named the Alaskan Humanist of the Year (1980), she won the Alaska Governor's Award for the Arts (1990), the Before Columbus Foundation's American Book Award (1991), and the Community Spirit Award from First People's Fund of Rapid City, SD (2005). From 1983 to 1997, she was principal researcher in language and cultural studies at Sealaska Heritage Foundation in Juneau. She is married to Richard Dauenhauer, writer and former poet laureate of Alaska, with whom she has co-authored and co-edited several editions of Tlingit language and folklore material. She has four children, twelve grandchildren, and eight great-grandchildren. She lives in Juneau, where she is semi-retired but still continues with research, writing, consulting, and volunteer work with schools and community.

**Richard Dauenhauer**, born and raised in Syracuse, New York, has lived in Alaska since 1969. He is widely recognized as a translator, and several hundred of his translations of poetry from German, Russian, classical Greek, Swedish, Finnish, and other languages have appeared in a range of journals and little magazines since 1963. He holds degrees in Slavic languages, German, and comparative literature. Since he came to Alaska, much of his professional work has focused on applied folklore and linguistics in the study, materials development, and teacher training of and for Alaska Native languages and oral literature. He has taught at Alaska Methodist University and Alaska Pacific University in Anchorage, and part time at the University of Alaska Southeast in Juneau; he also served as director of language and cultural studies at Sealaska Heritage Foundation, Juneau. In August 2005, he accepted the position as president's professor of Alaska Native languages and culture at the University of Alaska Southeast. He is married to Nora Marks Dauenhauer, widely published and anthologized Native American writer, transcriber, and translator of Tlingit oral literature. He lives in Juneau, where he teaches and works as a freelance writer and consultant. His honours include Humanist of the Year by the Alaska Humanities Forum (1980), poet laureate of Alaska (1981-88), Alaska State Governor's Award for the Arts (1989), and an American Book Award from the Before Columbus Foundation (1991).

**Michael Harkin** is professor of anthropology at the University of Wyoming. He received his PhD in anthropology from the University of Chicago and has conducted fieldwork in British Columbia, Wyoming, North Carolina, and France. He is the author of *The Heiltsuks: Dialogues of Culture and History on the Northwest Coast* (1997); he edited *Reassessing Revitalization Movements: Perspectives from North America and the Pacific Islands* (2004), *Coming to Shore: New Perspectives on Northwest Coast Ethnology*, with Marie Mauzé and Sergei Kan (2004), and

*Perspectives on the Ecological Indian: Native Americans and the Environment*, with David Rich Lewis (2007). He is editor of the journal *Ethnohistory* and theme editor for cultural anthropology in the *Encyclopedia of Life Support Systems*, published by UNESCO.

**John Sutton Lutz** teaches and researches the history of indigenous-newcomer relations in the Pacific Northwest at the University of Victoria. Temporally, his research projects run from first contact to the current day and the impact of the welfare state. They are united by an overriding interest in the different modes of communication and transmission of knowledge between natives and newcomers. He is the author of several articles and a forthcoming book on the impact of the Euro-Canadian economy on indigenous people in British Columbia, and is co-editor, with Jo-Anne Lee, of *Situating Race and Racism in Time, Space and Theory* (2005). He has a strong interest in disseminating history via the new media and is co-director of the Great Unsolved Mysteries in Canadian History project (http://canadianmysteries.ca) as well as other websites accessible from http://web.uvic.ca/~jlutz.

**I.S. MacLaren** is a professor at the University of Alberta in the Departments of History and Classics, and English and Film Studies. Early Canadian literature, exploration and travel in the North American Arctic and west, national parks history, and travel literature past and present are the subjects he teaches and researches regularly. His latest book is *Mapper of Mountains: M.P. Bridgland in the Canadian Rockies, 1902-1930* (2005), with Eric Higgs and Gabrielle Zezulka-Mailloux. This biography of a Dominion land surveyor and co-founder of the Alpine Club of Canada also places on view the work of the current Rocky Mountain Repeat Photography Project (http://bridgland.sunsite.ualberta.ca/) which studies landscape change by comparing Bridgland's original photographs to rephotographs being made today by an interdisciplinary research team.

**Patrick Moore** is assistant professor of anthropology at the University of British Columbia. He has worked extensively with the Slavey, Kaska, Tagish, and Beaver First Nations in northern Alberta, British Columbia, and the Yukon to document their languages and oral traditions. His books include *Wolverine Myths and Visions*, with Angela Wheelock (1990); *Traditional Lifestyles of Kaska Women*, with Angela Wheelock (1996); *Guzāgi K'úgé': Our Language Book, Nouns, Kaska, Mountain Slavey* (1991); and *Dene Gudeji: Kaska Narratives* (1999).

**Wendy Wickwire** is an associate professor in the Department of History at the University of Victoria. With Okanagan elder Harry Robinson, she has produced *Write It on Your Heart: The Epic World of an Okanagan Storyteller* (1989); *Nature Power: In the Spirit of an Okanagan Storyteller* (2004); and *Living by Stories: An Okanagan Journey of Landscape and Memory* (2005). With Michael M'Gonigle, she co-authored *Stein: The Way of the River* (1988); later, also with M'Gonigle, she co-edited *Victory Harvest: The Diary of a Canadian in the British Women's Land Army, 1940-1944* (1997). Most recently, she has guest-edited a special double issue of *BC Studies*, "Ethnographic Eyes: In Memory of Douglas L. Cole"

(2000). Her research interests include the oral traditions of the Aboriginal peoples of southcentral British Columbia and the history of anthropology in British Columbia. She is currently completing a book on early BC ethnographer James A. Teit.

# Index

Printed and bound in Canada by Friesens
Set in Stone by Artegraphica Design Co. Ltd.
Copy editor: Deborah Kerr
Proofreader: Sarah Munro
Indexer: Noeline Bridge
Cartographer: Eric Leinberger